D0065501

Keynes and the Market

Keynes and the Market

How the World's Greatest Economist Overturned Conventional Wisdom and Made a Fortune on the Stock Market

Justyn Walsh

WILEY

John Wiley & Sons, Inc.

Published by John Wiley & Sons, Inc., Hoboken, New Jersey.
Published simultaneously in Canada.

For general information on our other products and services or for technical support, please
contact our Customer Care Department within the United States at (800) 762-2974,
outside the United States at (317) 572-3993 or fax (317) 572-4002.

Wiley also publishes its books in a variety of electronic formats. Some content that appears
in print may not be available in electronic books. For more information about Wiley
products, visit our web site at www.wiley.com.

Library of Congress Cataloging-in-Publication Data:

Walsh, Justyn, 1970–
    Keynes and the market : how the world's greatest economist overturned conventional
wisdom and made a fortune on the stock market/Justyn Walsh.
        p.   cm.
    Includes bibliographical references and index.
    ISBN 978-0-470-28496-4 (cloth)
        1. Keynes, John Maynard, 1883-1946.   2. Investments.   3. Investment analysis.
I. Title.
HB103.K47W25   2008
332.6092—dc22

                                                                          2008014646

Printed in the United States of America

10 9 8 7 6 5 4 3 2 1

Contents

Introduction

John Maynard Keynes conferred a distinct glamor on the dismal science of economics. He was a Cambridge don, key member of the Bloomsbury set, best-selling author, husband of a world-famous ballerina, father of modern macroeconomics, valued government adviser, ennobled member of the House of Lords, and midwife to the IMF and the World Bank. His bracing response to the doldrums of the Great Depression—"The patient needs exercise, not rest"—heralded the Keynesian era of managed capitalism and pump-primed Western economies. Renowned almost as much for the variability of his opinions as for the vigor, style, and intelligence with which they were advanced, Keynes delighted in assaulting conventional wisdom and deployed pungent prose as his weapon of choice.

Despite affecting an aristocratic disdain for the profession of money-making, Keynes was also an incredibly successful stock market player. At the time of his death, his net worth—largely accrued through his investment activities—amounted to the present-day equivalent of $30 million. The Cambridge college fund administered by Keynes recorded a twelve-fold increase in its value while under his stewardship, a period during which the broader market averages failed even to double.

In his role as chairman of one of Britain's most venerable life assurance companies his speeches were, according to a journalist at the time, "so highly regarded by the City that his prediction of a trend was enough to jiggle the stock market." Keynes was that rarest of beasts—an economist who, having clambered down from his ivory tower, mastered the financial markets in practice as well as in theory.

Notwithstanding his financial success, one might reasonably query how an analysis of Keynes' stock market techniques can profit the modern investor. Keynes was, after all, a child of the Victorian era and died over half a century ago. He lived in a different, more decorous time than our own—Keynes could have been describing himself when he conjured the image of "the inhabitant of London . . . sipping his morning tea in bed," languidly contemplating whether to "adventure his wealth in the . . . new enterprises of any quarter of the world." He invested in whaling companies and other now-defunct industries, and was directed by editors to ensure that his magazine articles were of sufficient length to allow readers to work through at least three glasses of port. Redolent as he is of another age, is there anything to be gained from an appraisal of Keynes' investment principles in this era of day traders, delta ratios, and dot-coms?

The answer, perhaps surprisingly, is a resounding "yes". After a couple of false starts, Keynes alighted on a set of precepts that won him singular stock market success. In the twilight of his long investment career, he declared with characteristic immodesty that:

> The financial concerns where I have had my own way have been uniformly prosperous . . . My difficulties in financial quarters all through have been the difficulty of getting unorthodox advice accepted by others concerned.

These unorthodox tenets anticipated, to a remarkable degree, the investment philosophies of some conspicuously successful contemporary "value investors," most notably Warren Buffett of Berkshire Hathaway. Noting that Keynes' "brilliance as a practicing investor matched his brilliance in thought," Buffett has on a number of occasions recognized his intellectual debt to the English economist. Just as importantly to the modern reader, Keynes' observations were set out in the limpid, casually elegant language for which he was rightly acclaimed. As his friend, the newspaper baron Lord Beaverbrook, averred, Keynes made "exciting literature out of finance"—truly a Herculean feat.

Keynes' upbringing and personal philosophy deeply influenced his attitude toward money and its pursuit. Any investigation of the man's investment principles must, therefore, also chart some of the key landmarks of his life. One of Keynes' closest friends, the iconoclastic Lytton Strachey, remarked that his professional task as a biographer was to:

> . . . row out over that great ocean of material, and lower down into it, here and there, a little bucket, which will bring up to the light of day some characteristic specimen, from those far depths, to be examined with a careful curiosity.

Our inquiry is necessarily very focused—we will be hauling to the surface those "characteristic specimens" relating chiefly to Keynes' investment precepts. Nevertheless, in carrying out these soundings, hopefully at least a flavor of Keynes' ample life will also be conveyed to the reader. To extend Strachey's metaphor, occasionally we will have cause to divert our gaze beyond the objects of our immediate scrutiny and toward the expansive, sometimes turbulent ocean that constituted the life of John Maynard Keynes.

Chapter 1

The Apostle Maynard

The Worldly Philosopher

Some surprise has been expressed about the large fortune left by Lord Keynes. Yet Lord Keynes was one of the few economists with the practical ability to make money.
— *FINANCIAL TIMES*, SEPTEMBER 30, 1946

In September 1946, five months after his death, the bequest of John Maynard Keynes was made public. His net assets totaled just under £480,000, or around $30 million in today's money. Although Keynes had secured a number of board positions at leading City institutions and had received considerable royalties from some of his better-selling books, general amazement greeted news of his fortune. He had, after all, spent most of the preceding six years as an unpaid Treasury adviser; his parents had outlived him and therefore provided no inheritance; and Keynes, a great arts patron, had funded many cultural ventures out of his own pocket.

As suggested in the salmon-pink pages of the *Financial Times*, it was indeed Keynes' skill in the art of moneymaking that contributed to the bulk of his riches. Keynes' facility with money was not just limited to his own account, however. King's College—Keynes' spiritual, intellectual, and sometimes temporal home—was also a beneficiary of his financial acumen. In its obituary on Keynes, the *Manchester Guardian* reported that:

> As bursar of his own college in Cambridge . . . he was conspicuously successful, and by bold and unorthodox methods he increased very greatly the value of its endowments.

Although little known to the wider world, in certain circles Keynes' investment expertise was prized. There are stories of other college bursars making the pilgrimage to King's College, where Keynes would lounge Buddha-like and regally impart investment wisdom to an eager audience. A colleague noted that "such was his influence in the City and his reputation abroad" that markets would move in response to his speeches delivered as Chairman of the National Mutual Life Assurance Society. He sat on the boards of numerous investment companies, from which he would, with the unwavering conviction of a papal nuncio, declaim his views on the stock market and government economic policy.

This aspect of Keynes—the shrewd investor, the canny player of financial markets—is rather unexpected in light of the man's early life and beliefs. Keynes was an aesthete, his first allegiance to philosophy and the art of living well. At school and university he displayed little interest in worldly matters, and for the remainder of his life exhibited an intensely ambivalent attitude to the pursuit of wealth. He believed in Francis Bacon's dictum that money makes a good servant but a bad master—in Keynes' formulation, money's merit lay solely in its ability to secure and maintain the conditions allowing one to "live wisely and agreeably and well." Like economics itself, money was a mere expedient, nothing other than "a means to the enjoyment and realities of life," and moneymaking little more than an "amusement."

Before proceeding to an examination of Keynes' investment activities and techniques, a brief survey of the early influences on the man's life is appropriate. For although Keynes did not take up speculation and investing with any particular ardor until his mid-thirties, the attitudes that shaped his views on moneymaking were largely formed in his early years.

Enter the Hero

I like the name suggested—John Maynard Keynes sounds like the substantial name of the solid hero of a sensible novel.
—KEYNES' GRANDFATHER, JUNE 6, 1883

In the late nineteenth century, Britain was still the world's most powerful nation—"workshop of the world" and boasting an empire on which, famously, the sun never set. Other than occasional episodes of colonial disobedience, it had been decades since Britannia had been obliged to flourish her spear at an enemy of any substance. Before the Crimean War of the mid-1850s the last general European conflict was the Battle of Waterloo in 1815, in which the United Kingdom and its allies finally ended Napoleon's quest for French glory. Compared with the horrors and madness of the succeeding century, the Victorian era was a remarkable oasis of peace.

Emboldened by Adam Smith's paradoxical doctrine that selfish private actions transmuted into public virtues, and later by Darwin's observations on natural selection and survival of the fittest, *fin de siècle* British society embraced free trade and a substantially laissez-faire government. The spirit of competition and endeavor pervaded Queen Victoria's nation. Notwithstanding attacks on the flanks by the likes of Oscar Wilde and George Bernard Shaw, Britons fervently believed in the virtues of duty, hard work, and thrift. The stiff upper lip would, just occasionally, quiver and curl into a slight smirk of satisfaction when the British contemplated the patent superiority of their race.

Into this world of security, prosperity, and solid bourgeois values came John Maynard Keynes. He was born in June 1883 in the university town of Cambridge, his father an economics fellow at the University and his mother one of its first female graduates. Maynard, as he was known to family and friends, was subsequently joined by two siblings who themselves would figure in English public life—Geoffrey, later an eminent surgeon and bibliographer, and husband to Charles Darwin's granddaughter; and Margaret, like her mother a prominent social reformer and destined to marry a Nobel Prize winner in medicine.

A Privileged Boy

Education: the inculcation of the incomprehensible into the indifferent by the incompetent.

—KEYNES (ATTRIBUTED)

Appropriately for one of the first true offspring of Cambridge University—for it was only in the late 1870s that the ancient statutes preventing Cambridge dons from marrying were repealed—Keynes shone intellectually. After a precocious childhood, bolstered by a rigorous study regimen devised by his father, Keynes secured a scholarship to Eton College, school of choice for British royalty and the nation's elite. Once at Eton, Keynes maintained his academic ascendancy, winning over sixty prizes during his five years there. Unlike some other Old Etonians such as Eric Blair—better known to the reading public as George Orwell—he also prospered socially and was elected College prefect in his final year at school.

Even at Eton, an institution not generally known for the humility of its incumbents, Keynes displayed an inordinate degree of intellectual haughtiness. One schoolmaster remarked, "I should like in certain things to see him a little more dissatisfied, a little more ready to note the points in which he fails." Another observed that "[Keynes] gives one the idea of regarding himself a privileged boy with perhaps a little intellectual conceit." He was quick-witted and cutting—he wrote of one of Charles Darwin's sons that "his hands certainly looked as if he might be descended from an ape," and complained that one particular schoolmaster was "dull and soporiferous beyond words . . . I shall not suffer from want of sleep this half." He embraced the prejudices of the upper middle class, holding in equal contempt the "absurd" aristocracy and the "boorish" lower classes—only the "intelligentsia," of which the Keynes family was a prime example, commanded his respect.

Like most other Establishment institutions of the time, Eton evinced a snobby disregard for commercial matters. The school had long been the proving ground for young gentlemen of the Empire—the Duke of Wellington famously, if apocryphally, affirmed that the Battle of Waterloo was won on Eton's playing-fields—and there was little room for the ungallant trade of the businessman in this sanctuary of old-world values. The only hint of Keynes' subsequent career as an economist and investor was the schoolboy's almost autistic preoccupation with lists and numbers—Keynes obsessively recorded cricket scores, train times, hours worked, variations in his body temperature, and even "the comparative lengths of some long poems" during his time at Eton.

The Cambridge Idyll

The appropriate subjects of passionate contemplation and communion were a beloved person, beauty and truth, and one's prime objects in life were love, the creation and enjoyment of aesthetic experience and the pursuit of knowledge.
　　　　　—KEYNES ON THE APOSTLES, *MY EARLY BELIEFS*

On the back of a scholarship to King's College, Keynes returned to Cambridge in 1902 to study mathematics and classics. With customary chutzpah, he announced in his freshman year that "I've had a good look round the place and come to the conclusion that it's pretty inefficient." Although a gifted mathematician, he was by no means a prodigy, and in late 1905 placed twelfth of those receiving a First Class degree. While at university Keynes also found time to cultivate his social interests, and in his final undergraduate year became president of the Cambridge Union and president of the Liberal Club.

The most important influence on Keynes while at Cambridge was a secret society known to initiates as "the Apostles." This group recruited from the promising young men of Cambridge—E. M. Forster, Wittgenstein, and Bertrand Russell were fellow members—and its defining principles were best expressed in G. E. Moore's *Principia Ethica*, published during Keynes' first year at Cambridge. Moore's philosophy was profoundly nonmaterialistic and unworldly—Keynes once commented that, in comparison to the *Principia*, "the New Testament is a handbook for politicians." Moore, a Cambridge academic, believed that:

> By far the most valuable things, which we know or can imagine, are certain states of consciousness, which may be roughly described as the pleasures of human intercourse and the enjoyment of beautiful objects.

Many of the Apostles applied a very particular interpretation to Moore's endorsement of the pleasures of human intercourse. In the cloistered and covert world of the society, where aesthetic experience and intimate friendships were paramount, relations often transcended the merely platonic. Keynes reminisced many years later that "we repudiated entirely customary morals, conventions, and traditional wisdom . . . [and] recognized no moral obligation on us, no inner sanction, to conform or to obey."

Standing aloof from the masses, the Apostles developed a superiority complex to match the belief that only they possessed the requisite sensitivity to truly appreciate the finer things in life. Keynes likened the group to "water-spiders, gracefully skimming, as light and reasonable as air, the surface of the stream without any contact at all with the eddies and currents underneath." Others, less charitably, dismissed the group as self-indulgent and ridiculous, twisting Moore's philosophy into "a metaphysical justification for doing what you like and what other people disapprove of."

An India Man

Cecily, you will read your Political Economy in my absence. The chapter on the Fall of the Rupee you may omit. It is somewhat too sensational. Even these metallic problems have their melodramatic side.
—OSCAR WILDE, *THE IMPORTANCE OF BEING EARNEST*

Reality eventually intruded into Keynes' life and, after graduating in mathematics, the practical question of how to earn a living confronted him. He toyed with the idea of undertaking a second degree in economics, and for a while attended lectures given by Professor Alfred Marshall, a personal friend of the Keynes family and probably the world's most influential economist at the time. Despite Marshall's entreaties—"I trust your future career may be one in which you will not cease to be an economist," the Professor implored—Keynes eventually opted for a career as a government man. In August 1906 he sat for the nationwide Civil Service examination, where he placed second overall. Ironically, his worst mark was in economics, prompting Keynes to remark that "the examiners presumably knew less than I did."

Unable to secure his first choice of government department—the Treasury—Keynes became a cog in the machine of Empire, moving to London and joining the India Office as a junior clerk in October 1906. In those days of the "gold standard"—the convention then prevailing in most Western nations, whereby a country's exchange rate was determined by its reserves of gold—India's rather less domesticated monetary system attracted considerable interest among theoretical economists, and may have been influential in Keynes' career choice. Despite the alleged allure of the maverick rupee, however, Keynes found the India Office singularly unexciting. Unedifying tasks such as arranging the shipment of ten stud bulls to Bombay, Keynes' first assignment, undoubtedly presented a rude contrast to the rarefied climes he had inhabited in Cambridge.

The Bloomsbury Rebellion

We were out to construct something new; we were in the van of the builders of a new society which should be free, rational, civilized, pursuing truth and beauty. It was all tremendously exhilarating.
      —Leonard Woolf on the Bloomsbury group

Offsetting the dullness of the Civil Service was the loose and fluctuating coterie of artists, writers, and philosophers who coalesced at the residence of Virginia Woolf and her siblings. Like the Apostles before them, the Bloomsbury group—named after the London district of garden squares and grand houses—reveled in confounding the traditional pieties and restraints of society. A herald of the counterculture movement later that century and the original bourgeois Bohemians, one "Bloomsberry" later recounted:

> We found ourselves living in the springtime of a conscious revolt against the social, political, religious, moral, intellectual, and artistic institutions, beliefs, and standards of our fathers and grandfathers.

The group's willingness to slough conventional modes of thought and behavior naturally extended to the more intimate domain of personal relationships. Bloomsbury affairs were notoriously labyrinthine and prickly—it was said that Bloomsberries "lived in squares but loved in triangles." Romantic intrigues, betrayals, and sniping provided a diversion from earnest discussions on art, ideas, and the meaning of life, and members of the group sometimes used their artistic gifts in the service of less than genteel verbal assaults. Virginia Woolf, in a fit of pique, once likened Keynes to "a gorged seal, double chin, ledge of red lip, little eyes, sensual, brutal, unimaginative," although this outburst could quite possibly have been in response to Keynes' gentle suggestion that she stick to nonfiction.

The more conservative elements of society regarded the Bloomsberries with open hostility. John Buchan, author of *The Thirty-Nine Steps* and a stalwart Victorian, dismissed them as:

> . . . the usual round-up of rootless intellectuals . . . terribly knowing and disillusioned and conscientiously indecent . . . a smattering not so much of facts as of points of view . . . They took nothing for granted except their own surpassing intelligence . . .

Although indeed possessed of a stratospheric self-importance, the group's pretensions were not completely unfounded. They were outriders for new styles of thought and artistic expression, and—ironically for a medley of such unrestrained egos—were instrumental in shepherding other, greater, artists and thinkers before the public eye. Picasso, Freud, Proust, Cézanne, and Matisse, among others, entered the English-speaking world largely through the Bloomsbury portal.

The Uncivil Servant

I work for a Government I despise for ends I think criminal.
—Keynes to Duncan Grant, December 15, 1917

Defeated by the tedium of the job, Keynes resigned from the India Office in June 1908 and returned to King's College, where he submitted a dissertation on probability—according to one newspaper, "a thesis on mathematics so advanced that it was said that only three people on earth could understand it." He was elected to a fellowship in March 1909 and, although having no formal qualifications in the subject, taught economics and finance at Cambridge. Keynes became a polished and popular teacher, with some lectures—particularly those relating to the stock exchange—drawing capacity crowds.

During this time at Cambridge Keynes began to ascend the ladder of academia and public life. In 1911 he was appointed editor of the *Economic Journal*, perhaps the world's leading professional economics periodical at the time. Less than two years later, his first book, *Indian Currency and Finance*, was published and Keynes became a member of the Royal Commission on Indian Finance—a prestigious appointment for someone not yet thirty years of age. Keynes' Cambridge idyll was shattered, however, in the balmy summer of 1914 when Queen Victoria's grandsons Willy and Georgie—Kaiser Wilhelm II of Germany and King George V of Britain—led their nations into the first great conflict of the new century.

The declaration of war in August 1914 drew Keynes back to the Civil Service, this time at Treasury where he advised on the financing of the British war effort. Keynes' Bloomsbury acquaintances, fiercely pacifist, objected to his new role. One challenged Keynes:

> What are you? Only an intelligence that they need in their extremity ... A genie taken incautiously out of King's ... by savages to serve them faithfully for their savage ends, and then—back you go in to the bottle.

Despite their high-minded criticism of his role as a hired gun in the "European blood feud," as Keynes labeled the Great War, the

Bloomsberries were not averse to exploiting Keynes' increasing influence within the Establishment. He often appeared before tribunals as an advocate for those male members of the group seeking to avoid the draft. In a hearing for Lytton Strachey—delicate aesthete and Keynes' one-time paramour—the army prosecutor demanded to know what Strachey would do if a Hun attempted to rape his sister. Poker-faced, he replied in his peculiarly squeaky voice, "I should try and come between them."

Keynes was "absolutely and completely desolated" by the carnage of the war and the government's determination to pursue victory at any cost. Many of his university friends, including the celebrated poet and patriot Rupert Brooke, remained forever on the foreign fields where they fell. In a tragic ambush of the old world by the new, these sons of the upper classes were invariably ordained "officer material" and, honoring the traditions of ages past, obliged to march into battle at the head of their men—only to be met by the murderous steel storms of modern weaponry. Keynes' letters to his former classmates were sometimes returned to him unopened, the bleak epitaph "Killed" scrawled across them.

Frustrated and conflicted over his role as an intellectual mercenary for the war effort, Keynes' reputation for arrogance and condescension ripened. On a trip to the United States in 1917 he made a "terrible impression for his rudeness." The British Ambassador to the United States noted in his high camp style that:

> This morning we got a visit from [Keynes] . . . who was very Treasuriclarkacious and reduced Dicky to silentious rage and Malcolm to a high treble. He was really too offensive for words and I shall have to take measures. He is also a Don and the combination is not pleasing. He is also a young man of talent and I presume the rule for such nowadays is to show his immense superiority by crushing the contemptible insignificance of the unworthy outside.

Keynes was beginning to find his voice—the impudent junior rebuking his masters, the gadfly nipping at the flanks of a complacent Establishment, the double agent within the citadel, valuing truth above expediency.

A Carthaginian Peace

Words ought to be a little wild, for they are the assault of thoughts upon the unthinking.

—KEYNES, *NATIONAL SELF-SUFFICIENCY*

Expected by most to last only a few months, it was four years before the war finally gave way to an armistice in November 1918. France, which lost a staggering 1.4 million men during the conflict, was determined to make Germany pay dearly for its perceived belligerence. Britain, which together with its dominions recorded close to a million men dead, was initially more conciliatory. The British Prime Minister, David Lloyd George, observed in March 1919 that the preservation of peace on the Continent would depend "upon there being no causes of exasperation constantly stirring up either the spirit of patriotism, of justice, or of fair play, to achieve redress." Accordingly, he advocated peace terms:

> . . . dictated . . . in the spirit of judges sitting in a cause which does not personally engage their emotion or interests, and not in a spirit of savage vendetta, which is not satisfied without mutilation and the infliction of pain and humiliation.

Despite these lofty words, the Paris Peace Conference degenerated into an unseemly auction of the aggrieved, a contest among the victors as to which could carve the most from the husk of central Europe. In an effort to appease constituents at home and deliver on promises to "make Germany pay," the Allied leaders imposed a war guilt clause on Germany—an explicit statement that the German state and its confederates were solely responsible for the Great War—and also a reparations clause requiring Germany to "make compensation for all damage done to the civilian population of the Allied and Associated Powers and to their property."

Keynes, attached to the British delegation as an economic adviser, scorned the shortsightedness of the Allied leaders:

> The future life of Europe was not their concern; its means of livelihood was not their anxiety. Their preoccupations, good and bad alike, related to frontiers and nationalities, to the balance of power, to imperial aggrandizements, to the future enfeeblement of a strong

and dangerous enemy, to revenge, and to the shifting by the victors of
their unbearable financial burdens on to the shoulders of the defeated.

On his thirty-sixth birthday, June 5, 1919, and as the Treaty of Versailles
was being finalized, Keynes resigned in protest at the "Carthaginian
peace" to be imposed on the vanquished nations.

Freed from the constraints of the Civil Service, he produced
in only a few months a withering critique of the Conference. *The
Economic Consequences of the Peace*, published in December 1919, was
a sensation—translated into eleven languages and selling over 100,000
copies in its first full year of publication. The book was celebrated as
much for its bravura portraits of key Conference participants as for
its political and economic arguments. Keynes depicted the American
President Woodrow Wilson as a "blind and deaf Don Quixote" who
"like Odysseus . . . looked wiser when he was seated," and the French
leader Georges Clemenceau as a xenophobe with "one illusion—
France; and one disillusion—mankind." Warming to his theme, he par-
odied Lloyd George as "this goat-footed bard, this half-human visitor
to our age from the hag-ridden magic and enchanted woods of Celtic
antiquity." Cooler heads eventually persuaded Keynes to withhold this
last pen portrait from the published version of his book.

In a conclusion of frightening prescience, Keynes declared that the
aggressive reparations terms would return to haunt the Continent:

> If we aim deliberately at the impoverishment of Central Europe,
> vengeance, I dare predict, will not limp. Nothing can then delay for
> very long that final civil war between the forces of reaction and the
> despairing convulsions of revolution, before which the horrors of
> the late German war will fade into nothing, and which will destroy,
> whoever is victor, the civilization and the progress of our generation.

Disestablished

*The book in a certain sense was the turning point in Lord Keynes'
career. Thereafter he was no longer a mere economist but a prophet
and pamphleteer, a journalist and the author of a best seller.*
　　　　　　　　　—THE NEW YORK TIMES ON THE ECONOMIC
　　　　　　　　　　　CONSEQUENCES OF THE PEACE

In a pattern that would be repeated over the rest of his life, Keynes' robust take-no-prisoners style polarized opinions. Many derided his perceived pro-German sympathies—some mockingly referring to him as "Herr Johann von Keynes," others suggesting he be awarded an Iron Cross—and he was cast on the outer by the government he had so effectively ridiculed. *The Economic Consequences of the Peace* marked Keynes' transformation from a mere government functionary operating on the periphery of diplomacy and academia to an influential and dissident public figure—he commented that, following publication of the book, "I woke up like Byron, famous and disreputable."

Notwithstanding his newfound notoriety, Keynes—jobless after resigning from Treasury—desperately needed another source of income to sustain the rather lavish lifestyle to which he and the Bloomsbury circle had become accustomed. Putting his money where his mouth was, Keynes decided to back the pessimistic views expressed in *Economic Consequences* by speculating heavily on the foreign exchange market, taking short positions on key Continental currencies and long positions on the U.S. dollar. Keynes believed he was ideally equipped to play the speculation game—having lectured on the subject at Cambridge, he knew something of finance and exchanges; his stint at Treasury had provided an insight into global realpolitik and the interplay of capital flows; and he had ready access to a pool of investors willing to back his trading activities.

Additionally, speculation offered the pleasing prospect of earning considerable amounts of money relatively painlessly. Like his contemporary Winston Churchill, much of Keynes' business was transacted while lounging in his bed. As one of his biographers noted:

> Some of this financial decision-making was carried out while he was still in bed in the morning; reports would come to him by phone from his brokers, and he would read the newspapers and make his decisions.

It is to this incarnation of Keynes—the aesthete, the outsider, the languid speculator—that we now turn.

Chapter 2

Citizen Keynes

The Lapsed Apostle

. . . Yet I glory
More in the cunning purchase of my wealth
Than in the glad possession . . .

—BEN JONSON, *VOLPONE*

Maynard Keynes was a paradoxical figure—a Bohemian eventually embraced by the Establishment, an aesthete who prospered in the world of Mammon, the savior of capitalism with scant regard for the free enterprise system. In his opinions, too, Keynes was mercurial, embodying Emerson's dictum that a foolish consistency is the hobgoblin of little minds. He was notoriously contradictory and capricious—Churchill is said to have remarked that "whenever I ask England's six leading economists a question, I get seven answers—two from Mr. Keynes." David Lloyd George—still smarting from Keynes' hatchet job in *The Economic Consequences of the Peace*—complained that Keynes "dashed at conclusions with acrobatic ease. It made things no better that he rushed into opposite conclusions with the same agility."

Perhaps nowhere was Keynes' capacity for contradiction more evident than in his attitude to money and the pursuit of wealth. The righteous author who railed against the "rentier bourgeoisie" for subordinating "the arts of . . . enjoyment" to compound interest in *Economic Consequences* considerably softened his invective only a couple of years later. In a 1921 speech to a new batch of Apostles, Keynes referred to a recently deceased member of the club who had forsaken academia for life in the business world—a man whose intellectual capacities, Keynes remarked acidly, "were much in excess of those usually associated with the love of money." Keynes ventured the opinion that the deceased's mercantile acts were perhaps more in the nature of "artistry, not of avarice," and he summoned the image of a curious hybrid, a type of poet-plutocrat, participating in "the stir and bustle of the world, pitting his wits, at a price, against all comers . . . [and] exercising a variety of conjoined gifts." Moneymaking, Keynes suggested to the undergraduates, could be viewed as a great game, a kind of high-stakes chess where the nimble minded could cash in on their intellectual superiority.

Although ostensibly a valedictory to a former Apostle, there is little doubt that Keynes was attempting to justify his own move into the world of finance and speculation. One part of Keynes despised the pursuit of wealth. In a later paper he would invoke a glowing future where:

> The love of money as a possession . . . will be recognized for what it is, a somewhat disgusting morbidity, one of those semi-criminal, semi-pathological propensities which one hands over with a shudder to the specialists in mental disease.

The more pragmatic side of Keynes accepted, however, the incontrovertible fact that money was, to use Dostoyevsky's phrase, "coined liberty" and that "the enjoyments and realities of life" were withheld from those of little means.

From these two competing insights arose a typically Keynesian compromise: Keynes would leap headlong into the world of finance, but the task of moneymaking would not consume him. It would remain an amusement, a means to an end, a way of supporting his more worthy ventures. And if he could win at the expense of those who professed an overweening love of money, then so much the better.

The Speculation Racket

[Speculation is] my diversion, to avoid the possibility of tedium in a country life.

—KEYNES TO HIS MOTHER, SEPTEMBER 3, 1919

Before 1919, Keynes had shown only fitful interest in the financial markets. His first recorded investment was in 1905, at twenty-two years of age, when he bought shares in an insurance company and later an engineering firm using his "special fund" of birthday money and cash from academic prizes. Clive Bell, a close acquaintance, hazarded a guess that Keynes' real interest in the markets was not sparked until early 1914:

> Maynard, who at Cambridge and in early London days had barely glanced at "Stock Exchange Dealings," grew so weary . . . of reading the cricket-scores in *The Times* that, while drinking his morning tea, he took to studying prices instead.

Keynes' investments until 1919 were relatively sporadic, but his portfolio—principally in the form of ordinary shares—enjoyed a steady increase in value, and by the end of 1918 he owned securities worth £9,428, around $625,000 in today's money.

Keynes began speculating in earnest in August 1919, in between correcting drafts of *The Economic Consequences of the Peace*. His activities were focused on the currency markets, where exchange rates, shorn free from the bedrock of the prewar gold standard, would often jag wildly. Keynes' strategy was simple—backing the views expressed in his book, he was bearish on certain Continental currencies and bullish on the U.S. dollar. This policy proved extremely successful, and in the space of five months Keynes realized profits of just over £6,000, the equivalent of around $375,000 today. Buoyed by this, Keynes wrote to his mother that:

> Money is a funny thing . . . As the fruit of a little extra knowledge and experience of a special kind, it simply (and undeservedly in any absolute sense) comes rolling in.

Keynes' initial triumph engendered a grander scheme. He teamed up with a former Treasury colleague, Oswald Falk, to form a syndicate to speculate on currency movements. "Foxy" Falk, a partner in the aptly named stockbroking firm Buckmaster and Moore, was, like Keynes, a charismatic figure of firm views. One City acquaintance recalled of Falk that he:

> . . . would not look after any private client unless he was given *carte blanche* to do what he liked. The poor victim either made a killing in the market or was wiped out completely.

Although Keynes had predicted that his financial speculation "will shock father," the enterprise was enthusiastically supported by family and friends, and the sum of £30,000 was quickly raised.

Keynes and Falk embarked upon their trading scheme in January 1920. Due to a perceived lack of liquidity in the currency market, Falk withdrew from the syndicate shortly afterward, but Keynes persevered and had realized profits of £9,000 after the first three months of operations. However, in May the market turned against the syndicate and losses began to swell—by midyear Keynes noted that the partnership had witnessed the "slaughter of a large part of our holdings." Keynes was stoic—"It has been a beastly time, but I have kept fairly philosophical," he confided to Bloomsbury Vanessa Bell—and his parents also seemed to accept the losses with good grace. Keynes' mother mused that:

> It was perhaps necessary to throw something overboard to propitiate the Gods—if they are content with mere money, we will not grudge it to them.

Undaunted, Keynes remounted the horse that had thrown him. He liquidated securities from his personal stock portfolio, procured an advance payment for royalties due on sales of *Economic Consequences*, and inveigled a £5,000 loan from King Edward's private banker, Sir Ernest Cassel. In his letter to Cassel, Keynes, despite having "quite exhausted my resources," thought that the foreign exchange market offered "an unequalled opportunity for speculation" and anticipated that Cassel would be rewarded with "very substantial profits with very good probability if you are prepared to stand the racket for perhaps a couple of months." Keynes' optimism was justified—toward the end of 1920 he repaid Cassel, and by December 1922 he had cleared all his syndicate debts and boasted net assets of just over £21,000, around $1.5 million in today's money.

The Economist and the Showgirl

As for Loppi don't *marry her. Flight to India may save you. However charming she may be, she'd be a very expensive wife & would give up dancing & is altogether I'm sure much to be preferred as a mistress . . .*
—VANESSA BELL TO KEYNES, JANUARY 1, 1922

Keynes' career as a City man was not, however, confined to the tumult of the currency market. Befitting a son of the Establishment, he fulfilled his gentlemanly destiny and accepted board positions at a number of insurance and investment companies. Keynes' first directorship was secured in September 1919 at the National Mutual Life Assurance Society, and throughout the early 1920s he continued to collect board appointments at various London finance houses. Away from the City, Keynes was elected Second Bursar of King's College in late 1919 and succeeded to First Bursar, or chief treasurer of the College, five years later.

Keynes' détente with mainstream respectability continued in 1925 when, to the absolute disbelief of the Bloomsbury set, the confirmed bachelor married the Russian prima ballerina Lydia Lopokova. The union garnered international headlines, with Keynes—despite his fame following *The Economic Consequences of the Peace*—playing a distinctly second fiddle to his exotic bride. Lydia was something of a tabloid darling—not only had she danced for the Tsar as a child, performed vaudeville in New York with Al Jolson, and been a lover of the composer Stravinsky, but had commandeered London headlines in 1919 when she fled the Ballets Russes, allegedly to elope with a Russian general. On the day of their marriage, a press scrum jostled outside the St. Pancras registry office to document the celebrity wedding—the lanky and slightly stooped figure of Keynes, grave in a dark suit and looking uncharacteristically abashed, and the tiny Lydia, presenting herself to the battery of photographers with the practised ease of a professional.

Lydia's childlike enthusiasms and stumbling misadventures with the English language—"You must come and see Lady B's ovary; she says it's the largest in England!" she once exclaimed, having glimpsed an acquaintance's collection of caged birds—charmed Keynes and proved a welcome diversion from the cynical Bloomsberries. Notwithstanding Keynes' previous romantic predilections—and an unpromising start to the marriage when the gloomy Austrian philosopher Ludwig Wittgenstein gatecrashed the couple's honeymoon—"Pupsik" and "Maynarochka," as they labeled themselves in their many letters, would remain a devoted pair for the rest of their married life.

In Gold We Trust

In truth, the gold standard is already a barbarous relic.
—KEYNES, *A TRACT ON MONETARY REFORM*

Paralleling Keynes' transformation from libertine to faithful husband was his move away from the hustle and commotion of the currency markets and toward the slightly more civilized milieu of the stock exchange. Keynes' drift from currency speculation was largely prompted by the decision of Winston Churchill, then Chancellor of the Exchequer, to restore sterling to the gold standard in 1925. Tethering the pound to a fixed benchmark radically reduced relative price movements—and hence a speculator's opportunity for profit—in the currency market. Keynes strenuously opposed this move, but not just because it robbed him of a livelihood.

He asserted in *The Economic Consequences of Mr. Churchill*— published in August 1925, the same month as his marriage to Lydia— that the Chancellor had been "deafened by the clamorous voices of conventional finance . . . and . . . gravely misled by his experts" who recommended that sterling be restored to its prewar exchange rate against the U.S. dollar. These "experts," Keynes thought, were unwilling to countenance the possibility that the pound had effectively weakened in the decade or so since the start of the Great War. He argued that their insistence on maintaining a strong currency—partly motivated, one suspects, by a vague and misplaced sense of national pride—would price many British exports out of the market, leading to unemployment and a further weakening of an already fragile economy. Despite the vigor of his protests, Keynes' jeremiad passed largely unheeded. As he remarked forlornly in a letter to *The Times*, "To debate monetary reform with a City editor . . . is like debating Darwinism with a bishop sixty years ago."

Compound Interest Machines

*... Money is of a prolific generating Nature. Money can beget Money,
and its Offspring can beget more ...*
—BENJAMIN FRANKLIN, *ADVICE TO A YOUNG TRADESMAN*

Rather serendipitously, at around the same time Britain was cajoled
back on to the gold standard—and, in consequence, currency trading opportunities dwindled—Keynes came across an "interesting little
book" on equities. Edgar Lawrence Smith's *Common Stocks as Long-
Term Investments* analyzed the relative performance of American common stocks and bonds from 1866 to 1922. Smith's original hypothesis
was that an investment in common stocks would outperform an investment in bonds in a period of inflation, but the converse would be true
in times of falling prices. This was an eminently reasonable assumption: businesses can generally hedge against inflation by increasing their
prices to offset costs, but bond coupons remain fixed even in an environment of consistently rising prices.

By the early 1920s, the role of stocks as an "inflationary shield"
was more than a mere academic footnote. Many Continental European
nations, destabilized by the ravages of the Great War and struggling
to service reparations obligations, suffered mind-boggling inflation.
The German government, to cite the most extreme example, printed
money at such a rate that hyperinflation seized the country—a loaf of
bread costing less than 200 marks in 1922 escalated to 200 *billion* marks
by November 1923. In an inversion of the conventional consumer
experience, shoppers entered a store with a trolley-full of cash and left
with only a handful of items. In this environment, the value of bonds
and bank deposits, which pay a fixed money amount regardless of any
erosion in purchasing power, was destroyed.

Although the value of stocks as a hedge against inflation was readily
understood by the mid-1920s, accepted wisdom also held tenaciously
to the assumed flip side of this finding—that in deflationary periods,
bonds should outperform stocks. The results of Smith's study on the
relative merits of stocks and bonds were, however, quite unexpected.
Smith found that, overwhelmingly, ordinary shares outperformed bonds
not only in inflationary periods but also in times of falling prices.

Smith attributed this result to a number of factors, the most important of which was the "compound interest" effect inherent in ordinary shares. As Keynes summarized in a review of Smith's book:

> Well-managed industrial companies do not, as a rule, distribute to the shareholders the whole of their earned profits. In good years, if not in all years, they retain a part of their profits and put them back into the business. Thus *there is an element of compound interest* operating in favor of a sound industrial investment. Over a period of years, the real value of the property of a sound industrial is increasing at compound interest, quite apart from the dividends paid out to the shareholders. Thus . . . an index of shares yields *more* in the long run than its initial apparent rate of interest.

Smith's simple but profound observation—that equities were, in effect, "compound interest machines," offering not just dividends but capital growth through reinvestment of undistributed earnings—was a key factor in kick-starting the "cult of the common stock" in the mid-1920s.

A Devotee of the Cult

[Ordinary shares] represent the live large-scale business and invest-ment world of today, and any investment institution which ignores or is not equipped for handling their shares is living in a backwater.
                    —Keynes, National Mutual annual meeting,
                                                   January 25, 1928

Seduced by "the dizzy virtues of compound interest," Keynes became a lead evangelist of the cult of the common stock. He extolled the merits of equities in book reviews, at shareholder meetings, and in memo-randa to his investment brethren. Notwithstanding Keynes' considerable powers of persuasion—and despite common stocks being anointed as a legitimate investment vehicle as a result of Smith's study—convincing investment company boards and college funds to invest in equities was no easy task. Most financial institutions at the time considered stocks—which paid a variable dividend dependent on the underlying com-pany's profits—to be far riskier than the comforting predictability of bond yields and property rents. In the first quarter of the twentieth century at least, gentlemen most definitely preferred bonds.

Undeterred, and with the fervor of any new convert, Keynes unceasingly browbeat his colleagues and eventually prevailed. By as early as 1926 the proportion of National Mutual's funds invested in ordinary shares was over three times the average stock holding of other British life assurance societies. Similarly, and after sustained lobbying by Keynes, the investment remit of the King's College "Chest Fund"—an endowment fund over which Keynes enjoyed sole managerial discretion—was broadened from the traditional focus on property and fixed-yield securities to also include investments in shares. Keynes' campaign to widen the scope of the Chest Fund contended against not only the inherent conservatism of College custodians, but also hidebound rules proscribing particular investments. Indeed, one campus conspiracy theory at the time attributed Keynes' steadfast opposition to the appointment at a law don to King's to his fear that, under expert scrutiny, the Chest Fund would be found to be in breach of certain arcane university statutes forbidding investments in equities.

Gotham A-Go-Go

MAMMON, n: The god of the world's leading religion. The chief temple is in the holy city of New York.
      —AMBROSE BIERCE, *THE DEVIL'S DICTIONARY*

Unfortunately for Keynes, the fledgling investment manager, British stocks were at the time an exceptionally unexciting investment prospect—after a fleeting boom in 1920, the United Kingdom settled into a long economic winter. The defeat of Germany and its allies proved a Pyrrhic victory, and the power shift from the Old World to the New had been hastened to its conclusion by the Great War. By the end of the fighting, Britain had lost around a quarter of its offshore assets—the bulk of these pawned to the United States in return for wartime supplies—and had ceded its position as the world's largest creditor to its former colony. Efforts to boost Britain's industrial production—which, even by 1925, was still considerably less than its prewar level—were hampered by what Keynes derided as the "gold fetters" of the re-introduced gold standard. With around one in ten of the workforce jobless during the 1920s, the British economy stalled, and for the remainder of the decade the stock market stagnated in sympathy.

In contrast to the situation in Britain, a "high tide of prosperity," as Keynes termed it, washed the shores of the United States. An already faltering international gold standard had obliged the Federal Reserve to lower American interest rates, and—partly fuelled by this cheap money—the richest society ever known to the world had embarked on what F. Scott Fitzgerald later described as "the most expensive orgy in history." Seemingly defying gravity and the tenets of common sense, the Dow Jones index—that seismograph of investor confidence—traced an almost vertical ascent in the last years of the 1920s. Wall Street climbed more in the eighteen months to September 1929 than it had in the previous five years combined, and market darlings such as the Radio Corporation of America doubled and then doubled again over this period.

Although Keynes' attitude to America was ambivalent—he once commented that "I always regard a visit [to the United States] as in the nature of a serious illness to be followed by a convalescence"—his enthusiasm for Wall Street was sincere. Like so many others in benighted Europe, Keynes looked longingly across the Atlantic to the bright lights and palpable energy of New York. The advent of wire services made offshore investment practicable and a buoyant Wall Street became the natural destination for European speculative capital. Although Keynes' dollar exposure during the 1920s represented only a very small portion of his personal portfolio, some of his investment companies were heavily invested in American securities, and in consequence he became an avid observer of the New York exchange. And it was to be on the febrile and frenetic Wall Street of the late 1920s that Keynes would encounter the extremes of investor psychology and discern the true nature of the stock market.

Chapter 3

Snap, Old Maid, and Musical Chairs

Nothing but Blue Sky

. . . all people are most credulous when they are most happy.
—WALTER BAGEHOT, *LOMBARD STREET*

President Calvin Coolidge was not known for his verbosity. It was said by one hostess that he spoke so infrequently that every time he opened his mouth a moth flew out. Once, responding to a dinner guest's confession of a bet that she could get the President to say at least three words during the meal, he replied, "You lose." However, in December 1928, in one of his last addresses as President, "Silent Cal" was moved to a rare eloquence. He proudly boasted that:

> No Congress of the United States ever assembled, on surveying the state of the Union, has met with a more pleasing prospect than that which appears at the present time . . . The country can regard the present with satisfaction and anticipate the future with optimism.

At the end of 1928, a certain smugness about the state of the American economy seemed justified. Uncle Sam had grown fat on the remains of a Europe still recovering, dazed and haltingly, from the Great War. America was the world's undisputed economic superpower, but paradoxically it had turned inward, shaken by its brief, bloody excursion to the Old World. Exploiting its newfound wealth, the country instead sought consolation in a massive binge of retail therapy. The techniques of mass production, honed during the war, were now applied to the civilian sphere, and radios, automobiles, and myriad domestic appliances spilled off America's assembly lines. A nation of consumers was created to absorb this productive capacity—advertising and easy credit persuaded Americans to abandon their puritan peccadillos and embrace materialism.

The Jazz Age was born—that curious mix of moneymaking and frivolity, parties and Prohibition. It was as if the whole country was animated by the relentless tempo of the production line. In this feverish environment of getting and spending, the stock market became a national obsession. As one British visitor noted in 1929:

> You could talk about Prohibition, or Hemingway, or air conditioning, or music, or horses, but in the end you had to talk about the stock market, and that was when the conversation became serious.

Bellhops and shoe-shine boys dispensed stock tips, punters bought shares on margin, brokers opened offices on ocean liners so transatlantic passengers could imbibe the bounty of Wall Street. Borne aloft on updrafts of investor euphoria, the Dow Jones index doubled in only a couple of years.

Some commentators—noting a global system unbalanced by wartime debts and a domestic economy giddy on easy money—shook their heads and predicted an almighty financial hangover to follow the riotous Roaring Twenties. These Cassandras were, however, largely ignored. Wall Street pundits cited the improving effects of Prohibition on workers' productivity and the steadying influence of the Federal Reserve, among other factors, to support their contention that stock prices were fundamentally sound. Perhaps the most potent rejoinder to the doomsayers, however, was an explanation appealing to that most American of traits—faith in the democratic process. The argument was best summarized by Professor Joseph Stagg Lawrence of Princeton University who, late in the summer of 1929, posed the following rhetorical challenge:

> ... the consensus of judgment of the millions whose valuations function on that admirable market, the Stock Exchange, is that stocks are not at present prices over-valued ... Where is that group of men with the all-embracing wisdom which will entitle them to veto the judgment of this intelligent multitude?

The Collective Mind

If everyone is thinking alike then somebody isn't thinking.
—GENERAL GEORGE S. PATTON (ATTRIBUTED)

Professor Lawrence's reverence for the "intelligent multitude" anticipated the dogma later to be known as the "efficient markets hypothesis." This theory states that the stock exchange—meeting house, in Professor Lawrence's words, of "the consensus of judgment of the millions"—incorporates all public information which could possibly affect a stock's price, drawing on that sprawling resource, the investing public. Eugene Fama, the patriarch of the efficient markets theory, explains the hypothesis in the following terms:

> In an efficient market, competition among the many intelligent participants leads to a situation where, at any point in time, actual prices of individual securities already reflect the effects of information based both on events that have already occurred and on events which, as of now, the market expects to take place in the future.

In defense of Professors Lawrence and Fama, there is considerable empirical evidence supporting the notion of the "intelligent multitude"—the idea that a group of decision makers can be greater than the sum of its parts. Prosaically, we have the so-called "*Who Wants to Be a Millionaire* phenomenon," where studio audiences give the correct answer around 90 percent of the time, significantly outperforming the nominated experts. Other examples—predicting election results, or setting the odds at horse races, or even guessing the number of jellybeans in a jar—all confirm that a group can be much smarter than most of its constituents. In the right environment, the unique opinions, knowledge, and perspectives of each component member of the group are brought to bear on the decision-making process, and from the rough and tumble of competing opinions emerges the polished stone of precision.

Intelligent group behavior, however, only flourishes where there is independence and diversity of opinion. As James Surowiecki explains in *The Wisdom of Crowds*:

> Independence is important to intelligent decision making for two reasons. First, it keeps the mistakes that people make from becoming correlated. Errors in individual judgment won't wreck the group's collective judgment as long as these errors aren't systematically pointing in the same direction . . . Second, independent individuals are more likely to have new information rather than the same old data everyone is already familiar with.

Paradoxically, group intelligence will only manifest when participants act as if they are *not* part of a group.

The Price Is Right

The god of the cannibals will be a cannibal, of the crusaders a crusader, and of the merchants a merchant.
—RALPH WALDO EMERSON, *THE CONDUCT OF LIFE*

The intelligent multitude thesis works best where the group draws on diverse knowledge sets, can make individual judgments independently, and has a mechanism for assimilating these judgments into a collective prediction or decision. The Internet—an agglomeration of informed, atomistic individuals largely unconstrained by real-world complications, and the closest thing we have to the classical economic ideal of a "perfect market"—perhaps best illustrates the power of group intelligence. Google, for example, harnesses the decisions of millions of Internet users to identify web pages most relevant to particular search criteria.

Through the operation of abstruse algorithms, links from one web page to another are interpreted as a "vote" for that page, with these votes weighted so that the most visited pages are accorded greater influence than more obscure sites. Google—a meritocracy of millions of individuals' choices—generates an uncannily effective search tool from the distilled wisdom of the crowd.

In a similar manner, stock exchanges absorb the myriad views of thousands of individuals, all of whom may "vote" by electing to buy or sell their securities. In theory, the stock market should be a highly effective forum for the exercise of collective intelligence: it incorporates the decisions of many independent actors, each motivated by the opportunity of financial return, and aggregates these judgments rapidly and transparently. Stockholders "voting" on the price of a security will bring their diverse perspectives to the process—including alternative information sources, differing time horizons, and contrasting investment styles. Efficient markets proponents argue that this arena of robustly competing opinions produces stock prices that embody, and appropriately weight, *all* publicly known information about a particular stock.

A corollary of the efficient markets hypothesis is that it is futile to try to beat the market. As Nobel laureate Paul Samuelson explains, the efficient markets theory teaches that there are no undiscovered bargains or overpriced time bombs lurking on the exchanges:

> If intelligent people are constantly shopping around for good value, selling those stocks they think will turn out to be overvalued and buying those they expect are now undervalued, the result of this action by intelligent investors will be to have existing stock prices already have discounted in them an allowance for their future prospects. Hence, to the passive investor, who does not himself search out undervalued and overvalued situations, there will be presented a pattern of stock prices that makes one stock about as good or bad a buy as another. To that passive investor, chance alone would be as good a method of selection as anything else.

Efficient markets fundamentalists deem the market—like God or his representative on earth—to be omniscient and infallible. Better for the individual to submit to this all-knowing entity, they argue, than waste his or her time trying to best it.

The Pike in the Carp-Pond

As in the case of the bow and the lyre, there is harmony in the tension of opposites.

—Heraclitus

Despite the best efforts of orthodox dogma—which, at its simplest, assumes that all economic actors are members of that elevated species, the ultrarational, perfectly knowledgeable *homo economicus*—it is an incontrovertible fact that some individuals fall far short of the exacting standards of theory. In any stock market there will always be a proportion of participants willing to slipstream behind other investors, relying perhaps on the efficient markets theory to absolve them of the need to apply their own analysis. A market which counts the irrational, the uninformed, or the just plain lazy among its number can still, however, be efficient—provided there are enough sophisticated investors to rein in pricing anomalies caused by the less astute.

A Treasury official once recalled of Keynes that he:

> . . . accepted a description of his functions as those of the pike put into the Roman carp-ponds to chase the carp around and keep them from getting lousy.

Within the Civil Service, Keynes saw himself as a sort of devil's advocate, spurring his colleagues into action and attacking any perceived complacency. The efficient markets theory assumes a similar dynamic. Although there may indeed be slow-witted and inattentive investors in the market, the theory affirms, aberrations caused by their shortcomings will be exploited by their more sophisticated and nimble counterparts. Apparently underpriced stocks will be bid up, and overpriced stocks sold down, by the more efficient predators, maintaining the soundness of the market.

The efficient markets theory does not, therefore, demand that all market participants be the finely calibrated calculating machines of classical theory—merely that sufficient numbers of discerning investors exist so as to countervail the actions of the less sophisticated. In other words, there must be enough investors in any particular market who—disregarding the implications of the efficient markets theory—believe that there *are* in fact bargains to be had. It is these discriminating investors who ensure that markets remain efficient—they are the ever-vigilant pike, securing the overall health of the pond. The efficient markets theory, then, is like a perverse fairytale—one that comes true only if enough people do *not* believe in it.

Safety in Numbers

One dog barks at something, and a hundred bark at the bark.
—CHINESE PROVERB

Unfortunately for efficient markets proponents, individuals often cast aside their independence and instead seek the comfort of the crowd. Man, after all, is a social animal and, where possible, will rely on cues from his fellow creatures. The tendency to accede to the crowd may well be hardwired: the caveman who, on seeing a torrent of people rushing past him, their faces contorted in a rictus of fear, declines to join the stampede is unlikely to have passed his genes on to posterity. Running with the mob is a primal response, particularly in times of panic or uncertainty, but even in more settled circumstances an individual will often seek the imprimatur of the majority.

"Social proof "—the belief that if a large number of people behave in a particular manner there must be a good reason for doing so—is a well-established psychological phenomenon. In the Asch conformity experiments of the 1950s, for example, a group of students was asked to judge the relative lengths of several lines. The catch was that all but one of the students were "insiders" instructed to give answers that were clearly incorrect. Despite obvious discomfort with their responses, around a third of the test subjects conformed to the erroneous view— they believed that the majority could simply not be wrong.

In circumstances such as these, the wisdom of the crowd degenerates into "groupthink"—a situation where each member of a group complies with the perceived consensus. Stock markets are particularly prone to this follow-the-crowd tendency. The bandwagon most conspicuously traverses the uncharted promised land of "new economy" industries—railways in the 1840s, radio in the 1920s, transistors in the

1960s—where a technology is commercially unproven or not readily understood by the bulk of the investing public, and investors take their prompts from those seemingly in the know. The twentieth century's final speculative craze—the dot-com debacle of the 1990s—sported the holy trinity of bubble factors: an emerging technology, new commercial opportunities, and the means for groupthink to propagate itself in chat rooms where like-minded individuals could pontificate without fear of contradiction. Like some sinister self-replicating virus, fostering the conditions of its own flourishing, the Internet bubble fed off the Internet itself as day traders bid up "new economy" stock to unsustainable levels.

Nietzsche Market

When a hundred men stand together, each of them loses his mind and gets another one.
—FRIEDRICH NIETZSCHE (ATTRIBUTED)

There is also, as Keynes observed, "a peculiar zest in making money quickly." Emulation and envy are powerful stimulants, and the desire to keep up with the Joneses often fuels herd behavior. The economist Charles Kindleberger wryly noted that "there is nothing so disturbing to one's well-being and judgment as to see a friend get rich," and the prospect of easy money on the stock exchange inevitably encourages others to venture their hand. Indeed, during booms the more cautious among the investment community are often castigated for their lack of entrepreneurial zeal. One observer of the "vortex of speculation" that gripped English railway stocks in the 1840s commented that:

> The few quiet men who remained uninfluenced by the speculation of the time were, in not a few cases, even reproached for doing injustice to their families, by declining to help themselves from the stores of wealth that were poured out on all sides.

Perhaps the most compelling explanation for the stock market's susceptibility to "informational cascades," however, is that, in some circumstances, herd behavior can appear to be a rational strategy—in the short term at least. A trend of rising stock prices will encourage others to purchase equities, which, in turn, reinforces the upward price trend. The economist John Kenneth Galbraith outlined the mechanics of these "positive feedback loops" in his book *A Short History of Financial Euphoria*:

> Some artifact or some development, seemingly new and desirable . . . captures the financial mind . . . The price of the object of speculation goes up . . . This increase and the prospect attract new buyers; the new buyers assure a further increase. Yet more are attracted; yet more buy; the increase continues. The speculation building on itself provides its own momentum.

With magnificent circularity, rising prices lead to rising prices. Stock market players no longer apply their own judgment in valuing a particular stock, but rather look to trends in the market as their trading guide.

Mob Rule (Sometimes)

They called me mad, and I called them mad, and damn them, they outvoted me.
— NATHANIEL LEE, RESTORATION PLAYWRIGHT
AND BEDLAM INMATE

Financial exchanges, then, are particularly predisposed to informational cascades—episodes where the polarity of the market changes, and speculators predominate over more reasoned elements. The market reaches a pivot point where the intelligent multitude mutates into the unreasoning rabble, or, to use Keynes' metaphor, the schooling carp overwhelm the predatory pike. When the "smart money" is swamped by those scrambling aboard the bandwagon, the group is no longer intelligent and the market forfeits any claim to efficiency.

To paraphrase Oscar Wilde, a speculator is a man who knows the price of everything and the value of nothing. The speculator's concern is not to independently assess the value of a particular stock, but rather to divine the future movement of the market in an attempt to on-sell the stockholding at a profit. Keynes captured the mindset of the speculator perfectly:

> . . . most of these persons are, in fact, largely concerned, not with making superior long-term forecasts of the probable yield of an investment over its whole life, but with foreseeing changes in the conventional basis of valuation a short time ahead of the general public. They are concerned, not with what an investment is really worth to a man who buys it "for keeps," but with what the market will value it at, under the influence of mass psychology, three months or a year hence.

It is the "greater fool" trading strategy—where, as Keynes noted, the speculators' objective is "to outwit the crowd, and to pass the bad, or depreciating, half-crown to the other fellow."

Pass the Parcel

In skating over thin ice, our safety is in our speed.
—RALPH WALDO EMERSON, *PRUDENCE*

Speculators walk a tightrope between staying in the market long enough to optimize trading gains, but not so long that the individual is caught in a bearish lurch downward. Keynes likened trading on a speculation-riven exchange to:

> . . . a game of Snap, of Old Maid, of Musical Chairs—a pastime in which he is victor who says *Snap* neither too soon nor too late, who passed the Old Maid to his neighbor before the game is over, who secures a chair for himself when the music stops. These games can be played with zest and enjoyment, though all the players know that it is the Old Maid which is circulating, or that when the music stops some of the players will find themselves unseated.

The key task for the speculator is, therefore, to correctly *time* the purchase and sale of securities. Based on this belief, Keynes, in the early part of his investment career, thought that success on the stock market required little more than anticipating the anticipations of others.

The rationale behind this strategy was set out in *A Treatise on Money,* written in the late 1920s:

> . . . it may often profit the wisest [stock market player] to antici-
> pate mob psychology rather than the real trend of events, and to ape
> unreason proleptically [i.e. in anticipation] . . . Thus, so long as the
> crowd can be relied on to act in a certain way, even if it be mis-
> guided, it will be to the advantage of the better-informed professional
> to act in the same way—a short period ahead.

Keynes' principal stock market trading strategy in the 1920s—which he christened "credit cycle investing"—faithfully reflected the market-timing approach of the typical speculator. Credit cycling was an application of the oldest stock market maxim in the book: buy low and sell high. As Keynes explained many years later, credit cycling in respect of common stocks "means in practice selling market leaders on a falling market and buying them on a rising one." It was a "top-down" approach to stock market investment, involving "a general systematic movement out of and into ordinary shares as a whole at different phases of the trade cycle." This approach—sometimes dignified with the slightly more scientific-sounding appellations of "momentum investing" or "anticipatory trading"—relies on the speculator's ability to apprehend turns in the market and time trades accordingly. For the "credit cycler," price momentum is the fundamental trading driver, rather than any assessment of the inherent value of a stock relative to its price.

An investment approach requiring the individual to anticipate something as fluid and capricious as "mob psychology" is, as Keynes would later discover, no easy undertaking. He compared the task to:

> . . . those newspaper competitions in which the competitors have to
> pick out the six prettiest faces from a hundred photographs, the prize
> being awarded to the competitor whose choice most nearly cor-
> responds to the average preferences of the competitors as a whole;
> so that each competitor has to pick, not those faces which he him-
> self finds prettiest, but those which he thinks likeliest to catch the
> fancy of the other competitors, all of whom are looking at the prob-
> lem from the same point of view. It is not a case of choosing those
> which, to the best of one's judgment, are really the prettiest, nor even

those which average opinion genuinely thinks the prettiest. We have reached the third degree where we devote our intelligences to anticipating what average opinion expects the average opinion to be. And there are some, I believe, who practice the fourth, fifth and higher degrees.

Momentum investors operate in an Alice in Wonderland world of second-guesses—a crazy, reflexive hall of mirrors where individuals attempt to fathom "what average opinion expects the average opinion to be."

Running of the Bulls

When stock prices are rising, it's called "momentum investing"; when they are falling, it's called "panic."
—PAUL KRUGMAN, *THE NEW YORK TIMES*

Drawing on vast reserves of confidence and self-regard, Keynes convinced himself that he possessed the requisite foresight, skill, and agility to navigate the shifting shoals of market sentiment. Twenty years earlier, he had boasted to his undergraduate friend Lytton Strachey that:

I want to manage a railway or organize a Trust, or at least swindle the investing public. It is so easy and fascinating to master the principles of these things.

Now, at last, Keynes had his opportunity to exploit the mob—to profit from the "gulls" and prove his intellectual superiority. He would, he assumed, successfully ride the cycle—dexterously picking market peaks and bottoms, second-guessing the enthusiasms and fears of the mass of individuals known in the abstract as "the market."

Keynes' unshakeable confidence in his own ability was a trait shared by many in those heady days of the late 1920s. Wall Street was firmly in the grip of a wave of investor euphoria, and while the stock exchange boomed, momentum investing was a game in which almost everyone could be a winner—as the old Wall Street saw reminds us, a rising tide lifts all boats. Although some naysayers liquidated their stockholdings in the summer of 1929, most others—reluctant to be the first to leave the party—maintained their portfolios, anticipating even greater profits in the future.

Charles Mitchell, Chairman of the National City Bank of New York and a noted market bull, typified the exuberant optimism of the time. He asserted in September 1929 that the market was "like a weather-vane pointing into a gale of prosperity." Unfortunately for Keynes and millions of others, Mitchell's meteorological metaphor was only half-right. Rather than a gale of prosperity, a perfect storm of financial destruction was bearing down on Wall Street.

Chapter 4

The Reckoning

The Music Stops

Booms go boom.
—FRED SCHWED, *WHERE ARE THE CUSTOMERS' YACHTS?*

By the late 1920s, Irving Fisher was America's most famous economist and financial pundit—a man who, like Keynes, achieved distinction in both academia and business. A professor of economics at Yale University, Fisher became a multimillionaire after his Index Visible Company, producer of an early version of the Rolodex, merged with Rand in 1925, with Fisher becoming a major shareholder in the new entity. In his unique position as theoretician, entrepreneur, and market player, Fisher was a shaman of the stock market, called upon at regular intervals to read the auguries of Wall Street—especially when the great god Market seemed restive and disobliging.

Fisher was Wall Street's Pollyanna, always ready to offer a reassuring comment or upbeat prognostication to the investing congregation. His great friend, but professional nemesis, was the securities analyst

Roger Babson, dubbed "the Prophet of Loss" by New York newspapers. Babson had presaged a stock market correction since 1926, but, like his fellow unbelievers, had been dismissed as little more than a "sandbagger of American prosperity" by most market watchers. However, on September 5, 1929—just two days after the Dow Jones Industrial Average had recorded an all-time high of 381.2 points—Babson's apprehensions finally found an audience. In a speech to group of businessmen, he warned:

> Sooner or later a crash is coming, and it may be terrific . . . factories will shut down . . . men will be thrown out of work . . . the vicious circle will get in full swing and the result will be a serious business depression.

Wall Street fell around 3 percent that day, and the "Babson break" marked the beginning of six weeks of erratic trading.

Fisher, unsurprisingly, disputed Babson's dark and destabilizing predictions. In mid-October 1929, less than a fortnight before the Great Crash, the Professor stated, "Stock prices have reached what looks like a permanently high plateau . . . I expect to see the stock market a good deal higher . . . within a few months." His effort to quell the bears was, however, unsuccessful. On the morning of October 24, 1929—"Black Thursday," as it later became known—the Wall Street bubble was pricked. Panic selling gripped the exchange in the morning, the financial hemorrhaging staunched only when a cabal of influential bankers ostentatiously stepped on to the trading floor, brandishing a pocketful of buy orders.

The intervention assuaged skittish investors, but only temporarily. Although the weekend break provided a respite from the gyrations of Wall Street, distance from the market also afforded a disturbingly grim vista to spooked shareholders. "Black Monday," October 28, was a financial bloodbath. The Dow Jones index fell by almost a quarter in a single day—the largest one-day decline in Wall Street's history—and in some cases only a lack of buyers arrested the precipitate fall in stock prices. The following day—maintaining the swarthy theme, "Black Tuesday"—witnessed another calamitous decline, this time by a further 13 percent. In that last week of October, stock ticker machines—overwhelmed by the unprecedented trading volume and disgorging tape long after the market had closed—tapped out a staccato requiem for the Great Bull Market of the 1920s.

Nightmare on Wall Street

Some of the people I knew lost millions. I was luckier. All I lost was two hundred and forty thousand dollars . . . I would have lost more but that was all the money I had.
—GROUCHO MARX, *GROUCHO AND ME*

Irving Fisher, that unconquerable optimist, naturally imparted a sanguine spin to the October meltdown. He attributed the severe decline in the Dow Jones index to a "shaking out of the lunatic fringe" and in November 1929 volunteered the opinion that "the end of the decline of the Stock Market will probably not be long, only a few more days at most." In early 1930 he again tried to convince the market—and, in light of his massive exposure, perhaps himself—that "for the immediate future, at least, the outlook [for stocks] is bright." Many others shared Fisher's dogged optimism—even Wall Street's archrealist, the financier Bernard Baruch, felt confident enough by mid-November to cable Winston Churchill with the unequivocal message that the "financial storm [has] definitely passed."

For a while, it looked as if the black days of late 1929 had indeed been nothing more than a pit stop on the road to prosperity. Wall Street was unusually volatile in the wake of the October tempest, but the overall trend was positive—by April 1930 the Dow Jones index was almost 30 percent above the depths plumbed six months earlier. But these brief flares of confidence turned out to be no more than "suckers' rallies," the last instinctive convulsions of a dying market. Wall Street resumed its descent in mid-1930, and by 1932 the Dow Jones Industrial Average stood at a miserable 41.2 points, a drop of almost 90 percent from its September 1929 peak. It would be a quarter of a century before the Dow Jones again reached the heights scaled during the Roaring Twenties.

Irving Fisher, like myriad other speculators and investors, was wiped out. He and his immediate family had borrowed money to buy additional Rand shares at the bull market's pinnacle, and his son later estimated Fisher's loss at around $10 million, well over $100 million in present-day terms. Fisher's insolvency obliged Yale University to buy his house and rent it back to him, with Fisher often unable to pay his new landlord. He came to the attention of the IRS for nonpayment of tax, and was forced to borrow money from his wealthy sister-in-law. As a neoclassical economist whose professional interest was the study of rational markets, he was, for the remainder of his life, the butt of never-ending jokes for his naïve faith in ever-ascending stock prices.

Prophet Warning

Wall Street did *have a go yesterday. Did you read about it? The big-gest crash ever recorded . . . I have been in a thoroughly financial and disgusting state of mind all day.*
　　　　　　　—KEYNES TO LYDIA, OCTOBER 25, 1929

In contrast to his American confrere, Keynes had substantially reduced his exposure to the stock market prior to the Great Crash of 1929. This move was not, however, attributable to any superior foresight on Keynes' account. Rather, his "terrifying adventures" on the speculative markets—this time, the commodities market—had once again brought him undone. In 1928, after several years of profitable trading, Keynes' positions in the rubber, corn, cotton, and tin markets turned against him, and he was obliged to liquidate the bulk of his equities to cover these losses. The stock exchange upheavals of late 1929 then exacted a heavy toll on what little remained of Keynes' stock portfolio: his main holding—the Austin Motor Car Company—lost over three-quarters of its value in the final two years of the 1920s. In aggregate, Keynes' net worth declined by more than 80 percent over this period—from £44,000 at the start of 1928 to less than £8,000 two years later—and, for the second time in his life, he found himself poised on the precipice of financial ruin.

　　Despite the assault on his wealth, Keynes initially shared Fisher's confidence that the events of late 1929 were mere "corrections." He assured readers of the *New York Evening Post* the day after Black

Thursday that "commodity prices will recover and farmers will find themselves in better shape." However, by as early as November 1929 his view on the situation had darkened considerably. Keynes thought that a major economic downturn was imminent and recommended to his fellow directors that the Independent Investment Company, which was heavily invested in Wall Street, sell its securities and repay outstanding debts. By May 1930, Keynes was broadcasting his bleak message to a much wider audience:

> The fact is—a fact not yet recognized by the great public—that we are now in the depths of a very severe international slump, a slump which will take its place in history amongst the most acute ever experienced. It will require not merely passive movements of bank rates to lift us out of a depression of this order, but a very active and determined policy.

The Canary in the Coal Mine

It was borrowed time anyhow—the whole upper tenth of a nation living with the insouciance of grand dukes and the casualness of chorus girls.
　　　　—F. SCOTT FITZGERALD, *ECHOES OF THE JAZZ AGE*

The events of October 1929 were in fact an early symptom—rather than the cause—of a far more malignant malady. The Wall Street side-show had diverted attention away from unsustainable imbalances within the wider community—as the economic historian Robert Heilbroner noted, just prior to the Crash, "some twenty-four thousand families at the apex of the social pyramid received a stream of income three times as large as six million families squashed at the bottom." Credit had largely been channeled away from the real economy and into financial speculation and conspicuous consumption, and while easy money stoked the speculative inferno of the late 1920s, farmers and other primary producers struggled with poor prices and mounting debts.

　　The gilded mansion of American prosperity proved to be top-heavy and teetering, perched precariously on the sandy foundations of installment credit and margin loans. The tremors on Wall Street had finally brought down this house of cards. There were foreclosures, runs on banks, and, ultimately, masses of men laid off. By 1933, a quarter of the United States work force was unemployed, industrial production was only half that of 1929, and real income per capita had fallen to levels not seen since the start of the century. Over 5,000 banks had gone to the wall and "Hoovervilles"—shanty towns of the dispossessed—scarred the country, like open sores on the body politic.

The Wall Street contagion quickly spread beyond American frontiers, the web of obligations arising from the Versailles settlement entangling nations and frustrating their best efforts to quarantine the growing financial pandemic. Worse still, in a Canute-like effort to hold back the deadening tide, Western governments sought refuge behind ever-higher trade barriers. In dismantling the structure of free trade, the developed world was slowly dismembering its golden goose—this protectionist race to the bottom halved the volume of international trade in the four years following the Crash. Deprived of the oxygen of commerce, the world swooned into a state of near-paralysis.

Carpe Diem

But this long run *is a misleading guide to current affairs.* In the long run *we are all dead. Economists set themselves too easy, too useless a task if in tempestuous seasons they can only tell us that when the storm is long past the ocean is flat again.*
— KEYNES, *A TRACT ON MONETARY REFORM*

With increasing urgency, Keynes exhorted governments to act decisively to wrest the Western world from "the bog" into which it had sunk—"Activity and boldness and enterprise," he told a radio audience in early 1931, "must be the cure." His pleas were, however, largely ignored by the practitioners of sound finance. Conventional wisdom counseled a policy of "liquidationism"—letting the hard times "purge the rottenness out of the system," in the words of Andrew Mellon, then the United States Secretary of the Treasury. These high priests of orthodox finance argued that the slump was no more than a rather spectacular manifestation of the "business cycle" which coursed through all developed economies, and that, ultimately, the Western world would right itself and full employment be restored.

Business cycles had long been viewed as an inevitable feature of advanced societies. The first recorded economic forecast had, after all, been Joseph's prediction of seven years of plenty followed by seven years of famine in Pharaonic Egypt, and Keynes himself had been born in the middle of what had been termed "the Great Depression" until it was trumped by the far more serious calamity of the 1930s. Indeed, downturns were welcomed by many as a type of Darwinian spring-cleaning, in which underperforming enterprises are winnowed from the commercial weal. Certain "austere and puritanical souls," Keynes would later remark, even viewed slumps as a kind of divine retribution by the market, as:

> . . . an inevitable and a desirable nemesis on so much overexpansion, as they call it; a nemesis on man's speculative spirit. It would, they feel, be a victory for the mammon of unrighteousness if so much prosperity was not subsequently balanced by universal bankruptcy.

Implicit in the idea of business *cycles,* however, is the notion that—as surely as spring follows winter—the economy will at some stage revert to its previous prosperity. Classical economics, as Keynes summarized, presumed that:

> . . . the existing economic system is, in the long run, a self-adjusting system, though with creaks and groans and jerks, and interrupted by time lags, outside interference and mistakes.

Despite the ferocity of the Great Depression, orthodoxy's faith in the efficacy of markets remained largely intact, seemingly unperturbed by the millions of unemployed, the destitution of families, and the unraveling of nations. Keynes abhorred the easy complacency of classical hardliners, and their serene assurances to the masses that society would *eventually* emerge from the Great Slump. In a stark rejoinder to the liquidationists selling their scorched earth policies, he reminded them that "in the long run we are all dead." In the time of its greatest crisis, capitalism simply did not have the luxury of waiting for the economy to heal itself.

The Croakings of a Cassandra

During the past 12 years I have had very little influence, if any, on policy. But in the role of Cassandra, I have had considerable success as a prophet.

—KEYNES, SPEECH TO MEMBERS OF PARLIAMENT,
SEPTEMBER 16, 1931

As the 1930s stuttered on, there was scant evidence that the developed world was returning to health. Economies wallowed, unemployment levels remained stubbornly persistent, rumblings of discontent grew bolder, and men became restive. In 1932 U.S. Army units—commanded by Douglas MacArthur and George Patton, and assisted by Dwight Eisenhower in his first taste of armed conflict—brutally cleared with bayonets and tanks and teargas the makeshift camps of thousands of war veterans who had marched on the Capitol demanding government aid. That same year in Britain—where official unemployment levels averaged 20 percent nationally, and up to 70 percent in some regions— Sir Oswald Mosley, a former Government minister, seeded the British Union of Fascists in the fertile soil of discontent and despair. And on Continental Europe, the Great Depression acted as a kind of giant centrifuge—hurling men and women away from the political center, toward the extremes of socialism and fascism.

Keynes' gravest forebodings had come to pass. He had warned that the harsh tribute extracted from the Central Powers under that "damnable and disastrous document," the Versailles Treaty, would create insoluble international tensions. Later, he predicted that a return to the gold standard at prewar exchange rates would severely distort trade and capital flows. And, now, as the world lurched even further into the morass, he despaired at the "beggar-thy-neighbor" policies of increasingly protectionist governments, remarking that:

> The modern capitalist is a fair-weather sailor. As soon as a storm rises, he abandons the duties of navigation and even sinks the boats which might carry him to safety by his haste to push his neighbor off and himself in.

Civilization, Keynes realized, rested on "a thin and precarious crust." He believed that the standard nostrum of classical theory—letting "matters take their natural course"—was inadequate and, moreover, misguided. Keynes, with the dubious advantage of already having lived through a decade-long recession in Britain, realized that the Great Depression was more than a merely cyclical phenomenon, and that there were fundamental structural factors which prevented the world from hauling itself out of the quagmire. He had previously used newspaper articles, pamphlets, open letters to heads of state, and what he coyly described as "suggestions to the Treasury" as his soapbox. But despite the energy with which Keynes prosecuted his case, he realized something more was needed—nothing less than a new economic theory which would explain, and solve, "the enormous anomaly of unemployment in a world full of wants."

Keynes would utilize the insights gained from his roller-coaster ride on the financial markets to develop a revolutionary theory that accounted for the booms and busts of modern economies. A central contention of Keynes' radical thesis would be that financial markets were not always efficient, and that upheavals in the world of money could lead to disturbances in the real economy. As a not unwelcome incidental, Keynes would also alight on a set of investment principles— one of the earliest formulations of the value investing philosophy sub- sequently adopted by the likes of Warren Buffett—which would propel him to immense wealth. Like his contemporary Irving Fisher, Keynes had been financially mauled by the volatile markets of the late 1920s. Unlike the unfortunate Fisher, however, Keynes would emerge from the slump with his professional reputation burnished and his riches even greater.

Chapter 5

Raising a Dust

Into the Daylight

. . . the problem of want and poverty and the economic struggle between classes and nations is nothing but a frightful muddle, a transitory and an unnecessary *muddle.*

—KEYNES, *ESSAYS IN PERSUASION*

In 1930—as stock markets faltered, dole queues lengthened, and dark clouds of despair shadowed the Western world—John Maynard Keynes, in a characteristically contrarian mood, proffered a vision of civilization one hundred years hence. He invoked a world where, due to the supreme efficiency of the capitalist system, the "struggle for subsistence" has been overcome and man has at last been led "out of the tunnel of economic necessity into daylight." In this utopia, economists are at last relegated to their proper place in society—"as humble, competent people, on a level with dentists," mere technocrats piloting with a delicate touch the ship of state.

Keynes predicted that when this economic Eden has finally been reached:

> We shall be able to rid ourselves of many of the pseudo-moral principles which have hag-ridden us for two hundred years, by which we have exalted some of the most distasteful of human qualities into the position of the highest virtues.

For Keynes, the cult of capitalism fostered a bizarre parallel universe of inverted values, sanctifying some of man's least attractive tendencies—"avarice and usury and precaution"—into a credo for society. He accepted, however, that the means justified the ends—"wisely managed, [capitalism] can probably be made more efficient for attaining economic ends than any alternative system yet in sight." Keynes' attitude to capitalism was rather like that of Churchill's to democracy—the worst system ever invented, except for all the others. It was a necessary crutch until man finally reached the sunlit uplands of abundance, upon which time a more noble means of administering society could be implemented.

Capitalism's chief virtue, and saving grace, had been its efficacy. If the free market system relinquished its claim to matchless productivity there was a danger that other, ostensibly less morally repugnant, social models would be preferred. As Keynes observed:

> Modern capitalism is absolutely irreligious, without internal union, without much public spirit, often, though not always, a mere congeries of possessors and pursuers. Such a system has to be immensely, not merely moderately, successful to survive.

The apparent failure of the free market system to "deliver the goods," Keynes noted in 1933, meant that Western nations were increasingly willing to abandon their Faustian pact with capitalism and instead embark "on a variety of politico-economic experiments."

Despite his own antipathy to many aspects of the system, Keynes believed that capitalism was not fatally flawed. The profound problems of chronic unemployment and economic stagnation had a simple cause, he asserted, and were amenable to a simple remedy. All that was required was to dethrone the existing orthodoxy, and to ground a new theory more firmly in the realities of everyday economic life—an environment in which individuals grappled with an uncertain future and were prey to greed, fear, and irrationality.

Casting Out the Money Changers

There is always an easy solution to every human problem—neat, plausible, and wrong.

—H. L. MENCKEN, *PREJUDICES*

In March 1933, the recently installed leader of a great but humbled nation addressed his countrymen for the first time in his new capacity. Like an Old Testament firebrand, the leader fulminated against the men of finance who had imperiled his beloved country:

> The money changers have fled from their high seats in the temple of our civilization. We may now restore that temple to the ancient truths. The measure of the restoration lies in the extent to which we apply social values more noble than mere monetary profit.

Noting that "this Nation asks for action, and action now," he urged his compatriots to "move as a trained and loyal army willing to sacrifice for the good of a common discipline . . . because it makes possible a leadership which aims at a larger good." If the national emergency remained critical, the leader cautioned, he would seek "broad Executive power . . . as great as the power that would be given to me if we were in fact invaded by a foreign foe."

Franklin Delano Roosevelt's Inaugural Address as President of the United States was delivered in the depths of the Depression—when, as FDR observed apocalyptically, "the withered leaves of industrial enterprise lie on every side . . . [and] the savings of many years in thousands of families are gone." It disturbingly echoed the messianic platform of the German Nazi Party, which, just two days after Roosevelt's inauguration, garnered the largest number of votes in the country's last free election before the Second World War. The Western world was becoming increasingly desperate—the capitalist system that had served it so well now seemed irremediably broken, and only extreme measures appeared capable of tearing it from its torpor.

This sense of despondency was deepened by the apparent triumphs of Soviet Russia, the country that had most emphatically broken with the free market. Under the uncompromising Five Year Plans issued from the Kremlin, the Soviet Union massively increased its industrial output in the 1930s, almost quadrupling its share of global manufactured products. Seduced by communism's fraternal ideals and its material successes, and perhaps unaware of the human suffering that underwrote these achievements, many of Keynes' friends and students turned "Bolshie" in the Depression decade. Others—generally those in the City or Whitehall—instead sought refuge in the stern, reassuring order of corporatism or fascism. Although the Bolsheviks, the Colonel Blimps, and the Blackshirts squared-off from different ends of the political spectrum, they did have one thing in common—a conviction that the free enterprise system no longer did the job, and needed to be replaced. It seemed, in the mid-1930s, that Marx's grim prognosis of the inbuilt obsolescence of capitalism may have been correct after all.

A New Wisdom

Half of the copybook wisdom of our statesmen is based upon assumptions that were at one time true, or partly true, but are now less and less true by the day. We have to invent new wisdom for a new age.
                                        —KEYNES, *ESSAYS IN PERSUASION*

Keynes was not impressed by the arguments of those wishing to depose capitalism. He seemed to regard communism as more Groucho Marx than Karl Marx, dismissing it as "complicated hocus-pocus" and remarking to his students that he had read *Das Kapital* "as if it were a detective story, trying to find some clue to an idea in it and never succeeding." Similarly, he had no time for fascism as a political solution—Keynes' call to action, he informed the British Fascist leader Oswald Mosley, "was to save the country from [you], not to embrace [you]." In Keynes' opinion, the most serious threat to capitalism came not from the aspiring revolutionaries peddling their "quack remedies," but rather from those who most strenuously proclaimed their fealty to the existing order.

Orthodox finance argued that just as in hard times a household should exercise strict financial discipline, so, too, should slump-afflicted governments practice financial sobriety. As Adam Smith reasoned, "What is prudence in the conduct of every private family, can scarce be folly in that of a great kingdom," and conventional wisdom merely extrapolated good housekeeping to the national arena. Backing up orthodoxy's intuitions were the maxims of classical economics, which posited that the free market system benefited from a system of checks and balances that ensured that the economy always tended toward full employment.

In the Panglossian world of classical theory, all savings would be invested, all workers employed, and all products consumed. Consequently, as Keynes remarked, any interference with this self-adjusting system was viewed as:

> . . . not merely inexpedient, but impious, as calculated to retard the onward movement of the mighty process by which we ourselves had risen like Aphrodite out of the primeval slime of ocean.

However, like the Greek philosopher Thales, who stumbled into a well while gazing at the stars, classical fundamentalists were so dazzled by the beauty of their theoretical superstructure that they disregarded the inadequacies of its foundations. Keynes argued that classical theory's "tacit assumptions are seldom or never satisfied, with the result that it cannot solve the economic problems of the actual world." Rather than reprimand reality for failing to live up to the exacting standards of theory, Keynes would develop a model that embraced and explained real-world imperfections.

Bowling Over the Frock Coats

All successful revolutions are the kicking in of a rotten door.
—JOHN KENNETH GALBRAITH, *THE AGE OF UNCERTAINTY*

Keynes, the proud iconoclast, was never one to be fettered by the accepted economic verities. He exhibited the underrated English virtue of pragmatism, of not being too tightly wed to any particular world view—as he airily informed a Parliamentary Committee in 1930, "I am afraid of 'principle.'" Keynes maintained that economics "is a technique of thinking . . . not a body of settled conclusions." Although originally a zealous defender of the classical tradition, by the mid-1920s he increasingly ranged himself with the "cranks," asserting that a free market economy could stall at "underemployment equilibrium" for lengthy periods.

Keynes observed that classical economics—built on an assumption of scarcity of resources—was poorly equipped to deal with the situation of excess, squandered resources. The orthodoxy, he stated, "has ruled over us rather by hereditary right than by personal merit," and its policy prescriptions often confounded common sense. Keynes mercilessly attacked the "timidities and mental confusions of the so-called 'sound' finance"—those who recited, as if by rote, the tired tenets of classical theory in support of a policy of financial rectitude and caution:

> When we have unemployed men and unemployed plant . . . it is utterly imbecile to say that we cannot *afford* these things. *For it is with the unemployed men and the unemployed plant, and with nothing else, that these things are done.*

Assailing the "deadhead" liquidationists, Keynes argued that the classical paradigm was not inviolate, was not Holy Writ, and by extension the slump was not akin to an Act of God—it was a human problem, and could be solved by the application of sound thinking and courageous initiatives. As Keynes declared in late 1934, "We are . . . at one of those uncommon junctures of human affairs where we can be saved by the solution of an intellectual problem, and in no other way." In arriving at a solution to the overwhelming social problem of his time, Keynes would jettison many of the assumptions and conclusions underwriting classical theory. As he declared to a radio audience:

> There is no reason why we should not feel ourselves free to be bold, to be open, to experiment, to take action, to try the possibilities of things. And over against us, standing in the path, there is nothing but a few old gentlemen tightly buttoned-up in their frock coats, who only need to be treated with a little friendly disrespect and bowled over like ninepins.

The General Theory

I want, so to speak, to raise a dust; because it is only out of the controversy that will arise that what I am saying will get understood.
—KEYNES TO A FELLOW ECONOMIST, AUGUST 27, 1935

The General Theory of Employment, Interest and Money, published in February 1936, disputed the orthodox doctrine that free markets always produce optimal results. Like its namesake, Einstein's General Theory of Relativity, Keynes' magnum opus overthrew the accepted theoretical structure, showing that markets were not necessarily analogous to the clockwork precision of Newtonian physics. Keynes likened classical economists to "Euclidean geometers in a non-Euclidean world who, discovering that in experience straight lines apparently parallel often meet, rebuke the lines for not keeping straight." In his opinion, parts of the classical doctrine, although theoretically elegant, were based on flawed assumptions and deduced outcomes clearly diverging from those in the real world. Keynes set himself the task of overturning the redundant truths of his predecessors. As he prophesied to his friend George Bernard Shaw in 1935, *The General Theory* would "largely revolutionize . . . the way the world thinks about economic problems."

The General Theory was written at a time when most of the developed world had already endured years of chronic unemployment and stagnation—a situation that orthodox economic doctrine deigned impossible, as theory dictated that markets were self-correcting and naturally worked toward full employment. Classical economists argued that the economy was languishing partly because workers were not sufficiently flexible—if only they would behave more like the rational automatons of classical economic theory, willing to take a cut in wages sufficient to justify their employment, then the labor market would self-correct and full employment return.

Keynes believed the orthodox theory—which essentially blamed the unemployed for their plight—to be "wicked" and, moreover, wrongheaded. A central conclusion in *The General Theory*—informed by Keynes' own experience as a speculator—was that the psychology of uncertainty impaired the efficient operation of the market. The existence of uncertainty would periodically result in bouts of underinvestment and oversaving, leading in turn to underutilization of an economy's resources. The Keynesian solution to this state of affairs was, in essence, to boost an economy's aggregate expenditure by increasing government spending to offset lower business and consumer activity.

Money Matters

Speculation improved his economics and economics improved his speculation.

—Nicholas Davenport on Keynes,
Memoirs of a City Radical

The Keynesian prescription was not unlike one of those Eastern sects which hold that worldly temptations and vices can only be defeated through overindulgence. In the same way that Adam Smith thought that the "vain and insatiable desires" of consumers led by the operation of an invisible hand to the advancement of society as a whole, so, too, did Keynes propose a type of hidden hand which transformed the perceived vices of deficit financing into the virtues of full employment and economic stability. In challenging the paradoxical doctrine of the invisible hand, Keynes, the great perverter, proposed an equally counterintuitive proposal—that at certain times, state profligacy could be the most responsible policy.

This idea was deeply offensive to the laissez-faire orthodoxy and to the precepts of sound finance, which clung rigidly to balanced budgets and the principle that expenses should not outrun revenue. Russell Leffingwell, an American banker who had known Keynes since the days of the Paris Peace Conference, typified the City's condescending response to his ideas:

> . . . Keynes and all his school . . . have not the judgment of practical men . . . They are civil servants. They are professors of political economy. They are not bankers and they are not business men.

In fact, it was precisely because Keynes was *more* than just a civil servant or economist that he could break free from the orthodox mindset and develop a theory to explain persistent underemployment, for it was Keynes' experiences on the financial markets that gave him an insight into the true workings of modern economies. Traditional theory had largely overlooked the importance of money and financial exchanges—in the classical realm they were little more than conduits, a veil over "real economy" processes. As the Scottish philosopher David Hume had summarized two centuries before, money in orthodox theory is "none of the wheels of trade: It is the oil which renders the motion of the wheels more smooth and easy."

Rather than abstracting money and financial markets from economic theory, Keynes saw them as a driving force. He realized that money was far more than a medium of exchange or the insubstantial shadow of real economy activities—it was "above all, a subtle device for linking the present to the future." Keynes noted that:

> . . . our desire to hold Money as a store of wealth is a barometer of the degree of our distrust of our own calculations and conventions concerning the future . . . The possession of actual money lulls our disquietude; and the premium which we require to make us part with money is the measure of the degree of our disquietude.

"Liquidity preference"—the desire to hold cash or near-cash—is a gauge of individuals' wariness about the future. When money moves from "industrial circulation" to "financial circulation"—when, rather than being invested in enterprise, savings instead lie fallow—slumps can occur. The flow of money can be thought of as an economy's metabolism, and when individuals hoard their savings because of fears for the future, or when investors lack confidence to embark on new projects, the daisy chain of prosperity breaks and "enterprise will fade and die."

Spender of Last Resort

. . . this is not a crisis of poverty, but a crisis of abundance . . . The voices which—in such a conjuncture—tell us that the path of escape is to be found in strict economy and in refraining, wherever possible, from utilizing the world's potential production are the voices of fools and madmen.
—Keynes, *The World's Economic Outlook*

Rather than having complex and profound causes requiring a radical remedy, Keynes argued that the protracted slump had a simple cause and was capable of a simple solution. The economic engine, he asserted, was suffering from nothing more than "magneto trouble." The motor was largely sound and there was plenty of fuel in reserve—all that was required was a transforming spark to kick-start the machine and return it to the road to prosperity. In the depths of the Great Slump, Keynes buoyantly informed radio listeners that "we are suffering from the growing pains of youth, not from the rheumatics of old age." The celebrated invisible hand, Keynes implied to his audience, merely needed a helping hand.

Like the humanists of an earlier age who rejected the notion of man as a passive plaything of God's will, the Keynesian prescription did not abdicate responsibility for economic welfare to an omniscient, all-powerful market. Rather, man's economic destiny was firmly within his own hands—governments could actively intervene to smooth the business cycle by "spending against the wind," as Keynes termed fiscal fine-tuning. As he declared:

> The important thing for government is not to do things which individuals are doing already, and to do them a little better or a little worse; but to do those things which at present are not done at all.

The General Theory polarized opinion. Some commentators, although admiring the book's cleverness, believed it to be intellectually flawed, "a farrago of confused sophistication." Arthur Pigou, a Cambridge economics professor, was complimentary in a rather backhanded way. "We have watched an artist firing arrows at the moon," he commented. "Whatever be thought of his marksmanship, we can all admire his virtuosity." Others, such as the Austrian economist Friedrich von Hayek, thought it a first step to the totalitarian states that had developed in Germany and Russia. Keynes robustly rejected "the pessimism of the reactionaries who consider the balance of our economic and social life so precarious that we must risk no experiments." In moderating the excesses of capitalism— by introducing an element of "socialization of investment"—Keynes believed that society would, in effect, be inoculated against the far more serious threats of collectivism and authoritarianism.

Keynes thought his "monetary theory of production" to be "moderately conservative in its implications." The Keynesian blueprint merely advocated an external stimulus—"an impulse, a jolt, an acceleration," as Keynes put it—when Adam Smith's invisible hand becomes atrophied through inaction. Once the economic engine had been reignited and "our central controls succeed in establishing an aggregate volume of output corresponding to full employment as nearly as is practicable," then, he commented, "the classical theory comes into its own again from this point onwards." In the previous century Lord Salisbury had stated that British foreign policy was "to float lazily downstream, occasionally putting out a diplomatic boathook to avoid collisions." Keynes's proposed economic policy was similar in conception but somewhat more vigorous in execution—the government would act as a rudder on the ship of state, guiding the economy out of danger when unemployment and stagnation loomed.

The Mark of Keynes

All truth passes through three stages. First, it is ridiculed. Second, it is violently opposed. Third, it is accepted as being self-evident.
    —ARTHUR SCHOPENHAUER, ON THE WISDOM OF LIFE

Considering that Keynes' theory told many politicians exactly what they wanted to hear—that the path to recovery lay not in austerity but in higher spending and lower taxes—it is somewhat surprising that his ideas took so long to be accepted by policymakers. It would not be until that period of sustained global public expenditure otherwise known as the Second World War that "Keynesianism" became the dominant creed of Western nations. Keynes had written in *The General Theory* that:

> Practical men, who believe themselves to be quite exempt from any intellectual influences, are usually the slaves of some defunct economist. Madmen in authority, who hear voices in the air, are distilling their frenzy from some academic scribbler of a few years back.

Keynes' academic scribblings—the belief that fiscal policy should be used to fine-tune an economy's "aggregate demand"—usurped the laissez-faire theories of the classical school almost as comprehensively as Darwin's narrative had displaced that of Genesis.

For three decades after the war, as the Western world luxuriated in conditions of "permanent boom," even Keynes' most vehement ideological adversaries reluctantly conceded that "we are all Keynesians now." Keynes had dragged economics, kicking and screaming, into the twentieth century—from a study of choice under conditions of scarcity to a study of choice under conditions of uncertainty, and from an emphasis on microeconomic factors to an emphasis on aggregates. In his own way, he contributed to the Bloomsbury mission to introduce modernism into Western society, for his economics owed perhaps more to Sigmund Freud's conception of the primal mind than to earlier notions of economic rationality and mechanistic order.

The Keynesian hegemony would finally yield to a counterrevolution of sorts in the 1970s, when conditions of "stagflation"—consistently rising prices in an environment of high unemployment—fostered the revival of neoclassical economics in general, and monetarism in particular. But just as the embers of the first Keynesian coup were flickering out, a second Keynesian revolution was being kindled. In the late 1970s, the emerging discipline of behavioral finance—a melding of economics and psychology—rediscovered Keynes' views on investor psychology and stock market behavior. Having comprehensively overthrown many of the confident conclusions of classical economics over half a century ago, *The General Theory*—perhaps the world's first major work on behavioral economics—would once again prove a foundation text for new ways of thinking.

Chapter 6

Animal Spirits

What Goes Up . . .

To every action there is always opposed an equal reaction.
—Sir Isaac Newton, *Philosophiae Naturalis Principia Mathematica*

In July 1936, only a few months after the release of *The General Theory*, Keynes acquired at auction a large steel trunk from a financially embattled English aristocrat. The box contained some of the personal papers of Isaac Newton, Cambridge's most famous son. Newton is venerated as a giant of science, the son of an illiterate farmer who ushered the world into the Age of Enlightenment. In the words of Alexander Pope:

> Nature and Nature's laws lay hid in night: God said, Let Newton be! and all was light.

In the year 1666 alone—the "Year of Wonders"—the young Newton, locked away at home after the Plague had forced the closure of Cambridge's colleges, invented differential calculus, formulated the

Law of Universal Gravitation, and proposed his Theory of Light. He was celebrated as the discoverer of "the grand secret of the whole Machine," a man whose incandescent intelligence snuffed out the shadows of medieval superstition and ignorance.

The High Priest of Reason was, however, something of a heretic behind closed doors. Much of Newton's early life was spent in his "elaboratory," where, according to his assistant, his "chemical experiments . . . aimed at something beyond the reach of human art and industry." Newton was no dry geometer of the universe—despite the mechanistic conception of the world he propounded, he was obsessed with alchemy and the supernatural. He never completely accepted the notion of "inanimate brute matter," suspecting instead that life was invigorated by unseen "animal spirits" in the ether.

Newton was also an ardent pursuer of material wealth. Unsuccessful in his alchemical effort to transmute base metals into gold, he eventually found his own Philosopher's Stone as Master of the Royal Mint. In this capacity, Newton oversaw the recoinage of England's currency, receiving a commission on all coins struck under his supervision and becoming extraordinarily rich in the process. In 1720, toward the end of his long life, Newton ventured some of his fortune in stock of the South Sea Company. After selling his initial holding for a considerable profit, Newton was induced by rising stock prices to re-enter the market. The second time around he was not so lucky. The South Sea Bubble burst and Newton lost around £20,000—more than $6 million in today's money. Chastened by this demonstration of gravity in the world of finance, he remarked ruefully, "I can calculate the motions of heavenly bodies, but not the madness of people."

Like his hero Newton, Maynard Keynes also learned the hard way that—largely due to the unavoidable fact of uncertainty—financial markets were sometimes buffeted by unpredictable squalls of "whim or sentiment or chance" and prey to "purely irrational waves of optimism or depression." Having spent a decade trying to anticipate the quicksilver tacks of the market—and having been wrong-footed on more than one occasion—Keynes finally concluded that those who run with the crowd are apt to be trampled. Better to stand back from the thundering herd, he decided, than be torn asunder in the running of the bulls or the flight from the bears.

The Uncertainty Principle

. . . in the greatest part of our Concernment, [God] has afforded us only the twilight.

—JOHN LOCKE, *AN ESSAY CONCERNING HUMAN UNDERSTANDING*

Among his other accomplishments, Keynes was also a leading authority on Newton, a position enhanced by his acquisition of the scientist's papers. Keynes brought to the world's attention the occult-obsessed, metaphysical side of Newton—portraying him as a man with "one foot in the Middle Ages, and one foot treading a path for modern science." He also appropriated Newton's idea of "animal spirits"—arguing that in the supposedly mechanistic world of financial markets, investors were often propelled by something other than a clinical analysis of expected outcomes.

Keynes' *General Theory* explained that financial markets are not only prone to periodic informational cascades that compromise efficiency, but also that investors cannot be the rational actors of classical theory because a cold calculation of expected outcomes is simply not possible. With incontrovertible common sense, Keynes observed that there are some events for which "there is no scientific basis on which to form any calculable probability whatever":

> The outstanding fact is the extreme precariousness of the basis of knowledge on which our estimates of prospective yield have to be made. Our knowledge of the factors which will govern the yield of an investment some years hence is usually very slight and often negligible. If we speak frankly, we have to admit that our basis of knowledge for estimating the yield ten years hence of a railway, a copper mine, a textile factory, the goodwill of a patent medicine, an Atlantic liner, a building in the City of London amounts to little and sometimes to nothing . . .

"Wishes are fathers to thoughts," Keynes once observed. Remarkably, it seemed that in championing the case for efficient markets, orthodox theory had glossed over the fact that "core risk"—uncertainty that cannot be assigned a probability—precludes a precise calculation of a stock's expected yield. Keynes therefore rejected orthodox theory's blithe assumption that, in valuing a security, financial market participants could perform "a good Benthamite calculation of a series of prospective advantages and disadvantages, each multiplied by its appropriate probability, waiting to be summed." Despite the assumptions of classical theory, there are, as Keynes pointed out, many factors about which "we simply do not know."

My Indecision Is Final

Prediction is very difficult, especially about the future.
—NIELS BOHR (ATTRIBUTED)

Keynes invoked a paradox beloved of philosophers—that of "Buridan's ass"—to illustrate why "the necessity for action and for decision compels us as practical men" to overlook the "awkward fact" that a uniquely correct valuation of a stock is impossible. Buridan's ass is an apocryphal beast that, faced with two equally attractive and accessible bales of hay, starved while deliberating which one was preferable. Like the donkey of the parable, stock market participants—if they were to attempt to apply a purely rational approach to their investment decisions—would also be rendered immobile by the daunting "what ifs" of an unknowable future. Instead, they resort to less analytical factors when assessing stock market opportunities:

> To avoid being in the position of Buridan's ass, we fall back . . . on motives . . . which are not "rational" in the sense of being concerned with the evaluation of consequences, but are decided by habit, instinct, preference, desire, will etc.

The stock market player is impelled—in part at least—by factors that, although not rational, are nevertheless legitimate in some sense. Unlike the situation with, say, government bonds—which pay a fixed coupon, and whose present investment value can be determined with reasonable precision—stocks exist in a twilight zone of ambiguity. This uncertainty gap is a blank canvas on which the investor projects his or her most fervent hopes or darkest fears. "Animal spirits"—the "spontaneous urge to action rather than inaction," as Keynes defined them—embolden individuals and allow them to bridge the uncertainty gap inherent in any investment decision.

The investor, Keynes concluded, is not the perfectly knowledgeable calculating machine of orthodox theory. Despite the assertions of efficient markets proponents, stock market behavior is not—*cannot be*—governed by purely rational factors. *Investor psychology* plays an integral role in the decision to buy, sell, or hold a stock. As Keynes summarized:

> . . . a large proportion of our positive activities depend on spontaneous optimism rather than on a mathematical expectation, whether moral or hedonistic or economic. Most, probably, of our decisions to do something positive, the full consequences of which will be drawn out over many days to come, can only be taken as a result of animal spirits . . . and not as the outcome of a weighted average of quantitative benefits multiplied by quantitative probabilities.

Jumping at Shadows

The stock market has predicted nine out of the last five recessions.
—Paul Samuelson, *Newsweek*

Not only does the presence of uncertainty mean that investors fall back on their "state of confidence" or "animal spirits" when making investment decisions, but it also exaggerates the impact of near-term factors on a stock's performance. In his *A Treatise on Money*, published in 1930, Keynes noted:

> . . . how sensitive—over-sensitive if you like—to the near future, about which we may think we know a little, even the best-informed must be, because, in truth, we know almost nothing about the more remote future.

Not unreasonably, Keynes conceded, investors attach greater weight to matters about which they are relatively more confident, "even though they may be less decisively relevant to the issue than other facts about which our knowledge is vague and scanty." In consequence:

> ... the facts of the existing situation enter, in a sense disproportionately, into the formation of our long-term expectations; our usual practice being to take the existing situation and to project it into the future, modified only to the extent that we have more or less definite reasons for expecting a change.

The broad assumption that "the existing state of affairs will continue indefinitely" means that:

> Day-to-day fluctuations in the profits of existing investments, which are obviously of an ephemeral and non-significant character, tend to have an altogether excessive, and even an absurd, influence on the market.

As an example of this tendency, Keynes claimed—not without a touch of hyperbole—that "the shares of American companies which manufacture ice tend to sell at a higher price in summer when their profits are seasonally high than in winter when no one wants ice" and that the "recurrence of a bank-holiday may raise the market valuation of the British railway system by several million pounds."

The focus on the shorter term means that investor expectations—and therefore stock prices—are extremely sensitive to new information, and that:

> Faced with the perplexities and uncertainties of the modern world, market values will fluctuate much more widely than will seem reasonable in the light of after-events ...

In simple terms, the unavoidable fact of uncertainty prompts stock market players to latch on to new information, causing stock prices to overshoot. Empirical evidence supports Keynes' thesis—studies show that stock prices display far greater volatility than would be expected relative to changes in underlying earnings and dividends. Exacerbating this tendency to overweight new information is the "risk averse" nature of the average investor—his or her propensity to feel financial losses more keenly than equivalent gains. Risk aversion may cause stock prices to react disproportionately to negative news, as investors overdiscount security prices affected by unfavorable new information.

Confidence Trick

Randolph Duke: *Exactly why do you think the price of pork bellies is going to keep going down, William?*

Billy Ray Valentine: *Okay, pork belly prices have been dropping all morning, which means that everybody is waiting for it to hit rock bottom, so they can buy low. Which means that the people who own the pork belly contracts are saying, "Hey, we're losing all our damn money, and Christmas is around the corner, and I ain't gonna have no money to buy my son the G. I. Joe with the kung-fu grip! And my wife ain't gonna f—my wife ain't gonna make love to me if I got no money!" So they're panicking right now, they're screaming "SELL! SELL!" to get out before the price keeps dropping. They're panicking out there right now, I can feel it.*

—TRADING PLACES

The stock market, Keynes demonstrated, was not always the unassailable paragon of efficiency that orthodox financial theorists claimed it to be. It was prone to informational cascades—episodes where prices would snowball in one direction or the other merely because momentum had seized the market—and, more fundamentally, investment decisions were impelled to some extent by necessarily nonrational factors. As Keynes pointed out, due to the inescapable fact of uncertainty, "all sorts of considerations enter into the market valuation which are in no way relevant to the prospective yield."

To take but one example, a biographer of Marcel Proust, that rich but troubled neurasthenic of the early twentieth century, noted that the French author:

> . . . made many ruinous investments but refused to listen to his banker
> . . . More often than not he purchased a stock because of its poetic name ("The Tanganyika Railway," "The Australian Gold Mines"); in fact, these stocks were a substitute for the travels to exotic places he longed to make.

Like Tolstoy's unhappy families, all irrational investors are irrational in their own particular way. Proust's purchases, made in the antiseptic emptiness of his cork-lined bedroom, were guided by the evocativeness of a company name, their words as charged with associations as his tea-soaked madeleine biscuits. Other, perhaps less poetically inclined, market players might equally be influenced by a perceived trend in a stock's price, an inside tip, or what the chap next door is doing.

Keynes' view of the stock market was diametrically opposed to that of orthodox financial theory, where, as the reference books inform the reader, "investors are unromantically concerned with the firm's cash flows and the portion of those cash flows to which they are entitled." In the make-believe world of classical theory, the stock market was conceived as an infallible machine for crystallizing the present value of future income from a security. Real world complications such as uncertainty and the state of investor confidence were conveniently disregarded in the interests of theoretical elegance. Orthodox theory did not admit the possibility that the virus of animal spirits could infect the machine, causing it to generate numbers which could depart widely from any reasonable assessment of true value.

State of Emergency

Under certain circumstances . . . an agglomeration of men presents new characteristics very different from those of the individuals comprising it.
—GUSTAVE LE BON, *THE CROWD*

Economics has been greatly influenced by discoveries in the "hard" sciences—the clockwork precision of Newtonian physics was reflected in classical theory's mechanistic conception of the world; Darwin's doctrine of survival of the fittest inspired the muscular free-trade policies of the Victorian era; and Einstein's bizarre theories of relativity were mirrored in the Keynesian universe, where money—like time—was sometimes more than a mere inert cipher. Keynes argued, however, that economics seemed to depart from the comforting resemblance to science in at least one key respect. In the discipline of economics, he asserted, "the atomic hypothesis that has worked so splendidly in physics breaks down," and consequently:

We are faced at every turn with the problems of organic unity, of discreteness, of discontinuity—the whole is not equal to the sum of the parts, comparisons of quantity fail us, small changes produce large effects, the assumptions of a uniform and homogeneous continuum are not satisfied.

The economy, as Keynes noted, exhibits what have come to be called "emergent properties": complex, sometimes unpredictable, collective behavior in a system, arising out of the multiplicity of interactions between its individual constituents.

Behavior in the atomistic world of microeconomics cannot always be extrapolated to the sphere of macroeconomics, the study of aggregates. Keynes' most famous example of the "fallacy of composition" was the so-called Paradox of Thrift—which notes that saving is good for the individual, but if all individuals increase their savings then aggregate demand will fall, eventually leading to lower savings for the population as a whole. Similarly, the stock market—one of the purest expressions of the free market system—can, on occasions, display emergent properties, where individual behavior mutates into mob irrationality. Even for someone of Keynes' protean interests and abilities, the stock market was simply too vast and too complex a mechanism to second-guess.

A Sentimental Education

Don't try to buy at the bottom and sell at the top. This cannot be done—except by liars.
—BERNARD BARUCH, *MY OWN STORY*

Keynes eventually concluded that because of the utter capriciousness and complexity of the stock market, a short-term "momentum investing" approach rarely rewarded its followers with financial success. As he conceded to a colleague in May 1938:

> I can only say that I was the principal inventor of credit cycle investment and have seen it tried by five different parties acting in detail on distinctly different lines over a period of nearly twenty years, which has been full of ups and downs; and I have not seen a single case of a success having been made of it.

Keynes thought that credit cycling not only demanded "abnormal foresight" and required "phenomenal skill to make much out of it," but that transaction expenses from such a necessarily active investment policy tended to erode trading profits. He expanded on this theme in a memorandum to the King's College Estates Committee:

> . . . I am clear that the idea of wholesale shifts [out of and into stocks at different stages of the business cycle] is for various reasons impracticable and indeed undesirable. Most of those who attempt it sell too late and buy too late, and do both too often, incurring heavy expenses and developing too unsettled and speculative a state of mind . . .

Keynes' realization that there was no method to the market's madness prompted a radical change in his investment approach. Following the Great Crash, he completely inverted his investment principles, becoming an investor rather than a speculator—one who focuses on likely future performance rather than past trends, expected yield rather than disposal price, particular stocks rather than the broader index, and relying on his own judgment rather than that of the market. Simply stated, Keynes switched from market timer to value investor, seeking to profit from swings in the market rather than participating in them.

Chapter 7

Game Players

Flowering Inferno

"It's always best on these occasions to do what the mob do."
"But suppose there are two mobs?" suggested Mr. Snodgrass.
"Shout with the largest," replied Mr. Pickwick.
　　　　　　　—CHARLES DICKENS, *THE PICKWICK PAPERS*

"Tulipomania" saw the pathogen of animal spirits visit that most stolid of people, the Dutch burghers of the seventeenth century. As Charles Mackay recalls in his catalog of human folly, *Extraordinary Popular Delusions and the Madness of Crowds,* the "rage to possess" tulips was so powerful that:

> Nobles, citizens, farmers, mechanics, seamen, footmen, maidservants, even chimney-sweeps and old clotheswomen, dabbled in tulips. People of all grades converted their property in cash, and invested it in flowers.

Speculative fervor for the exotic plants was such that traders, in an early version of a futures contract, started to sell the rights to bulbs they had not yet even planted. This innovation—dismissively labeled *windhandel,* or "wind trade," by those untouched by the mania—encouraged even more speculation, as trading moved from the physical to the abstract.

"Broken" flowers—cultivars with flares of blazing color—were the most highly valued. By early 1637, one bulb of the *Semper Augustus* strain—its blood-red flames vivid against a pure white—commanded the same price as a large canal-side house in Amsterdam. The variegated hues of these prized flowers were caused by a virus, and, as was later discovered, it was the virus that both increased the attractiveness of the flowers and also contributed to their frailty. As Mackay explained:

> When it has been weakened by cultivation, [the tulip] becomes more agreeable in the eyes of the florist . . . Thus this masterpiece of culture, the more beautiful it turns, grows so much the weaker, so that, with the greatest skill and most careful attention, it can scarcely be transplanted, or even kept alive.

The Dutch tulipomania eventually, and inevitably, unwound in a most spectacular manner. Bulbs that had sold for 5,000 guilders in January 1637 fetched only 50 guilders a month later. The Dutch courts correctly diagnosed the malady that had temporarily seized the population—characterizing the transactions as nothing more than gambling operations, they declined to enforce outstanding contracts of sale.

The tulipomania—in addition to providing another illustration of the periodic irrationality that ensnares markets—also affords a metaphor for financial exchanges generally. Like the tulip, whose refinement and frailty move in tandem, the more highly evolved a stock market, the greater the risk that it will be susceptible to the contagion of animal spirits. As Keynes noted in *The General Theory,* when "the organization of investment markets improves, the risk of the predominance of speculation does, however, increase."

Having disposed of the fiction of investors as rational calculating machines summing risk-weighted expected cash flows, Keynes then proceeded in *The General Theory* to identify other factors, largely attributable to the increasing sophistication of financial exchanges, that he believed compromised the efficiency of markets. When discriminating investors are "so much in the minority that their behavior does not govern the market," Keynes argued, a stock exchange could assume the traits of its "game players," evincing an excessively short-term approach and presenting with bipolar tendencies.

The Dangers of Democracy

I don't want to belong to any club that will accept me as a member.
—GROUCHO MARX, *GROUCHO AND ME*

Keynes, unapologetic elitist that he was, believed that the increasing democratization of stock investing adversely affected the stability of the system. As he observed in *The General Theory*:

> That the sins of the London Stock Exchange are less than those of Wall Street may be due, not so much to differences in national character, as to the fact that to the average Englishman Throgmorton Street is, compared with Wall Street to the average American, inaccessible and very expensive.

Keynes thought that "liquid" financial exchanges—those with low transaction costs and that are effectively open to all—encouraged the entry of dilettante investors who "have no special knowledge of the circumstances, either actual or prospective, of the business in question."

He believed that the lack of real knowledge about the underlying business increased the stock market's fickleness and its propensity to overreact to new information, "since there will be no strong roots of conviction to hold [a valuation] steady." Keynes also lamented that the financial exchanges—with their constant price quotations and potential to readily monetize investments—gave:

> . . . a frequent opportunity to the individual . . . to revise his commitments. It is as though a farmer, having tapped his barometer after breakfast, could decide to remove his capital from the farming business between 10 and 11 in the morning and reconsider whether he should return to it later in the week.

Greater liquidity, lower transaction costs, and the advent of the Internet combine to make shares even easier to trade today, and in consequence have further exacerbated the flightiness of capital. These factors also make stocks increasingly abstract concepts, disembodied from the businesses they represent—"an abstraction, a name, a symbol interchangeable with a certain amount of money," as one commentator described the transformation of the humble tulip during the Dutch derangement of the seventeenth century. The perception by many market participants that stocks are little more than a number in a newspaper column or on a computer screen—a mere trading chip divorced from the underlying business, rather than a part-interest in the business itself—further inflames the speculative mindset.

Outrunning the Bear

Worldly wisdom teaches that it is better for reputation to fail conventionally than to succeed unconventionally.
— KEYNES, *THE GENERAL THEORY*

The story is told of two hunters, madly scrambling through a forest, trying to evade a particularly cantankerous and agile bear. Mid-pursuit, one stops, reaches into his backpack, and changes into running shoes. The other man tells him he is crazy—there is no way he will be able to outrun the bear, even with his new footwear. "I don't need to outrun the bear," he replies, "I just need to outrun *you*." A similar dynamic exists on modern stock markets, where fund managers and other financial institutions are largely assessed on performance relative to their peers over short intervals, rather than by reference to their absolute investment performance over the longer term. This benchmarking practice naturally encourages fund managers to adopt a near-term focus—for even if the institutions themselves are impervious to the siren calls of the mob, their unit-holders may not possess the same forbearance.

The efficient markets hypothesis states that although some stock market participants may not boast Spock-like levels of rationality and cool-headedness, the smart money will nevertheless act to rein in any pricing anomalies produced. Keynes dismissed this belief as little more than a convenient fiction:

It might have been supposed that competition between expert professionals, possessing judgment and knowledge beyond that of the average private investor, would correct the vagaries of the ignorant individual left to himself. It happens, however, that the energies and skill of the professional investor and speculator are mainly occupied otherwise. For most of these persons are, in fact, largely concerned, not with making superior long-term forecasts of the probable yield of an investment over its whole life, but with foreseeing changes in the conventional basis of valuation a short time ahead of the general public.

Professional investors, in practice, rarely accept the role of market monitor assigned to them by orthodox theory. As Keynes noted, there is overwhelming institutional pressure to conform, even among allegedly sophisticated investors:

> . . . it is the long-term investor, he who most promotes the public interest, who will in practice come in for most criticism, wherever investment funds are managed by committees or boards or banks. For it is in the essence of his behavior that he should be eccentric, unconventional and rash in the eyes of average opinion. If he is successful, that will only confirm the general belief in his rashness; and if in the short run he is unsuccessful, which is very likely, he will not receive much mercy.

Like the mass of investors, fund managers are more often concerned with not underperforming than trying to outperform. In practice, they do not provide a countervailing force against the more flighty investors—indeed, on many occasions they actually amplify the swings of investor irrationality.

Intensifying the short-term focus of many institutional investment managers are two additional factors—an emphasis on "total returns" as a performance guide, and the presence of "index-tracking funds." Total returns measures—comprising dividend payments and any increase or decrease in the price of a given stock—are usually dominated by unrealized capital gains or losses, which once again focuses attention on short-term stock price fluctuations. Index-tracking funds—investment vehicles that seek to replicate market performance by holding a representative portfolio of stocks—aggravate the market's tendency to overshoot by reinforcing trends in the market. Index funds are momentum investors *in excelsis*—they automatically buy more of a stock as its price, and therefore its value relative to the broader market, increases, and sell as its price decreases—thus adding to overshoots and further eroding the purported efficiency of financial exchanges.

Bipolar Bears (and Bulls)

[Bipolar Affective Disorder] is . . . characterized by repeated . . . episodes in which . . . mood and activity levels are significantly disturbed, this disturbance consisting on some occasions of an elevation of mood and increased energy and activity (mania . . .), and on others of a lowering of mood and decreased energy and activity (depression). Characteristically, recovery is usually complete between episodes . . .
—CLASSIFICATION OF MENTAL AND BEHAVIOURAL DISORDERS, WORLD HEALTH ORGANIZATION

The stock market, Keynes showed, could move violently in response to changes in investor psychology, was susceptible to informational cascades, could overshoot based on new information, was excessively focused on near-term price performance, and was populated by investors having "no special knowledge" of the stocks in which they trade. One financial markets practitioner who shared Keynes' rather jaundiced view was Benjamin Graham, an American investor and academic. Like Keynes, Graham had been badly burnt by the Great Crash, his stock portfolio losing almost three-quarters of its value during the slump. And again like Keynes, this loss—combined with observations picked up while working on Wall Street—motivated Graham to think deeply about financial exchanges and their frailties.

Graham believed that stock markets were periodically influenced by pendulum swings of investor sentiment, when quoted prices depart significantly from a stock's underlying value, and that these swings could be exploited by the rational, patient investor:

> . . . price fluctuations have only one significant meaning for the true investor. They provide him with an opportunity to buy wisely when prices fall sharply and to sell wisely when they advance a great deal.

To illustrate his thesis, Ben Graham proposed a novel way to think about the stock market. He encouraged investors to imagine that they are dealing with an individual who, each trading day, offers to buy or sell stocks at a given price. As Graham explained, "Mr. Market":

> . . . is very obliging indeed. Every day he tells you what he thinks your interest is worth and furthermore offers either to buy you out or sell you an additional interest on that basis.

Mr. Market is often a relatively stable and rational entity, offering to deal in stocks at prices which approximate their true worth. Sometimes, however, Mr. Market lapses into mania or depression, is panicked by a negative piece of news or elated by apparently positive developments, or focuses excessively on short-term factors while missing the bigger picture. When Mr. Market "lets his enthusiasm or his fears run away with him," Graham observed, "the value he proposes seems to you a little short of silly."

The stock market, Graham implied, could sometimes be neurotic, paranoid, myopic, and afflicted by mania or depression—if it were an individual, it would be medicated. Yet despite all his pathologies and character flaws, Mr. Market possesses one sterling virtue—that of perseverance. He is not offended if an investor is unresponsive to his constant solicitations, and will unfailingly return every trading day with renewed offers to buy and sell securities. Using Mr. Market as an investment adviser, Graham cautioned, could be ruinous for an investor. On the other hand, the poor fellow could be exploited when he was in the throes of an irrational episode—for although Mr. Market frequently degenerated into a form of madness, he would eventually come to his senses, and stock prices would in due course revert toward their fundamental value.

Buffy the Empire Slayer

Charlie Munger: *If you mix raisins with turds, they're still turds.*
Warren Buffett: *That's why they have me write the annual report.*
    —BERKSHIRE HATHAWAY ANNUAL MEETING, 2000

Ben Graham's investment company spawned a number of highly successful value investors, the most famous of whom is Warren Buffett.

Buffett is one of the world's richest men, but unlike most other members of the billionaires' club, his wealth was built entirely from stock market and other company investments. As *Time* magazine noted in a profile on Buffett:

> We've seen oil magnates, real estate moguls, shippers, and robber barons at the top of the money heap, but Buffett is the first person to get there just by picking stocks.

Buffett has been investing for over half a century, and his record is remarkable. In the four decades or so since he acquired Berkshire Hathaway as his investment vehicle, the company has outperformed the broader market by a fiftyfold margin. This investment performance represents an average compounded return of more than 20 percent a year—a record unmatched by any other large, long-term investor.

Buffett and his vice chairman at Berkshire Hathaway, Charles Munger, are the Butch Cassidy and Sundance Kid of the investment world. Buffett is a wisecracking, Coke-swigging septuagenarian dispensing pithy financial wisdom in perfectly honed epigrams, while the octogenarian Munger revels in the role of straight man and resident curmudgeon. In his letters to stockholders and at Berkshire Hathaway's annual meetings—labeled "Woodstock for Capitalists" by the Chairman—Buffett plays up the image of himself as a gauche but deceptively wise Midwesterner, possessed of deep reserves of folksy common sense. The phlegmatic Buffett is the antithesis of the edgy, volatile stock market players depicted in popular culture, and there is a satisfying moral resonance to his message—the meek and unflashy may indeed inherit the earth.

Warren Buffett is not the "Wizard of Wall Street" or the "Sage of Silicon Valley," but rather the "Oracle of Omaha." Berkshire Hathaway is headquartered in Omaha, Nebraska—about equidistant from Wall Street and Silicon Valley, as if reluctant to get too close to either. The positioning seems uncannily appropriate. The Berkshire Hathaway duo dismiss many of the maxims of conventional finance, and their consistent outperformance of the broader indices is a living reproof to the efficient markets hypothesis. They are proud Luddites, famous abstainers during the dot-com delirium, and merciless critics of the hyperactivity of day traders and some investment funds. In a feat of exquisite symmetry—and as if to underline Buffett's contrarian invest-ment style and his absolute antipathy to the financial fads that periodi-cally hijack the market—during the rollicking dot-com days of early 2000, Berkshire Hathaway stock fell to a three-year low on the same day the NASDAQ reached its record high.

Buffett owes much of his success to Ben Graham's insights on stock market behavior. He has embraced Graham's Mr. Market analogy—frequently referring to the "various forms of mass hysteria that infect the investment markets from time to time"—and has also wholeheart-edly adopted some of Graham's other principles, such as ensuring that a significant "margin of safety" exists when purchasing securities. But in many ways Buffett's stock market philosophy is far closer to that practiced by Keynes decades earlier. Noting that Keynes "began as a market-timer . . . and converted, after much thought, to value invest-ing," Buffett often cites his philosophical fellow traveler when musing on the stock market.

Far From the Madding Crowd

When the facts change, I change my mind—what do you do, sir?
                                                    —KEYNES (ATTRIBUTED)

Keynes' break with credit cycling marked his transformation from spec-ulator to investor. He defined speculation as "the activity of forecasting the psychology of the market," in contrast to "enterprise," or true invest-ment, which involves "forecasting the prospective yield of assets over their whole life." The investor focuses on the income that a security is expected to produce, not the possible sale price of that security in the near term. Or, to employ Keynes' terminology, the true investor is con-cerned more with "ultimate values" than "exchange values."

Rather than trying to be a type of market barometer—gauging whether fair winds or foul would visit the exchange—Keynes decided to take advantage of the stock market's "bull tacks" and "bear tacks" in another way. He would no longer attempt to *time*, or anticipate, *general* movements in the market; instead, he would use the *value* of a *particular* stock as his investment guide. Only when the pendulum of investor sentiment had swung too far in respect of a given stock—such that the quoted price veered significantly from assessed fundamental value— would Keynes consider buying or selling that security.

As Keynes summarized, this alternative investment policy:

> . . . assumes the ability to pick specialties which have, on the average, prospects of rising enormously more than an index of market leaders . . . this practice does, in my opinion, in fact enable one to take at least as good an advantage of fluctuations as credit cycling, though in a rather different way. It is largely the fluctuations which throw up the bargains and the uncertainty due to fluctuations which prevents other people from taking advantage of them.

Keynes realized that the distance from manic to panic on the stock market could be vanishingly short. Rather than trying to outwit the mercurial mob and anticipate inflections in the investment cycle, he concluded it was far more preferable to pick the low-hanging fruit that occasionally presented itself to the investor.

The Prodigal Son

There are two times in a man's life when he should not speculate:
when he can't afford it, and when he can.
    —MARK TWAIN, *PUDD'NHEAD WILSON'S NEW CALENDAR*

Keynes' switch from speculator to value investor delivered a radical change in his fortunes. In contrast to the grim days of the early 1930s— where, "although not quite destitute," he had been obliged to put two of his best-loved paintings, a Matisse and a Seurat, up for sale—Keynes had again become "horribly prosperous" by the time *The General Theory* was published. In the years between the Wall Street Crash and the end of 1936, Keynes multiplied his wealth more than sixtyfold, parlaying net assets of just under £8,000 at the end of 1929 to more than £500,000 only six years later.

Just as impressive as his financial recovery was his return to the Establishment fold. The man who had likened himself to Cassandra of Greek mythology—gifted with the powers of prophecy, but fated never to be believed—found himself embraced once again by the ruling elite. Like Churchill, Keynes was drafted into deal with a situation he had long presaged, when in 1940 he became an unpaid adviser to the Chancellor—in his words, a "demi-semi-official" with a wide-ranging brief to formulate economic policy for war-pressed Britain. The following year he was installed as a director of the Bank of England—on his appointment he quipped to his mother that it could only be a matter of time before he became a bishop—and in 1942 elevated to a peerage, becoming Lord Keynes, Baron of Tilton. In the closing stages of the war he continued to straddle the worlds of Mammon and of Art—acting as Britain's chief representative at both the international monetary conference at Bretton Woods and in loan negotiations with the United States, and becoming the United Kingdom's first arts tsar as inaugural chairman of what would evolve into the British Arts Council.

Remarkably, these various offices were carried out while Keynes was in extremely frail health. In mid-1937, just before his fifty-fourth birthday, he suffered his first heart attack, and was confined to a sanatorium and later his country house in Sussex for much of his convalescence. Paralleling Keynes' physical breakdown was a short, sharp economic recession in late 1937 and 1938, accompanied by another severe "sinking spell" on major stock markets. Unable to attend many board and investment committee meetings due to his enforced confinement, and obliged to defend his stock market techniques amid yet another bout of pervasive pessimism, Keynes explained his investment philosophy in a series of letters and memoranda to his colleagues.

It is from this rich documentary legacy that we distill Keynes' six key investment principles, representing a straightforward and time-tested system for exploiting the periodic irrationality of stock markets.

Chapter 8

Searching for Stunners

The Damn'd South Sea

The additional rise of this stock above the true capital will be only imaginary; one added to one, by any rules of vulgar arithmetic, will never make three and a half; consequently, all the fictitious value must be a loss to some persons or other, first or last. The only way to prevent it to oneself must be to sell out betimes, and so let the Devil take the hindmost.

—UNKNOWN CONTEMPORARY COMMENTATOR,
ON THE SOUTH SEA BUBBLE

The South Sea Company, when established in 1711, seemed an elegant solution to a number of disparate problems. It would take over Britain's burgeoning public debt by converting government borrowings into Company equity, its trading rights to Spain's American colonies could be used as a bargaining chip with the belligerent Spanish king, and the venture, if successful, promised to fill the coffers of the Exchequer with

substantial trading profits. Yet despite support from the highest levels—
King George was appointed Governor of the Company in 1715—
the enterprise initially languished. The "trade monopoly" secured over the
Spanish Americas was pitiful, in both senses of the word: an annual quota
of 4,800 *piezas de Indias* (male African slaves, no defects, at least 58 inches
in height), as well as one ship per year carrying miscellaneous commercial
goods. The venture yielded no substantial profit and, in any case, war with
Spain in 1718 effectively terminated the trading rights of the Company.

The fortunes of the South Sea Company were, however, reinvigor-
ated in March 1720 when it won a bidding contest against the Bank
of England to acquire more government debt in another stock-for-
borrowings swap. In an effort to procure a favorable exchange rate
for the conversion, promoters talked up the prospects of the Company
and circulated "the most extravagant rumors" of the potential value
of its trading concessions with the New World. Stock prices rocketed
from £128 per share in January 1720 to just over £1,000 less than six
months later. Prefiguring day traders' chat rooms of our era, the boost-
erism of Company directors was abetted by stimulant-stoked chatter in
coffee houses and wildly optimistic reports in the newfangled medium
of newspapers.

London was caught up in a fetish for easy money. Samuel Johnson
later noted that "even poets panted after wealth"—Alexander Pope, he
wrote, "ventured some of his money . . . and for a while he thought
himself the lord of thousands." Although himself caught in the riptide
of greed, Pope still had an eye to the deleterious effect of South Sea
hysteria, which diverted the populace from the banal, but necessary,
responsibilities of everyday life:

> No Ships unload, no Looms at Work we see,
> But all are swallow'd by the damn'd South Sea.

Women, constrained in their dealings in real property, were particularly enthusiastic participants in the stock market frenzy. One lady,
Sarah, Duchess of Marlborough, realized that prices for South Sea stock
were not anchored to any bed of true value:

> Every mortal that has common sense or that knows anything of fig-
> ures, sees that 'tis not possible by all the arts and tricks upon earth

long to carry £400,000,000 of paper credit with £15,000,000 of specie. This makes me think that this project must burst in a little while and fall to nothing.

The Duchess—who, her great-grandson Winston Churchill would later remark, possessed an "almost repellent common sense"—sold her shares near the market peak, pocketing the then astronomical sum of £100,000. For the following couple of months, she continued to profit from the mob by extending heavily secured loans to some of her more bullish peers. Ultimately, they did not share the Duchess's good fortune—prompted by the failure of a similar scheme in France, spooked by the closure of trading ports due to the Plague, and perhaps affected by a general credit squeeze, the bubble eventually burst. By December 1720 the stock had sputtered back to ground—describing an almost perfect parabola on the share price chart, South Sea paper traded at exactly the same level as at the start of the year.

As the Duchess of Marlborough shrewdly observed, stock exchanges can at times confect prices which veer considerably from any reasonable estimate of underlying value. Almost three centuries later, despite—and often because of—the sophistication of modern exchanges, stock markets are still prone to episodes in which pricing and value radically diverge. Like the Duchess, Maynard Keynes concluded by the early 1930s that, as one of his biographers put it, "the laws of arithmetic were more reliable than the winds of rumor"—far better, he decided, to ground investment decisions in the firm foundation of hard analysis than in something as impalpable as "market sentiment."

Nullius in Verba

The seekers after perpetual motion are trying to get something from nothing.

—SIR ISAAC NEWTON (ATTRIBUTED)

In July 1720, the British parliament passed the "Bubble Act," which prohibited the formation of joint stock companies unless expressly authorized by Royal Charter. Although some cynics suggested that the real purpose of the legislation was to allow the South Sea Company to corner the market on investor credulity, the ostensible explanation for the Act was to curb the speculative wildfire ignited by the South Sea bubble. Exploiting the "inordinate thirst of gain that had afflicted all ranks of society" during the mad days of early 1720, other company promoters had attempted to raise money for projects of dubious merit, including a hush-hush enterprise "for carrying on an undertaking of great advantage, but nobody to know what it is," and another to build a wheel for perpetual motion.

Isaac Newton—the practitioner of "cold and untinctured reason" in his scientific endeavors—became the most famous "cully", or victim, of the South Sea hysteria. Perhaps the continued rise of South Sea stock in the summer of 1720 convinced him that the market could simply not be wrong, that Britain had indeed stumbled on a corporate El Dorado. In any case, the man who was once a dirt-poor student among the Cambridge toffs, supporting himself by scrubbing the floors and emptying the bedpans of his more affluent classmates, was beguiled by the vision of abundant wealth shimmering on the horizon. He, like so many others, became intoxicated by the "unwholesome fermentation" produced by the action of animal spirits, in which "the hope of boundless wealth for the morrow made [men] heedless and extravagant for to-day."

Newton, then the President of the Royal Society, the world's oldest existent academy of science, failed to heed its eminently wise motto, *Nullius in Verba*—don't take anyone's word for it. Had he applied the same rigor to his stock speculations as he did to his scientific speculations, Newton would have realized that, just as certain fundamental laws in physics mandate that a perpetual motion machine cannot exist, so too the inexorable rise of South Sea stock could not last. Instead of following the crowd, he would have been far better served exercising "his unusual powers of continuous concentrated introspection," as Keynes characterized what he considered Newton's chief strength. Upon even a cursory analysis, Newton would have concluded that the prices of South Sea shares were levitating entirely as a result of the collective will of speculators, rather than by reference to any economic fundamentals.

The Economist and the $100 Bill

A neoclassical economist and his pupil are sauntering across a university green one day, discussing the finer points of financial theory, when the undergraduate sights what seems to be a $100 bill skipping across the grass. The student quickens his pace to intercept the fugitive note, but the economist indulgently restrains his young charge. "If it really were a $100 bill," the older man advises, "someone would have picked it up by now."

—MARKET ANECDOTE

After his own stock market reverses, Keynes determined that value investing—basing the investment decision on a comparison of the likely future returns from a security against its asking price—was the best corrective to the periodic visitations of animal spirits. Value investing repudiates a fundamental tenet of the efficient markets hypothesis by asserting that there can in fact be a sustained divergence between the quoted price of a stock and its underlying value. Value investors are fond of citing the rather arch parable of the economist and the $100 bill to parody the "strong form" of the efficient markets theory, which states that there are no hitherto undiscovered bargains—and, conversely, no overpriced lemons—lurking on sophisticated financial exchanges.

As characterized by some financial commentators, an efficient financial market is one in which the sheep are protected from the wolves by other wolves—that is, discerning investors will operate to trim any disparity between quoted price and true worth by bidding up apparently underpriced stocks and selling down overpriced paper. By so doing, these stock market vigilantes—the pike in the carp-pond, to borrow Keynes' metaphor—ensure that, in theory, unsophisticated investors will not be at the mercy of the smart money. As the authors of *Principles of Corporate Finance,* the bible in undergraduate finance classes around the world, assure their readers: "In an efficient market you can trust prices. They impound all available information about the value of each security."

Efficient markets proponents will often go to great lengths to defend their theory. They may argue, for example, that the ever-ascending prices of a fervid bull market are justified by a particular innovation or improvement in the economic environment—"This time it's different," they persuade themselves, as old valuation metrics are casually discarded. Former President Herbert Hoover, for instance, recalled the self-serving fictions invented to justify the extravagant stock prices of the late 1920s:

> With the growing optimism, they gave birth to a foolish idea called the "New Economic Era." The notion spread over the whole coun- try. We were assured that we were in a new period where the old laws of economics no longer applied.

Stock market players, it is apparent, are sometimes more adept at ration- alization than rationality.

Other adherents to the orthodoxy simply proffer the circular argu- ment that prices must always be correct because they are the product of an all-knowing exchange. The comforting conceit of efficient markets seemingly blinds some to the common-sense observation that financial exchanges periodically experience spasms of irrationality, where security prices diverge considerably from any reasonable assessment of underly- ing value. The backers of the efficient markets hypothesis simply do not accept that on occasions there are not enough wolves to corral the sheep, and that the bleating flock can blindly file into a chasm.

The Weighting Game

> *It is impossible to avoid a precipice, when one follows a road that leads nowhere else.*
> —JEAN-BAPTISTE SAY, *A TREATISE ON POLITICAL ECONOMY*

Efficient markets fundamentalists, in arguing that stock prices *always* incorporate *all* public information impacting the value of a security, succumb to an absurdly basic error. As Warren Buffett has noted:

> Observing correctly that the market was *frequently* efficient, [many academics and investment professionals] went on to conclude incor- rectly that it was *always* efficient. The difference between these prop- ositions is night and day.

Value investors, by definition, do not accept the strong form of the efficient markets theory. There are times when the quoted price of a security departs from its underlying value, these investors believe, and it is on these occasions that the intelligent investor seeks to exploit the mispricing that results.

Despite their skepticism about the effectiveness of the stock market in the short run, value investors generally accept that over the longer term stock markets price securities efficiently. As Keynes commented in a letter to a colleague, "when the safety, excellence, and cheapness of a share is generally realized, its price is bound to go up." Ben Graham offers another arresting analogy to illustrate this tendency:

> . . . the market is not a *weighing machine,* on which the value of each issue is recorded by an exact and impersonal mechanism, in accordance with its specific qualities. Rather should we say that the market is a *voting machine,* whereon countless individuals register choices which are the product partly of reason and partly of emotion.

In the near term, stock prices oscillate around true worth, and at times the amplitude of divergence can be significant. In the longer term, however, the truth will out. As Buffett comments, "The market may ignore business success for a while, but eventually will confirm it."

Market efficiency, for value investors, is therefore a question of timing—although not agreeing that financial exchanges are invariably efficient in the short run, they generally accept that in the long run stock markets are indeed very effective "weighing machines." As pioneering fund manager John Bogle observes, "The fact is that when the perception—interim stock prices—vastly departs from the reality—intrinsic corporate values—the gap can only be reconciled in favor of reality." This is due to a simple and indisputable mathematical identity—over time, stockholders, in aggregate, can only earn what the underlying business earns. Animal spirits lack endurance—they may deflect prices from underlying value for a period of time, but ultimately the hard realities of earnings and dividends will determine the value of a business to its owners. Empirical evidence confirms the effectiveness of stock markets as a weighing machine over the longer term. As one report concludes, although year-to-year stock performance is heavily influenced by price movements:

> For the seriously long-term investor, the value of a portfolio corresponds closely to the present value of dividends. The present value of the (eventual) capital appreciation dwindles greatly into insignificance.

Bargain Hunting

Annual income twenty pounds, annual expenditure nineteen nineteen and six, result happiness. Annual income twenty pounds, annual expenditure twenty pounds ought and six, result misery.
—CHARLES DICKENS, *DAVID COPPERFIELD*

Intelligent investors, then, look for stocks where the quoted price has for some reason uncoupled from any reasonable assessment of earnings potential. Value investing, at its simplest, is the act of getting more than is given—for a buyer of stocks, securing a stream of cash flows whose present value is expected to exceed the purchase price, for a seller of stocks, pocketing sale proceeds which exceed any reasonable estimate of future dividends. As Warren Buffett summarizes, value investors:

> . . . search for discrepancies between the *value* of a business and the *price* of small pieces of that business in the market . . . The investors simply focus on two variables: price and value.

It is on expected earnings and dividends, therefore, that the value investor concentrates, rather than short-term price fluctuations. The quoted price of a stock is useful only as a point of reference, in determining whether the market is offering substantially more or less than the estimated underlying value of the security. In explaining his investment philosophy to a colleague, Keynes remarked that:

> My purpose is to buy securities where I am satisfied as to assets and ultimate earning power and where the market price seems cheap in relation to these.

As Keynes emphasized, when ascertaining the underlying value of a stock, it is the company's net assets or, more often, its "ultimate earning power" that is relevant. The "intrinsic" or "fundamental" value of a stock is simply the sum of expected cash flows from a given security, appropriately discounted for the effects of time. Other measures commonly thought to satisfy value investment precepts—such as low price-to-earnings ratios, low price-to-book value, and a high dividend yield—are, at best, tools for identifying possibly underpriced stocks. Ultimately, however, it is the expected earning power of a stock that counts.

The value investor, therefore, adopts a "bottom-up," rather than "top-down," investment style—that is, the investor scrutinizes *particular* stocks in an effort to determine whether there exists a discrepancy between the quoted price of the business and its assessed underlying value. Other factors—whether the stock price has trended up or down in recent times, what other stock markets are doing, whether a particular sector is "hot" at the moment—are of no interest to the intelligent investor. As renowned stock-picker and financier Sir John Templeton counseled, the disciplined investor should "buy value, not market trends or the economic outlook." The value investor focuses on specific stocks rather than the broader index, and remembers always that there is no such thing as an undifferentiated "stock market"—there is only a market for individual stocks.

Eyes Forward

The future ain't what it used to be.

—YOGI BERRA (ATTRIBUTED)

Man is a pattern-making animal, and seeks to impose order or a *raison d'être* where it does not necessarily exist. He discerns faces in clouds and winning streaks in a coin toss, and three dots on a piece of paper will always resolve into a triangle. Likewise in the stock market, many game players believe that the trend is their friend—that what happened in the recent past is as good a guide as any as to what might happen in the future. As Keynes observed in one of his Chairman's speeches at a National Mutual annual meeting, "Speculative markets . . . are governed . . . by fear more than by forecast, by memories of last time and not by foreknowledge of next time." Speculators generally rely on *past* events—price momentum and perceived market trends—as buying or selling cues.

In contrast, value investors—those who scrutinize individual stocks rather than attempting to take the temperature of the market—focus only on the likely *future* income from a particular security. For these individuals, the investment decision is driven not by a mere expectation that prices will rise or fall over the short term, but rather by an assessment of whether stock prices appear cheap or expensive, based on an estimate of what earnings are likely to do in the long term. Intelligent investors concentrate on the business behind the stock, speculators on the stock price independent of the business. Practitioners of value investing always have intrinsic value as the bedrock of their decision-making—price merely offers a point of entry (or exit) to the investor, should it move far enough from the estimated underlying value of the security.

Virtue Rewarded

I am still convinced that one is doing a fundamentally sound thing, that is to say, backing intrinsic values, enormously in excess of the market price, which at some utterly unpredictable date will in due course bring the ship home.
—KEYNES TO THE MANAGING DIRECTOR OF PROVINCIAL INSURANCE COMPANY, APRIL 10, 1940

Keynes, as one of his Bloomsbury contemporaries observed, "loved a bargain." Notwithstanding his growing wealth and generous financial support of the arts, he watched over his personal finances with surprisingly keen eyes. Keynes was not above haggling with tradesmen over a few pence, would buy large consignments of war-issue bully beef because it was only a penny a tin, and hosted dinner parties that were legendary for their frugality. Virginia Woolf noted that on one occasion Keynes served a miserly three grouse to his eleven guests—the visitors' "eyes gleamed as the bones went round," she later remarked with a regulation Bloomsbury barb. The Bloomsberries, grousing about the grouse, may have extracted a few sardonic laughs at Keynes' expense, but perhaps they missed a key point about the man. The remarkable fact was not that Keynes was a resolute bargain hunter despite his great wealth, but rather that the bulk of his riches were derived precisely *because* he was a bargain hunter.

In the final phase of his investment career, Keynes focused on identifying "stunners"—those stocks which offered "intrinsic values . . . enormously in excess of market price." Although Keynes professed scant faith in the efficiency of financial exchanges at any given point in time, he did concede that, in the longer term, the stock market would recognize the value inherent in a security and reward performance. The intelligent investor, therefore, focuses on the *future earnings ability* of a *particular* stock, rather than being diverted by past trends in the market as a whole. Short-term price fluctuations, the excitement generated by an influx of animal spirits, stock market whims and fashions—all these are of absolutely no import to the discriminating investor. The only relevant factor is the disparity, if any, between price and the estimated intrinsic value of a stock.

Keynes' value investing discipline effectively shielded him from the assaults of animal spirits during the 1930s and 1940s. Unlike Newton, who during the South Sea imbroglio followed the crowd and neglected to flex his mental muscles in the field of finance, Keynes applied his own analysis rather than trying to anticipate the market. In a letter to Richard Kahn, a former pupil and Second Bursar at King's, Keynes summarized his value investing philosophy as follows:

> It is a much safer and easier way in the long run by which to make investment profits to buy £1 notes at 15*s.* than to sell £1 notes at 15*s.* in the hope of repurchasing them at 12*s.* 6*d.*

Or, rephrasing this maxim in decimal terms, we could say that it is preferable to buy one-dollar bills at seventy cents, rather than selling them at seventy cents in the hope of subsequently repurchasing the notes at fifty cents.

To return to the beauty contest analogy in *The General Theory,* a value investor—after proper reflection—will determine whom he or she thinks is the prettiest contestant, rather than trying to second-guess the second-guesses of others. The intelligent investor has faith that, eventually, the prettiest girl will indeed step up to the podium.

Chapter 9

Safety First

The Fall of the Nous of Ussher

I would rather be vaguely right, than precisely wrong.
—KEYNES (ATTRIBUTED)

James Ussher was a man of many talents—Archbishop of Armagh, Primate of All Ireland, Privy Councillor, and Vice-Provost of Dublin's Trinity College. But perhaps his greatest gift to posterity was his detailed study on the chronology of the Bible, undertaken in the mid-seventeenth century during the last decade of his life. By adding up the genealogies of Adam and his brood, and painstakingly cross-referencing these against other classical texts, Ussher deduced the exact date of Creation. The world, he declared, saw its first sunrise on Sunday, October 23, 4004 BC. Working from this absolute base, he could then calculate other key dates from Genesis—Adam and Eve, for example, were ejected from Paradise on Monday, November 10, 4004 BC, and Noah's Ark finally bumped into Mount Ararat on May 5, 2348 BC, a Wednesday.

Archbishop Ussher's ecclesiastical exactitude—subsequently modified by Isaac Newton in his own quest to fathom the secrets of the scriptures—is an object lesson in the perils of precision. Likewise, in the sphere of stock market investing, Keynes recognized that—due to unavoidable uncertainty surrounding future earnings—determining the intrinsic value of a stock was a necessarily fuzzy art. He had little time for the "brand of statistical alchemy" that many stock analysts brought to their calculations, in which the alleged value of a security was derived with pinpoint accuracy. Precision in stock valuation was nothing more than a consoling fiction, Keynes thought, perhaps designed to provide the illusion of certainty in an inherently unpredictable world.

Like Warren Buffett after him, Keynes rejected the application of a bogus precision when estimating the intrinsic value of a stock. He realized that not only does an overemphasis on quantitative factors downplay non-numerical elements that may impact on the value of a stock, but—due to uncertainty—any stock valuation must of necessity be inexact, lying at best within a range of possible values. The prudent investor, therefore, incorporates a wide margin of error into any assessment of the relative merits of a security. Inverting the mindset of the typical speculator, value investors focus as much on not losing money as on potential gains—they are concerned with the return *of* capital, not just the potential return *on* capital. In his effort to avoid what he called "stumers"—situations "where the fall in value is due not merely to fluctuations, but to an intrinsic loss of capital"—Keynes focused on a policy of "safety first", of ensuring that a protective buffer exists between a stock's price and its perceived underlying value.

Omission Possible

Life is the art of drawing sufficient conclusions from insufficient premises.
—SAMUEL BUTLER, *THE NOTE-BOOKS OF SAMUEL BUTLER*

In 1922, while in Germany to advise on currency reform, Keynes found himself seated next to Max Planck at a dinner for Berlin's financial and academic elite. Planck, a recent Nobel Prize winner for his pioneering work in quantum physics, revealed to his dinner companion that—perhaps influenced by a Munich professor's rueful observation years earlier that in the field of physics "almost everything is already discovered, and all that remains is to fill a few holes"—he had at one stage considered studying economics. Ultimately, however, Planck had declined the opportunity to join the ranks of the dismal scientists— economics, he had decided, was simply too difficult.

What Planck meant, Keynes later explained, was that economics was an "amalgam of logic and intuition," incapable of distillation into the flinty certainties of the physical sciences, and it was this lack of precision that made it "overwhelmingly difficult" for a man of Planck's rigorous and deductive disposition. Although Keynes' response to Planck's observation was not recorded, he no doubt would have congratulated the esteemed professor on his perspicacity. Keynes believed that, in a misguided effort to mimic the theoretical rigor of the physical sciences, classical economics clung too tightly to a "specious precision," at the expense of "concealed factors" that are not capable of quantification.

Friedrich von Hayek—Keynes' philosophical antipode in most other areas—shared these reservations. In his Nobel Prize lecture, he noted that "in the study of such complex phenomena as the market . . . [many factors] will hardly ever be fully known or measurable." Classical economists laboring under a "scientistic" attitude, Hayek observed, simply disregard those factors which "cannot be confirmed by quantitative evidence" and "they thereupon happily proceed on the fiction that the factors which they can measure are the only ones that are relevant." Keynes similarly deplored the "Ricardian vice" which he believed pervaded classical economic thought—the crystallization of all interrelationships, all activities into mathematical formulas, and the dismissal of qualitative elements as unworthy of analysis. "When statistics do not seem to make sense," he once remarked, "I find it is generally wiser to prefer sense to statistics!"

Origins of the Specious

There are three kinds of lies: lies, damned lies and statistics.
—MARK TWAIN, *THE AUTOBIOGRAPHY OF MARK TWAIN*

Despite the fact that the only certainty about future returns from a security is their very uncertainty, a similar defect afflicts the stock market—analysts solemnly apply rigorous quantitative techniques to derive a valuation, down to the last cent, for a particular stock. Berkshire Hathaway's Charlie Munger has labeled this bias toward quantification, at the expense of qualitative factors, as the "man with a hammer" syndrome—"To the man with only a hammer," he observes, "every problem looks like a nail." Echoing Hayek's criticisms, Munger notes that:

> . . . practically everybody (1) overweighs the stuff that can be num-bered, because it yields to the statistical techniques they're taught in academia, and (2) doesn't mix in the hard-to-measure stuff that may be more important.

It appears that human psychology demands this spurious precision in an effort to mask the uncertainty inherent in any investment deci-sion. As Fred Schwed observed in *Where Are the Customers' Yachts?*, his classic account of Wall Street's foibles:

> It seems that the immature mind has a regrettable tendency to believe, as actually true, that which it only hopes to be true. In this case, the notion that the financial future is not predictable is just too unpleas-ant to be given any room at all in the Wall Streeter's consciousness.

Keynes agreed that this sham exactitude was the stock market's equiva-lent of whistling in the dark, noting that "peace and comfort of mind require that we should hide from ourselves how little we foresee."

Elaborate quantitative analysis may also be an attempt to clothe mere hunches in a cloak of intellectual respectability. The economist Robert Shiller, author of the book *Irrational Exuberance*, remarks that sometimes:

> . . . institutional investors do not feel that they have the authority to make trades in accordance with their own best judgments, which are often intuitive, that they must have reasons for what they do, reasons that could be justified to a committee.

Complex and comprehensive spreadsheets—calculating cash flows, risk-adjusting returns, deriving stock valuations with unimpeachable certitude—are often nothing more than an elaborate alibi, designed to confer a bogus authority to inherently uncertain subject matter.

Girl in the Gorilla Suit

Not everything that counts can be counted, and not everything that can be counted counts.
—Sign hung in Albert Einstein's Princeton study

The psychology experiment sometimes known as "the girl in the gorilla suit" illustrates how focusing too tightly on some factors can distort the bigger picture. In this experiment, subjects were shown a short video of two teams passing a basketball among themselves, and were asked to count the number of passes made by one of the teams. While team members are firing basketballs at each other, a woman in a gorilla suit lopes on to the court, stops, faces the camera and pounds her chest before moving off-screen. Around half of the participants in the exercise claimed not to have seen the apish apparition—they were simply too preoccupied with diligently counting the number of passes made by "their" team.

In a similar way, an excessive focus on quantitative data can warp stock valuations. As Ben Graham commented:

> . . . the combination of precise formulas with highly imprecise assumptions can be used to establish, or rather to justify, practically any value one wishes . . . in the stock market the more elaborate and abstruse the mathematics the more uncertain and speculative are the conclusions we draw therefrom.

Graham's own solution to this problem was not to reduce his reliance on quantitative factors, but rather to impose a more onerous test on potential acquisitions. In his book *The Intelligent Investor*, Graham suggested "readers limit themselves to issues selling not far above their tangible-asset value." Such a high hurdle would, he thought, ensure that investors secured a sufficient "margin of safety" in their stock purchases.

Fingers and Toes Investing

Charlie Munger: *We have such a "fingers and toes" style around here. Warren often talks about these discounted cash flows, but I've never seen him do one . . .*

Warren Buffett: *That's true. It's sort of automatic. If you have to actually do it with pencil and paper, it's too close to think about. It ought to just kind of scream at you that you've got this huge margin of safety.*

—Berkshire Hathaway annual meeting, 1996

In determining whether a stock displayed the necessary margin of safety—a sufficiently wide gap between assessed intrinsic value and quoted price—Ben Graham exhibited his own particular variant of the "man with a hammer" syndrome. His valuation approach was essentially a static one, concentrating mainly on the value of a company's physical assets. This technique might have been appropriate in the wake of the Great Depression—where stocks were sometimes offloaded at fire-sale prices and physical assets constituted the bulk of a firm's worth—but it is of limited practical value in today's world, where it is estimated that almost three-quarters of the market value of companies in the Standard & Poor's 500 comprises intangible assets, such as brand names, patents and "human capital."

Keynes, like Warren Buffett after him, practiced a more dynamic valuation methodology—one focused on projected earnings accruing to a particular firm. The notional tool used in this type of analysis is the "dividend discount model." This model states that the intrinsic value of a given security is determined by the stream of its prospective dividend payments over time, discounted back to a present value. Warren Buffett highlighted the tasks required of an investor using this technique:

> If you buy a bond, you know exactly what's going to happen, assuming it's a good bond . . . If it says 9 percent, you know what the coupons are going to be for maybe thirty years . . . Now, when you buy a business, you're buying something with coupons on it, too, except, the only problem is, they don't print the amount. And it's my job to print in the amount on the coupon.

Unlike government or corporate bonds—which carry a known coupon and a predetermined maturity date—the expected income flow from a security cannot be determined with any degree of precision. Instead, the investor must refer to qualitative factors when determining the value of a stock. Warren Buffett provides an everyday analogy to describe the derivation of intrinsic value:

> It's exactly what I would do if I were going to buy a Ford dealership in Omaha—only with a few more zeros. If I were going to try and buy that business—let's say I weren't going to manage it—I'd try to figure out what sort of economics are attached to it: What's the competition like? What can the return on equity likely be over time? Is this the guy to run it? Is he going to be straight with me? It's the same thing with a public company. The only difference is that the numbers are bigger and you buy them in little pieces.

Ascertaining the intrinsic value of a stock is a necessarily inexact art— as Buffett observes, the underlying or fundamental value of a stock is "a number that is impossible to pinpoint but essential to estimate."

The Half-Empty Glass

Fish see the bait, but not the hook; men see the profit, but not the peril.
—CHINESE PROVERB

Intrinsic value, then, is a nebulous measure, existing at best within a range of possibilities. The importance of qualitative elements means that calculations of intrinsic value, properly done, cannot move beyond a fairly basic level of analysis—as Ben Graham observed, he had never "seen dependable calculations made about common-stock values . . . that went beyond simple arithmetic or the most elementary algebra." The benefit of intrinsic value calculations lies as much in providing a checklist to ensure that the investor has turned his or her mind to all major factors potentially impacting the price of a security as in ascertaining an actual range of values. As Warren Buffett explains:

> Just as Justice Stewart found it impossible to formulate a test for obscenity but nevertheless asserted, "I know it when I see it," so also

can investors—in an inexact but useful way—"see" the risks inherent in certain investments without reference to complex equations or price histories.

Compensating for this necessary imprecision is the concept of a *margin of safety*—a buffer, in Ben Graham's words, "for absorbing the effect of miscalculations or worse than average luck." Value investors, accepting the inexactness of intrinsic value measures, seek to identify those stand-out stocks that appear to display an undeniably large gap between underlying worth and quoted price. Although these "ultra favorites" or "stunners," as Keynes called them, may not display a sharply defined intrinsic value, a sufficient margin of safety should nevertheless be evident. Ben Graham and his co-author David Dodd explained the concept in their book *Security Analysis*:

> To use a homely simile, it is quite possible to decide by inspection that a woman is old enough to vote without knowing her age or that a man is heavier than he should be without knowing his exact weight.

Value investing is, in essence, a "glass half-empty" rather than "glass half-full" approach—it focuses on downside risks rather than those on the upside. By selecting only those stocks that appear to be priced at a substantial discount to intrinsic worth, the investor ensures that there is a "floor" of underlying value that should support pricing over the longer term. The speculator, in contrast, is principally concerned not with the underlying earnings of a business but rather whether the stock can be offloaded at a higher price. As Fred Schwed observed:

> Speculation is an effort, probably unsuccessful, to turn a little money into a lot. Investment is an effort, which should be successful, to prevent a lot of money from becoming a little.

Keynes noted that for those seized by animal spirits, "the thought of ultimate loss . . . is put aside as a healthy man puts aside the expectation of death." Value investors, on the other hand, focus heavily on downside risks before investing, by seeking to ensure a sufficient margin of safety exists in respect of any potential purchase.

Pick-a-Number

Having a past actually counted against a company, for a past was a record and a record was a sign of a company's limitations . . . You had to show that you were the company not of the present but of the future.
—MICHAEL LEWIS ON DOT-COMS, *THE NEW NEW THING*

Reviewing a journal article on statistical methods, Keynes recalled the mythical account of the seventy scholars asked to translate the Old Testament into Greek for inclusion in the Library of Alexandria:

> It will be remembered that the seventy translators . . . were shut up in seventy separate rooms with the Hebrew text and brought out with them, when they emerged, seventy identical translations. Would the same miracle be vouchsafed if seventy [analysts] were shut up with the same statistical material?

Keynes had very little faith in the ability of purely quantitative methods to come up with meaningful estimates of intrinsic worth. Quoting the nineteenth-century journalist Walter Bagehot, he agreed that "there is no place where the calculations are so fine, or where they are employed on data so impalpable and so little 'immersed in matter'" as on the stock exchange. Consequently, there exists a very frail foundation for the calculation of a stock's underlying value, and there may be widely divergent opinions on the worth of a security.

Recognizing that, due to both uncertainty and the presence of qualitative factors, a range of possibilities was the best that could be expected when assessing the underlying worth of a stock, Keynes adopted a "safety first" policy that sought to identify those stocks trading at a substantial discount to even low-range estimated intrinsic value. He realized that "the amount of the risk to any investor principally depends, in fact, upon the degree of ignorance respecting the circumstances and prospects of the investment he is considering." In other words, as uncertainty surrounding expected future cash flows increases, so too does the "fuzziness" of intrinsic value measures—consequently, a greater margin of safety is required.

Keynes observed that some stocks are more amenable to a tighter calculation of intrinsic value than others, and are therefore more compatible with a safety first policy. In *The General Theory* he noted that:

> . . . there are many individual investments of which the prospective yield is legitimately dominated by the returns of the comparatively near future . . . In the case of . . . public utilities [for example], a substantial proportion of the prospective yield is practically guaranteed by monopoly privileges coupled with the right to charge such rates as will provide a certain stipulated margin.

Warren Buffett repeated the point in a letter to Berkshire Hathaway stockholders, in which he commented that "the more uncertain the future of a business, the more possibility there is that the calculation will be wildly off-base."

A Bird in the Hand

Unquestionably, the really right policy would be to aim at as high an income as possible, and not to trouble too much about capital valuations.
—KEYNES TO THE CHIEF OFFICER OF NATIONAL MUTUAL,
JANUARY 19, 1939

The tenets of value investing—which demand a wide margin of safety in respect of securities acquired—will naturally bias investors toward stocks with a relatively stable and sustainable earnings profile. Serial acquirers—corporate Pacmen with the capacity to hide earnings performance behind the latest acquisition—are of little interest to the value investor, nor are stocks offering the promise of "blue sky" returns at some indefinite point in the future. Warren Buffett—a famous no-show at the Internet bender of the late 1990s—explained his preference, as an investor, for those stocks sometimes dismissively labeled as "boring":

> With Coke I can come up with a very rational figure for the cash it will generate in the future. But with the top 10 Internet companies, how much cash will they produce over the next 25 years? If you say you don't know, then you don't know what it is worth and you are speculating, not investing. All I know is that I don't know, and if I don't know, I don't invest.

In an undergraduate essay on the British philosopher and statesman Edmund Burke, Keynes noted in passing that:

> Our power of prediction is so slight, our knowledge of remote consequences so uncertain, that it is seldom wise to sacrifice a present benefit for a doubtful advantage in the future.

Keynes' observation was a rather baroque restatement of the proverb "a bird in the hand is worth two in the bush." In the stock market arena, too, Keynes eventually adhered to this principle—"ultimate earning power," not the vague promise of riches in some undefined future period, was fundamental in determining the worth of a stock.

Warren Buffett similarly insists on "demonstrated consistent earning power" before he commits capital to a particular security. He notes that:

> The key to investing is not assessing how much an industry is going to affect society, or how much it will grow, but rather determining the competitive advantage of any given company and, above all, the durability of that advantage.

It is earnings—not market capitalization, revenue growth, or the novelty of an industry—that will ultimately determine the value of a company, and therefore its stock price. A business that draws in $50 billion of revenue but, because of poor margins, ekes out the profit of a market stall is worth very little to the rational investor. Similarly, companies lacking defensible barriers to competitive entry may not have sustainable long-term earnings, and therefore will be of little interest to the disciplined stock-picker.

Maintaining an Edge

> *. . . I am generally trying to look a long way ahead and am prepared to ignore immediate fluctuations, if I am satisfied that the assets and earning power are there . . . If I succeed in this, I shall simultaneously have achieved safety-first and capital profits.*
> —KEYNES TO THE CHAIRMAN OF PROVINCIAL
> INSURANCE COMPANY, FEBRUARY 6, 1942

Unlike many of his peers, Keynes did not harbor a secret desire to make economics as inflexible and austere as Euclidean geometry. "Economics is essentially a moral science and not a natural science," he maintained, "that is to say, it employs introspection and judgments of value." Similarly, Keynes disclaimed the need for—or possibility of—precision in the stock market domain. The unavoidable presence of uncertainty—the fact that, in regard to the future, "we simply do not know"—combined with the existence of factors which impact on a stock's value but cannot be quantified, means that the task of ascertaining the underlying value of a stock is a necessarily inexact art.

Accepting that intrinsic value can, at best, lie somewhere within a range of values, Keynes developed a safety first policy in respect of his stock acquisitions. Considering both quantitative and non-numerical factors, he assessed a firm's "assets and ultimate earning power" and compared the implied value of the entire company against the market's asking price for part-shares in that business. By "backing intrinsic values . . . enormously in excess of the market price," Keynes was confident that he would achieve his stated objectives of both "safety first" and, eventually, capital gains.

Warren Buffett's investment policy is very similar to that of Keynes. He accepts that "valuing a business is part art and part science" and therefore advocates a margin of safety—a financial shock absorber—to compensate for this lack of precision:

> You also have to have the knowledge to enable you to make a very general estimate about the value of the underlying businesses. But you do not cut it close. That is what Ben Graham meant by having a margin of safety. You don't try and buy businesses worth $83 million for $80 million. You leave yourself an enormous margin. When you build a bridge, you insist it can carry 30,000 pounds, but you only drive 10,000 pound trucks across it. And that same principle works in investing.

Exactitude in the stock market arena is a fiction—because of uncertainty, no one can value a security precisely. The best response to this uncertainty, Keynes and Buffett argue, is to ensure a wide buffer exists between perceived value and quoted price. Eventually, as the stock market reasserts its function as a weighing machine, this margin of safety should be converted into an investor's margin of gain.

Chapter 10

Leaning into the Wind

Apples for Peanuts

Necessity never made a good bargain.
— BENJAMIN FRANKLIN, *POOR RICHARD'S ALMANACK*

In March 1918 the German army—its eastern forces loosed after a treaty with newly Bolshevik Russia—gambled on a massive assault on the Western Front before the resources of that awakened giant, America, could be fully deployed. Ground which had been so expensively purchased in previous years—thousands of men killed for every few hundred yards of swampy, torn earth—now yielded itself freely to the Central Powers, and in just a few days *Sturmtruppen* were encamped on the outskirts of Paris. From these redoubts the Germans employed a fearsome new weapon, gigantic guns capable of hurling payloads high into the stratosphere and more than 80 miles distant—well within range of the center of Paris.

Unsurprisingly, the success of the German Spring Offensive and the destruction inflicted by the unseen "Big Berthas" generated enormous panic in the French capital. Thousands of Parisians streamed west from the city, but battling against this current of people was Maynard Keynes. He had heard from his friend, the painter Duncan Grant, that the private collection of Edgar Degas was to be auctioned in Paris in late March. Grant and the Bloomsbury set urged Keynes to deploy his government connections to obtain funds to bid for these artworks. By proposing an ingenious scheme to offset any purchases against existing French debts to Britain, and arguing that "fine specimens of Masters" would be a much better bet than financially distressed French Treasury bills, Keynes extracted more than half a million francs from the Exchequer. Keynes was so taken with the operation, in fact, that not only did he secure the means for the National Gallery to bid for the Degas collection, but he also decided to attend the auction in person.

As Big Bertha periodically belched forth another shell, Keynes and the Director of the National Gallery—who, in true cloak-and-dagger style, had shaved off his moustache and donned spectacles to avoid detection by art dealers and the press—purchased twenty-seven paintings and drawings from the collection. Prices were so depressed by the fear and uncertainty caused by the encircling enemy that—despite the quantity and quality of the acquisitions, including works by Gauguin, Manet, and Delacroix—a quarter of the Treasury's grant remained unspent. Not only did this coup earn the grudging respect of the Bloomsberries—one offered the backhanded compliment that "your existence at the Treasury is at last justified"—but it also proved a personal boon for Keynes. Failing to convince his covert traveling partner of the merits of Cezanne, Keynes bought the post-impressionist's celebrated still life, *Apples*, on his own account for the ridiculously small sum of £327.

It would take more than a decade before Keynes applied the lessons learned in the Paris showroom to the domain of stock market investing. Abandoning the bandwagon-jumping approach of "credit cycling" during the turmoil of the late 1920s and early 1930s, he turned instead to a diametrically opposed investment style—one that focused on acquiring a handful of stocks at prices offering a substantial discount to expected future earnings potential, regardless of the whims and fashions of the market. After many successes and reversals, Keynes had eventually discerned that the stock market could, on occasion, be myopic, excessively optimistic or pessimistic, flighty, or propelled by informational cascades. It was at these times that the value investor's contrarian mantra that "one should be greedy when others are fearful, and fearful when others are greedy" came into its own.

Fashion Victim

What is pronounced strengthens itself.
What is not pronounced tends to nonexistence.
        —CZESLAW MILOSZ, "READING THE JAPANESE POET ISSA"

Belying his impeccable Establishment credentials, Keynes was the scion of a long line of religious dissenters on both sides of his family. This ancestral trait of nonconformism, in Maynard's case, seemed to extend well beyond matters of the spirit—in everyday life he delighted in paradoxes, opposed accepted wisdom, and, as the social reformer Beatrice Webb observed, disliked "all the common-or-garden thoughts and emotions that bind men together in bundles." A policy of "leaning into the wind," as he sometimes called contrarian investing, was ideally suited to Keynes' temperament—not only did it allow him to indulge the "perverse, Puckish" side of his nature, but his natural inclination to run counter to conventional thinking also offered the tangible satisfaction of financial gain.

Keynes rejected the more strident claims of efficient markets proponents, believing instead that, on occasions, a preponderance of "game players" over "serious-minded individuals" could produce a sustained divergence between quoted prices and underlying stock value. Like many other spheres of activity, stocks could be subject to the whims of fashion, caught up in the roiling currents of informational cascades where rising prices produce rising prices or falling prices engender further declines. Fred Schwed applied a characteristically cynical interpretation to this phenomenon:

> Those classes of investments considered "best" change from period to period. The pathetic fallacy is that what are thought to be the best are in truth only the most popular—the most active, the most talked of, the most boosted, and consequently, the highest in price at that

time. It is very much a matter of fashion, like Eugenie hats or waxed mustaches.

The stock exchange is, at times, patently *not* the exemplar of efficiency that orthodox theorists claim it to be. Notwithstanding its proclaimed role as a machine to crystallize expected future cash flows, the market on occasions succumbs to the fundamental fundamental—in an exuberant bull market, more willing buyers than sellers; in a despondent bear market, more willing sellers than buyers.

The ripples from these waves of optimism or pessimism affect even those stocks initially untouched by investor irrationality, as capital is channeled into "hot" stocks and away from others. As Ben Graham commented in *The Intelligent Investor*:

> The market is fond of making mountains out of molehills and exaggerating ordinary vicissitudes into major setbacks. Even a mere lack of interest or enthusiasm may impel a price decline to absurdly low levels.

This displacement effect was particularly evident, for example, in the dying days of the 1990s, when the rush to "new economy" shares created a two-speed market—on many exchanges the "TMT" trinity of telecommunications, media, and technology stocks broadly doubled in only a couple of years, while the derisively labeled "old economy" stocks languished out of the limelight.

The Perils of Popularity

If fifty million people say a foolish thing, it is still a foolish thing.
       —ANATOLE FRANCE (ATTRIBUTED)

Even Berkshire Hathaway, that beacon of levelheadedness and contrarian values, appears itself to have been the periodic plaything of fashion. As Charlie Munger—who jokingly describes himself as "assistant cult leader" at the company—comments, "what we have created at Berkshire . . . is, to some extent, a cult . . . [and] I think it's had effects on the stock prices of . . . Berkshire." Some individuals have been known to acquire one or two Berkshire Hathaway shares merely for the right to attend the stockholders' annual meeting and sit at the feet of Buffett and Munger. Conversely, in the last years of the 1990s—when Buffett was dismissed by many as a ponderous investment dinosaur doomed to extinction in the brave new world of dot-coms—Berkshire's stock became less modish and, in consequence, suffered a rare period of underperformance relative to the market.

Berkshire Hathaway's experience is a case study in the life cycle of stocks-as-fashion accessories. A stock is first picked up by the cognoscenti because of some particular attribute—in Berkshire's case, the immoderate success of its value investing approach. As enthusiasm for the stock percolates through the wider market and investors jump on the brimming bandwagon, prices may overshoot any reasonable estimate of intrinsic value. And when the stock inevitably falls out of favor—as happened with Berkshire Hathaway in the late 1990s, when investors deserted old economy stocks for the blue sky of Internet plays—prices "overcorrect" on the downside.

A similar process—although far more exaggerated—was seen on Wall Street in the late 1920s and early 1930s. When Edgar Lawrence Smith published his seminal book in 1924, his key conclusion—that through the operation of retained earnings, stocks were effectively "compound interest machines"—launched the cult of the common stock. American equities—which had previously displayed no strong price trend, either up or down, over time—enjoyed annual growth rates of around 30 percent in the three calendar years following publication of Lawrence's study. Light-headed at these dizzying altitudes, the market subsequently overbalanced and fell into a chasm. As Warren Buffett remarked, "What the few bought for the right reason in 1925, the many bought for the wrong reason in 1929." Stocks are contrary creatures—when they are most despised they promise the greatest rewards, and when most loved they present the greatest potential hazard.

Backing the Right Horse

A difference of opinion is what makes horse racing and missionaries.
—WILL ROGERS, *THE AUTOBIOGRAPHY OF WILL ROGERS*

The model that perhaps most resembles that of the stock market is the humble racetrack. At the races, bettors compete against other bettors, the odds on horses constantly moving to reflect the perceived favorites. Additionally, horses are handicapped with varying weights in an attempt to level the playing field—horses with a good win record will carry heavier weights than less successful nags. The stock market displays a very similar dynamic—investors compete with each other, buying and selling stocks based on their apparent prospects, and stocks perceived to have more potential are "handicapped" by higher price-to-earnings multiples than those securities deemed to be less promising.

In an ideal world—the world posited by efficient markets die-hards—prices generated on the stock exchange by buyers and sellers will reflect the relative merits, in terms of earnings potential, of a security, so that each share is as good a bet as the other. In an interview with *Outstanding Investor Digest*, Berkshire Hathaway's Charlie Munger expanded on this point:

> Everybody goes [to the racetrack] and bets and the odds change based on what's bet. That's what happens in the stock market. Any damn fool can see that a horse carrying a light weight with a wonderful win rate and a good post position . . . is way more likely to win than a horse with a terrible record and extra weight and so on . . . But if you look at the odds, the bad horse pays 100 to 1, whereas the good horse pays 3 to 2. Then it's not clear which is statistically the best bet . . . The prices have changed in such a way that it's very hard to beat the system.

In a broadly efficient stock market—as with a correctly priced horse race—it is indeed extremely difficult to beat the system. The key to success in both these arenas, therefore, is to identify the radically mis-priced bet—the horse or stock that offers good odds *and* has a strong chance of performing.

Increasing the difficulty of the investor's or bettor's task is the fact that "the house"—the stock exchange for the investor, the racing authority for the bettor—retains a percentage of each wager laid. Although the stock market's take is not nearly as large as that of the racetrack, and historically the stock market pie generally grows larger over time, the principle still holds—successful investors and bettors must not only out-bet the rest of the market, but also receive a margin large enough to compensate for the transaction costs incurred in laying the wager. Success on the stock market, as Charlie Munger reminds us, requires the individual "to understand the odds and have the discipline to bet only when the odds are in your favor."

Fear Factor

Our distrust is very expensive.
                              —RALPH WALDO EMERSON, *NATURE*

Stock markets, although bedevilled by uncertainty, exist *because* of uncertainty. As John Kenneth Galbraith noted:

> Were it possible for anyone to know with precision and certainty what was going to happen to . . . the prices of stocks and bonds, the one so blessed would not give or sell his information to others; instead, he would use it himself, and in a world of uncertainty his monopoly of the certain would be supremely profitable. Soon he would be in possession of all fungible assets, while all contending with such knowledge would succumb.

Simply stated, financial markets exist because certainty does not—markets are as much an exchange of opinions as an exchange of capital and securities.

Keynes realized that radically mispriced stock market bets are most abundant when there exists great uncertainty and, in consequence, widely divergent opinions about the value of a stock. As he explained to a colleague, "The art of investing, if there is such an art, is that of taking advantage of the consequences of a mistaken opinion which is widespread." In making this observation, Keynes echoed an insight of Frank Knight, a University of Chicago academic. Knight noted that there were two types of uncertainty—measurable probability, which he labeled "risk," and unquantifiable ambiguity, which was true uncertainty. "Risk" can be assigned a probability value—such as the 50 percent chance of throwing heads in a coin toss or the one-in-six prospect of rolling a particular number on a die—whereas "uncertainty" is utterly unmeasurable. In the free enterprise system, Knight asserted, only true uncertainty—"ignorance of the future," as he described it—can consistently create potentially profitable situations, as quantifiable risk should, in theory, already be factored into the pricing of an asset.

Those investors wishing to profit from the stock market, therefore, are those who embrace uncertainty. As Keynes noted, "It is because particular individuals, fortunate in situation or in abilities, are able to take advantage of uncertainty and ignorance . . . that great inequalities of wealth come about." Uncertainty, in respect of stocks, may be attributable to ambiguity about the business prospects of a particular company, more generalized misgivings about the state of the stock market or the broader economy, or some combination of these factors. The value investor—fortified by a perceived margin of safety operating to his or her advantage—exploits uncertainty, rather than being cowed by it.

Groceries, Not Perfume

People always clap for the wrong things.
—HOLDEN CAULFIELD,
IN J.D. SALINGER'S *THE CATCHER IN THE RYE*

The stock market—the apotheosis of the free market system—frequently confounds a fundamental tenet of economics. When the price of a stock goes up, demand for that stock tends to *increase*, often merely because the price has risen. Similarly, when the price of a stock falls, demand for the stock often subsides. In so doing, the market betrays its true nature—it is under the influence of "game players," stock market participants concerned primarily with short-term price movements rather than longer-term earnings profiles. Warren Buffett provides a contrarian reality check on this behavior:

> . . . many [investors who expect to be net buyers of investments throughout their lifetimes] illogically become euphoric when stock prices rise and unhappy when they fall. They show no such confusion in their reaction to food prices: Knowing they are forever going to be buyers of food, they welcome falling prices and deplore price increases. (It's the seller of food who doesn't like declining prices.)

If stocks are perceived as dividend-paying vehicles, then the investor is not afraid of corrections—indeed, a decline in exchange value should be viewed favorably, as it allows the investor to get more "quality for price" in terms of income as a proportion of initial outlay. Only speculators—those who perceive stocks as trading assets—will ordinarily view stock price declines negatively. The rules of price theory and utility maximization deem that the rational individual will be disposed to buy more of something the cheaper it becomes. With stocks, price and demand are often correlated because the "return" most people consider is capital gain, and as the market declines the prospect of trading profits falls commensurately.

It was on this psychological quirk—the tendency for the market to be influenced by short-term price patterns—that Keynes based much of his investment philosophy. Discussing the disposition of the American stock market, he commented to a colleague that:

> Very few American investors buy any stock for the sake of something which is going to happen more than six months hence, even though its probability is exceedingly high; and it is out of taking advantage of this psychological peculiarity that most money is made.

Value investors focus on long-term earnings, not short-term price cascades. As Ben Graham noted, intelligent investors buy their stocks as they buy their groceries, not as they buy their perfume—*value* is the key consideration, not the short-winded enthusiasms of the rabble.

Kissing Toads

If you can keep your head when all about you are losing theirs . . . then maybe they know something you don't.

—MARKET MAXIM

Adhering to a policy of value investing—basing investment decisions on an analysis of intrinsic value rather than price momentum—means that value investors are often on the "other side" of the market. A contrarian policy is not, however, simply one of automatically opposing the mob, reflexively zigging when others zag. The practice of blind contrarianism is just as dangerous as bandwagon-jumping investing styles—like momentum investing, it dispenses with fundamental value analysis in favor of market timing and requires the speculator to divine something as fickle as mob psychology. As always, the investment decision should be motivated by an assessment of the estimated intrinsic value of a particular stock relative to its quoted price, not by market sentiment one way or another.

One of Keynes' first recorded contrarian forays, for example, foundered on the rocks of reality. In late July 1914, on the same day that the Austro-Hungarian Empire declared war on Serbia and markets recoiled at the prospect of a pan-European conflict, Keynes bought a parcel of mining and transport shares. In effect, he wagered that hostilities would remain localized—"The odds appear to me *slightly* against Russia and Germany joining in," he wrote to his father on the day of purchase— and that stock prices would, in consequence, rebound. Keynes' optimism proved to be woefully misplaced—two days later, Russia ordered the general mobilization of its army, and the Germans then formally declared war on Russia. The dominoes were toppling and the Great War would embroil a large proportion of the developed world. In the arrogant flush of youth, Keynes had forgotten that markets, on many occasions, successfully execute their idealized role as an "intelligent multitude."

Ironically, the world's most successful investment institution, Berkshire Hathaway, draws its name from a failed business investment— a "turnaround" that failed to turn. In the mid-1960s, when Warren Buffett acquired the company, Berkshire Hathaway seemed to satisfy many of the rule-of-thumb measures used in identifying potentially underpriced opportunities—low price-to-book value, low price-to-earnings ratio, and so on. But the market, in this case, had been correct in marking down the price of Berkshire stock, as Buffett recounts:

> [Berkshire Hathaway] made over half of the men's suit linings in the United States. If you wore a men's suit, chances were that it had a Hathaway lining. And we made them during World War II, when customers couldn't get their linings from other people. Sears Roebuck voted us "Supplier of the Year." They were wild about us. The thing was, they wouldn't give us another half a cent a yard because nobody had ever gone into a men's clothing store and asked for a pin striped suit with a Hathaway lining.

Berkshire lacked pricing power—its products were mere commodities and therefore subject to fierce competitive pressure. Two decades after his acquisition of the company, Buffett was forced to shut down the last of Berkshire Hathaway's textile operations.

Monopoly Money

Better a diamond with a flaw than a pebble without.
—CONFUCIUS

The early misadventures of Berkshire Hathaway illustrate a broader lesson learned by both Keynes and Buffett—the importance of acquiring interests in businesses possessing a sustainable competitive advantage, or commercial "moats" as Buffett describes them. Berkshire Hathaway's original business, textile manufacturing, was a commodity-type industry requiring high capital expenditure and delivering generally poor returns. Better long-term business investment prospects, Buffett discovered, lay in those companies possessing sturdy barriers to competition, such as unique franchises, settled oligopolies, or well-known brand names.

Buffett emphasizes "the importance of being in businesses where tailwinds prevail rather than headwinds"—the ultimate investment opportunity presents itself, he advises, "when a great company gets into temporary trouble." In this respect, Buffett departs from the practice of his mentor, Ben Graham. Graham believed in buying average businesses at cheap prices—he would build a widely diversified portfolio of those stocks meeting his simple but rigorous quantitative measures, in the expectation that a sufficient number of these businesses would surmount their vicissitudes and eventually increase in price. Buffett's investment criteria, in contrast, focuses more on qualitative factors—he looks for "great companies with dominant positions, whose franchise is hard to duplicate and has tremendous staying power or some permanence to it."

In this emphasis on quality—buying companies with defensible moats at fair prices—Buffett reflects the approach of Keynes. In an early magazine article, Keynes endorsed the virtues of "blue chips":

> It is generally a good rule for an investor, having settled on the class of security he prefers—. . . bank shares or oil shares, or investment trusts, or industrials, or debentures, preferred or ordinary, whatever it may be—to buy only the best within that category.

Most alleged "turnaround" plays offer a very flimsy margin of safety to the value investor—predictions of future income based on optimistic "blue sky" projections will always be highly speculative. For the long-term investor, quality companies are a much better bet. As Charlie Munger explains:

> Over the long term, it's hard for a stock to earn a much better return than the business which underlies it earns. If the business earns 6 percent on capital over 40 years and you hold it for . . . 40 years, you're not going to make much different than a 6 percent return—even if you originally buy it at a huge discount. Conversely, if a business earns 18 percent on capital over 20 or 30 years, even if you pay an expensive looking price, you'll end up with a fine result.

A long-term investor, harnessing the enormous cumulative power of compounding, will reap a greater return from steadily increasing earnings than from a one-off bargain purchase.

Minority Report

> *Many shall be restored that are now fallen and many shall fall that are now in honor.*
>
> —HORACE, *ARS POETICA*

Empirical evidence, generally speaking, tends to support a policy of contrarian investing. Numerous studies show that, over the longer term, "value" stocks outperform "growth" stocks—that is, securities with relatively low price-to-earnings multiples and price-to-book value ratios, and relatively high dividend yields, have provided better returns to the investor over time. Even Professor Eugene Fama, the University of Chicago academic known as "the father of efficient markets theory," has himself become something of a heretic among orthodox financial theorists with his findings that value stocks tend to produce higher returns than growth stocks in most of the world's major exchanges.

The phenomenon of "reversion to the mean" has also been observed on stock markets. The economist Robert Shiller, citing one study, notes that:

. . . ten-year real returns on the Standard & Poor's index have been substantially negatively correlated with price-earnings ratios at the beginning of the period.

What this means in practice, Shiller explains, is that "when the market gets high, it has tended to come down." The behavioral economists Richard Thaler and Werner De Bondt, examining a broad sample of underperforming stocks, found that "a strategy of buying extreme losers over [the preceding two to five years] . . . earns significant excess returns over later years," with prior "losers" outperforming prior "winners" by around 8 percent per year. Reversion to the mean—the tendency for stocks that have beaten the index in the short term to underperform the market in the longer term, and vice versa—can be viewed as a visible manifestation of the stock market reasserting itself as a weighing machine rather than a voting machine by eventually reining in pricing overshoots.

A number of market practitioners have used these findings—the outperformance of value stocks, and the tendency for unusually volatile securities to swing back to the mean—to develop simple contrarian strategies. Perhaps the best-known approach is the "Dogs of the Dow" system, in which the ten highest yielding Dow Jones Industrial Average stocks are acquired at the beginning of each year. The rationale behind this strategy is that all stocks in the Dow Jones index are "blue chip" companies paying relatively stable dividends, and thus a high dividend yield may be an indication that the stock is relatively underpriced and trading at the bottom of its price cycle. Although statistical analysis of the Dogs of the Dow effect confirms that over most periods the "Dow-10" has indeed produced excess returns, Keynes and Buffett would no doubt reject such a system on the basis that it dispenses with reasoned analysis in favor of a mechanical application of rules.

Buy on the Sound of Cannons

*Even outside the field of finance, Americans are apt to be unduly inter-
ested in discovering what average opinion believes average opinion to
be; and this national weakness finds its nemesis in the stock market.*
                                    —KEYNES, *THE GENERAL THEORY*

One of Keynes' colleagues at the Provincial Insurance Company
recalled an occasion when a member of the Investment Committee
suggested buying Indian government bonds. "By all means," Keynes
responded, "but timing is important. Wait 'til a Viceroy has been assassi-
nated!" Maynard Keynes realized that it was periods of uncertainty that
produced the conditions necessary for "stunners" to emerge. A rather
extreme example of this tendency—and one that gives credence to
the charge of economics as the dismal science—was the experience of
Keynes' protégé, the Italian economist Piero Sraffa. According to one
story circulating within Cambridge, Sraffa—who was in possession of
a substantial family inheritance—waited patiently for "the one perfect
investment." Shortly after the bombing of Hiroshima and Nagasaki by
the Allies, he invested heavily in Japanese government bonds—and subsequently reaped a fortune in Japan's postwar "miracle years."

Keynes himself exploited the tremendous uncertainty and fear created during the Great Depression to effect his greatest contrarian triumph. In late 1933, when shell-shocked American investors flinched at
FDR's robust anticorporate rhetoric, Keynes started buying preferred
shares of utility companies, reasoning that they were "now hopelessly
out of fashion with American investors and heavily depressed below
their real value." Despite fears that Roosevelt would nationalize electric-
ity utilities, Keynes acquired significant shareholdings in the belief that:

> . . . some of the American preferred stocks offer today one of those
> outstanding opportunities which occasionally occur of buying cheap
> into what is for the time being an irrationally unfashionable market.

In the following year alone, Keynes' net worth would almost triple,
largely on the back of his plunge on Wall Street.

Similarly, Warren Buffett achieved perhaps his most spectacular
contrarian coup during another deep stock market slump. In 1974,

when many pundits were proclaiming that "the Death of Equities" was imminent, Buffett acquired a large stake in *The Washington Post*. As Buffett explains, due to the overwhelming pessimism oppressing the market, the company was undervalued on any reasonable measure:

> In '74 you could have bought *The Washington Post* when the whole company was valued at $80 million. Now at that time the company was debt free, it owned *The Washington Post* newspaper, it owned *Newsweek*, it owned the CBS stations in Washington, D.C. and Jacksonville, Florida, the ABC station in Miami, the CBS station in Hartford/New Haven, a half interest in 800,000 acres of timberland in Canada, plus a 200,000-ton-a-year mill up there, a third of the *International Herald Tribune*, and probably some other things I forgot. If you asked any one of thousands of investment analysts or media specialists about how much those properties were worth, they would have said, if they added them up, they would have come up with $400, $500, $600 million.

The radically mispriced bet—in this case, one evidenced by even a fairly basic sum-of-parts calculation of key assets—is most often thrown up amidst conditions of great uncertainty. As Buffett continually reminds his disciples, "Fear is the foe of the faddist, but the friend of the fundamentalist." Bolstered by a perceived margin of safety, the value investor exploits this uncertainty, rather than being intimidated by it.

Lonesome in the Crowd

> *[Stock market investing] is the one sphere of life and activity where victory, security, and success is always to the minority and never to the majority. When you find anyone agreeing with you, change your mind. When I can persuade the Board of my Insurance Company to buy a share, that, I am learning from experience, is the right moment for selling it.*
>
> —KEYNES TO A FELLOW STOCK INVESTOR,
> SEPTEMBER 28, 1937

Keynes was a defiant individualist and very diffident team player. He once joked that his chief hobby was "fluttering dovecotes, particularly in the City," and the man sometimes seemed constitutionally incapable of finding accord with the majority. In the closing stages of World War II, during loan negotiations with the United States, Keynes' frustration with consensus-building excited some of his finest invective. He called Leo Crowley, the American administrator of the Lend-Lease scheme, a "Tammany Polonius" whose "ear [was] so near the ground that he was out of range of persons speaking from an erect position," and observed for good measure that the unfortunately florid Crowley had a face like "the buttocks of a baboon." Of Marriner Eccles, chairman of the Federal Reserve and a key member of the American negotiating team, he commented: "No wonder that man is a Mormon. No single woman could stand him." James Meade, later a winner of the Nobel Prize in economics, unsurprisingly described the fiercely independent Keynes as "a menace in international negotiations."

Similarly, Keynes—the instinctive contrarian—was uncomfortable with an investment-by-committee approach. In a contrite letter to a fellow member on the Eton finances committee, he explained:

> My central principle of investment is to go contrary to general opinion, on the ground that, if everyone agreed about its merits, the investment is inevitably too dear and therefore unattractive. Now obviously I can't have it both ways—the whole point of the invest-ment is that most people disagree with it. So, if others concerned don't feel enough confidence to give me a run, it is in the nature of the case that I must retire from unequal combat.

Keynes discerned that one is unlikely to be able to consistently out-perform the crowd when one is part of it—as Ben Graham advised, sustained success on the stock market can only be achieved by follow-ing an investment policy that is "(1) inherently sound and promising, and (2) not popular on Wall Street." Unlike some of his investment committee colleagues, Keynes realized that value investing is a matter of facts, not fashion—ascribing an intelligence to the masses, as if knowledge could be weighed rather than evaluated, is a sure path to underperformance.

Value investors are almost by definition contrarians—an under-priced stock implies that the broader market has not recognised, or at least has underestimated, the earnings potential of that security.

Contrarian investing, however, demands more effort than a mere reflexive opposition to prevailing market sentiment—one needs to be a good swimmer to go against the flow. Stock market "dogs" can bite, and the value investor must be satisfied, after his or her own independent analysis, that the underlying company possesses a sustainable earnings flow. Warren Buffett distinguishes "extraordinary business franchises with a localized excisable cancer" from turnarounds "in which the managers expect—and need—to pull off a corporate Pygmalion." Value investors—realizing that, all other things being equal, a fall in stock prices will allow them to acquire more earnings for a given outlay—are not upset by a decline in prices, provided that the earnings prospects of the underlying business remain substantially unchanged. The intelligent investor understands that lack of present popularity does not necessarily translate into lack of future profitability.

Chapter 11

Being Quiet

Homage to Catatonia

Wisely and slow; they stumble that run fast.
—SHAKESPEARE, *ROMEO AND JULIET*

King's College, Keynes' alma mater, is famed for its medieval chapel, considered one of the finest examples of late-Gothic architecture anywhere in the world. Declared the most beautiful church in England by Henry James, it was immortalized by William Wordsworth as a "glorious work of fine intelligence ... Where light and shade repose, where music dwells." It was into this place of otherworldly beauty, built by Henry VI to redound the glory of God, that Maynard Keynes strode one day in the mid-1930s with a very specific task in hand. He surveyed the chapel's lofty pillars and vaulted ceilings, but not, on this occasion at least, for their aesthetic charms. Rather, Keynes—mathematician that he originally was—proceeded with a rough reckoning of the cubic capacity of the building. His purpose was to determine whether the chapel could accommodate a large and imminent shipment of grain from South America.

Owing to one of his more flamboyant commodity plays, Keynes was about to be encumbered with the equivalent of a month's supply of wheat for the whole of the United Kingdom. Rather than pay the difference between the spot price of wheat and the contract price—the conventional method for settling a futures contract—Keynes elected to back his judgment and take physical delivery of the grain, confident that the market rate would eventually rise beyond his contracted price. In a rare victory for aesthetics over commerce, Keynes' impertinent scheme to convert the King's College chapel into a granary was averted—apparently the building was simply not big enough to store the consignment. Instead, Keynes stalled by objecting to the quality of the cargo, complaining that the wheat contained more than the permitted number of weevils per cubic foot. By the time the grain was cleaned, the market price had risen such that the wily economist eventually made money on the contract.

Keynes' preposterous plan to turn the hallowed chapel into one of history's more elegant barns was emblematic not only of his transformation from callow aesthete to hardheaded money-man, but also the change in his investment philosophy from momentum investing to one of "faithfulness" in respect of a handful of "pets." As an early value investor, Keynes believed that "'Be Quiet' is our best motto"—short-term price fluctuations could be ignored as mere "noise" and the disciplined investor should patiently wait for the market to reassert itself as a weighing machine rather than a voting machine. The only rational response to irrational mob behavior, he determined, was to let the game players have the short term to themselves, while Keynes instead practiced a policy of "steadiness" in respect of his select portfolio of shares.

This buy-and-hold strategy was not only the natural complement to an investment philosophy that assessed stocks on the basis of future income streams, but it also offered long-term investors the not inconsiderable advantages of significantly lower transaction costs, and allowed them to reap the enormous power of compound interest.

Whirlpools of Speculation

Speculators may do no harm as bubbles on a steady stream of enterprise. But the position is serious when enterprise becomes the bubble on a whirlpool of speculation. When the capital development

*of a country becomes a by-product of the activities of a casino, the job
is likely to be ill-done.*

—KEYNES, *THE GENERAL THEORY*

Teddy Roosevelt, the trust-busting American President of the early twentieth century, once averred that "there is no moral difference between gambling at cards or in lotteries or on the race track and gambling in the stock market." Keynes disagreed with this assessment—he thought that gambling on the stock market was far more deleterious to a nation's health than the innocent pleasures of the track or the gambling den. In an appearance before a Royal Commission in 1932, he argued that "it is much better that gambling should be associated with frivolous matters of no great significance rather than be bound up with the industry and trade of the country." Keynes believed that racecourses and the like were a relatively harmless safety valve for the speculative urge. "Industrial betting" on stock exchanges, on the other hand, could lead to "the whole of [a nation's] industry becoming a mere by-product of a casino."

Keynes contrasted the socially destructive effects of stock market game players with those of speculators in the commodity and currency markets. This latter class of speculator, Keynes asserted, provided "a useful, indeed almost an essential, service" by providing certainty in otherwise risky situations:

> Where risk is unavoidably present, it is much better that it should be carried by those who are qualified or are desirous to bear it, than by traders, who have neither the qualification nor the desire to do so, and whose minds it distracts from their own business.

In contrast, the "proper social purpose" of the stock market was, as Keynes explained, "to direct new investment into the most profitable channels in terms of future yield." The price performance of a stock will influence not only the ability of the underlying company to raise capital on the equity market, but will also affect the company's borrowing capacity, its ability to make acquisitions, and the types of strategies it seeks to implement. A fundamental tenet of discriminating capitalism is that the stock market should reward those businesses that are the most successful. Success in the capitalist system is defined in brutally reductionist terms—the ability to earn sustainable profits over time.

Only "enterprise" investing, where the investment decision is informed by an estimate of the total prospective yield of a security, facilitates this social purpose. Stock market speculation—which, as Ben Graham remarked, "is largely a matter of A trying to decide what B, C, and D are likely to think—with B, C, and D trying to do the same"—merely serves to distort capital flows, by potentially diverting capital and kudos away from performing businesses. As Keynes noted in *The General Theory*, "The social object of skilled investment should be to defeat the dark forces of time and ignorance which envelop our future." In Keynes' perfect world, the stock market would be populated by individuals buying securities "for keeps," based on "long-term forecasts of the probable yield of an investment over its whole life"—not by trigger-fingered game players attempting to anticipate short-term swings in mass psychology.

Time on Your Side

Foul-cankering rust the hidden treasure frets,
But gold that's put to use more gold begets.
　　　　　　　—SHAKESPEARE, *VENUS AND ADONIS*

Keynes had a happy ability to produce economic theories that conformed to his own personal beliefs. One of the chief conclusions of *The General Theory*—that moribund economies could be kick-started by government spending—coincided perfectly with his view that money was meant to be spent, not hoarded. Keynes' advocacy of "a somewhat comprehensive socialization of investment" reflected his faith in state-appointed mandarins to, in certain circumstances, do a better job than the mobbish market. And his views on speculation in the stock market—as opposed to the currency and commodity markets—were in tune with his later incarnation as a value investor, while still allowing Keynes an occasional flirtation with the commodity and foreign exchange pits.

Both during his life and posthumously, Keynes weathered many attacks accusing him of a form of intellectual contortionism: essentially, molding his theories so that they satisfied his personal predilections. In his defense, however, socially responsible stock market investing—a policy of "steadfast holding" of stocks acquired on the basis of anticipated yield—also happened to be most congenial to the creation of wealth in the long term. A long investment horizon not only allows investors to look beyond the distractions of constantly fluctuating prices, but also shields them from the erosion of capital inevitably produced by transaction costs inherent in trading.

Perhaps more importantly, a philosophy of "being quiet"—of limiting activity in the market only to those occasions when quoted prices appear to stray far from intrinsic value—allows the investor to reap the tremendous power of compound interest. Compound interest works like a kind of financial snowball—if income from an asset is reinvested, this income will in turn earn income, and the original capital contribution grows at a geometric rate. The "rule of 72" neatly illustrates the exponential increases available from compounding. Dividing the number 72 by the yield earned on an investment provides a close approximation of the amount of time required for a sum of income-earning capital to double in value—for example, a sum yielding 6 percent return per year, if re-invested, will double in twelve years, and an asset with a 9 percent per annum yield will double in value in only eight years.

The intelligent investor, recruiting time as his ally in the value-creation process, relies on what Keynes called the "powerful . . . operation of compound interest" rather than the vagaries of the market. For the buy-and-hold value investor, it is time in the market—rather than market timing—that is important.

Errors of Commission

Stockjobber: a low wretch who gets money by buying and selling shares in the funds.

—SAMUEL JOHNSON,
A DICTIONARY OF THE ENGLISH LANGUAGE

Even from a relatively early age, Keynes viewed brokers and investment managers in an unfavorable light. In *Indian Currency and Finance*, his first book, Keynes asked rhetorically:

. . . how long will it be found necessary to pay City men so entirely out of proportion to what other servants of society commonly receive for performing social services not less useful or difficult?

Later in life, he advised his nephew—just setting out in the world of investment—not to take any notice of brokers' suggestions. Keynes hinted that a type of reverse Darwinism operated among the broking fraternity, a survival of the dimmest. "After all," he reasoned with his young charge, "one would expect brokers to be wrong. If, in addition to their other inside advantages, they were capable of good advice, clearly they would have retired a long time ago with a large fortune."

The Berkshire Hathaway duo share Keynes' distaste for the financial advisory profession. Warren Buffett drolly notes that "Wall Street is the only place that people ride to work in a Rolls Royce to get advice from those who take the subway," and Charlie Munger has drafted in Keynes to support his argument:

> I join John Maynard Keynes in characterizing investment management as a low calling. Because most of it is just shifting around a perpetual universe of common stocks. The people doing it just cancel each other out.

As Gordon Gekko, that famous demystifier of Wall Street, explained, stock market investing, in aggregate, is "a zero sum game—somebody wins, somebody loses." Interposing another level of intermediaries must, therefore, necessarily reduce the aggregate returns available to investors as a whole.

But brokers and investment managers exert a far more insidious effect on stock market game players. Like sharks, appropriately, brokers and other financial intermediaries require constant movement in order to survive. The interests of investors and brokers are poorly aligned—brokers are geared toward "churning" trades, thereby maximizing commissions, at the expense of the investor. Not only do brokers encourage excessive trading—"Never ask a barber if you need a haircut," Warren Buffett quips—but commissions, bid-ask spreads, and other agency costs can seriously erode the capital base of an active investor.

Capital Punishment

The avoidance of taxes is the only intellectual pursuit that still carries any reward.

—KEYNES (ATTRIBUTED)

Brokers' charges and other transaction costs do, however, possess one
positive attribute—they may act as something of a brake on excessive
trading, encouraging stock market players to think twice before buying
and selling, thereby sparing them from a potentially more punitive cost.
The various forms of "capital gains taxes"—a levy imposed on profits realized on the sale of assets, including stocks—are not in fact taxes
on capital gains; rather, they are a *transaction* tax. An investor holding a
stock that has improved in price merely incurs a *nominal* tax liability in
respect of his gains—only when the security is sold will the tax liability
crystallize.

Buy-and-hold investors sometimes receive concessions on "long-
term capital gains"—the tax rate may, for example, be lower for investments held for more than a year. In addition to this explicit reduction
in the tax rate, deferring a tax liability can—due to the power of compounding—have significant positive effects on the after-tax value of
an investor's portfolio. An active market player who turns his portfolio
over each year will incur an annual tax liability. The buy-and-hold
investor, on the other hand, only incurs a *theoretical* tax liability for as
long as he holds the stocks, and therefore still has his "before-tax" gains
working for him—in effect, the investor receives an interest-free loan
from the tax office. Due to the exponential effects of compounding,
the buy-and-hold investor will—all other things being equal—record a
significantly larger after-tax return.

Warren Buffett and Charlie Munger are particularly fierce critics
of the "self-inflicted wounds" sustained from excessive market activity. Buffett cautions that a "hyperactive stock market is the pickpocket
of enterprise," and Charlie Munger commends a policy of minimizing
"frictional costs":

> There are *huge* advantages for an individual to get into a position
> where you make a few great investments and just sit back and wait:
> You're paying less to brokers. You're listening to less nonsense. And
> if it works, the governmental tax system gives you an extra 1, 2 or 3
> percentage points per annum compounded.

As Buffett noted in a letter to Berkshire stockholders, "For investors as
a whole, returns decrease as motion increases."

To Have and to Hold

I believe now that successful investment depends on . . . [among other things] a steadfast holding of . . . fairly large units through thick and thin, perhaps for several years . . .
　　　—KEYNES TO THE KING'S COLLEGE ESTATES COMMITTEE,
　　　　　　　　　　　　　　　　　　　　　　　MAY 8, 1938

Keynes, better than most, understood the fleeting but intense satis-factions of the successful speculator. Writing in *The General Theory* with the guilty knowledge of the poacher-turned-gamekeeper, he observed that "human nature desires quick results . . . and remoter gains are discounted by the average man at a very high rate." It was upon this psychological peculiarity—now pathologized as the condition of "hyperbolic discounting" by the behavioral finance fraternity—that Keynes laid the foundation for his tremendous stock market success in the latter part of his investment career. Not only was a long-term hori-zon consistent with an investment policy based on realizing the latent potential of underpriced stocks, but this "steadiness" also protected the investor from transaction costs that can seriously erode the capital of the active investor.

In *The General Theory* Keynes suggested that compelling stock mar-ket participants to adopt a long view would cure them of the malaise of short-termism and hyperactivity. "The introduction of a substantial government transfer tax on all transactions," he mused, "might . . . [mit-igate] the predominance of speculation over enterprise." This idea was later taken up by Warren Buffett, who argued that a 100 percent tax should be applied to profits made on stocks held for less than a year. Buffett's refusal to effect stock splits on Berkshire paper—the company has the highest priced stock on the New York Stock Exchange, breach-ing the US$100,000 per share barrier in late 2006—is his own way of attempting to curtail the liquidity of, and therefore the speculative pressure on, Berkshire securities.

In considering the merits of a long-term approach to stock market investments, Keynes opined that:

> . . . to make the purchase of an investment permanent and indissolu-
> ble, like marriage, except by reason of death or other grave cause,

might be a useful remedy for our contemporary evils. For this would force the investor to direct his mind to the long-term prospects and to those only.

For Keynes at least, the marriage metaphor was apt. He had evolved from a type of financial philanderer—engaging in the monetary equivalent of one-night stands on the foreign exchange and commodities markets—to a more steadfast individual, remaining loyal to his select group of stock market "pets."

Warren Buffett also adopts a matrimonial analogy when discussing investment strategy, calling his stock market approach "our 'til-death-do-us-part policy" and remarking on Berkshire's "determination to have and to hold." Jesse Livermore, a famous stock trader and market bear in the early part of the last century, once likened Wall Street to a "giant whorehouse" where brokers pimped their stocks to the average Joe. Extending this admittedly crude metaphor, it might be said that Keynes—the reformed sinner, the speculator who eventually embraced the buy-and-hold approach—perhaps wanted to make honest women out of his stocks, seeking a faithful and fruitful relationship with his select handful of "stunners." As Buffett reminded his stock holder congregation in one of his missives, investors are not rewarded for activity—they are rewarded for being right.

Chapter 12

Eggs in One Basket

A Fugitive from the Law of Averages

Too much of a good thing can be wonderful.
—MAE WEST, IN *MY LITTLE CHICKADEE*

Keynes' paternal grandfather, like his illustrious descendant, was adept at turning a profit. Exploiting England's enduring obsession with gardening, he accrued a small fortune from his flower-growing business, making his first financial killing during the "dahlia craze" of the 1840s. Keynes senior was a shrewd businessman who resolutely focused on only the most lucrative flower strains—first dahlias, later roses and carnations—rather than, in the words of one gardening magazine of the time, "embark[ing] money and strength in dubious enterprises." Like his forebear, Maynard Keynes also believed that investing heavily in a few "pets" would typically deliver much better returns than an indiscriminate policy of diversification.

Keynes was repeatedly reprimanded for making big plays on only a small number of stocks. In response to criticism from a colleague at

Provincial for purchasing "a large and exceptional unit" in a shipping company, Keynes bristled:

> Sorry to have gone too large in Elder Dempster . . . I was . . . suffering from my chronic delusion that one good share is safer than ten bad ones, and I am always forgetting that hardly anyone else shares this particular delusion. The price has, I think, now gone up by about 6*d*, so you can get rid of any surplus without loss that you would like to.

In his indomitably contrarian way, Keynes rejected the orthodox view that an optimal stock portfolio is one that is widely diversified. Conventional financial theory decrees that markets are efficient—that is, all stocks are correctly valued and one stock is just as likely as another to rise or fall in price in response to unknowable future events. Building on this assumption, accepted wisdom argues that it is better to hold a large number of stocks so as to minimize the impact of random under-performance by any particular share. Diversification is the stock market application of the maxim "don't put all your eggs in one basket."

Keynes, like Warren Buffett after him, did not agree with this approach—he thought that a patient and informed investor could select a small group of "ultra favourites" having "prospects of rising enormously more than an index of market leaders." When these few "stunners"—or, as Buffett calls them, "superstars" and "grand-slam home runs"—are periodically thrown up by the market, intelligent investors should not be afraid to invest a relatively large proportion of their funds in these stocks.

Accordingly, in the latter half of his investment career Keynes maintained an extremely compact stock portfolio, with over half the value of his total stockholding represented by the shares of only a few firms. For his faith in portfolio concentration, Keynes was rewarded with an investment performance far superior—albeit more volatile—than that of the broader market.

Basket Case

I puts it all away, some here, some there, and none too much anywheres, by reason of suspicion.
> —LONG JOHN SILVER, IN ROBERT LOUIS STEVENSON'S
> *TREASURE ISLAND*

Portfolio diversification is essentially a defensive strategy—by spreading funds between a large number of stocks, the extent to which poorly performing shares affect overall portfolio value is reduced. Further, the greater the diversification within a stock portfolio—that is, the more representative it becomes of the market as a whole—the lesser the risk of underperforming *relative to the market.* This outcome is important to both orthodox theorists and the average investor. Conventional financial wisdom defines "risk" as the *volatility* of a portfolio relative to the broader market, and therefore asserts that a diversified portfolio must, by definition, be less "risky" than a more compact suite of stocks. The average investor, too, is generally risk averse and accepts that lower potential portfolio gains is the price to be paid for reducing the risk of potential losses.

Although Keynes himself was never satisfied with a merely middling result, he did concede that a policy of "scattering one's investments over as many fields as possible might be the wisest plan" for an individual with no special knowledge of the stock market. Warren Buffett repeated the point in a shareholder letter:

> Diversification serves as protection against ignorance. If you want to make sure that nothing bad happens to you relative to the market, you should own everything. There's nothing wrong with that. It's a perfectly sound approach for somebody who doesn't know how to analyze businesses.

Keynes thought that, for an individual who cannot or will not rigorously apply the precepts of value investing, "it ought to be considered as imprudent for such a man to make his own investments as to be his own doctor or lawyer."

For these investors, index funds—investment vehicles that mimic broad market performance by building an appropriately weighted portfolio of stocks—offer low-cost exposure to the stock market. As Buffett explained to Berkshire Hathaway shareholders, an unsophisticated investor seeking "to be a long-term owner of . . . industry" should:

> . . . both own a large number of equities and space out his purchases. By periodically investing in an index fund, for example, the know-nothing investor can actually out-perform most investment professionals. Paradoxically, when "dumb" money acknowledges its limitations, it ceases to be dumb.

Moreover, an investor committing a fixed sum to an index fund at regular intervals—a practice known as "dollar cost averaging"—will automatically counteract the excesses of Mr. Market. When Mr. Market is in his manic phase—bidding up prices way above their fundamental value—the investor will buy fewer shares per investment contribution, due to the higher cost per share. Conversely, when Mr. Market is in a down period—with shares sinking far below fundamental value—the investor will purchase more shares for the same outlay. Dollar cost averaging is a simple, self-regulating contrarian strategy, absolving the unsophisticated investor from any misguided efforts to second-guess the market.

If You Can Beat Them, Don't Join Them

A man must consider what a rich realm he abdicates when he becomes a conformist.

—RALPH WALDO EMERSON, *JOURNALS*

The price of joining the crowd, however, is that one will never stand out from it—diversification limits volatility not only on the downside, but on the upside also. For an individual with a good understanding of the market, Keynes believed that a diversified stock portfolio made no sense whatsoever. He thought that those investors who could properly analyze stocks should focus only on potential "stunners" and—when the market occasionally presents them to the investing public—buy them in meaningful quantities.

Toward the end of his investment career, Keynes concluded that:

> . . . it is out of these big units of the small number of securities about which one feels absolutely happy that all one's profits are made . . . Out of the ordinary mixed bag of investments nobody ever makes anything.

Similarly, the Berkshire Hathaway duo endorse the idea of "loading up" on "grand-slam home runs"—Charlie Munger commends an investment policy of "making a few great investments and sitting back," and Buffett advises that "the important thing is that when you do find [a 'superstar'] where you really do know what you are doing, you must buy in quantity." To borrow one of Buffett's aphorisms, "If something is not worth doing at all, it's not worth doing well": the impact of scoring a "home run" will be diluted if the stock constitutes only a small portion of total portfolio value.

Portfolio concentration can produce better results than diversification due to a number of factors, including lower transaction costs—broker commissions proportionately decrease as deal size increases—and potentially lower administration costs. But perhaps the most compelling argument for portfolio concentration by informed investors is the simple logic expressed in one of Warren Buffett's shareholder letters:

> I cannot understand why an [educated] investor . . . elects to put money into a business that is his 20th favorite rather than simply adding that money to his top choices—the businesses he understands best and that present the least risk, along with the greatest profit potential.

The same impulse that propels stock market speculation also motivates the drive toward diversification—the desire to be part of the crowd. As the financier Gerald Loeb recognized, a widely diversified portfolio "is an admission of not knowing what to do and an effort to strike an average"—for those investors who believe that they can in fact rank stocks, a policy of portfolio *concentration* is preferable.

Keeping It Simple

The art of being wise is the art of knowing what to overlook.
    —WILLIAM JAMES, THE PRINCIPLES OF PSYCHOLOGY

Diversification is the tribute paid by investors to uncertainty. In what may well be the world's first pro-diversification tract, the Book of Ecclesiastes counsels the reader to:

> Send your grain across the seas, and in time you will get a return. Divide your merchandise among seven ventures, eight maybe, since you do not know what calamities may occur on earth.

This biblical injunction to go forth and diversify reflects the conventional reaction to uncertainty—moderate risks by diluting them as much as practicable. Diversification is, in reality, more a strategy of risk *dispersion* than risk reduction.

Keynes' response to uncertainty and risk in the share market was radically different to the prevailing wisdom—as he explained in a letter to one of his business associates:

> . . . my theory of risk is that it is better to take a substantial holding of what one believes shows evidence of not being risky rather than scatter holdings in fields where one has not the same assurance.

To ascertain which stocks "show evidence of not being risky," the value investor searches for those securities that exhibit a sufficiently large margin of safety—that is, those stocks with a substantial gap between estimated intrinsic value and the quoted price.

In undertaking this analysis, the intelligent investor will necessarily focus only on those businesses he or she understands. Keynes noted that he would prefer "one investment about which I had sufficient information to form a judgment to ten securities about which I know little or nothing." His contention was that intelligent, informed investors will reduce their downside risk by scrutinizing only those sectors within their "circle of competence"—to use Buffett's phrase—and then only investing in those stocks which exhibit a satisfactory margin of safety. Like Socrates, the intelligent investor is wise because he recognizes the bounds of his knowledge.

Searching for Holes in the Baskets

Put all your eggs in the one basket and—WATCH THAT BASKET.

—MARK TWAIN, *PUDD'NHEAD WILSON*

Paradoxically, diversification—like all forms of insurance—can actually encourage riskier behavior. Just as those with flood insurance may be tempted to build their houses closer to the water, or motorists wearing seatbelts may become more aggressive drivers, so, too, highly diversified investors may similarly feel that they can afford to have a flutter on a speculative stock play if there is relatively little at stake—as the economist-stockbroker David Ricardo rationalized, "I play for small stakes, and therefore if I'm a loser I have little to regret." Or, to quote Bob Dylan, a more modern authority on this phenomenon, "When you got nothing, you got nothing to lose."

In contrast to the diversified stockholder, the focus investor will ordinarily demand a significant margin of comfort prior to allocating substantial funds to a single stock. Fear of loss can concentrate the mind wonderfully, and the investor staking a large proportion of his or her total funds on only one security is more likely to rigorously scrutinize this potential investment. As Buffett summarizes, a policy of portfolio concentration should serve to increase "both the intensity with which an investor thinks about a business and the comfort-level he must feel with its economic characteristics before buying into it."

Focusing on only a handful of stocks should not, therefore, increase portfolio "risk," at least as it is defined by the layperson—that is, the possibility of incurring financial loss. The intelligent investor will only select those stocks that exhibit the largest shortfall between quoted price and perceived underlying value—that is, those securities that are likely to provide the greatest margin of safety against financial loss in the long term. Although a compact suite of stocks will be undeniably more volatile than a diversified holding, short-term price fluctuations are of little concern to a long-term holder of stocks who focuses on income rather than capital appreciation. Indeed, value investors favor those stocks that display the potential for extreme volatility—the difference is that these investors expect predominantly *upside* volatility. Risk, for value investors, is not a four-letter word—it is embraced and addressed proactively, not defensively.

Waiting for a Fat Pitch

I call investing the greatest business in the world because you never have to swing. You stand at the plate, the pitcher throws you General Motors at 47! US Steel at 39! and nobody calls a strike on you. There's no penalty except opportunity lost. All day you wait

*for the pitch you like; then when the fielders are asleep, you step up
and hit it.*

—WARREN BUFFETT, QUOTED IN *FORBES* MAGAZINE

A policy of portfolio diversification is the logical outcome of a belief
in efficient markets. As Keynes noted, it is "false to believe that one
form of investment involves taking a view and that another does not.
Every investment means committing oneself to one particular side of
the market." A strategy of extreme diversification is, at its core, a con-
cession by the investor that stock-picking is futile for that particular
individual—that, indeed, one stock is as good as another. It is a candid
admission that the market knows more than that person.

Keynes rejected the notion that markets always priced securities
correctly based on publicly available information and that, therefore,
it was pointless to search for potential stunners. His view was much
more pragmatic, and was grounded in his experience as an investor and
financial theorist: Keynes believed that financial exchanges—although
perhaps *usually* efficient—were not *always* efficient. On occasions,
the stock market generates prices that veer radically from underlying
value—Mr. Market is perhaps in the throes of a particularly acute
bipolar episode—and it is at these times that the intelligent investor
should buy in quantity.

The poet Paul Valery once asked Albert Einstein if he kept a note-
book to record his ideas—Einstein is said to have replied, "Oh, that's
not necessary—it's so seldom I have one." Similarly, opportunities to
buy quality stocks at a material discount to fundamental value are infre-
quent. As stock investor and author Philip Fisher commented:

> . . . practical investors usually learn their problem is finding enough
> outstanding investments, rather than choosing among too many . . .
> Usually a very long list of securities is not a sign of the brilliant inves-
> tor, but of one who is unsure of himself.

Agreeing that "ultra-favorites" are usually thin on the ground, Keynes
noted that "there are seldom more than two or three enterprises at
any given time in which I personally feel myself entitled to put *full*
confidence."

When the market does offer a security at a substantial discount to
its intrinsic worth the investor should, therefore, acquire meaningful

amounts of that stock. Charlie Munger opts for a metaphor close to his heart when explaining Berkshire Hathaway's policy of "loading up" on mispriced bets:

> Playing poker in the Army and as a young lawyer honed my business skills. What you have to learn is to fold early when the odds are against you, or if you have a big edge, back it heavily because you don't get a big edge often. Opportunity comes, but it doesn't come often, so seize it when it does come.

Good investment opportunities are too scarce to be parsimonious with, Buffett often reminds his acolytes—when a stunner presents itself, the value investor should not be afraid to back his or her judgment with relatively large capital outlays.

Crossing the Jordans

> *You won't improve results by pulling out the flowers and watering the weeds.*
>
> —PETER LYNCH, ONE UP ON WALL STREET

For an investor who—like Keynes and Buffett—adopts a buy-and-hold policy in respect of stocks, portfolio concentration is something that tends to happen naturally over time. Inevitably, some stocks within a portfolio will perform better than others and these "stunners" will come to constitute a large proportion of total value. A policy of portfolio concentration cautions against an instinctive desire to "re-balance" holdings just because an investor's stock market investments are dominated by a few companies.

Buffett illustrates this point with an analogy. If an investor were to purchase a 20 percent interest in the future earnings of a number of promising basketball players, those who graduate to the NBA would eventually represent the bulk of the investor's royalty stream. Buffett says that:

> To suggest that this investor should sell off portions of his most successful investments simply because they have come to dominate his portfolio is akin to suggesting that the Bulls trade Michael Jordan because he has become so important to the team.

Buffett cautions against selling off one's "superstars" for the rather perverse reason that they have become too successful. The decision to sell or hold a security should be based solely on an assessment of the stock's expected future yield relative to its current quoted price, rather than any measure of past performance.

Eggs in a Couple of Baskets

. . . half of [my speculative positions] go up and half of them go down when the news is bad, and vice versa when the news is good; so I have what is called a "well-balanced position" . . .
—KEYNES TO HIS MOTHER, SEPTEMBER 2, 1922

During his interview for a director's seat at National Mutual, Keynes ventured the opinion that "the right investment policy for [the Society] would be to hold one security only and change it every week at the board meeting." This rather hyperbolic remark was, no doubt, designed to dislodge the old guard from their stubborn attachment to a passive and property-oriented investment style. But although it was an ambit claim—intended to startle the frock-coated gents out of their comfortable complacency—it did reflect, to a large extent, Keynes' faith in "focus investing."

However, for all his enthusiasm for a compact portfolio, even Keynes conceded that the principle of concentration "ought not to be carried too far." Keynes accepted that the maintenance of "a balanced investment position" justified a certain degree of diversification within any stock holding. He defined a "balanced position" as one in which there were:

. . . a variety of risks in spite of individual holdings being large, and if possible opposed risks (e.g. a holding of gold shares amongst other equities, since they are likely to move in opposite directions when there are general fluctuations).

A portfolio of stocks with opposed risk characteristics—to take another example, oil producers and airline companies—will serve to offset, at least in part, the effect of unforeseen and unpredictable shocks to any particular security.

Additionally, investors may obtain some of the benefits of diversification, while still maintaining a focused portfolio, by spreading their capital between different asset classes—by holding not only stocks but also, for example, investments in property or bonds. Although Keynes' wealth was particularly concentrated in the stock market—he never owned a house or any other form of real property, and by the time of his death his securities portfolio represented over 90 percent of his total assets—most other investors display a preference for considerably less reliance on just one asset class. "Sell down to your sleeping point," the American financier J. Pierpont Morgan reportedly advised a friend whose slumber was being compromised due to worries about his stock portfolio. Similarly, most value investors may elect to adopt a slightly more wide-ranging investment approach than that of Keynes.

Loading Up

To suppose that safety-first consists in having a small gamble in a large number of different directions . . ., as compared with a substantial stake in a company where one's information is adequate, strikes me as a travesty of investment policy.
—KEYNES TO THE CHAIRMAN OF PROVINCIAL INSURANCE COMPANY, FEBRUARY 6, 1942

Value investment emphasizes the *quality* of stocks rather than the quantity of stocks. For those investors who believe they know something of the market, or at least certain sectors within the market, it makes sense to focus on what Keynes called the "ultra-favourites." This handful of stocks—Keynes never prescribed an exact number, Buffett in one communiqué suggested "five to ten sensibly-priced companies"—will absorb the bulk of investible funds. Intelligent investors—because they know the companies they are analyzing and because their comfort levels will need to be high to justify such relatively large outlays—will satisfy themselves, after diligent analysis, that the investment is not too risky. They will not merely cast their money on a wide range of stocks about which they know very little, relying on a belief in the efficiency of markets to absolve them from any need to carefully analyze the underlying companies.

Focus investing, then, refers not just to the maintenance of a targeted portfolio of stocks, but also to the limited pool of stocks evaluated (those within an investor's "circle of competence"), and the laser-like intensity with which those stocks are assessed. The intelligent investor will not reflexively spread his or her funds across the universe of investment opportunities, for, as Keynes noted:

> To carry one's eggs in a great number of baskets, without having time or opportunity to discover how many have holes in the bottom, is the surest way of increasing risk and loss.

Contrary to conventional financial wisdom, Keynes argues that a focused portfolio should be *less* risky than a diversified portfolio, as investors will restrict their analysis to those stocks within their circle of competence and will also demand a wide margin of comfort prior to allocating a substantial proportion of total funds to a single stock.

It is ironic that in the high temple of capitalism, Adam Smith's commandment to specialize has been so comprehensively ignored. Dismissing the dogma of diversification, Keynes noted in a letter to the Chairman of the Provincial Insurance Company that:

> As time goes on I get more and more convinced that the right method in investment is to put fairly large sums into enterprises which one thinks one knows something about and in the management of which one thoroughly believes. It is a mistake to think that one limits one's risk by spreading too much between enterprises about which one knows little and has no reason for special confidence.

The level of investment risk in respect of a particular stock, Keynes emphasized, was commensurate with the level of ignorance and uncertainty surrounding that security. Value investing inverts the risk-return trade-off suggested in orthodox texts—those stocks offering the greatest apparent margin of safety, and therefore by definition the least downside risk, also potentially offer the greatest returns. By "loading up" only in respect of "stunners," as Keynes suggested, investors should both reduce the riskiness of their portfolio *and* give themselves the best chance of outperformance relative to the broader market.

Chapter 13

A Sense of Proportion

The Stock Market Stoic

Of all existing things some are in our power, and others are not in our power . . . Let him then who wishes to be free not wish for anything or avoid anything that depends on others; or else he is bound to be a slave.

—EPICTETUS, *THE HANDBOOK*

Maynard Keynes granted only conditional assent to Saint Timothy's belief that the love of money was the root of all evil. True, he had little time for the "strenuous purposeful moneymakers" motivated by "the love of money as a possession," but he also agreed with Samuel Johnson that there are few ways in which a man can be more innocently employed than in getting money. Keynes observed in *The General Theory* that:

> . . . dangerous human proclivities can be canalized into comparatively harmless channels by the existence of opportunities for money-making and private wealth, which, if they cannot be satisfied in this

147

way, may find their outlet in cruelty, the reckless pursuit of personal power and authority, and other forms of self-aggrandizement. It is better that a man should tyrannize over his bank balance than over his fellow-citizens . . .

In any case, those touched with "the moneymaking passion" were, as Keynes conceded, a necessary evil—it would be in the wake of these men, impelled by their striving after profit, that the rest of mankind would be dragged to the promised land of "economic bliss" and material abundance.

Keynes, in contrast to the energetic worshippers of Mammon, professed a much more utilitarian conception of money. As he coolly commented to his friend Duncan Grant, who was "very much enraged" to have received mere cash as a birthday gift, "The thing is good as a means and absolutely unimportant in itself." Later, in *A Tract on Monetary Reform*, he would return to the theme of money as a simple expedient:

> It is not easy, it seems, for men to apprehend that their money is a mere intermediary, without significance in itself, which flows from one hand to another, is received and is dispensed, and disappears when its work is done from the sum of a nation's wealth.

Moneymaking, Keynes thought, should be accorded its proper place— as an amusement, an intellectual game, a means to secure the good things in life.

Keynes' pragmatic attitude conferred on him a hardy resistance to the assaults of animal spirits, and engendered a more clear-sighted approach to stock market investing. After the false starts of his early investment career, Keynes realized that enduring success in the stock market accrued to those who exploited mob behavior rather than those who participated in it, and that a businesslike approach to investment decisions was infinitely preferable to blindly following the crowd. Keynes' lesson from the 1920s was that financial exchanges were inherently unpredictable, at least in the short term. Intelligent investors, then, accept that they cannot control the market's behavior and instead focus on controlling their own behavior—what is required, as Warren Buffett would later affirm, is "a sound intellectual framework for making decisions and the ability to keep emotions from corroding that framework."

Don't Just Do Something, Stand There . . .

Investing should be more like watching paint dry or watching grass grow. If you want excitement, take $800 and go to Las Vegas.
— PAUL SAMUELSON (ATTRIBUTED)

Keynes was not unaware of the tribute exacted by stock trading. In one biographical sketch, he described the German representatives at the Paris Peace Conference as a "sad lot . . . with drawn, dejected faces and tired staring eyes, like men who had been hammered on the Stock Exchange." At first blush, this seems a curiously inappropriate simile— comparing the representatives of a vanquished nation to victims of a mere financial defeat—but the memoir was written in the summer of 1931, in the trough of the Great Depression and with the death of a former student still fresh in Keynes' mind. Sidney Russell Cooke, a fellow director at National Mutual and a "brilliant and engaging personality" in Keynes' estimation, took his own life the previous year as a result of losses on the stock exchange. Reversals in the world of money could, as Keynes discovered, claim a heavy toll on those weakened by the contagion of animal spirits.

In the subsequent calm, after he had restored his fortune on the back of value investing principles, Keynes concluded that the intelligent investor needed "as much equanimity and patience" as possible to withstand the periodic incursions of animal spirits and the distractions of fluctuating prices. Market liquidity and its concomitant, constant price quotation, is a double-edged sword—it enables investors to easily enter and exit the market, and thereby makes them "much more willing to run a risk," as Keynes noted, but minute-by-minute changes in stock prices can also foster a short-term mindset among stock market players. Keynes cautioned that:

> One must not allow one's attitude to securities which have a daily market quotation to be disturbed by this fact or lose one's sense of proportion. Some Bursars will buy without a tremor unquoted and unmarketable investments in real estate which, if they had a selling quotation for immediate cash available at each Audit, would turn their hair gray.

The intelligent investor, Keynes asserted, maintains "a sense of proportion" by accepting that for sustained periods a stock's price may split from its underlying value. The investor is not overwhelmed by constant price quotation, by Mr. Market's ceaseless urgings to buy or sell. Rather, the disciplined investor applies his or her own analysis in identifying mispriced stocks and adheres to a long-term time horizon, confident that the stock market will eventually revert to its professed role as a machine for crystallizing expected future cash flows and, ultimately, will reward those businesses with a sustainable earnings profile. The value investor must, as a colleague noted of Keynes' own temperament, maintain a "robust faith in the ultimate rightness of a policy based on reason and common sense."

Do-It-Yourself

For my own part, I can certainly claim to be a Buddhist investor, in the sense of depending wholly on my own meditations.
—KEYNES TO A FELLOW STOCK INVESTOR,
MARCH 28, 1945

As Ben Graham observed, "Buying a neglected and therefore undervalued issue for profit generally proves a protracted and patience-trying experience," and the value investor must resist strong social forces that encourage conformism and a short-term mindset. Not only can constant price quotation distract undisciplined investors from the long-term merits of an investment, but stock market participants must also battle against an institutional apparatus geared to high turnover. Brokers and investment managers have a vested interest in promoting active markets, and even orthodox financial theory conspires with the speculator to assert the pre-eminence of short-term price movements over long-term income flow by defining "risk" as volatility in prices rather than volatility of earnings.

Value investors are not swayed by these factors. Rather, they recognize that the stock market is there to serve investors, not to instruct them. In the dark days of the early 1930s, after the stock market had suffered another of its sinking spells, Keynes remarked defiantly that:

...I do not draw from this the conclusion that a responsible investing body should every week cast panic glances over its list of securities to find one more victim to fling to the bears.

Value investors like Keynes rely on their own independent analysis rather than seeking guidance from the crowd. They practice, as Keynes did, "a certain continuity of policy"—a strategy that limits trading activity to those occasions when price departs widely from underlying value.

Stock market prices are only relevant to the value investor as a benchmark against assessed intrinsic value, to determine whether a sufficient margin of safety exists. It is a potential entry or exit point for the investor, but past price patterns should not influence the investment decision. As Keynes said:

... it seems to me to be most important not to be upset out of one's permanent holdings by being too attentive to market movements ... Of course, it would be silly to ignore such things, but one's whole tendency is to be too much influenced by them.

It is a market truism that in times of crisis money moves from weak hands to strong hands—the disciplined investor must therefore cultivate, as Charlie Munger advises, a "disposition to own stocks without fretting."

Going for It

A nimble sixpence is better than a slow shilling.
—ENGLISH PROVERB

One of the first trading ventures established by Keynes and "Foxy" Falk was the P.R. Finance Company, founded in early 1923 and engaged mainly in commodities speculation. The initials of the company—an allusion to the ancient Greek aphorism *Panta rei, ouden menei* ("All things flow, nothing abides")—were perhaps a subtle salute to the mercurial nature of the commodities market. In the stock market, too, all is in a state of flux—prices jump about and the intrinsic value of a stock alters as conditions affecting the underlying business change. Value investors, therefore, cannot let their professed bias toward a long-term investment horizon acquit them of the duty to always remain vigilant, to be alert to changes in the value of stocks relative to their price.

A philosophy of "being quiet"—of trading only when a substantial gap is identified between a stock's intrinsic value and its quoted price— in no way implies a complacent or passive investment style. In his role as chairman of National Mutual, Keynes repeatedly emphasized that investors cannot adopt a "set and forget" investment policy:

> The inactive investor who takes up an obstinate attitude about his holdings and refuses to change his opinion merely because facts and circumstances have changed is one who in the long run comes to grievous loss.

Value investors must, Keynes asserted, exercise "constant vigilance, constant revision of preconceived ideas, constant reaction to changes in the external situation." In stock market investing, he implied, the price of success is eternal vigilance.

The intelligent investor, by focusing only on those stocks within his or her circle of competence, will in fact be far more attuned to shifts in their relative value than market participants monitoring a much wider universe of securities. And by concentrating on a smaller pool of stocks, the value investor is in a better position to make a judgment on the merits of a particular security and act decisively. One observer of Keynes' methods with the King's College Chest Fund noted that:

> The great point about King's has been that when a good opportunity is pointed out to them, they "go for it." The swiftness of decision which marked their policy is due to Mr. Keynes.

Nicholas Davenport, a fellow board member at National Mutual, agreed that Keynes' stock market success was due to "beating the other fellow to the gun," adding that "I have never known a man so quick off the mark in the stock exchange race." Value investing, conducted properly, is not unlike Keynes' beloved cricket—vast longueurs occasionally punctuated by episodes of intense activity.

Debt-Defying

Creditors are a superstitious sect, great observers of set days and times.
—BENJAMIN FRANKLIN, *POOR RICHARD'S ALMANACK*

During the effervescent days of the late 1920s—when Keynes still clung to the tenets of momentum investing, attempting to anticipate the anticipations of others, flitting in and out of the market—well over half of his investment portfolio was underwritten by borrowings. The idea was that he could leverage his bets on the financial exchanges— by borrowing money to speculate on the currency, commodity, and stock markets, Keynes would multiply his capital gains if his hunches were correct. Although he enjoyed intermittent success during these years, Keynes found that—like Irving Fisher, Ben Graham, and millions of others operating on credit during the Great Boom—leverage also works in reverse.

To take an extreme example, an investor buying a security on a 10 percent margin—that is, 90 percent of the purchase price is supported by borrowings—requires just a 10 percent increase in stock price to double his or her money. But with this greater potential reward comes a commensurate increase in risk—a 10 percent decline in price will effectively wipe out *all* the investor's capital contribution. Leverage works when markets are rising but can be catastrophic when they are falling. Margin loans and other forms of credit are an essential adjunct to many speculators' tool kits—they often work on fine margins, and borrowing funds allows them to raise the stakes on their stock market wagers. The power of leverage gives these game players the chance to potentially magnify capital profits, while "market liquidity" confers the illusion that there exists a fire escape should things get too hot.

The problem with fire escapes, however, is that they do not work particularly well when everyone is rushing the door at the same time. Those who believe that they can divine the tides of sentiment are often caught short when the market suddenly turns. Empirical evidence has, broadly speaking, failed to identify any single news factor that could explain some of the great "corrections" of the last century: the Crash of October 1929, "Black Monday" in 1987, the bursting of the dot-com bubble in March 2000. Those investors with leveraged positions—where market exposure far exceeded real capital resources—found themselves with financial obligations they simply could not meet. As Warren Buffett dryly comments, "You only find out who is swimming naked when the tide goes out."

Value investors—those who buy a stock on the expectation that, in the longer term, its quoted price will rise to meet intrinsic value— are particularly circumscribed when it comes to borrowings. Keynes observed that the market can stay irrational longer than game players can stay solvent—Alan Greenspan, after all, made his famous "irrational exuberance" remark a full three years before the dot-com bubble finally burst. The value investor must therefore be prepared to wait potentially considerable periods before the stock market weighing machine usurps the voting machine. Keynes consequently concluded that:

> . . . an investor who proposes to ignore near-term market fluctuations needs greater resources for safety and must not operate on so large a scale, if at all, with borrowed money . . .

Something of a debt junkie in the 1920s and early 1930s, Keynes considerably reduced his borrowings in the latter part of his investment career, with loans constituting around 10 percent of his assets in the last years of his life. This financial conservatism is repeated in the practices of Berkshire Hathaway, which, as Charlie Munger comments, is "chicken about buying stocks on margin." As Munger suggests, "The ideal is to borrow in a way no temporary thing can disturb you."

Mind Control

I still suffer incurably from attributing an unreal rationality to other people's feelings and behavior . . .
—KEYNES, *My Early Beliefs*

Value investors require a dispassionate framework for investment decision-making, one that screens them from the insidious effects of animal spirits and short-termism. As Warren Buffett comments:

> Investing is not a game where the guy with the 160 IQ beats the guy
> with the 130 IQ . . . Once you have ordinary intelligence, what you
> need is the temperament to control the urges that get other people
> into trouble in investing.

Cultivating the correct temperament—one that couples, in Buffett's
words, "good business judgment with an ability to insulate . . . thoughts
and behavior from the super-contagious emotions that swirl about the
marketplace"—requires the investor to focus on just two variables,
the price and the intrinsic value of a stock.

The intelligent investor, although skeptical of the stock market's ability to always price securities correctly, nevertheless maintains
an appropriately humble outlook. The investor not only accepts that
on many—if not most—occasions the market is approximately efficient in terms of pricing, but also remains firmly within his or her
circle of competence. Similarly, the investor does not succumb to the
trait of overconfidence. Adam Smith, in his seminal work *The Wealth of
Nations*, wryly remarked on:

> The overweening conceit which the greater part of men have of their
> own abilities . . . and . . . their absurd presumption in their own good
> fortune . . . There is no man living, who, when in tolerable health and
> spirits, has not some share of it. The chance of gain is by every man more
> or less overvalued, and the chance of loss is by most men undervalued . . .

Empirical evidence supports Smith's insight—individuals typically exag-
gerate their skills (to take an everyday example, considerably more than
half of survey respondents believe they are much better drivers than the
average motorist), and harbor overly optimistic views in respect of
future events (research has shown, for instance, that game show contest-
ants massively overestimate their chances of success).

Guilt-Edged Securities

. . . in the stock market the facts of any situation come to us through a curtain of human emotions.
— BERNARD BARUCH, *MY OWN STORY*

In addition to the traits of overconfidence and overoptimism, there are other cognitive biases that may affect investor behavior. Most important, perhaps, is the "endowment effect"—the tendency for people to apply an "ownership premium" to their possessions. A simple experiment conducted by the economist Richard Thaler—which showed that the average asking price of an object already owned by a person, in this case a coffee mug, was more than double the offer price of an equivalent object they did not yet own—illustrates the general principle that an individual will typically demand significantly more to give up something they already hold than they would be willing to pay to acquire the very same object.

In a similar manner, many stock market players appear to invest more than just dollars into their securities—a well-performed stock may garner positive emotional associations, and consequently the stockholder may be reluctant to sell his or her "pet" even when the quoted price far exceeds assessed intrinsic value. Conversely, an underperforming stock—whatever its future prospects—may be sold by the rash investor, rather in the manner of a guilty party anxious to dispose of incriminating evidence. Perhaps a more likely scenario—in light of findings by behavioral economists that financial losses exacted more than twice the emotional impact of an equivalent gain—is that some stockholders may be reluctant to sell underperforming securities, even those unlikely to return to favor, because to do so would crystallize a loss and confirm their original investment error.

The intelligent investor does not lapse into these episodes of transference, and remembers that, as Warren Buffett puts it rather poignantly, "The stock doesn't know you own it." Value investors focus on the perceived value of a stock based on expected future cash flows, and do not fixate on the original acquisition price. If investors are to anchor themselves to any particular number, it should be to anticipated future earnings rather than historical prices. The decision to buy, sell, or hold a security should be determined by reference to "a policy based on reason," one free from the taint of animal spirits and emotional baggage. Value investors concentrate unwaveringly on the economics of the underlying business—they are security analysts rather than insecurity analysts.

Pride Goeth before Destruction . . .

. . . while enthusiasm may be necessary for great accomplishments elsewhere, on Wall Street it almost invariably leads to disaster.
—BEN GRAHAM, THE INTELLIGENT INVESTOR

Aware of these psychological quirks, value investors work diligently within their circle of competence, practicing what Buffett terms "emotional discipline" and dealing only in stocks displaying a wide margin of safety. In an early press interview, Buffett compared investing to being in "a great big casino . . . [where] everyone else is boozing." He suggested that if the intelligent investor can stick to Pepsi (or, given his subsequent acquisitions, Coke), then that individual will do fine. Charlie Munger made the same point in a letter to shareholders of Wesco Financial Corporation, a Berkshire Hathaway subsidiary:

> It is remarkable how much long-term advantage people like us have gotten by trying to be consistently not stupid, instead of trying to be very intelligent. There must be some wisdom in the folk saying, "It's the strong swimmers who drown."

It was once remarked of Foxy Falk and his hyperintelligent merchant banking colleagues that "their brains make them dangerous, for they arrive at their errors more rapidly." Mere intelligence is not sufficient for stock market success—the disciplined investor must possess a robust and objective framework for investment decision-making, and a temperament that, as Keynes suggested, exhibits "much patience and courage." In a similar vein, Ben Graham noted that "the investor's chief problem—and even his worst enemy—is likely to be himself," and suggested that the successful stock market participant requires not only intelligence and an understanding of value investing principles, but also—and most importantly—"firmness of character."

Forewarned, Forearmed

. . . the modern organization of the capital market requires for the holder of quoted equities much more nerve, patience, and fortitude than from the holder of wealth in other forms.
—KEYNES TO THE KING'S COLLEGE ESTATES COMMITTEE,
MAY 8, 1938

The man who confirmed the primacy of money in economic theory thought very little of it in practice. To Keynes it was nothing more than a means to an end, a passport to the possibilities of life. It was this equivocal, utilitarian attitude to moneymaking that bestowed the sangfroid required for a businesslike attitude to stock market investing. Keynes realized that successful stock market players could not be distracted by constant price quotations, which were driven, by definition, by the greediest buyers and most jittery sellers. Rather, investors needed to cultivate "a sense of proportion"—the confidence that, despite short-term gyrations, in the longer term the market would recognize and reward those stocks with sustainable earnings.

Keynes cautioned that the intelligent investor must think independently, unaffected by the views of the pack. The disciplined stock-picker cannot be seduced by the siren calls of continuous price quotation, and must negotiate a course between excessive activity and an unresponsive passivity. The market is no respecter of the debt-servicing timetables of creditors, the expiry dates of derivatives, or the margin requirements of brokers—the intelligent investor does not, therefore, give hostages to fortune by borrowing excessively or relying on options.

Investing, in the style of Keynes and Buffett, may seem an easy game, but this simplicity of approach is deceptive. The investor must remain uninfluenced by the bipolar tendencies of the market and ensure that he or she is not tainted by the pathogen of animal spirits. As Keynes remarked to a colleague, successful investing may in fact require "more temperament than logic"—the ability to invest with one's head rather than one's glands, to paraphrase a Buffett observation. The intelligent investor—armed with the knowledge of concepts such as intrinsic value and safety first, and aware of the stock market's dual personality as a voting machine and a weighing machine—will be much better placed to cultivate the right temperament for successful investing.

Chapter 14

Post Mortem

The Establishment Rebel

I agree with everything in this if not *is put in front of every statement.*
—KEYNES' VERDICT ON A GOVERNMENT MEMORANDUM

There is a story that toward the end of Maynard Keynes' life, when he had once again returned to the warm and secure embrace of the Establishment, he was gently reproved for becoming orthodox in his old age. Keynes gave short shrift to such a foolish charge—"Orthodoxy has at last caught up with me," he replied with customary aplomb. After innumerable battles with what he mockingly called "sound finance," Keynes was justified in claiming, finally, to be on the right side of conventional wisdom. The central conclusions of *The General Theory*—that financial markets can misbehave, that disturbances in the world of money can blight the real economy, and that government intervention is required to remedy these dislocations—were accepted with the same certitude that classical dogma had been accorded only a few years earlier, and the "Keynesian consensus" ruled the developed world for the next three decades.

It has taken far longer for Keynes' views on stock market investing to move into the mainstream. Orthodox financial theorists, until
recently, have doggedly maintained that modern financial exchanges
are efficient mechanisms for pricing securities, that one share is as
good a bet as another, and that diversification is indeed the most prudent policy for stock market investors. The emergence of "behavioral
finance"—integrating psychological insights with economics—has at
last overturned the flawless fairytale world of classical economics, in
which all men are not only unfailingly rational, but also invested with
a divine omnipotence. Once again, *The General Theory* has proved the
harbinger for an intellectual revolution.

As Keynes would no doubt have asserted, however, a set of principles are only as good as their practical efficacy. Keynes himself was
prepared to change his mind when the facts warranted such a move—
like his sometimes sparring partner, sometimes ally, Winston Churchill,
Keynes never developed indigestion from eating his words. Ever the
pragmatist, each year he applied the blowtorch of analysis to his investment performance, "partly with a view to comparing our [stock mar-
ket] experiences with those of other investors and partly to discover
what lessons were to be learnt." These "post mortems", as he termed
them, were valuable not only in determining "whence the satisfactory
results came," but also—and perhaps more importantly—in identifying
where performance was susceptible to improvement.

The final part of our investigation into Keynes' stock market experiences will, in due homage to the man, therefore comprise an over-
view of his unorthodox investment tenets and an appraisal of his stock
market performance.

Every Crowd Has a Silver Lining

*If God didn't want them sheared, he would not have made them
sheep.*
—THE BANDIT-LEADER CALVERA, *THE MAGNIFICENT SEVEN*

Ben Graham applied a measure of anthropomorphic sleight of hand to
beget that embodiment of an irrational stock exchange, Mr. Market.

Warren Buffett, Graham's most renowned disciple, provides a concise character sketch of this creation:

> [Mr. Market] has incurable emotional problems. At times he feels euphoric and can see only the favorable factors affecting the business. When in that mood, he names a very high buy–sell price because he fears that you will snap up his interest and rob him of imminent gains. At other times he is depressed and can see nothing but trouble ahead for both the business and the world. On these occasions he will name a very low price, since he is terrified that you will unload your interest on him.

Mr. Market is riddled with a complex array of character pathologies. Afflicted by periodic "waves of irrational psychology," he can suffer from alternate bouts of mania and depression. Mr. Market can meta-morphose into Mr. Magoo—an extremely myopic character, congeni-tally unable to take the long view. And he can also be psychosomatic, with disturbances in his state of mind impacting not only the stock market but also the real economy.

In contract law, agreements with individuals of an unsound mind are generally unenforceable. In the dog-eat-dog world of the stock market, however, investors are free to exploit the periodic madness of others. Rather than being influenced by short-term price fluctuations—by Mr. Market's interminable yammerings—intelligent investors instead concentrate on the underlying value of a business. The phrase "value investing", then, is something of a tautology, for all true investing—as opposed to speculation—involves an assessment of intrinsic value. The value investor—realizing that a stock price is transitory, a snapshot of jostling views and emotions—views Mr. Market's prices as nothing more than a possible entry or exit point on to the market.

Price trends and market fashions are of no concern to the disci-plined stock-picker—instead, the investor applies his or her own inde-pendent analysis to the investment decision-making process. Intelligent investors buy for value reasons and capitalize on the mistakes of those who do not. Stocks, for these individuals, are not mere tracings on a chart but real entities producing real goods and services. At Berkshire Hathaway's annual meetings, Buffett emphasizes the ultimate con-creteness of his stock holdings by gulping Coke, offering discounts to

Berkshire-owned jewelry stores, and promoting the company's candy shops. Value investors focus on the attributes of the *business*—particularly future earnings—and when Mr. Market casts aside his accountant's eye-shade and dons his party hat, or assumes dark robes of mourning, they search carefully for the radically mispriced bet.

Stock Market Jujitsu

. . . the way is to avoid what is strong and to strike at what is weak.
—SUN TZU, *THE ART OF WAR*

Keynes' experiences on the stock market read like some sort of morality play—an ambitious young man, laboring under the ancient sin of hubris, loses almost everything in his furious pursuit of wealth; suitably humbled, our protagonist, now wiser for the experience, applies his considerable intellect to the situation and discovers what he believes to be the one true path to stock market success. Somewhat ironically for a man who remarked that "in the long run we are all dead," Keynes—in his new guise as value investor—became particularly scornful of the stock market's insistence on taking the short view. In his later incarnation, Keynes looked beyond short-term price trends and events, instead focusing on the long-term earnings potential of a stock and adopting a steadfast holding of his "pets."

The practice of value investing involves identifying those stocks displaying a wide gap between quoted prices and a reasonable estimate of future income potential, and often requires the investor to battle against the prevailing currents of crowd sentiment. The value investor favors a long-term investment horizon, and is content to wait for the ephemera of constantly quoted prices to eventually reconcile with the reality of earnings. Keynes' additional gloss to the value investing canon is a policy of portfolio concentration—of putting one's eggs in only a handful of baskets—a strategy practiced by Buffett, but not by some other notable value investors, such as Ben Graham.

In a memorandum written for the King's College Estates Committee in 1938, Keynes set out the most concise summary of his stock market investment philosophy:

I believe now that successful investment depends on three principles:–

(1) a careful selection of a few investments (or a few types of invest-ment) having regard to their cheapness in relation to their probable actual and potential *intrinsic* value over a period of years ahead and in relation to alternative investments at the time;

(2) a steadfast holding of these in fairly large units through thick and thin, perhaps for several years, until either they have fulfilled their promise or it is evident that they were purchased on a mistake;

(3) a *balanced* investment position, i.e. a variety of risks in spite of individual holdings being large, and if possible opposed risks (e.g. a holding of gold shares amongst other equities, since they are likely to move in opposite directions when there are general fluctuations).

In effect, Keynes proposed a form of stock market jujitsu. Rather than trying to run just ahead of the inconstant mob, attempting to pick the bull and bear tacks of the stock market before they actually happen, Keynes determined that a better approach for disciplined investors was to use the kinetic energy of an irrational market to their own advantage. Instead of contributing to market volatility, caught up in the pendulum swings of sentiment, the value investor stands apart from the wildly flail-ing market and waits for it to overbalance. When excessive exuberance or pessimism throws up a "stunner" or a "grand-slam home run," the intelligent investor—working within his circle of competence and con-fident of a wide margin of safety—can act decisively and commit a rela-tively large amount of capital to the transaction.

The Investment Principles

Everything interested him because everything in his mind fitted instantaneously into its place in the conflict between Wisdom and Folly.
—TREASURY COLLEAGUE ON KEYNES

Keynes' stock market activities were but one aspect of an enormously productive life. As *The New York Times* noted in its obituary on Keynes, in addition to his better known accomplishments as an economist and statesman, he also cultivated an astoundingly wide range of interests in other fields:

> He was a Parliamentary orator of high order, a historian and devotee of music, the drama and the ballet. While at Cambridge University, he founded an arts theatre there because he wanted to go to a good theatre. A successful farmer, he was an expert on development of grass feeding stuffs.

Drawing on his vast and divergent knowledge base, and emboldened by a refusal to walk the worn paths of convention, Keynes distilled a set of investment principles that not only brought him great personal prosperity but also provided a template for stock market investors generally.

Keynes' six key investment rules, which have been embraced by some of the world's most successful stock market investors, suggest that the value investor should:

1. Focus on the estimated *intrinsic value* of a stock—as represented by the projected earnings of the particular security—rather than attempt to divine market trends.
2. Ensure that a sufficiently large *margin of safety*—the difference between a stock's assessed intrinsic value and price—exists in respect of purchased stocks.
3. Apply independent judgment in valuing stocks, which may often imply a *contrarian* investment policy.
4. Limit transaction costs and ignore the distractions of constant price quotation by maintaining a *steadfast holding* of stocks.
5. Practice a policy of *portfolio concentration* by committing relatively large sums of capital to stock market "stunners."
6. Maintain the appropriate *temperament* by balancing "equanimity and patience" with the ability to act decisively.

Keynes' investment principles are disarmingly simple, and may seem at first instance to be little more than applied common sense, especially when compared to the elaborate mathematics and complex concepts of modern financial theory. Value investing does not rely on academic esoterica like "beta," the "capital asset pricing model," or "optimized portfolios"—rather, it focuses on just two variables: price and intrinsic value. As Warren Buffett has remarked, "It's a little like spending eight years in

divinity school and having somebody tell you that the ten commandments were all that counted."

Keynes was aware of the insidious power of accepted wisdom, its
ability to "ramify . . . into every corner of our minds." Despite recent
incursions by new disciplines such as behavioral finance, orthodox
theory obstinately asserts that financial markets are broadly efficient—
as Buffett notes with palpable resignation, "Ships will sail around the
world but the Flat Earth society will flourish." Yet the sustained success
of value investors such as Maynard Keynes and, more recently, Warren
Buffett is perhaps the most eloquent testimony to the inadequacy of
orthodox dogma.

Investment Performance

Results must be judged by what one does on the round journey.
   —KEYNES TO A NATIONAL MUTUAL BOARD MEMBER,
                                    MARCH 18, 1938

Keynes' omnivorous interests in the wider world were matched by
those in the financial arena. Not only was he involved in investment
and speculation in various capacities—on his own account, as College
bursar with a large degree of discretion, and as a board member with
less influence on investment decisions—but his moneymaking activities
encompassed many different types of financial assets, from pig lard to
preferred stock. Most importantly for our purposes, Keynes' investment
style also changed radically around the time of the Great Crash—from
one of market timing to a more measured policy of value investing.

This eclectic approach, although providing a broad base from
which to develop his theories on investment, also highlights the importance of selecting an appropriate benchmark to assess Keynes' stock
market performance. Some of Keynes' financial ventures, such as the
P.R. Finance Company, can be ignored on the basis that they were
principally involved in currency or commodities speculation. Others
can be dismissed due to Keynes' limited tenure as an investment adviser
or board member—for example, Keynes left the A.D. Investment Trust,
the first investment company he founded with Foxy Falk, in late 1927,

well before his transfiguration into value investor. Likewise, Keynes effectively absented himself from an active management role at the Independent Investment Company in the mid-1930s and resigned from his position as Chairman of the National Mutual in 1938.

In some undertakings Keynes was hindered by institutional inertia and a stubbornly reactionary mindset. A letter from the Provost of Eton College to Keynes captures the frustrations of group decision-making:

> I find Governing Bodies meetings usually very entertaining. I like to hear the naked covetousness with which you recommend Southern Preferred Stock, the austere puritanism with which Lubbock meets such suggestions and the tergiversation of Ridley, who, agreeing with Lubbock, nevertheless votes with you because it is a poor heart that never rejoices and one must have a flutter sometimes.

Keynes' advocacy of "buying against the stream" more often than not met with fierce resistance from his fellow board members—as Keynes commented wearily, "All orthodox suggestions are too expensive, and all unorthodox are too unorthodox, so I am rather discouraged about making any further suggestion."

The Chest Fund

> *As regards the Railway Stocks, I am amused that they are at last*
> *dear enough for Francis to be inclined to buy them.*
> —KEYNES TO HIS STOCKBROKER, JANUARY 1943

There were only two investment concerns that focused on stocks and in which Keynes retained a large measure of decision-making discretion. The first was the Provincial Insurance Company, a small company "rather in the nature of a family affair," according to Keynes. Donald Moggridge, editor of Keynes' *Collected Writings,* notes that:

> [Keynes] was an extremely active director [of Provincial] throughout the years after 1930 . . . On investments, Keynes had fairly complete discretion within the guidelines set by the board at its monthly meetings and successfully persuaded the firm of the virtues of equities.

As Keynes observed with evident satisfaction in a memorandum for the Provincial board in 1938, the company "gave a good thrashing" to comparable market indices while under his stewardship. Keynes' influence on the board declined, however, after 1940, when he was called back to the Treasury.

The best benchmark for assessing Keynes' stock market performance is undoubtedly the King's College Chest Fund—for not only did it focus on equities, but management of the fund remained with Keynes until his death. The Chest Fund, established in June 1920 and capitalized at £30,000, was one of the few college funds permitted to invest in stocks, and Keynes exploited this freedom to achieve astonishing results. Taking 1931 as the base year—admittedly a relatively low point in the Fund's fortunes, but also on the assumption that Keynes' value investment style began around this time—the Chest Fund recorded a roughly tenfold increase in value in the fifteen years to 1945, compared with a virtual nil return for the Standard & Poor's 500 Average and a mere doubling of the London industrial index over the same period.

This vast outperformance relative to comparable indices is even more impressive in light of the fact that all income generated by the Chest Fund was spent on college building works and the repayment of loans—in other words, the capital appreciation from £30,000 in 1920 to around £380,000 at the time of Keynes' death solely comprised capital gains on the portfolio. An empirical study of the performance of the Chest Fund concluded that, although far more volatile than the broader averages, "the Fund's performance was clearly superior to that of the market." The authors of the study noted that "on the basis of modern performance evaluation measures, the evidence indicates that Keynes was an outstanding portfolio manager, 'beating the market' by a large margin."

The Positives

Rule No. 1: Never lose money. Rule No. 2: Never forget Rule 1.
                                        —Warren Buffett

Two broad trends are discernible in Keynes' stock market performance—the first is that, as his biographer Robert Skidelsky notes, "the more directly under Keynes' control the investments were, the better they performed," the second is the marked improvement in investment performance dating from the early 1930s. As Donald

Moggridge observes in his assessment of the performance of Keynes' personal holdings:

> Whereas in the 1920s Keynes was generally less successful than the market, after 1929 his investments (treating Wall Street and London separately) outperformed the market on 21 of the 30 available accounting years and did so cumulatively by a large margin.

Keynes attributed his stock market success to "a safety first policy" which resulted in "the avoidance of 'stumers' with which many investment lists are disfigured." In a letter to a colleague at Provincial, Keynes expanded on the importance of minimizing losses:

> . . . there had scarcely been a single case of any large-scale loss. There had been big fluctuations in market prices. But none of the main investments had, in the end, turned out otherwise than all right. Thus, against the profits which inevitably accumulate, there were comparatively few losses to offset. Virtually *all* our big holdings had come right.

Keynes' investment performance confirms that successful stock market investing is, as Charles Ellis described it in the title of one of his books, a "loser's game." The key task for the investor is to *avoid mistakes*—this is done by working within one's circle of competence and ensuring that a substantial margin of safety exists in respect of each stock purchase. As Ben Graham commented in *The Intelligent Investor*, "The really dreadful losses . . . were realized in those common-stock issues where the buyer forgot to ask 'How much?'"

The Negatives

I made my money by selling too soon.
                    —BERNARD BARUCH (ATTRIBUTED)

If some commentators have found fault with Keynes' investment performance, it was in his apparent inability to dispose of overpriced stocks. One academic described Keynes as a "one-armed contrarian who bought at the bottom but could never get out at the top"—an investor who could identify underpriced stocks but was less adroit when it came to jettisoning overpriced paper. Keynes was perhaps aware of his particular susceptibility to holding on to his "pets" even after they had become too expensive based on his own value investing principles. In a post mortem written for King's College, he defended himself as follows:

> One may be, and no doubt is, inclined to be too slow to sell one's pets after they have had most of their rise. But looking back I don't blame myself *much* on this score;—it would have been easy to lose a great deal more by selling them too soon.

In early 1936, for example, Keynes noted at the annual meeting of National Mutual unit holders that prices of British industrial shares were very high and presumed:

> . . . not merely a maintenance of the present industrial activity for an indefinite period to come but a substantial further improvement. Not that many people actually believe this, but each is hopeful of unloading on the other fellow in good time.

Despite this unequivocal view, Keynes held on to most of his stocks and suffered a significant fall in portfolio value when the stock markets experienced yet another severe decline in 1937.

Keynes' tendency to hold on to some of his pets for too long may have been due to his overwhelmingly optimistic nature—as Clive Bell commented, "Maynard's judgment would have been as sound as his intellect was powerful had it really been detached; but Maynard was an incorrigible optimist." All investors are, of course, optimists to some extent—they defer present consumption, commending capital to the uncharted land of the future, in the hope of a return. With reassuring infrequency, Warren Buffett also candidly pleads guilty to the same crime. "I made a big mistake in not selling several of our larger holdings during The Great Bubble," he confessed in the wake of the Internet boom and bust. Keynes' and Buffett's errors of omission in this regard are a reminder to investors that, as Charlie Munger stresses, "If you stick with stocks that are underpriced, you must keep moving or switching them around as they move closer to their true value."

The Wheel Turns

In Washington Lord Halifax
Whispered to Lord Keynes
"It's true they've all the money bags.
But we've got all the brains."

— NOTE PASSED AROUND AMONG THE
BRITISH LOAN NEGOTIATION TEAM

In the summer of 1940, the treadmill of time seemed to have spun full revolution for Keynes. War had been declared the previous year, and once again Keynes found himself back in the Treasury. "Well here am I, like a recurring decimal, doing very similar work in the same place for a similar emergency," he lamented to Russell Leffingwell in July 1942. As in the Great War, Britain again found herself a supplicant at the feet of Uncle Sam, and this time Keynes—given "a sort of roving commission" by the Chancellor—was assigned the task of negotiating the American loans. The quintessential Englishman, a man of vast independent wealth, was dispatched to Washington to shake the begging bowl on behalf of his country.

Despite his poor health, Keynes tackled these new responsibilities with vigor and panache. The economist Lionel Robbins, who accompanied Keynes to the United States for the American loan negotiations, was dazzled by Keynes' initial performances:

> . . . Keynes must be one of the most remarkable men that have ever lived—the quick logic, the birdlike swoop of intuition, the vivid fancy, the wide vision, above all the incomparable sense of the fitness of words, all combine to make something several degrees beyond the limit of ordinary human achievement . . . The Americans sat entranced as the God-like visitor sang and the golden light played round.

Notwithstanding the beatific vision summoned by Robbins, the hardnosed U.S. contingent remained largely unmoved by this wizardry. Keynes—who, like Churchill, initially had great faith in the purported brotherhood of "the English-speaking peoples"—became increasingly frustrated with what he perceived to be the harsh conditions its putative ally was seeking to impose on Britain.

Keynes remarked of one U.S.-based Treasury colleague that "he could be silent in several languages." Although professing admiration for the eloquent polyglot silence of his workmate, Keynes possessed no such diplomatic reserve. His arguments with the Americans became increasingly heated—Keynes objected to his counterparts "picking out the eyes" of the Empire, while the U.S. contingent was wary of Britain, the cunning Old World fox, whom many Americans believed had "bamboozled" their nation into the Great War and later had the impudence to default on its war loans. James Meade later noted that Keynes and Harry Dexter White, the co-architect of the IMF and the World Bank, would "go for each other in a strident duet of discord which after a crescendo of abuse on either side leads up to a chaotic adjournment."

After the war Keynes' task became, if anything, even more difficult. The Labor Party won a surprise landslide victory over the British bulldog, Winston Churchill, in July 1945, and the United States became even more chary of giving money to a newly socialist government. Under this pressure, Keynes reported that his body gave "ominous signs of conking out." His health was so fragile, in fact, that some German newspapers had published his obituary as early as mid-1944 after news was received that he had suffered another heart attack. As was the case with Mark Twain, reports of Keynes' death were greatly exaggerated. But after making six exhausting trips to the United States to negotiate loans and formulate the structure of a new global monetary scheme, Keynes was fatally weakened. He would not live to see the international monetary system he promoted, the global economic boom his theories forged, nor even the country-saving loan installments he had negotiated.

Laid to Rest

Fears and doubts and hypochondriac precautions are keeping us muf-
fled up indoors. But we are not tottering to our graves. We are healthy
children. We need the breath of life. There is nothing to be afraid of.
On the contrary. The future holds in store for us far more wealth and
economic freedom and possibilities of personal life than the past has
ever offered.

—KEYNES, *ESSAYS IN PERSUASION*

On May 2, 1946, a memorial service was held for Keynes in that
mausoleum to Old England, Westminster Abbey. Joining Lydia and
Keynes' immediate family at the ceremony were representatives from
the many different spheres of the man's life—the Prime Minister,
Bank of England directors, the Provost and fellows of Eton and King's
College, colleagues from the Arts Council, former students, and surviv-
ing members of the Bloomsbury group. Keynes' "wonky breathing muscles," laboring under the strain of ceaseless journeys to the United States
to simultaneously avert a "financial Dunkirk" and establish a new global
monetary body, had finally given out on Easter Sunday. World War II
claimed one of its last victims—as Lionel Robbins remarked, Keynes
had died "for the cause as certainly as any soldier on the field of battle."

Keynes' life had turned full circle—the prodigal son returned to
the heart of a grateful Establishment. The world was utterly unrecognizable from that which had beckoned in the hopeful and carefree days
of undergraduate Cambridge and the birth of Bloomsbury. The sun
was setting on Britain's Empire, which once proudly shaded a quarter
of the world's landmass in imperial pink. The India Office, Keynes' first
taste of public service, would be wound up the following year when
the subcontinent freed itself from the British Raj. And only a month
before Keynes' death, the recently deposed Churchill, on a speaking
tour of the United States, had warned of an "Iron Curtain" descending
on continental Europe. The war-weary world was entering another era,
a time of new anxieties and apprehensions.

To untrained eyes, Keynes, too, had changed beyond recognition. The
unworldly aesthete had become a rich man and a lord, a promoter of
investment companies and an emissary for his country. But this journey

from Apostle to apostate was illusory—in many ways, the course of Keynes' life can be seen as an effort to recapture the Edwardian insouciance of his youth, a mythical time when young men lazily punted down the River Cam and discoursed on the finer things in life. Keynes never lost the optimism, the belief in the perfectibility of society, characteristic of that time. "Progress is a soiled creed, black with coal dust and gunpowder; but we have not discarded it," he declared defiantly. Keynes' efforts in the public arena were designed to solve the economic problem so that mankind could "live wisely and agreeably and well." In the personal sphere, too, his moneymaking ventures aimed at the same end—as a means of securing the conditions for a well-lived life, and nothing more.

Keynes substantially achieved what he had preached. He brought confidence and buoyancy to troubled times and, in our field of particular interest, showed that investors could embrace uncertainty rather than be cowed by it. Friedrich von Hayek, who during the war shared with Keynes air-raid warden duties at King's College, wrote that Keynes "was the one really great man I ever knew"—his success as an investor was but a small part of a richly lived life. And his only regret? Some report that, tallying his achievements and disappointments toward the end of his life, Keynes remarked wistfully, "I wish I had drunk more champagne."

Notes

Further Reading

The definitive book for those wishing to examine Keynes' life in greater detail is Robert Skidelsky's *John Maynard Keynes 1883–1946: Economist, Philosopher, Statesman* (2003). Not only does Skidelsky's book provide a comprehensive account of Maynard Keynes' life and ideas, but—due to Keynes' Zelig-like ability to place himself at the heart of so many events of world import—it also offers a fascinating snapshot of Britain in the first half of the twentieth century.

Volume XII of *The Collected Writings of John Maynard Keynes* (1983) is the best general repository of Keynes' opinions on financial exchanges, speculation, and investment. Chapter 12 of *The General Theory of Employment, Interest and Money* (1936) also offers a very readable summary of Keynes' views on the fallibility of stock markets.

There are many books analyzing value investing techniques and, in particular, the stock market strategies of Warren Buffett. Perhaps the best entrée into the world of the Oracle of Omaha lies in Buffett's Chairman's Letters to Berkshire Hathaway stockholders, available online at www.berkshirehathaway.com/letters/letters.html.

Relative Monetary Values

All present-day monetary equivalents are given in U.S. dollars, and have been calculated by reference to the British retail price index series.

References

In the notes that follow, *CW* refers to *The Collected Writings of John Maynard Keynes* (variously edited by Donald Moggridge and Elizabeth Johnson), published in thirty volumes between 1971 and 1989 by Palgrave Macmillan for the Royal Economic Society. Catalog references are those of the Archive Centre, King's College, Cambridge, which holds the economic and personal papers of John Maynard Keynes.

Introduction

Page vii *The patient needs exercise* Keynes, J. M., "The Problem of Unemployment—Part II," *The Listener*, January 14, 1931. In a BBC radio broadcast, Keynes asserted: "The patient does not need rest. He needs exercise."

Page viii *so highly regarded by the City* Davenport, J., "Baron Keynes of Tilton," *Fortune*, May 1944

Page viii *the inhabitant of London* Keynes, J. M., *The Economic Consequences of the Peace* (*Collected Writings of John Maynard Keynes* [hereafter *CW*], *Vol. II*), Macmillan, 1919 (1971), p. 6

Page viii *the financial concerns* Letter from J. M. Keynes to the journalist John Davenport, March 21, 1944 (Catalog reference: JMK/A/44/37)

Page viii *brilliance as a practicing investor* Buffett, W., 1991 Chairman's Letter to the shareholders of Berkshire Hathaway Inc., February 28, 1992

Page viii *exciting literature out of finance* Letter from Lord Beaverbrook to J. M. Keynes, April 18, 1945 (quoted in R. Skidelsky, *John Maynard Keynes: Fighting for Britain 1937–1946* (Volume 3), Macmillan, London, 2000, p. 388)

Page ix *row out over that great ocean* Strachey, L., *Eminent Victorians*, Chatto & Windus, London, 1918, p. 7

Chapter 1: The Apostle Maynard

Page 1 *As bursar of his own college* Obituary published in the *Manchester Guardian*, April 22, 1946

Page 2 *such was his influence in the City* Davenport, N., *Memoirs of a City Radical*, Weidenfeld & Nicolson, London, 1974, p. 49

Page 2 *live wisely and agreeably and well* Keynes, J. M., "Economic Possibilities for Our Grandchildren," *Essays in Persuasion* (*CW, Vol. IX*), Macmillan, London, 1930 (1972), p. 328

Page 2   *a means to the enjoyment* Ibid.

Page 4   *I should like in certain things* Quoted in D. Moggridge, *Maynard Keynes: An Economist's Biography*, Routledge, London, 1992, p. 35

Page 4   *his hands certainly looked* J. M. Keynes, quoted in R. F. Harrod, *The Life of John Maynard Keynes*, Macmillan, London, 1951, p. 19

Page 4   *dull and soporiferous beyond words* J. M. Keynes, quoted in Moggridge, *Maynard Keynes: An Economist's Biography*, p. 35

Page 5   *the comparative lengths* J. M. Keynes, quoted in Harrod, *The Life of John Maynard Keynes*, p. 29

Page 5   *I've had a good look round* J. M. Keynes, quoted in C. R. Fay, "The Undergraduate," in Keynes, Milo (ed.), *Essays on John Maynard Keynes*, Cambridge University Press, Cambridge, 1975, p. 38

Page 6   *The New Testament is a handbook* Keynes, J. M., "My Early Beliefs," *Two Memoirs (CW, Vol. X)*, 1933 (1972), p. 444

Page 6   *By far the most valuable things* Moore, G. E., *Principia Ethica*, Cambridge University Press, Cambridge, 1903, pp. 188–189

Page 6   *we repudiated entirely customary morals* Keynes, J. M., "My Early Beliefs," *Two Memoirs*, p. 446

Page 6   *water-spiders, gracefully skimming* Ibid., p. 450

Page 6   *a metaphysical justification* Beatrice Webb, quoted in G. Himmelfarb, "From Clapham to Bloomsbury: A Genealogy of Morals," *Commentary*, February 1985

Page 7   *I trust your future career* Alfred Marshall, quoted in A. Robinson, "John Maynard Keynes: 1883–1946," *Economic Journal*, Vol. 57, No. 275, March 1947, p. 12

Page 7   *the examiners presumably knew* Ibid.

Page 8   *We found ourselves living* Woolf, L., *Sowing: An Autobiography of the Years 1880 to 1904*, Hogarth Press, London, 1960, pp. 160–161

Page 8   *a gorged seal* Woolf, V., *The Diary of Virginia Woolf: Volume 2, 1920–24*, Penguin, London, 1978 (1981), p. 69

Page 8   *the usual round-up of rootless intellectuals* Buchan, J., *The Island of Sheep*, Wordsworth Editions, Hertfordshire, 1936 (1998), p. 80

     Robert Skidelsky (*John Maynard Keynes: Fighting for Britain 1937–1946* (Volume 3), p. 19) notes that the character Joseph Bannatyne Barralty— "half adventurer, half squire"—in *The Island of Sheep* is a thinly disguised portrait of Keynes. In this novel, published the same year as *The General Theory*, Buchan derides Barralty as "the patron of every new fad in painting and sculpting and writing" and refers to Bloomsbury parties where Barralty "was a king among the half-baked." Buchan even furnishes Barralty with a "particular friend"—a "lovely creature" and actress calling herself "Lydia Ludlow." The narrator in *The Island of Sheep* ventures a rationale for Barralty's desire for wealth: "He must have money, great quantities of money, so that he can prove to the world that a fastidious and cynical intellectual can beat the philistines at their own game."

Page 9   *a thesis on mathematics* Obituary published in the *Daily Express*, April 22, 1946

Page 9   *What are you?* Letter from David Garnett to J. M. Keynes, undated (Catalog reference: JMK/PP/45/116/4 and 5)

Page 10   *I should try and come between them* Lytton Strachey, quoted in M. Holroyd, *Lytton Strachey: A Biography*, Penguin, London, 1971, p. 629

Page 10   *absolutely and completely desolated* Letter from J. M. Keynes to Lytton Strachey, November 27, 1914 (quoted in Harrod, *The Life of John Maynard Keynes*, p. 200)

Page 10   *a terrible impression for his rudeness* Letter from Basil Blackett to Granville Hamilton, January 1, 1918 (quoted in J. M. Keynes, *The Treasury and Versailles (CW, Vol. XVI)*, p. 264)

Page 10   *This morning we got a visit* Spring-Rice, C., Papers, Churchill College, Cambridge (quoted in R. Skidelsky, *John Maynard Keynes: Fighting for Britain 1937–1946* (Volume 3), p. 207)

Page 11   *upon there being no causes* Lloyd George, D., "Fontainebleu Memorandum," March 25, 1919

Page 11   *make compensation for all damage* Article 232, Treaty of Versailles, June 28, 1919

Page 11   *The future life of Europe* Keynes, J. M., *The Economic Consequences of the Peace*, p. 35

Page 12   *blind and deaf Don Quixote* Ibid., p. 26

Page 12   *like Odysseus* Ibid., p. 25

Page 12   *one illusion—France* Ibid., p. 20

Page 12   *this goat-footed bard* Keynes, J. M., "Mr. Lloyd George: A Fragment," *Essays in Biography (CW, Vol. X)*, 1933, p. 23

Page 12   *If we aim deliberately* Keynes, J. M., *The Economic Consequences of the Peace*, p. 170

Page 13   *I woke up like Byron* J. M. Keynes, quoted in J. Davenport, "Baron Keynes of Tilton," *Fortune*, May 1944

Page 13   *Some of this financial decision-making* Hession, C., *John Maynard Keynes*, Macmillan, New York, 1984, p. 175

Chapter 2: Citizen Keynes

Page 15 *dashed at conclusions with acrobatic ease* Lloyd George, D., *War Memoirs, Volume II*, Ivor Nicholson & Watson, London, 1933, p. 684

Page 16 *the arts of . . . enjoyment* Keynes, J. M., *The Economic Consequences of the Peace*, p. 12

Page 16 *were much in excess* Keynes, J. M., Presidential address to the Society of Apostles, June 21, 1921 (Catalog reference: JMK/66/UA/36)

Page 16 *the stir and bustle of the world* Ibid.

Page 16 *The love of money as a possession* Keynes, J. M., "Economic Possibilities for Our Grandchildren," *Essays in Persuasion*, p. 329

Page 16 *the enjoyments and realities of life* Ibid.

Page 17 *Maynard, who at Cambridge* Bell, C., *Old Friends: Personal Recollections*, Chatto & Windus, London, 1956, pp. 44–45

Page 17 *Money is a funny thing* Letter from J. M. Keynes to Florence Keynes, September 23, 1919 (Catalog reference: JMK/PP/45/168/10/17)

Page 18 *would not look after any private client* Davenport, N., *Memoirs of a City Radical*, p. 44

Page 18 *will shock father* Letter from J. M. Keynes to Florence Keynes, September 3, 1919 (*CW, Vol. XVII*, p. 125)

Page 18 *slaughter of a large part of our holdings* Letter from J. M. Keynes to Vanessa Bell, May 22,1920 (Catalog reference: CHA/1/341/3/2)

Page 18 *It has been a beastly time* Ibid.

Page 18 *It was perhaps necessary* Letter from Florence Keynes to J. M. Keynes, June 1, 1920 (Catalog reference: JMK/PP/45/168/10/38-9)

Page 18 *quite exhausted my resources* Letter from J. M. Keynes to Sir Ernest Cassel, May 26, 1920 (*CW, Vol. XII*, p. 7)

Page 18 *an unequalled opportunity for speculation* Ibid.

Page 18 *very substantial profits* Ibid.

Page 19 *You must come and see Lady B's ovary* Recounted in Davenport, N., *Memoirs of a City Radical*, p. 47

Page 20 *deafened by the clamorous voices* Keynes, J. M., *The Economic Consequences of Mr. Churchill* (*CW, Vol. IX*), 1925 (1981), p. 212

Page 20 *To debate monetary reform* Letter from J. M. Keynes to *The Times*, March 28, 1925 (*CW, Vol. XIX*, pp. 348–349)

Page 22 *Well-managed industrial companies* Keynes, J. M., "An American Study of Shares Versus Bonds as Permanent Investments," *The Nation and Athenaeum*, May 2, 1925 (*CW, Vol. XII*, p. 250)

Page 22 *the dizzy virtues of compound interest* Keynes, J. M., *The Economic Consequences of the Peace*, p. 13

Page 24 *gold fetters* Keynes, J. M., "The End of the Gold Standard," *Sunday Express*, September 27, 1931 (*CW, Vol. XI*, p. 245)

Page 24 *high tide of prosperity* Keynes, J. M., transcript of CBS broadcast, April 12, 1931 (*CW, Vol. XX*, p. 517)

Page 24 *the most expensive orgy in history* Fitzgerald, F. S., "Echoes of the Jazz Age," *Scribner's Magazine*, Vol. XC, No. 5, 1931, p. 182

Page 24 *I always regard a visit* Letter from J. M. Keynes to P. A. S. Hadley, September 10, 1941 (Catalog reference: JMK/PP/80/9/28)

Chapter 3: Snap, Old Maid, and Musical Chairs

Page 25 *No Congress of the United States* President Calvin Coolidge, State of the Union Address, December 4, 1928

Page 26 *You could talk about Prohibition* Brooks, J., *Once in Golconda*, Allworth Press, New York, 1969 (1997), p. 82

Page 27 *the consensus of judgment of the millions* Lawrence, J. S., *Wall Street and Washington*, Princeton University Press, Princeton, 1929, p. 179

Page 27 *In an efficient market* Fama, E., "Random Walks in Stock Market Prices," *Financial Analysts Journal*, Vol. 21, No. 5, September–October 1965, p. 56

Page 28 *Independence is important* Surowiecki, J., *The Wisdom of Crowds*, Doubleday, New York, 2004, p. 41

Page 29 *If intelligent people* Paul Samuelson, quoted in B. Malkiel, *A Walk Down Wall Street*, Norton, New York, 2003, pp. 196–197

Page 30 *accepted a description of his functions* Eady, W., "Maynard Keynes at the Treasury," *The Listener*, June 7, 1951, p. 920

Page 32 *a peculiar zest in making money quickly* Keynes, J. M., *The General Theory of Employment, Interest and Money* (*CW, Vol. VII*), 1936, p. 157

Page 32 *There is nothing so disturbing* Kindleberger, C., *Manias, Panics, and Crashes: A History of Financial Crises*, John Wiley & Sons, New York, 2000, p. 15

Page 32 *The few quiet men* Smiles, S., *The Life of George Stephenson*, John Murray, London, 1881, p. 172

Page 33 *Some artifact or some development* Galbraith, J. K., *A Short History of Financial Euphoria*, Penguin Books, New York, 1993, pp. 2–3

Page 34 *most of these persons* Keynes, J. M., *The General Theory of Employment, Interest and Money*, pp. 154–155

Page 34 *to outwit the crowd* Ibid., p. 155

Page 34 *a game of Snap, of Old Maid* Ibid., pp. 155–156

Page 35 *it may often profit the wisest* Keynes, J. M., *A Treatise on Money—Volume 2: The Applied Theory of Money (CW, Vol. VI)*, 1930 (1971), pp. 323–324

Page 35 *means in practice selling* Letter from J. M. Keynes to R. F. Kahn, May 5, 1938 (*CW, Vol. XII*, p. 100)

Page 35 *a general systematic movement* Memorandum from J. M. Keynes to the Estates Committee, King's College, Cambridge, May 8, 1938 (*CW, Vol. XII*, p. 106)

Page 35 *those newspaper competitions* Keynes, J. M., *The General Theory of Employment, Interest and Money*, p. 156

Page 36 *I want to manage a railway* Letter from J. M. Keynes to Lytton Strachey, November 15, 1905 (Catalogue reference: JMK/PP/45/316/5)

Page 37 *like a weather-vane* Cited in Chancellor, E., *Devil Take the Hindmost*, Macmillan, London, 2000, p. 200

Chapter 4: The Reckoning

Page 40 *Sooner or later a crash is coming* Babson, R., *The Commercial and Financial Chronicle*, September 7, 1929 (cited in Galbraith, J. K., *The Great Crash 1929*, Penguin, Middlesex, 1961, p. 108)

Page 40 *Stock prices have reached* For an entertaining account of Irving Fisher's disastrous prognoses, see John Kenneth Galbraith's *The Great Crash 1929*, p. 95, p. 116, and p. 119

Page 41 *for the immediate future at least* Fisher, I., *The Stock Market Crash—and After*, Macmillan, New York, 1930, p. 269

Page 41 *financial storm [has] definitely passed* Cablegram from Bernard Baruch to Winston Churchill, November 15, 1929 (quoted in J. Grant, *Bernard M. Baruch: The Adventures of a Wall Street Legend*, John Wiley & Sons, New York, 1997, p. 227)

Page 43 *commodity prices will recover* Keynes, J. M., "A British View of the Wall Street Slump," *The New York Evening Post*, October 25, 1929 (*CW, Vol. XX*, p. 2)

Page 43 *The fact is—a fact not yet recognized* Keynes, J. M., *The Nation*, May 10, 1930

Page 43 *Some twenty-four thousand families* Heilbroner, R. L., *The Worldly Philosophers: the Great Economic Thinkers*, Allen Lane, London, 1969, p. 242

Page 44 *Activity and boldness and enterprise* Keynes, J. M., "The Problem of Unemployment—Part II," *The Listener*, January 14, 1931

Page 44 *purge the rottenness out of the system* Andrew Mellon, quoted in H. Hoover, *The Memoirs of Herbert Hoover: The Great Depression 1929–1941*, Hollis and Carter, London, 1953, p. 30

Page 45 *an inevitable and a desirable nemesis* Keynes, J. M., "An Economic Analysis of Unemployment," notes for the Harris Foundation lecture, Chicago, June 1931 (*CW, Vol. XIII*, p. 349)

Page 45 *the existing economic system* Keynes, J. M., "Poverty in Plenty: Is the Economic System Self-Adjusting?," *The Listener*, November 21, 1934 (*CW, Vol. XIII*, pp. 486–487)

Page 46 *The modern capitalist* Keynes, J. M., "The World's Economic Outlook," *Atlantic Monthly*, May 1932

Page 47 *a thin and precarious crust* Keynes, J. M., "My Early Beliefs," *Two Memoirs*, p. 447

Page 47 *matters take their natural course* In response to a suggestion by Sir Harry Goschen, Chairman of the National Provincial Bank, that the Government should let "matters take their natural course," Keynes replied tartly: "Is it more appropriate to smile or to rage at these artless sentiments? Best of all, perhaps, just to leave Sir Harry to take his natural course." (Keynes, J. M., "Speeches of the Bank Chairmen," *Nation and Athenaeum*, February 23, 1924 (*CW, Vol. IX*, p. 189))

Page 47 *the enormous anomaly of unemployment* Keynes, J. M., "Economic Possibilities for Our Grandchildren," *Essays in Persuasion*, p. 322

Chapter 5: Raising a Dust

Page 49 *out of the tunnel of economic necessity* Keynes, J. M., "Economic Possibilities for Our Grandchildren," *Essays in Persuasion*, p. 331

Page 49 *as humble, competent people* Ibid., p. 332

Page 50 *We shall be able to rid ourselves* Ibid., p. 329

Page 50 *avarice and usury and precaution* Ibid., p. 331

Page 50 *wisely managed, [capitalism] can* Keynes, J. M., "The End of Laissez-Faire" (1926), *Essays in Persuasion*, p. 294

Page 50 *Modern capitalism is absolutely irreligious* Keynes, J. M., "A Short View of Russia" (1925), *Essays in Persuasion*, p. 267

Page 50 *deliver the goods* In a June 1933 article in the *Yale Review*, Keynes noted that:

"The decadent international but individualistic capitalism in the hands of which we found ourselves after the war is not a success. It is not intelligent. It is not beautiful. It is not just. It is not virtuous. And it doesn't deliver the goods." (Keynes, J. M., "National Self-Sufficiency," *Yale Review*, Vol. 22, No. 4, June 1933)

Page 51   *on a variety of politico-economic experiments* Keynes, J. M., "National Self-Sufficiency," *Yale Review*, Vol. 22, No. 4, June 1933, p. 761

Page 51   *The money changers have fled* President Franklin D. Roosevelt, Inaugural Address, March 4, 1933

Page 52   *complicated hocus-pocus* J. M. Keynes, quoted in M. Straight, *After Long Silence*, Collins, London, 1983, p. 67

Page 52   *as if it were a detective story* Ibid.

Page 52   *was to save the country from me, not to embrace me* Mosley, O., *My Life*, Thomas Nelson & Sons, London, 1968, p. 247

Page 53   *What is prudence in the conduct* Smith, A., *An Enquiry into the Nature and Causes of the Wealth of Nations*, William Pickering, London, 1805 (1995), p. 191

Page 53   *not merely inexpedient, but impious* Keynes, J. M., "The End of Laissez-Faire," *Essays in Persuasion*, p. 276

Page 53   *tacit assumptions are seldom* Keynes, J. M., *The General Theory of Employment, Interest and Money*, p. 378

Page 54   *I am afraid of "principle"* J. M. Keynes, quoted in D. Moggridge, *The Return to Gold*, Cambridge University Press, Cambridge, 1969, p. 90

Page 54   *has ruled over us rather by hereditary right* Keynes, J. M., "The End of Laissez-Faire," *Essays in Persuasion*, p. 287

Page 54   *timidities and mental confusions* Keynes, J. M., "How to Organize a Wave of Prosperity," *The Evening Standard*, July 31, 1928 (*CW, Vol. XIX*, pp. 761–766)

Page 54   *When we have unemployed men* Ibid.

Page 54   *We are . . . at one of those uncommon junctures* Keynes, J. M., "Poverty in Plenty: Is the Economic System Self-Adjusting?," *The Listener*, November 21, 1934 (*CW, Vol. XIII*, p. 492)

Page 54   *There is no reason why we should not* Keynes, J. M., "Can Lloyd George Do It?" (1929), *Essays in Persuasion*, p. 125

Page 55   *Euclidean geometers in a non-Euclidean world* Keynes, J. M., *The General Theory of Employment, Interest and Money*, p. 16

Page 55   *largely revolutionize . . . the way* Letter from J. M. Keynes to George Bernard Shaw, January 1, 1935 (Catalog reference: JMK/PP/45/291/16; also *CW, Vol. XIII*, pp. 492–493)

Page 56   *vain and insatiable desires* Smith, A., *The Theory of Moral Sentiments*, Cambridge University Press, Cambridge, 1759 (2002), p. 215

Page 56   *Keynes and all his school* Letter from Russell Leffingwell to Walter Lippmann, December 30, 1931 (quoted in R. Skidelsky, *John Maynard Keynes: The Economist as Savior 1920–1937* (Volume 2), Macmillan, London, 1992, pp. 398–399)

Page 57   *none of the wheels of trade* Hume, D., "Of Money", reprinted in *Essays: Moral, Political and Literary*, Cosimo Classics, New York, 1754 (2006), p. 289

Page 57   *above all, a subtle device for linking* Keynes, J. M., *The General Theory of Employment, Interest and Money*, p. 294

Page 57   *our desire to hold Money* Keynes, J. M., "The General Theory of Employment," *The Quarterly Journal of Economics*, Vol. 51, No. 2, February 1937, p. 216 (see also *CW, Vol. XIV*, p. 116)

Page 57   *enterprise will fade and die* Keynes, J. M., *The General Theory of Employment, Interest and Money*, p. 162

Page 58   *we are suffering from the growing pains* Keynes, J. M., "The Problem of Unemployment," BBC symposium, January 12, 1931 (Catalog reference: JMK/BR/1/121)

Page 58   *The important thing for government* Keynes, J. M., "The End of Laissez-Faire," *Essays in Persuasion*, p. 291

Page 58   *a farrago of confused sophistication* Letter from Hubert Henderson to Roy Harrod, April 2, 1936 (quoted in D. Besomi (ed.), *The Collected Interwar Papers and Correspondence of Roy Harrod, Volume II: Correspondence, 1936–39*, Edward Elgar Publishing, Cheltenham, p. 540)

Page 58   *We have watched an artist firing arrows* Pigou, A., "Mr. J. M. Keynes' General Theory of Employment, Interest and Money," *Economica*, Vol. 3, No. 10, May 1936, p. 132

Page 58   *the pessimism of the reactionaries* Keynes, J. M., "Economic Possibilities for Our Grandchildren," *Essays in Persuasion*, p. 322

Page 59   *moderately conservative in its implications* Keynes, J. M., *The General Theory of Employment, Interest and Money*, p. 377

Page 59   *our central controls succeed* Ibid., p. 378

Page 59   *Practical men, who believe themselves* Ibid., p. 383

Page 60   *We are all Keynesians now* Milton Friedman, quoted in "We Are All Keynesians Now," *Time*, December 31, 1965

Chapter 6: Animal Spirits

Page 61   *Nature and Nature's laws* Alexander Pope, "Epitaph for Sir Isaac Newton" (1727)

Page 62   *the grand secret of the whole Machine* John Arbuthnot, *An Essay on the Usefulness of Mathematical Learning* (1745)

Page 62   *chemical experiments . . . aimed at something* Letter from Humphrey Newton to John Conduitt, January 17, 1727 (quoted in J. M. Keynes, "Bernard Shaw and Isaac Newton," *Essays in Biography*, p. 377)

Page 62   *whim or sentiment or chance* Keynes, J. M., *The General Theory of Employment, Interest and Money*, p. 163

Page 62   *purely irrational waves of optimism or depression* Keynes, J. M., "Great Britain's Foreign Investments," *New Quarterly*, February 1910 (*CW, Vol. XV*, p. 46)

Page 63   *one foot in the Middle Ages* Keynes, J. M., "Newton, the Man," *Essays in Biography*, p. 370

Page 63   *there is no scientific basis* Keynes, J. M., "The General Theory of Employment," *Economica*, p. 214 (see also *CW, Vol. XIV*, p. 114)

Page 63   *The outstanding fact is the extreme* Keynes, J. M., *The General Theory of Employment, Interest and Money*, pp. 149–150

Page 63   *Wishes are fathers to thoughts* Keynes, J. M., "An Economic Analysis of Unemployment" (*CW, Vol. XIII*, p. 343)

Page 64   *a good Benthamite calculation* Keynes, J. M., "The General Theory of Employment," *Economica*, p. 214 (see also *CW, Vol. XIV*, p. 114)

Page 64   *we simply do not know* Ibid.

Page 64   *the necessity for action and for decision* Ibid.

Page 64   *To avoid being in the position of Buridan's ass* Letter from J. M. Keynes to Hugh Townsend, December 7, 1938, in *The General Theory and After: A Supplement* (*CW, Vol. XXIX*), p. 294

Page 65   *spontaneous urge to action rather than inaction* Keynes, J. M., *The General Theory of Employment, Interest and Money*, p. 161

Page 65   *a large proportion of our positive activities* Ibid.

Page 65   *how sensitive—over-sensitive if you like* Keynes, J. M., *Treatise on Money—Volume 2*, p. 322

Page 65   *even though they may be less* Keynes, J. M., *The General Theory of Employment, Interest and Money*, p. 148

Page 66   *the facts of the existing situation* Ibid.

Page 66   *the existing state of affairs* Ibid., p. 152

Page 66   *Day-to-day fluctuations* Ibid., pp. 153–154

Page 66   *the shares of American companies* Ibid., p. 154

Page 66   *recurrence of a bank-holiday may raise* Ibid.

Page 66   *Faced with the perplexities and uncertainties* Speech by J. M. Keynes to the Annual Meeting of the National Mutual Life Assurance Society, February 23, 1938 (*CW, Vol. XXI*, p. 445)

Page 67   *all sorts of considerations* Keynes, J. M., *The General Theory of Employment, Interest and Money*, p. 152

Page 67 *made many ruinous investments* White, E., *Proust*, Weidenfeld & Nicolson, London, 1999, pp. 84–85

Page 68 *investors are unromantically concerned* Brealey, R., and Myers, S., *Principles of Corporate Finance*, McGraw-Hill, New York, 1981, p. 266

Page 68 *The atomic hypothesis that has worked* Keynes, J. M., "Francis Ysidro Edgeworth, 1845–1926," *The Economic Journal*, March 1926 (*CW, Vol. X*, p. 262)

Page 68 *We are faced at every turn* Ibid.

Page 69 *I can only say that I was the principal inventor* Letter from J. M. Keynes to R. F. Kahn, May 5, 1938 (*CW, Vol. XII*, p. 100)

Page 69 *phenomenal skill to make much out of it* Ibid.

Page 70 *I am clear that the idea of wholesale* Memorandum from J. M. Keynes to the Estates Committee, King's College, Cambridge, May 5, 1938 (*CW, Vol. XII*, p. 106)

Chapter 7: Game Players

Page 71 *Nobles, citizens, farmers* Mackay, C., *Extraordinary Popular Delusions and the Madness of Crowds*, Wordsworth, Hertfordshire, 1841 (1995), p. 94

Page 72 *When it has been weakened by cultivation* Ibid., p. 90

Page 72 *the organization of investment markets* Keynes, J. M., *The General Theory of Employment, Interest and Money*, p. 158

Page 73 *so much in the minority* Ibid., p. 150

Page 73 *That the sins of the London Stock Exchange* Ibid., p. 159

Page 73 *have no special knowledge* Ibid., p. 153

Page 73 *since there will be no strong roots* Ibid., p. 154

Page 73 *a frequent opportunity to the individual* Ibid., p. 151

Page 74 *an abstraction, a name, a symbol* Herbert, Z., "The Bitter Smell of Tulips," in *Still Life with a Bridle*, The Ecco Press, Hopewell, New Jersey, 1993, p. 47

Page 75 *It might have been supposed* Keynes, J. M., *The General Theory of Employment, Interest and Money*, p. 154

Page 75 *it is the long-term investor* Ibid., pp. 157–158

Page 76 *price fluctuations have only one* Graham, B., *The Intelligent Investor*, Collins, New York, 2003, p. 205

Page 77 *is very obliging indeed* Ibid.

Page 77 *lets his enthusiasm or his fears* Ibid.

Page 78   *We've seen oil magnates* Rothchild, J., "How Smart is Warren Buffett?," *Time*, April 3, 1995

Page 79   *various forms of mass hysteria* Warren Buffett, quoted in J. Lowe, *Warren Buffett Speaks*, John Wiley & Sons, New York, 1997, p. 114

Page 79   *began as a market-timer* Buffett, W., 1988 Chairman's Letter, February 28, 1989

Page 79   *the activity of forecasting the psychology* Keynes, J. M., *The General Theory of Employment, Interest and Money*, p. 158

Page 79   *forecasting the prospective yield* Ibid.

Page 80   *assumes the ability to pick specialties* Letter from J. M. Keynes to R. F. Kahn, May 5, 1938 (*CW, Vol. XII*, pp. 100–101)

Page 81   *demi-semi-official* Quoted in Moggridge, *Maynard Keynes: An Economist's Biography*, p. 118

Chapter 8: Searching for Stunners

Page 84   *ventured some of his money* Johnson, S., "The Life of Pope," in *Lives of the Poets, Volume III*, John Henry and James Parker, Oxford and London, 1781 (1865), p. 49

Page 85   *Every mortal that has common sense* Sarah, Duchess of Marlborough, quoted in M. Balen, *A Very English Deceit: The Secret History of the South Sea Bubble and the First Great Financial Scandal*, Fourth Estate, London, 2002, p. 119

Page 85   *almost repellent common sense* Chancellor, E., *Devil Take the Hindmost*, Macmillan, London, 2000, p. 80 (n.)

Page 85   *The laws of arithmetic were more reliable* Harrod, *The Life of John Maynard Keynes*, p. 302

Page 86   *inordinate thirst of gain that had afflicted* Mackay, *Extraordinary Popular Delusions and the Madness of Crowds*, p. 52

Page 86   *for carrying on an undertaking* Ibid., p. 55

Page 86   *cold and untinctured reason* Keynes, J. M., "Newton, the Man," *Essays in Biography*, p. 363

Page 86   *unwholesome fermentation* Mackay, *Extraordinary Popular Delusions and the Madness of Crowds*, p. 71

Page 86   *the hope of boundless wealth* Ibid.

Page 86   *his unusual powers of continuous concentrated introspection* Keynes, J. M., "Newton, the Man," *Essays in Biography*, p. 364

Page 87   *In an efficient market you can trust* Brealey and Myers, *Principles of Corporate Finance*, p. 264

Page 88   *With the growing optimism* Hoover, *The Memoirs of Herbert Hoover: The Great Depression 1929–1941*, p. 5

Page 88   *Observing correctly that the market* Buffett, W., 1988 Chairman's Letter, February 28, 1989

Page 89   *when the safety, excellence and cheapness* Letter from J. M. Keynes to F. C. Scott, February 6, 1942 (*CW, Vol. XII*, p. 82)

Page 89   *the market is not a weighing machine* Graham, B. and Dodd, D., *Security Analysis*, McGraw-Hill, New York, 1940 (2005), p. 28

Page 89   *The market may ignore business success* Buffett, W., 1987 Chairman's Letter, February 29, 1988

Page 89   *The fact is that when the perception* Bogle, J., "Don't Count On It! The Perils of Numeracy," address to Princeton University, October 18, 2002

Page 90   *For the seriously long-term investor* Dimson, E., Marsh, P., and Staunton, M., *ABN Amro Global Investment Returns Yearbook 2005*, p. 36

Note also that in John Bogle's October 2002 address, referred to above, he provides further evidence to support the argument that markets are efficient in the long run:

". . . it is an irrefutable fact that in the long run it is economics that triumphs over emotion. Since 1872, the average annual real stock market return (after inflation but before intermediation costs) has been 6.5%. The *real* investment return generated by dividends and earnings growth has come to 6.6% . . . Speculative return slashed *investment* return by more than one-half during the 1970s and then *tripled*(!) it during the 1980s and 1990s. But measured today, after this year's staggering drop in stock prices, *speculative* return, with a *net* negative annual return of –0.1% during the entire 130-year period, on balance neither contributed to, nor materially detracted from, investment return."

Page 90   *search for discrepancies between* Buffett, W., "The Superinvestors of Graham-and-Doddsville," *Hermes* (magazine of the Columbia Business School), Fall 1984

Page 90   *My purpose is to buy securities* Letter from J. M. Keynes to F. C. Scott, February 6, 1942 (*CW, Vol. XII*, p. 82)

Page 91   *Speculative markets . . . are governed* Speech by J. M. Keynes at the Annual Meeting of National Mutual Life Assurance Society, February 23, 1938 (*CW, Vol. XII*, p. 238)

Page 92   *loved a bargain* Bell, *Old Friends: Personal Recollections*, p. 52

Page 92   *eyes gleamed as the bones went round* Virginia Woolf, quoted in R. Skidelsky, *John Maynard Keynes 1883–1946: Economist, Philosopher, Statesman*, Macmillan, London, 2003, p. 362

Page 93   *intrinsic values . . . enormously in excess* Letter from J. M. Keynes to F. C. Scott, April 10, 1940 (*CW, Vol. XII*, p. 77)

Page 93   *It is a much safer and easier way* Letter from J. M. Keynes to R. F. Kahn, May 5, 1938 (*CW, Vol. XII*, p. 101)

Chapter 9: Safety First

Page 96   *where the fall in value* Letter from J. M. Keynes to F. C. Scott, June 7, 1938 (*CW, Vol. XII*, p. 66)

Page 97   *amalgam of logic and intuition* Keynes, J. M., *Essays in Biography*, p. 186, *n*. 2

Page 97   *in the study of such complex* von Hayek, F., "The Pretence of Knowledge," Nobel Prize Lecture, December 11, 1974

Page 97   *cannot be confirmed by quantitative evidence* Ibid.

Page 97   *they thereupon happily proceed* Ibid.

Page 97   *When statistics do not seem to* Letter from J. M. Keynes to E. Rothbarth, January 21, 1940 (Catalog reference: JMK/W/4/69)

Page 98   *To the man with only a hammer* Charles Munger, quoted in "A Lesson on Elementary Worldly Wisdom As It Relates to Investment Management & Business," *Outstanding Investor Digest*, May 5, 1995, p. 49

Page 98   *practically everybody (1) overweighs* Munger, C., "Academic Economics: Strengths and Faults After Considering Interdisciplinary Needs," Herb Kay Undergraduate Lecture, University of California, Santa Barbara, October 3, 2003

Page 98   *It seems that the immature mind* Schwed, F., *Where Are the Customers' Yachts?*, John Wiley & Sons, New York, 1940 (1995), p. 19

Page 98   *peace and comfort of mind require* Keynes, J. M., *The General Theory and After: Part II* (*CW, Vol. XIV*), 1937 (1973), p. 124

Page 98   *institutional investors do not feel* Shiller, R., "Bubbles, Human Judgment and Expert Opinion," Yale International Center for Finance, February 5, 2001

Page 99   *the combination of precise formulas* Graham, *The Intelligent Investor,* pp. 564, 570

Page 99   *readers limit themselves to issues* Graham, *The Intelligent Investor,* p. 9

Page 101   *It's exactly what I would do* Buffett, B., transcript of a meeting of the New York Society of Financial Analysts, December 6, 1994

Page 101   *a number that is impossible to pinpoint* Buffett, W., 1994 Chairman's Letter, March 7, 1995

Page 101   *seen dependable calculations* Graham, *The Intelligent Investor,* p. 570

Page 101   *Just as Justice Stewart found it* Buffett, W., 1993 Chairman's Letter, March 1, 1994

Page 101   *for absorbing the effect of miscalculations* Graham, *The Intelligent Investor*, p. 518

Page 102   *To use a homely simile* Graham and Dodd, *Security Analysis*, p. 22

Page 102   *Speculation is an effort, probably unsuccessful* Schwed, *Where Are the Customers' Yachts?*, p. 172

Page 102   *the thought of ultimate loss* Keynes, J. M., *The General Theory of Employment, Interest and Money*, p. 162

Page 103   *It will be remembered that the seventy* Keynes, J. M., Review on "A Method and its Application to Investment Activity," *Economic Journal*, March 1940 (*CW, Vol. XIV*, p. 320)

Page 103   *there is no place where the calculations* Walter Bagehot, quoted in J. M. Keynes, "The Works of Bagehot," *The Economic Journal*, Vol. 25, No. 19, September 1915, p. 373

Page 103   *the amount of the risk to any investor* Keynes, J. M., "Great Britain's Foreign Investments," *New Quarterly*, February 1910 (*CW, Vol. XV*, p. 46)

Page 103   *there are many individual investments* Keynes, J. M., *The General Theory of Employment, Interest and Money*, p. 163

Page 104   *the more uncertain the future* Buffett, W., 2005 Chairman's Letter, February 28, 2006

Page 104   *With Coke I can come up with* Warren Buffett, quoted in A. Bianco, "Homespun Wisdom from the Oracle of Omaha," *BusinessWeek Online*, July 5, 1999

Page 104   *Our power of prediction is so slight* Keynes, J. M., "The Political Doctrines of Edmund Burke" (1904) (Catalog reference: JMK/UA/20/14)

Page 105   *demonstrated consistent earning power*, Buffett, W., 1982 Chairman's Letter, March 3, 1983

Page 105   *The key to investing is not assessing* Buffett, W. and Loomis, C., "Warren Buffett on the Stock Market," *Fortune*, December 10, 2001

Page 105   *Economics is essentially a moral science* Letter from J. M. Keynes to Roy Harrod, July 4, 1938 (quoted in Besomi, *The Collected Interwar Papers and Correspondence of Roy Harrod, Volume II*, p. 796)

Page 106   *Valuing a business is part art and part science* Warren Buffett, quoted in A. Smith, "The Modest Billionaire," *Esquire*, October 1988, p. 103

Page 106   *You also have to have the knowledge* Buffett, W., "The Superinvestors of Graham-and-Doddsville," *Hermes*, Fall 1984

Chapter 10: Leaning into the Wind

Page 108 *your existence at the Treasury* Letter from Vanessa Bell to J. M. Keynes, March 23, 1918 (quoted in Harrod, *The Life of John Maynard Keynes*, p. 226)

Page 109 *all the common-or-garden thoughts* MacKenzie, N. and MacKenzie, J. (eds), *The Diary of Beatrice Webb, Volume 4: 1924–1943, The Wheel of Life*, Virago, London, 1985, p. 94

Page 109 *Those classes of investments* Schwed, *Where Are the Customers' Yachts?*, p. 102

Page 110 *The market is fond of making mountains* Graham, *The Intelligent Investor*, p. 167

Page 110 *what we have created at Berkshire* Charles Munger, quoted in J. Lowe, *Damn Right! Behind the Scenes with Berkshire Hathaway Billionaire Charlie Munger*, John Wiley & Sons, New York, 2000, p. 162

Page 111 *What the few bought for the right reason* Buffett and Loomis, "Warren Buffett on the Stock Market," *Fortune*, December 10, 2001

Page 112 *Everybody goes [to the racetrack] and bets* Munger, C., "A Lesson on Elementary Worldly Wisdom As It Relates to Investment Management & Business," *Outstanding Investor Digest*, May 5, 1995, p. 57

Page 113 *to understand the odds* Charles Munger, quoted in "In the Money," *Harvard Law Bulletin*, Summer 2001

Page 113 *Were it possible for anyone* Galbraith, J. K., *A History of Economics: The Past as Present*, Penguin, London, 1989, p. 4

Page 113 *The art of investing, if there is such* Letter from J. M. Keynes to F. C. Scott, April 1944 (Catalog reference: JMK/PC/1/9/295)

Page 114 *It is because particular individuals* Keynes, J. M., "The End of Laissez-Faire," *Essays in Persuasion*, p. 291

Page 114 *many [investors who expect to be net buyers]* Buffett, W., 1990 Chairman's Letter, March 1, 1991

Page 115 *Very few American investors* Letter from J. M. Keynes to F. C. Scott, April 10, 1940 (*CW, Vol. XII*, p. 78)

Page 116 *The odds appear to me slightly against* Letter from J. M. Keynes to his father, John Neville Keynes, July 28, 1914 (Catalogue reference: JMK/PP/45/168/7/244)

Page 116 *[Berkshire Hathaway] made over half* Buffett. W., transcript of a lecture to Notre Dame faculty, Spring 1991

Page 117 *the importance of being in businesses* Buffett, W., 1977 Chairman's Letter, March 14, 1978

Page 117 *great companies with dominant positions* Warren Buffett, quoted in Lowe, *Warren Buffett Speaks*, p. 146

Page 117 *It is generally a good rule* Keynes, J. M., *The Nation and Athenaeum*, June 2, 1923 (*CW, Vol. XIX*, p. 93)

Page 118 *Over the long term, it's hard* Charles Munger, quoted in "A Lesson on Elementary Worldly Wisdom As It Relates to Investment Management & Business," *Outstanding Investor Digest*, May 5, 1995

Page 119 *ten-year real returns* Schiller, R., "Bubbles, Human Judgment, and Expert Opinion," Cowles Foundation Discussion Paper, May 2001

Page 119 *a strategy of buying extreme losers* De Bondt, W., and Thaler, R., "Financial Decision-Making in Markets and Firms: A Behavioural Perspective," in R. Jarrow, V. Maksimovic, and W. Ziemba, *Handbook in Operational Research and Management Science*, Elsevier Science, Amsterdam, 1995, p. 394

Page 120 *By all means, but timing is important* J.M. Keynes, quoted in D. Moggridge (ed.), *Economic Articles and Correspondence: Investment and Editorial* (*CW, Vol. XII*), 1983, p. 50

Page 120 *now hopelessly out of fashion* Letter from J. M. Keynes to F. C. Scott, November 23, 1933 (*CW, Vol. XII*, p. 61)

Page 120 *some of the American preferred stocks* Ibid.

Page 120 *In '74 you could have bought* Buffett, W., transcript of lecture to Notre Dame students, 1991

Page 121 *Fear is the foe of the faddist* Buffett, W., 1994 Chairman's Letter, March 7, 1995

Page 121 *fluttering dovecotes, particularly in the City* Obituary published in *The Daily Express*, April 22, 1946

Page 121 *Tammany Polonius* Letter from J. M. Keynes to Sir John Anderson, December 12, 1944 (*CW, Vol. XXIV*, p. 218)

Page 121 *ear [was] so near* Ibid., p. 204

Page 122 *the buttocks of a baboon* J. M. Keynes, quoted in Moggridge, *Maynard Keynes: An Economist's Biography*, p. 799

Page 122 *No wonder that man is a Mormon* J. M. Keynes, quoted in Skidelsky, *John Maynard Keynes: Fighting for Britain* (Volume 3), p. 435

Page 122 *a menace in international negotiations* Howson, S., and Moggridge, D. (eds), *The Wartime Diaries of Lionel Robbins and James Meade*, Palgrave Macmillan, Basingstoke, 1990, p. 122

Page 122 *My central principle of investment* Letter from J. M. Keynes to Sir Jasper Ridley, March 1944 (*CW, Vol. XII*, p. 111)

Page 122 *(1) inherently sound and promising, and* Graham, *The Intelligent Investor*, p. 31

Page 123 *extraordinary business franchises with* Buffett, W., 1980 Chairman's Letter, February 27, 1981

Chapter 11: Being Quiet

Page 125 *glorious work of fine intelligence* William Wordsworth, "Within King's College Chapel, Cambridge" (1825)

Page 126 *"Be Quiet" is our best motto* Memorandum from J. M. Keynes to the National Mutual Life Assurance board, February 18, 1931 (*CW, Vol. XII*, p. 19)

Page 127 *There is no moral difference* President Theodore Roosevelt, Annual Message to Congress, January 31, 1908, 42 Congressional Record, p. 1349

Page 127 *it is much better that gambling* J. M. Keynes, quoted in the minutes of evidence of the Royal Commission on Lotteries and Betting, December 15, 1932 (*CW, Vol. XXVIII*, p. 406)

Page 127 *the whole of [a nation's] industry* Ibid., p. 399

Page 127 *Where risk is unavoidably present* Keynes, J. M., *A Tract on Monetary Reform* (*CW, Vol. IV*), 1923, p. 136

Page 127 *proper social purpose is to direct* Keynes, J. M., *The General Theory of Employment, Interest and Money*, p. 159

Page 128 *is largely a matter of A trying to decide* Graham and Dodd, *Security Analysis*, p. 443

Page 128 *The social object of skilled investment* Keynes, J. M., *The General Theory of Employment, Interest and Money*, p. 155

Page 128 *a somewhat comprehensive socialization* Ibid., p. 378

Page 129 *powerful . . . operation of compound interest* Keynes, J. M., *The Economic Consequences of the Peace*, p. 126, *n.* 1

Page 129 *how long will it be found necessary* Keynes, J. M., *Indian Currency and Finance* (*CW, Vol. I*), 1913 (1971), p. 51

Page 130 *After all one would expect brokers* Letter from J. M. Keynes to David Hill, February 1, 1944 (Catalog reference: JMK/PP/45/143/2)

Page 130 *Wall Street is the only place* Warren Buffett, quoted in Lowe, *Warren Buffett Speaks*, p. 114

Page 130 *I join John Maynard Keynes* Comments by Charlie Munger at the 2005 Berkshire Hathaway Annual Meeting

Page 130 *Never ask the barber if you need a haircut* Warren Buffett, quoted in Lowe, *Warren Buffett Speaks*, p. 112

Page 131 *self-inflicted wounds* Buffett, W., 2005 Chairman's Letter, February 28, 2006

Page 131   *hyperactive stock market is the pickpocket* Buffett, W., 1983 Chairman's Letter, March 14, 1984

Page 131   *There are* huge *advantages* Munger, C., *Outstanding Investor Digest*, May 5, 1995

Page 131   *For investors as a whole* Buffett, W., 2005 Chairman's Letter, February 28, 2006

Page 132   *human nature desires quick results* Keynes, J. M., *The General Theory of Employment, Interest and Money*, p. 157

Page 132   *The introduction of a substantial* Ibid., p. 160

Page 132   *to make the purchase of an investment* Ibid.

Page 133   *our 'til-death-do-us-part policy* Buffett, W., 1986 Chairman's Letter, February 27, 1987

Page 133   *determination to have and to hold* Buffett, W., 1987 Chairman's Letter, February 29, 1988

Chapter 12: Eggs in One Basket

Page 135   *embark[ing] money and strength* Cited in R. Skidelsky, *John Maynard Keynes: Hopes Betrayed, 1883–1920 (Volume 1)*, Macmillan, London, 1983, p. 5

Page 136   *Sorry to have gone too large* Letter from J. M. Keynes to F. C. Scott, February 6, 1942 (*CW, Vol. XII*, p. 79)

Page 137   *scattering one's investments* Letter from J. M. Keynes to F. C. Scott, February 1945 (Catalog reference: JMK/PC/1/9/366)

Page 137   *Diversification serves as protection* Comments by Warren Buffett at the 1996 Berkshire Hathaway Annual Meeting

Page 137   *it ought to be considered as imprudent* Speech by J. M. Keynes at the National Mutual Life Assurance Society annual meeting, January 29, 1923 (*CW, Vol. XII*, p. 125)

Page 137   *both own a large number of equities* Buffett, W., 1993 Chairman's Letter, March 1, 1994

Page 138   *it is out of these big units* Letter from J. M. Keynes to F. C. Scott, April 10, 1940 (*CW, Vol. XII*, p. 78)

Page 138   *the important thing is that when you do* Comments by Warren Buffett at the 1998 Berkshire Hathaway Annual Meeting

Page 139   *If something is not worth doing at all* Buffett, W., 1994 Chairman's Letter, March 7, 1995

Page 139   *I cannot understand why* Buffett, W., 1993 Chairman's Letter, March 1,1994

Page 139 *is an admission of not knowing* Loeb, G., *The Battle for Investment Survival*, Wiley, New York, 1935 (1996), p. 119

Page 139 *Send your grain across the seas* Ecclesiastes 11:1–2

Page 140 *my theory of risk* Letter from J. M. Keynes to F. C. Scott, February 1945 (Catalog reference: JMK/PC/1/9/366)

Page 140 *one investment about which* Letter from J. M. Keynes to F. C. Scott, February 6, 1942 (*CW, Vol. XII*, p. 81)

Page 141 *I play for small stakes* David Ricardo, quoted in P. Sraffa (ed.), *The Works and Correspondence of David Ricardo: Biographical Miscellany, Volume X*, Cambridge University Press, Cambridge, 1955, p. 81

Page 141 *When you got nothing, you got nothing to lose* Bob Dylan, "Like a Rolling Stone," *Highway 61 Revisited*, Copyright © 1965; renewed 1993 Special Rider Music

Page 141 *both the intensity with which* Buffett, W., 1993 Chairman's Letter, March 1, 1994

Page 142 *false to believe that one* Keynes, J. M., "Foreword to *King Street, Cheapside* by G. H. Recknell," (*CW, Vol. XII*), 1936, p. 243

Page 142 *practical investors usually learn* Fisher, P., *Common Stocks and Uncommon Profits*, John Wiley & Sons, New York, 1958 (1996), p. 117

Page 142 *there are seldom more than two or three* Letter from J. M. Keynes to F. C. Scott, August 15, 1934 (*CW, Vol. XII*, p. 57)

Page 143 *Playing poker in the Army* Charles Munger, quoted in Lowe, *Damn Right! Behind the Scenes with Berkshire Hathaway Billionaire Charlie Munger*, p. 36

Page 143 *To suggest that this investor* Buffett, W., 1996 Chairman's Letter, February 28, 1997

Page 144 *the right investment policy for [the Society]* Keynes, J. M., quoted in N. Davenport, "Keynes in the City," in *Essays on John Maynard Keynes*, p. 225

Page 144 *ought not to be carried too far* Letter from J. M. Keynes to F. C. Scott, August 15, 1934 (*CW, Vol. XII*, p. 57)

Page 144 *a variety of risks in spite of* Memorandum from J. M. Keynes to the Estates Committee, King's College, Cambridge, May 8, 1938 (*CW, Vol. XII*, p. 107)

Page 145 *five to ten sensibly-priced companies* Buffett, W., 1993 Chairman's Letter, March 1, 1994

Page 146 *To carry one's eggs in a great* Memorandum from J. M. Keynes to the Provincial Insurance Company, March 7, 1938 (*CW, Vol. XII*, p. 99)

Page 146 *As time goes on I get more* Letter from J. M. Keynes to F. C. Scott, August 15, 1934 (*CW, Vol. XII*, p. 57)

Chapter 13: A Sense of Proportion

Page 147 *strenuous purposeful moneymakers* Keynes, J. M., "Economic Possibilities for Our Grandchildren," *Essays in Persuasion*, p. 328

Page 147 *dangerous human proclivities can be canalized* Keynes, J. M., *The General Theory of Employment, Interest and Money*, p. 374

Page 148 *The thing is good as a means* Letter from J. M. Keynes to Duncan Grant, January 22, 1909 (see Skidelsky, *John Maynard Keynes: Hopes Betrayed 1883–1920 (Volume 1)*, p. 202)

Page 148 *It is not easy, it seems, for men* Keynes, J. M., *A Tract on Monetary Reform* (*CW, Vol. IX*, p. 170)

Page 148 *a sound intellectual framework* Buffett, W., Preface to Graham, *The Intelligent Investor*, p. ix

Page 149 *sad lot . . . with drawn, dejected faces* Keynes, J. M., "Dr Melchior: A Defeated Enemy," *Two Memoirs*, p. 395

Page 149 *brilliant and engaging personality* Speech by J. M. Keynes at the National Mutual Life Assurance Annual Meeting, January 20, 1931 (*CW, Vol. XII*, p. 178)

Page 149 *as much equanimity and patience* Memorandum from J. M. Keynes to the Estates Committee, King's College, Cambridge, May 8, 1938 (*CW, Vol. XII*, p. 108)

Page 149 *much more willing to run a risk* Keynes, J. M., *The General Theory of Employment, Interest and Money*, p. 160

Page 149 *One must not allow one's attitude* Memorandum from J. M. Keynes to the Estates Committee, King's College, Cambridge, May 8, 1938 (*CW, Vol. XII*, p. 108)

Page 150 *robust faith in the ultimate rightness* Letter from F. C. Scott to J. M. Keynes, January 1939 (*CW, Vol. XII*, p. 50)

Page 150 *Buying a neglected and therefore* Graham, *The Intelligent Investor*, p. 32

Page 151 *I do not draw from this conclusion* Memorandum from J. M. Keynes to the National Mutual Life Assurance board, February 18, 1931 (*CW, Vol. XII*, p. 18)

Page 151 *a certain continuity of policy* Letter from J. M. Keynes to F. C. Scott, November 29, 1933 (*CW, Vol. XII*, p. 65)

Page 151 *it seems to me to be most important* Letter from J. M. Keynes to F. C. Scott, August 23, 1934 (*CW, Vol. XII*, pp. 58–59)

Page 151 *disposition to own stocks without fretting* Comments by Charles Munger at the 2003 Berkshire Hathaway Annual Meeting

Page 152 *The inactive investor who takes up* Keynes, J. M., "Investment Policy for Insurance Companies," *The Nation and Athenaeum*, May 17, 1924 (*CW, Vol. XII*, p. 243)

Page 152 *constant vigilance, constant revision* Ibid., p. 244

Page 152 *The great point about King's* Report by Ministry of Agriculture officials, December 18, 1926 (quoted in Moggridge, *Maynard Keynes: An Economist's Biography*, p. 411)

Page 152 *I have never known a man so quick* Davenport, N., *Memoirs of a City Radical*, p. 50

Page 154 *You only find out who is swimming* Buffett, W., 2001 Chairman's Letter, February 28, 2002

Page 154 *an investor who proposes* Keynes, J. M., *The General Theory of Employment, Interest and Money*, p. 157

Page 154 *chicken about buying stocks on margin* Charles Munger, quoted in R. Lenzner, and D. S. Fondiller, "Meet Charlie Munger," *Forbes*, January 22, 1996

Page 154 *The ideal is to borrow in a way* Ibid.

Page 155 *Investing is not a game where* Warren Buffett, quoted in an interview with *BusinessWeek*, June 25, 1999

Page 155 *good business judgment with an ability* Buffett, W., 1987 Chairman's Letter, February 29, 1988

Page 155 *The overweening conceit which the greater* Smith, A., *An Inquiry into the Nature and Causes of the Wealth of Nations*, Volume 1, p. 168

Page 156 *stock doesn't know you own it* Lecture by Warren Buffett to the University of Florida School of Business, October 15, 1998

Page 157 *a great big casino . . . [where] everyone else is boozing* Warren Buffett, quoted in an interview with *Forbes*, November 1, 1972

Page 157 *It is remarkable how much long-term* Munger, C., Wesco Financial Corporation Annual Report, 1989

Page 157 *their brains make them dangerous* Quoted in *Fortune* magazine, September 1933 (cited by Skidelsky, *John Maynard Keynes 1883–1946: Economist, Philosopher, Statesman*, p. 961)

Page 157 *much patience and courage* Letter from J. M. Keynes to G. H. Recknell, January 19, 1939 (*CW, Vol. XII*, p.49)

Page 157 *the investor's chief problem* Graham, *The Intelligent Investor*, p. 8

Page 158 *more temperament than logic* Letter from J. M. Keynes to Richard Kahn, May 5, 1938 (*CW, Vol. XII*, p. 100)

Chapter 14: Post Mortem

Page 159   *Orthodoxy has at last caught up with me* Obituary published in *The Daily Express*, April 22, 1946

Page 160   *partly with a view to comparing* Memorandum from J. M. Keynes to the Estates Committee, King's College, Cambridge, May 8, 1938 (*CW, Vol. XII*, p. 102)

Page 160   *whence the satisfactory results came* Letter from J. M. Keynes to F. C. Scott, February 6, 1942 (*CW, Vol. XII*, p. 83)

Page 161   *[Mr Market] has incurable emotional problems* Buffett, W., 1987 Chairman's Letter, February 29, 1988

Page 161   *waves of irrational psychology* Keynes, J. M., *The General Theory of Employment, Interest and Money*, p. 162

Page 162   *I believe now that successful investment* Memorandum from J. M. Keynes to the Estates Committee, King's College, Cambridge, May 8, 1938 (*CW, Vol. XII*, pp. 106–107)

Page 164   *While at Cambridge University* Obituary published in *the New York Times*, April 22, 1946

Page 164   *It's a little like spending eight years* Buffett, W., transcript of a meeting of the New York Society of Financial Analysts, December 6, 1994

Page 165   *ramify . . . into every corner of our minds* Keynes, J. M., Preface to *The General Theory of Employment, Interest and Money*, p. xxiii

Page 165   *Ships will sail around the world* Buffett, W., "The Superinvestors of Graham-and-Doddsville," *Hermes*, Fall 1984

Page 166   *I find Governing Bodies meetings* Letter from Lord Quickswood, Provost of Eton, to J. M. Keynes, December 17, 1943 (*CW, Vol. XII*, pp. 112–113)

Page 166   *All orthodox suggestions are too expensive* Letter from J. M. Keynes to R. E. Marsden, Bursar of Eton, March 8, 1944 (*CW, Vol. XII*, p. 111)

Page 166   *rather in the nature of a family affair* Letter from J. M. Keynes to John Davenport, March 21, 1944 (Catalog reference: JMK/A/44/37)

Page 166   *[Keynes] was an extremely active* Moggridge, (ed.), *Economic Articles and Correspondence: Investment and Editorial* (*CW, Vol. XII*), 1983, p. 51

Page 166   *gave a good thrashing* Memorandum from J. M. Keynes to the Provincial Insurance Company, March 7, 1938 (*CW, Vol. XII*, p. 97)

Page 167   *the Fund's performance was clearly* Chua, J., and Woodward, F., "J. M. Keynes's Investment Performance: A Note," *The Journal of Finance*, Vol. XXXVIII, No. 1, March 1983, p. 234

Page 167   *On the basis of modern performance* Ibid., p. 232

Page 167   *The more directly under Keynes' control* Skidelsky, *John Maynard Keynes: Fighting for Britain 1937–1946* (Volume 3), p. 524

Page 168   *Whereas in the 1920s Keynes was generally* Moggridge, *Maynard Keynes: An Economist's Biography*, p. 585

Page 168   *the avoidance of "stumers" with which* Letter from J. M. Keynes to F. C. Scott, June 7, 1938 (*CW, Vol. XII*, p. 66)

Page 168   *there had scarcely been a single case* Letter from J. M. Keynes to F. C. Scott, February 6, 1942 (*CW, Vol. XII*, p. 83)

Page 168   *The really dreadful losses* Graham, *The Intelligent Investor*, p. 8

Page 168   *one-armed contrarian who bought* Skousen, M., "Keynes as a Speculator: A Critique of Keynesian Investment Theory," in *Dissent on Keynes*, Praeger, New York, 1992, p. 166

Page 169   *One may be, and no doubt is* Letter from J. M. Keynes to R. F. Kahn, May 5, 1938 (*CW, Vol. XII*, p. 101)

Page 169   *not merely a maintenance of the present* Speech by J. M. Keynes at the Annual Meeting of National Mutual unit holders, February 19, 1936 (*CW, Vol. XXI*, p. 378)

Page 169   *Maynard's judgment would have been* Bell, *Old Friends*, pp. 45–46

Page 169   *I made a big mistake in not selling* Buffett, W., 2003 Chairman's Letter, February 27, 2004

Page 169   *If you stick with stocks that are underpriced* Comments by Charles Munger at the 2000 Berkshire Hathaway annual meeting

Page 170   *Well here am I, like a recurring decimal* J. M. Keynes, quoted in Skidelsky, *John Maynard Keynes: Fighting for Britain 1937–1946* (Volume 3), p. 135

Page 170   *a sort of roving commission* Ibid., p. 79

Page 170   *Keynes must be one of the most* Howson and Moggridge (eds), *The Wartime Diaries of Lionel Robbins and James Meade*, pp. 158–159

Page 170   *he could be silent* Keynes, J. M., obituary for Sir Frederick Phillips, August 13, 1943 (*CW, Vol. X*, p. 330)

Page 171   *go for each other in a strident duet* Howson and Moggridge (eds), *The Wartime Diaries of Lionel Robbins and James Meade*, p. 135 (see also *CW, Vol. XXV*, p. 364)

Page 172   *for the cause as certainly* Robbins, L., "John Maynard Keynes: Profound Influence on Thought and Policy," *The Times*, January 26, 1951, p. 7

Page 172 *Progress is a soiled creed* Keynes, J. M., "The Underlying Principles,"
Manchester Guardian Commercial, January 4, 1923 (*CW, Vol. XVII*, p. 448)

Page 173 *I wish I had drunk more champagne* George Rylands, the British theater
director and scholar, recalled that just a few months before he died,
Keynes "voiced his one regret that he had not drunk more champagne in his life" (see Keynes, Milo [ed.], *Essays on John Maynard
Keynes*, p. 48)

Index

Acknowledgments

Maynard Keynes once observed that his creative thinking generally began as a "gray, fuzzy, woolly monster" in his head. Only falteringly, and with much effort, were these thoughts given some semblance of shape and sense.

In the process of writing this book, and wrestling with my own particular species of woolly monster, I have built up substantial debts of gratitude to many people. Specifically, I would like to thank Steve Johnson of *The Intelligent Investor* publication and web site, and Dr. David Chambers of Judge Business School, University of Cambridge, for their comments on the manuscript. My thanks also to Patricia McGuire and Elizabeth Ennion of the Archive Centre, King's College, Cambridge, for their unfailing assistance and good humor.

My experience with John Wiley & Sons has been uniformly rewarding and productive, from initial pitch through to finished product. From Wiley, I would particularly like to thank David Pugh, Kelly O'Connor, Michelle Fitzgerald, Stacey Small, and Kevin Holm for their advice and patience.

Finally, I reserve my most heartfelt thanks and appreciation to Carmel, for giving me the support and encouragement to indulge my own—possibly irrational—fascination with Keynes and the stock market.

About the Author

Justyn Walsh is a Director at Renaissance Capital, an investment bank, and is based in London and Moscow. Prior to his career in investment banking, he worked as a corporate lawyer and financial journalist. *Keynes and the Market* is his first book.

D0065439

Recent Titles in
Contributions in Women's Studies

FILM
FEMINISMS

Library of Congress Cataloging in Publication Data

Gentile, Mary C.
  Film feminisms.

  (Contributions in women's studies, ISSN 0147-104X ;
no. 56)
  Bibliography: p.
  Includes index.
  1. Feminism and motion picture.   2. Moving-pictures—
Philosophy.   I. Title.   II. Series.
PN1995.9.W6G43   1985   791.43'09'09352042   84-19780
ISBN 0-313-24407-3 (lib. bdg.)

Library of Congress Catalog Card Number: 84-19780
ISBN: 0-313-24407-3
ISSN: 0147-104X

First published in 1985

Greenwood Press
A division of Congressional Information Service, Inc.
88 Post Road West
Westport, Connecticut 06881

Printed in the United States of America

10 9 8 7 6 5 4 3 2 1

Copyright Acknowledgments

Grateful acknowledgment is given for permission to use the following:

Excerpts from *Work 1961–73* by Yvonne Rainer, copyright 1974 by Yvonne
Rainer. Permission granted by Yvonne Rainer.

Excerpts from *What is Cinema? Volume II* by Andre Bazin (Essays Selected and
Translated by Hugh Gray), copyright 1971 by The Regents of the University of
California. Permission granted by The University of California Press.

Excerpts from *Women's Pictures: Feminism and Cinema* by Annette Kuhn, copyright 1982 by Annette Kuhn. Permission granted by Routledge & Kegan Paul Ltd.

Excerpts from *Women and Film: Both Sides of the Camera* by E. Ann Kaplan, copyright 1983 by E. Ann Kaplan. Permission granted by Methuen & Co.

Excerpts from *The Reader and the Writer—Essays, Sketches, Memories* by Christa
Wolf, copyright 1977 by Christa Wolf. Permission granted by International
Publishers.

FILM
FEMINISMS

THEORY AND PRACTICE

Mary C. Gentile

Contributions in Women's Studies, Number 56

GREENWOOD PRESS
Westport, Connecticut · London, England

To Mary
and Chris

Contents

Acknowledgments

I would like to acknowledge and thank the film programmers and distributors who assisted me in this research: Charles Silver and the Museum of Modern Art; Unifilm in New York City; Quartet/Films Incorporated in New York City; and Debi Weldon of New Cinema Ltd. in Toronto, Ontario. Debi Weldon, in particular, was generous and encouraging beyond all my expectations. Finally, I wish to thank Yvonne Rainer who, through Film-Makers' Cooperative in New York City, allowed me private screenings of all her films.

As well, I am grateful for the funds supplied by the Graduate Student Association through the Graduate Resource Access Development Project of the State University of New York at Buffalo.

I thank Thomas P. Adler, Co-Editor of the *Proceedings* of the Purdue University Seventh Annual Conference on Film, 1983, for permission to reprint my essay, "Feminist Film Theory and Practice."

FILM THEORIES AND FEMINISM

Introduction

Whenever we set out to construct a feminist aesthetic, or a feminist social theory, or a feminist politics, or a feminist mode of living, we see ourselves—and we are seen—as engaged in an "oppositional cultural practice."[1] Readings in feminist history and feminist social, political, cultural and psychological theory reinforce this perception. These writers offer new definitions, startling contexts for the old, "immutable experiences": Adrienne Rich gives us *Of Woman Born: Motherhood as Experience and Institution* and "Compulsory Heterosexuality and Lesbian Existence"; Audre Lorde offers *Uses of the Erotic: The Erotic as Power*; Mary Daly adds *Gyn/Ecology: The Metaethics of Radical Feminism*; and Sandra Gilbert and Susan Gubar write *The Madwoman in the Attic: The Woman Writer and the Nineteenth-Century Literary Imagination*.[2] The list goes on and on, and piece by piece, we assemble a new paradigm for ordering experience, particularly women's experience, a paradigm that stands in opposition to, and is rarely read without reference to the dominant order of physical, sexual, political, spiritual, psychological, or cultural practice.

This same dynamic holds true for film theory and film criticism. The earliest efforts were twofold: many writers began to build a scaffold of critical work addressing women directors, women scriptwriters, women editors, and even paying a new attention to the influence of actresses; this scaffold could be placed beside the pre-existing body of written work that addresses male filmmakers, scriptwriters, and so on. The second

impetus was to review those films by male directors that had already received a share of critical attention, but to read them, this time, "against the grain," to expose the ideological and aesthetic assumptions that had gone unnoticed and which underlie the cultural construction of Woman in film. These two examples of "oppositional cultural practice"—the creation of an alternate film tradition, the tradition of women filmmakers (Dulac, Arzner, Riefenstahl, Lupino, Deren, for example), and the development of alternate readings, alternate critiques, and ultimately, alternate evaluative judgments of the body of dominant (largely male-directed) cinema—have been noted and documented by Annette Kuhn in her book, *Women's Pictures: Feminism and Cinema* and by E. Ann Kaplan in *Women and Film: Both Sides of the Camera.*[3]

The earlier anthologies, *Women and the Cinema: A Critical Anthology* (edited by Karyn Kay and Gerald Peary) and *Sexual Stratagems: The World of Women in Film* (edited by Patricia Erens), can be read now as the tracks and traces of a developing aesthetic.[4] These books include examples of the two trends just noted, as well as early examples of a more self-conscious and theoretically sophisticated approach to the interface of feminism and film. For most of us, this approach was first expressed in Claire Johnston's pamphlet, *Notes on Women's Cinema* (1973) and Laura Mulvey's essay, "Visual Pleasure and Narrative Cinema" (1975).[5] Despite a move away, in this kind of work, from the assumption that a film will "give up" its one, true meaning to the viewer who is perceptive enough, this writing is still identified and, in fact, validated in terms of its oppositional nature. Kuhn and Kaplan both find themselves explaining, if not defending, the use of semiotic and psychoanalytic theory because, after all, it culminates in a critique of the existing system. In other words, we may be using the "dominant" tools but our finished product is still oppositional.

This passionate proclamation of "difference" has been and is necessary to the feminist critique of any aspect of society. As we shall discuss in chapter 1, it is only from the consciousness of our positioning as the "second sex," as "Other"—that is, from an awareness of our oppositional position—that an analysis of ideological practice and the construction of a female subjectiv-

ity can develop. The repression or denial of difference, we have learned from painful experience, leads to the repression of *women* and the denial of *women's* experience. Adrienne Rich exposes this dangerous elision in her critique of "compulsory heterosexuality," denouncing "the frequently heard assertion that in a world of genuine equality, where men were nonoppressive and nurturing, everyone would be bisexual. Such a notion blurs and sentimentalizes the actualities within which women have experienced sexuality; it is the old liberal leap across the tasks and struggles of here and now, the continuing process of sexual definition which will generate its own possibilities and choices."[6]

In this essay, however, Rich goes on to denounce those studies of female psychological development that present woman-woman bonding only in its relation to—that is, as an aberration of—the "primary heterosexual drive." She critiques those analyses that, although departing from traditional Freudian theory, still take their shape, their terminology from this tradition. The problem is not Chodorow or Dinnerstein's use of traditional psychoanalytic tools.[7] Rather the problem is that these studies find their origins in oppositionality to these traditional tools. Reactions to a given body of work are limited in the questions they may ask and the perspectives they may reflect. This work is still determined by traditional theories in the very fact of its opposition. The feminist analysis that Rich espouses, on the other hand, originates in open exploration of the "lesbian continuum," in practice, rather than in reaction to existing theoretical paradigms of sexuality.

Similarly, the pattern of feminist analysis I am positing calls for an alternative use of "difference." Let us not define feminist film theory, for example, by its opposition to or its exclusion of other film theories—the semiotic, psychoanalytic, structuralist, auteurist, or avant-garde. Rather let feminist film theory be that which exists in the spaces between all these theories. If feminist analysis finds its origins in the consciousness of gender-based oppression, it has continually opened out onto other fields of oppression. Socialist feminism has raised the question of class difference. Mothers have extended their analysis of women's oppression to the analysis of children's rights. Racial

oppression, ageism, the rights of the disabled—all these issues have found their way into the feminist politic.

By patriarchal standards of thought and ideological practice, this type of politic is a fiasco. Issues are not compartmentalized; directions are unclear; emphases spill over onto one another. How can one be "for" something if this does not imply one is "against" something else? Still, somehow this feminist politic comes closer to the personal reality of more individuals; this politic calls for a "complicated community" and a methodology that is more than dialectical.

The definition of feminism I posit here, therefore, is not that of an oppositional ideology. In fact, taking Bill Nichols' definition of ideology ("the image society gives of itself in order to perpetuate itself") feminism is more self-consciously a process than an ideology.[8] Feminism does not exist "in opposition to" so much as it incorporates opposition into itself.

All this is by way of introduction—proposing the model of feminism I utilize in this book and suggesting some of its features. I am interested here in presenting and exploring "difference," not as an instrument of division, but as a unifying force, a thread of commonality. For example, feminist film theorists have been asked, "How is your theory distinct from other avant-garde or anti-narrative theories?" Annette Kuhn raises a variant of this question in relation to Luce Irigaray's theory of "feminine discourse": "The theoretical groundings of the notion of a feminine text are complex and open to criticism, centering primarily on the fact that many of the arguments . . . seem to be suggesting that all radical signifying practice is, in some way, feminine."[9] Putting aside for a moment the problem of feminist discourse as opposed to feminine discourse (the latter raises questions of essentialism), these very questions arise from a view of feminism as oppositional. These questions develop from the notion that feminist film theory is somehow distinct from all other theories, standing in opposition to them. Rather, the feminist film theory I posit exists between and alongside these theories, revealing the contradictions and the questions that are common to them all—that is, the interrelations of ideology and subjectivity. Rather than grounding a feminist analysis solely on the examination of women's sta-

tus—or non-status—as "Other," I suggest we ground it in an analysis of the practice of constructing the "Other" in all individuals.

It seems that feminists have little choice but to open their analysis up in this manner. As soon as we begin to recognize the ways in which theory and practice—be it political, psychological, cultural, social—function so as to construct our image and our sense of ourselves, we also begin to recognize the ways in which this theory and practice create limitations and conflict for any group or individual that feels slightly out of sync with the "image in the mirror," the "ego ideal" reflected back to this group or this individual by society.[10] Any "marginal" group experiences this dissonance, be they women or men and women of color or the working class or the disabled or children or the elderly or gays and lesbians. I suggest, however, that individual members of the dominant class, race, sex and so on, also experience such a dissonance. Everyone is someone else's "Other." The dissonance may be less intense, easier to ignore, and it may not threaten their basic survival in the ways it does for marginal groups. It does, however, trigger a defensive reaction. Those who "just miss" the ideal will be more invested in presenting and defending it, in disguising all signs of nonconformity and in ".passing."

I am not suggesting the denial of difference mentioned earlier, the "liberal leap" that draws attention away from the oppression of women, for example, by asserting the victimization of all. Rather I wish to assert difference, to call attention to it, in all its forms and manifestations, to find a commonality in the experience of difference without compromising its distinctive realities and effects. I am positing a "multiple perspective" that can comprehend alternate viewpoints, not so as to excuse oppression but rather to clarify it, to expose the pain of one individual group without denying that of another. Placing the experience of many individuals or many groups in such a juxtaposition prevents oppressive simplifications and affirms Rich's "radical complexity," a concept she develops in her argument against lesbian separatism, "The Meaning of Our Love for Women Is What We Have Constantly to Expand."[11]

This multiple perspective is the feminism I build upon in this

book. I do not deny the origins of this perspective in the oppression of women. Neither do I deny the necessity to continue to focus upon this oppression—its history, its manifestations, its causes and implications, and the means to its eradication. However, I do place more emphasis upon this "way of seeing" than on "what is seen."[12] I am reluctant to make this distinction between a kind of "form" and "content," for one of the themes running through this work is the inseparability of the two. However, though form does determine content—the way we see does determine what we see—both the form and content still do have impact. Many complain that an emphasis upon the determinism of form relativizes content out of existence. I suggest rather that this emphasis upon "ways of seeing" is the only way we can understand and change the "content" of our daily experience. Understanding/experiencing the compelling quality of contradictory realities is the only way, short of violence, to resolve their differences.

With this definition of feminism in mind—multiple perspective—we can begin to reread the classical theorists and the dominant cinema in a new way. This concept of "re-reading" and "re-viewing" has been a staple of feminist analysis in all disciplines. Again, Adrienne Rich provides the vocabulary and the explanation, though not the impetus, in her essay, "When We Dead Awaken: Writing as Re-Vision":

Re-vision—the act of looking back, of seeing with fresh eyes, of entering an old text from a new critical direction—is for women more than a chapter in cultural history: it is an act of survival. Until we can understand the assumptions in which we are drenched we cannot know ourselves. . . . A radical critique of literature, feminist in its impulse, would take the work first of all as a clue to how we live, how we have been living, how we have been led to imagine ourselves, how our language has trapped as well as liberated us, how the very act of naming has been till now a male prerogative, and how we can begin to see and name—and therefore live—afresh.[13]

This essay, something of a manifesto, reflects the tack that many feminists have taken, re-reading old texts, written or filmed, for their exclusion of women, their manipulation of women, the assumptions concerning women's reality. These analyses fol-

low much the same course as the "ideological analyses," promoted and practiced by the writers of *Cahiers du Cinema* in their famous reading of John Ford's *Young Mr. Lincoln*. In *Women's Pictures: Feminism and Cinema*, Annette Kuhn distinguishes the practitioners of an "ideological analysis" who approach a film as if its gaps and assumptions and contradictions are somehow "present" causing tension within the text, from those who view the film purely as an expression of ideology to which the reader can bring a critical eye.[14] Kuhn concludes that:

Once a notion of reading as an active and situated practice is adopted, the distinction between films which embody an internal self-criticism and films which are completely ideologically complicit becomes redundant. This is because at this point the focus of analytical activity becomes the process of reading as much as the text itself: if reading is seen as dynamic and situated, then it is possible to argue that film texts are in some measure constituted or reconstituted in and through the act of reading.[15]

Although I accept Kuhn's analysis of the reader's active role in constructing a text's meaning, I maintain that a willingness to see multiple intention, multiple perspectives, and to entertain multiple readings of a particular text is essential to feminist critique. The feminist analysis I propose not only asks "feminist questions" of a text, it also actively entertains contradiction within and around the work.[16] Therefore, the readings I offer of particular films, later in this book, will center around the pivotal tensions in those works, the contradictory impulses— Yvonne Rainer's desire simultaneously to use and to free herself from narrative structure, for example. And, my readings are tentative and incomplete without the answering interpretations of other viewers of these films, viewers who may identify altogether different pivotal tensions.

As well, the analyses I will offer of the theories of Sergei Eisenstein and Andre Bazin will center around what I see as their contradictory impulses. I intend neither to wholly adopt nor reject their theories. Rather I try to see through their eyes, to present their impulses, and then to offer another perspective that contradicts or "cracks" their viewpoint. Intentionally I choose

these two classical film theorists, male theorists, for I hope to show the extent to which their contradictions are the contradictions feminist theory tries to confront.

Similarly, my use of the theories of Jacques Lacan and Louis Althusser are attempts to, again, place the issues of feminism in a continuum with the contradictions that plague dominant theorists of psychoanalysis and ideology. Just as Althusser and Lacan face the problems of ideology and subjectivity, so are these the issues that determine the limits of Eisenstein's and Bazin's theory. There is a continuity here and it is in feminism, the method and the multiple perspective of feminism, rather than in a feminist dogma, that these questions can be actively addressed. I draw these connections, not to disguise the distinctiveness or the unique origins of feminism, but rather to demonstrate its wider application and necessity.

Both Annette Kuhn and E. Ann Kaplan provide a historical summary of the most significant, or most sharply delineated, trends and developments in feminist film theory.[17] They position their analyses and their questioning within a chronological history of ideas, a theoretical time line. My focus in this book is rather the internalization of theory and its questions. How do Eisenstein's questions relate to those of Yvonne Rainer, or Bazin's to Laura Mulvey, or Althusser's to Helke Sander? And what do any of their questions have to do with the viewer, particularly the feminist viewer? What do they have to do with me? I want to bridge the arbitrary chasms between methodologies and styles to reveal the lines of connection, the common questions, that drive us all.

NOTES

1. Annette Kuhn, *Women's Pictures: Feminism and Cinema* (London: Routledge & Kegan Paul, 1982), p. 17.

2. Adrienne Rich, *Of Woman Born: Motherhood as Experience and Institution* (New York: Bantam Books, 1977); Adrienne Rich, "Compulsory Heterosexuality and Lesbian Existence," *Signs: Journal of Women in Culture and Society*, vol. 5, no. 4, 1980, pp. 631–60. Audre Lorde, *Uses of the Erotic: The Erotic as Power* (Brooklyn, N.Y.: Out & Out Books, 1978); Mary Daly, *Gyn/Ecology: The Metaethics of Radical Feminism* (Boston: Beacon Press, 1978); Sandra M. Gilbert and Susan Gubar, *The*

Madwoman in the Attic: The Woman Writer and the Nineteenth-Century Literary Imagination (New Haven: Yale University Press, 1979).

3. Kuhn, *Women's Pictures: Feminism and Cinema*; E. Ann Kaplan, *Women and Film: Both Sides of the Camera* (New York: Methuen, 1983).

4. Karyn Kay and Gerald Peary, eds., *Women and the Cinema: A Critical Anthology* (New York: E.P. Dutton, 1977); Patricia Erens, ed., *Sexual Stratagems: The World of Women in Film* (New York: Horizon Press, 1979).

5. Claire Johnston, ed., *Notes on Women's Cinema* (London: Society for Education in Film and Television, 1973). Laura Mulvey, "Visual Pleasure and Narrative Cinema," *Screen*, vol. 16, no. 3, Autumn 1975 p. 6–18.

6. Rich, "Compulsory Heterosexuality," p. 637.

7. Nancy Chodorow, *The Reproduction of Mothering: Psychoanalysis and the Sociology of Gender* (Berkeley: University of California Press, 1978); Dorothy Dinnerstein, *The Mermaid and the Minotaur: Sexual Arrangements and the Human Malaise* (New York: Harper & Row, 1976).

8. Bill Nichols, *Ideology and the Image: Social Representation in the Cinema and Other Media* (Bloomington: Indiana University Press, 1981), p. 1.

9. Kuhn, *Women's Pictures*, p. 12.

10. See chapter 1 for a discussion of Jacques Lacan and Louis Althusser.

11. Adrienne Rich, *On Lies, Secrets, and Silence: Selected Prose 1966–1978* (New York: W.W. Norton & Co., 1979), p. 227.

12. John Berger, *Ways of Seeing* (London and Harmondsworth: British Broadcasting Corporation and Penguin Books, Ltd., 1980).

13. Rich, *On Lies, Secrets, and Silence*, p. 35.

14. Kuhn, *Women's Pictures*, pp. 84–87.

15. Ibid., p. 92.

16. Ibid.

17. See Kuhn, *Women's Pictures*, chapter 4 and Kaplan, *Women and Film*, chapters 1 and 10.

1

Critical Subjectivity

What is our aim when we set out to develop a Feminist Film Theory? What roles does film theory serve and in what ways can it be feminist? J. Dudley Andrew defines the subject of film theory as the "cinematic capability" and its aim, "to formulate a schematic notion of the capacity of film."[1] Although these notions suggest a study of cinematic potential, they might become restrictive if we do not see theory as process or flux. Any theory of film capacity will have to adopt and change as cinema technology grows more sophisticated, and as our notions of aesthetics, of ideology, and of the function of art develop in relation to the social and political moment. Alongside a systematic analysis of how film has functioned, a more progressive theory might suggest new directions and new methods, thereby blurring a bit the distinctions between film theory and film practice. Add to this definition of film theory Nancy Hartsock's definition of feminist theory: "The role of theory, then, is to articulate for us what we know from our practical activity, to bring out and make conscious the philosophy embedded in our lives."[2] A feminist film theory, then, will not only describe *what* we construct in film and *how* we construct it, but also will explore and explain the ideologies that are served by our cinema. In other words, what assumptions about the nature of reality underlie Bazin's analysis of the Italian neorealist cinema? And what conscious and unconscious political commitments fuel Eisenstein's dream of an "Intellectual Cinema?"

So a feminist film theory will be an "engaged" theory, en-

gaged in making explicit the links between art and ideology.[3] And this theory will be openly engaged as far as its own assumptions go. Feminist theorists will attempt to interrogate their own thought process and analytical style, insofar as self-criticism or self-analysis is possible, providing the reader with insight and possible avenues for deconstruction and critique.[4] In this way the reader is actively called into the theoretical process.

Another characteristic of feminist film theory is the mingling of the categories filmmaker, film viewer, and film theorist. The film viewer actively constructs the meaning of a particular text, bringing to it her ideological and personal conditioning and experience, in as actual a sense as the filmmaker constructs the text itself. The activities of filmmaking, film viewing, and film theorizing exist on a sort of continuum. The more we emphasize the constructive process of film viewing, the closer the spectator comes to the filmmaker. And the more conscious this spectator becomes of her own viewing process, the closer she comes to the film theorist. Consequently, there is no artificial distinction between subject and object, between theorist and the text in the project of film theory. For the theorist and the spectator, like the maker, participate in the construction of the text they experience and similarly, in the construction of the theory that explores and explains these filmic texts.

This analysis of feminist film theory appears to give a central position to the individual spectator with his or her distinctive subjectivity or point of view. But this emphasis becomes problematic when we review the recent theories of Louis Althusser and Jacques Lacan. In these theories, subjectivity is under attack. In the past, we might have assumed that each individual has a unique consciousness or point of view through which he or she perceives and evaluates ideas and experience. Lacan suggests that a child first recognizes herself as a being distinct from the rest of the world in the "Mirror Phase," when she sees her image reflected back to her, autonomous and idealized. This mismatching or gap between the child herself and the ego-ideal, the image in the mirror, is the beginning of an endless stream of misnaming, misspeaking, and misrepresenting that characterizes, for Lacan, the child's entry into the symbolic. Entry into

the Symbolic occurs after the "Mirror Phase" and it refers to the child's acquisition of language.[5] With this language, the child can begin to speak her subjectivity; she acquires an "I." But although language provides the means to speak and therefore actualize one's subjectivity, it also, then, determines what and how the child can speak. Once again, there will be a gap between the child's desire and what the child is able to say. So as language enables the child to develop and express a full subjectivity, it also limits or in some ways determines what that subjectivity will be. For women, this determination is particularly repressive, if one follows Lacan's hypotheses. Woman, as mother, represents to the child a unity of subject and object, of desire and gratification, of self and other. When this unity is necessarily severed, the woman becomes the representation of lack, or desire unfulfilled, to the child. For Lacan, the original sense of unity or desire fulfilled is the phallus and once the mother's role as provider of this unity is shattered, the father's penis can become a symbol for this desire. The penis promises an eventual unity with the mother again. Meanwhile, the mother's role has become quite ambivalent, for although unity with her is still the child's desire, she has come to represent lack and absence of penis, and therefore the threat of castration or desire unfulfilled. In addition to the mother's ambivalent position, the girl child is similarly caught. When the boy recognizes the penis as a symbol for the phallus, he is able to enter the Symbolic Realm, that of language, and he is therefore able to speak his desire, although incompletely, and to assume an acting subjectivity. The girl, however, remains a symbol of lack, to men and to herself, and is unable to enter the Symbolic Realm or to acquire a full subjectivity in any but a "tentative, highly negotiated, and ambiguous" fashion.[6] Thus, Lacan's analysis leaves us with a male subjectivity that can function and name itself only through a preexistent language, a language that therefore determines and limits this subjective point of view. And we are left with a female subjectivity that is further limited by the fact that this determining language relegates her to the realm of "non-male" and of lack. Therefore, the language that would allow her a way to speak herself has already "written her out."

This problematic subjectivity is further elaborated and further complicated in the theory of Louis Althusser. Althusser writes: "*the category of the subject is only constitutive of all ideology in so far as all ideology has the function (which defines it) of constituting' concrete individuals as subjects.*"[7] In other words, ideology has a dual impact on individuals. Through the "Ideological State Apparatuses" of "Churches, Parties, Trade Unions, families, some schools, most newspapers, cultural ventures, etc., etc.,"[8] an interpretation or a version of "reality," a world view, is imparted and we see ourselves in the roles this world view affords us. We see ourselves as these apparatuses "reflect" our image back to us, much as Lacan's mirror reflects the child's image back to her. And more specifically, these apparatuses reveal the image of a thinking, self-determining individual; they convince us that we possess an identity, a subjectivity, thereby causing us to believe that the version of "reality" ideology creates for us is a perspective we have independently chosen. So if for Lacan, the form of our subjectivity is determined by a preexistent language, for Althusser our belief in the existence of subjectivity itself is an ideological effect. If we assume we are thinking for ourselves and making our own informed choices, how much more invisible will the workings of ideology become? In fact, according to Althusser, a recognition of the pervasive and determining function of ideology in an individual's life requires the recognition that one's sense of oneself has been constructed. Needless to say, an individual's reluctance to deny her own autonomy thus serves to preserve and protect the workings of ideology. Or as Althusser puts it, playing on the ambiguity of the term "subject:" "*the individual is interpellated as a (free) subject in order that he shall submit freely to the commandments of the Subject, i.e., in order that he shall (freely) accept his subjection.*"[9] So "Ideological State Apparatuses," although proceeding in this somewhat autonomous manner, all "contribute to the same result: the reproduction of the relations of production."[10] Integral to this project is the naming of individuals as subjects: individuals are addressed or "interpellated" as if they are subjects, conscious individuals, and so they think of themselves as such. Yet at the same time that we are addressed as subjects and in the same apparatuses, we are also provided with

models or "reflections" of what we "are." So our very sense of ourselves as conscious, acting individuals is stitched to a world view, a version of "reality" that limits or guides the ways in which we exercise our supposed autonomy.

Althusser recognizes the need to tear this ideological stitching[11] and he writes:

But to recognize that we are subjects and that we function in the practical rituals of the most elementary everyday life (the hand-shake, the fact of calling you by your name, the fact of knowing, even if I do not know what it is, that you "have" a name of your own, which means that you are recognized as a unique subject, etc.)—this recognition only gives us the "consciousness" of our incessant (eternal) practice of ideological recognition—its consciousness, i.e. its *recognition*—but in no sense does it give us the (scientific) *knowledge* of the mechanism of this recognition. Now it is this knowledge that we have to reach, if you will, while speaking in ideology, and from within ideology we have to outline a discourse which tries to break with ideology, in order to dare to be the beginning of a scientific (i.e. subjectless) discourse on ideology.[12]

What Althusser suggests here is, in a sense, a contradiction. How can subjects who are constructed by an ideology, speaking from within that ideology, break with that ideology? And how can subjects *ever* speak a "subjectless" discourse? On the other hand, if we can never speak but from within ideology, how can Althusser himself recognize and critique ideology? We seem to be caught within contradictions and paradox. And yet, perhaps Althusser does provide a key to our escape when he suggests the construction of a "subjectless" discourse. Cannot discourse be subjectless by being subject-full? Let me elaborate upon and explain this hypothesis.

In her introduction to *The Second Sex*, Simone de Beauvoir attempts to clarify Levi-Strauss' emphasis upon dualities or the capacity to perceive binary opposition when she writes: "Things become clear, . . . if, following Hegel, we find in consciousness itself a fundamental hostility toward every other consciousness; *the subject can be posed only in being opposed*—he sets himself up as the essential, as opposed to the other, the inessential, the object," (emphasis mine).[13] Following her observa-

tion, we can attempt to synthesize the views of subjectivity posed thus far. Lacan suggests that an individual achieves and expresses subjectivity when that individual enters the Symbolic Order—in other words, through language. If we follow Saussure's concept of language, it is a "system of differences with no positive terms."[14] In other words, language names an object by differentiating it from other objects. The meaning emerges from the opposition, or "the subject can be posed only in being opposed." Our subjectivity emerges in language when we speak the "I" instead of him or her, he or she, the "not-I."[15] Thus our sense of ourselves is based on our opposition to others. Obviously, this subjectivity is in line with the subjectivity that, according to Althusser, is constituted by ideology. For language itself is structured and coded to embody and express the prevailing ideology. For example, the "interpellation" or naming of an individual as a subject, achieved through the differentiated pronouns of our language, suggests a distinct and distinguishable identity for each individual, an identity that *belongs* to that individual. This suggests a possessiveness, a territoriality, a divisive individualism that serve the property-oriented ideology of our society all too well. It encourages the alienation of the individual, the sense that ego boundaries must be jealously guarded, and it discourages an actualization of the individual as "species being."[16] Thus, what we have posited is a subjectivity that is constructed through language and that is based upon binary opposition, the valorization of one term at the expense of another.

This subjectivity is obviously quite limited by its nature. For instance, it relies upon a focusing or narrowing down of attributes, of perspective and of alternatives in order to maintain one's sense of identity. The subsequent divisive individualism is compounded, on a broader level, by the treatment of an entire sex or class or race as the Other, the group in opposition to whom one's subjectivity can be established. To make matters worse, it is from within these groups that a critical perspective would most logically emerge, and yet the internalization of their status as Other blocks such a perspective. De Beauvoir elaborates upon the specific difficulties of women's position:

The reason why otherness in this case [women's] seems to be an absolute is in part that it lacks the contingent or incidental nature of historical facts. A condition brought about at a certain time can be abolished at some other time, as the Negroes of Haiti and others have proved; but it might seem that a natural condition is beyond the possibility of change. In truth, however, the nature of things is no more immutably given, once for all, than is historical reality. . . . Proletarians say "We;" Negroes also. Regarding themselves as subjects, they transform the bourgeois, the whites, into "others." But women do not say "We,". . . They do not authentically assume a subjective attitude.[17]

So this, then, is what is necessary: it is necessary for women[18] to develop an authentic subjectivity, to develop a voice and a confident perspective from which to critique a system that attempts to deny them just that. But isn't this a contradiction? It is the fact of the contradiction that makes this effort possible and necessary. It is unlikely that an awareness of the price they pay for their "autonomous subjectivity" will come from those who find a position of authority through it: "Refusal to pose oneself as the Subject, unique and absolute, requires great self-denial."[19] It is rather those who are in the place of the Other, the place of oppression, who must see through it. Furthermore, they must begin to construct a subjectivity that is not based upon the assertion of self at the expense of another if they wish to expand their perspectives. Women must find their way to a functional identity that does not rely upon the construction of an Other; they must move away from the binary opposition of "I" and "not-I." They must begin to see themselves as in a network of multiple possibilities, multiple perspectives, multiple identities, where there is no clear split between "I" and "not-I," but rather a range or continuum of existence. Women must function as a "subject-in-the-making."[20] Multiple perspectives allow this "subject-in-the-making" to find shifting alliances and differences between herself and others; there is no codified identity to which she must subscribe in order to function. If language allows us to express our subjectivity, there is also a gap between what language allows us to say and what we mean: "For when 'she' says something, it is already no longer identical to what she means."[21] And so "the subject is thus the site

of contradiction, thrown into crisis by alterations in language and in the social formation, capable of change. And in the fact that the subject is a *process* lies the possibility of transformation."[22]

But how can women become subjects at all, much less subjects who see beyond the oppressive base of the ideologically constructed subject? If subjectivity is constructed by ideology and expressed/determined through language, and if women's function in these orders is that of "Other," of non-male, how can they achieve the subjectivity necessary to see themselves in a network of multiple perspectives? The answer to this question lies in the very fact of women's exclusion from the ideological order, or their inclusion in a diminished position. Women exist, through language and ideology, as contradictions, or within contradictory frameworks.[23] They are loved as the site of potential unity with the mother, and they are hated as the reminder of that unity denied and as the representation of the castration threat. They are worshipped as purity and inspiring muse; they are defiled as the origin of a physical nature that speaks its own mortality. They are praised for their goodness, and they are accused of an underdeveloped super-ego. In fact, they are considered virtuous while at the same time they are not allowed the possibility of free action. The existence of this contradiction provides women with the key to a *critical subjectivity*. The pain and impossibility of the paradoxical role women are expected to play can force an insight into the construction of these contradictions and a critique of their oppressive nature. Place conflicting demands on an individual and she may try to satisfy them, despite the necessary pain and the ultimate defeat, or she may develop coping mechanisms. Sometimes these mechanisms may take the form of a quiet insight, a long-suffering awareness of the paradox and a patient effort to balance demands as best she may. In this case, her awareness of the paradox may save her from self-hatred, but that same awareness will serve to isolate her from those who make the demands upon her. On the other hand, an individual may recognize the impossibility of her position and try to make her insight known. This is the more militant, more radical position, it is also the position that may eventually allow women to find

a subjectivity *and* an identification with other women; finally women may be able to say "we."[24]

So women must develop a critical subjectivity and this subjectivity will develop through an awareness of contradiction within their ideologically created position and through an awareness of tension within the language they try to speak. The child's first recognition of itself in Lacan's "Mirror Phase" is characterized by a *mis*perception, a *mis*recognition. The child sees an idealized version of himself or herself and desires to achieve or unite with this ego-ideal. In a sort of "mirror reversal," a woman may begin to form a subjectivity for herself when she sees the gap between herself and the version of woman society reflects back to her, and when she stops trying to unite with this distorted reflection. The development of this critical subjectivity relies upon the perception of contradiction, and therefore this project is in opposition to a world view of an art "disposed to see things as a whole."[25]

The preceding discussion arose from an introductory definition of feminist film theory that placed great emphasis upon the individual and her distinctive point of view. We have learned through this reading of Lacan and Althusser that our point of view is constructed through language and ideology; that it must be deconstructed through the recognition and questioning of contradiction within the assumptions that form its base; and that we may then rebuild our point of view, constructing a critical subjectivity, a subjectivity that is critical of its own process and organization. This critical subjectivity knows no absolutes; the closest it comes to a sort of truth is the recognition of contradiction and tension. Rather than "the subject [that] can be posed only in being opposed,"[26] this subject exists only in the spaces in-between, *in* the contradiction between ideologies, between orders of language, and between experiences. Accepting Althusser's hypothesis, that our points of view are created by the ideology in which and through which we exist, we must still recognize that these points of view will differ according to our position within that ideology, and that our position will vary according to context. A black male who is illiterate will have a very different position and point of view within the ideological order, dependent upon whether he is seen as relative to white

men, black women, white women, black literate women in a situation which requires literacy, and so forth. Therefore, the closest this man can come to a critical subjectivity is his awareness of the contradictions within these varying points of view, and his questioning of such a conflicting order.

All of this suggests two major directions or purposes for feminist filmmaking, film viewing and film theorizing. The first involves the filmmaker and the film text itself, and the second involves the role of the film spectator and our attitude toward her. Beginning with the text, the feminist filmmaker may attempt to present a film that "means" multiply, a film that carries within it multiple perspectives and a key to its own contradictions. This is not simply a text that deconstructs itself, for in the process of deconstruction, the defusing of one system of form and content may yet imply the validity of some other system. Rather this is a text that attempts to hold contradictions in tension, to deconstruct and construct equally, to deflate no "truth" in favor of another but rather to affirm and deny them all. The only truth of this text lies in its contradictions. As for the film spectator, our analysis of critical subjectivity implies the validity and the necessity of her individual reading of a film.[27] The contradictions or conflicts a spectator may find in a particular film will emerge both from the film's content and from the position our spectator occupies within her ideological context. Thus multiplicity of perspective and the perception of contradiction can be triggered by the most traditional of films if the spectator is exercising a critical subjectivity in her viewing. This point is of particular importance for without it our suggestions for feminist film might become prescriptive and blindly limiting. Rather, this approach to film is multiple, appropriately enough, involving the spectator as well as the filmmaker and the film theorist.

In Chapters 2 and 3 that follow, I will discuss the film theories of Sergei Eisenstein and Andre Bazin. We will begin to see the seeds of a proposal for films that "mean" multiply in Bazin's discussion of the "ambiguity" of reality and in his insistence that film ought to portray this ambiguity. In Eisenstein's theory, we will begin to see a real concern for the role of the film spectator. Eisenstein will construct his films and his film theory in an effort to involve the spectator actively—emotionally and intellectually—in the film experience.

While an analysis of the theories of Bazin and Eisenstein will provide a basis for the development of this two-pronged feminist film aesthetic, it will also serve as a map of various ideological traps for the feminist theorist. I will locate fundamental points of difference of tension between their aims and their ideological frameworks, and the aims of a feminist film theory. Thus, in Chapter 4, it will become necessary to outline some of the *specifics* of this proposal for a feminist film that "means" multiply, and I will elaborate upon the theory of the spectator.

NOTES

1. J. Dudley Andrew, *The Major Film Theories: An Introduction* (London: Oxford University Press, 1976), pp. 4, 5.

2. Nancy Hartsock, "Feminist Theory and the Development of Revolutionary Strategy," in *Capitalist Patriarchy and the Case for Socialist Feminism*, ed. Zillah R. Eisenstein (New York: Monthly Review Press, 1979), p. 65.

3. Lillian S. Robinson, "Dwelling in Decencies: Radical Criticism and the Feminist Perspective," *Sex, Class and Culture* (Bloomington: Indiana University Press, 1978), p. 3.

4. For a possible guide to such self-analysis, see Norman Holland's discussion of Identity Theme analysis in *Poems in Persons: An Introduction to the Psychoanalysis of Literature* (New York: W.W. Norton, 1975.)

5. Background on Lacan from the following: Jacques Lacan, *Ecrits: A Selection*, trans. Alan Sheridan (New York: W.W. Norton, 1977); Catherine Belsey, *Critical Practice* (New York: Methuen & Co., 1980); Bill Nichols, *Ideology and the Image: Social Representation in the Cinema and Other Media* (Bloomington: Indiana University Press, 1981); Christine Gledhill, "Recent Developments in Feminist Criticism," *Quarterly Review of Film Studies*, vol. 3, no. 4, Fall 1978, p. 479.

6. Gledhill, "Recent Developments in Feminist Criticism," p. 479.

7. Louis Althusser, *Lenin and Philosophy and Other Essays*, trans. Ben Brewster (New York: Monthly Review Press, 1971), p. 171.

8. Althusser, *Lenin*, p. 144.

9. Ibid., p. 182.

10. Ibid., p. 154.

11. Note the analogy with Filmic "suture." Gledhill, "Recent Developments," p. 476.

12. Althusser, *Lenin*, p. 173.

13. Simone De Beauvoir, "Introduction to *The Second Sex*," *New French Feminisms*, ed. Elaine Marks and Isabelle de Courtivron (New York: Schocken Books, 1981), p. 45.

14. Belsey, *Critical Practice*, p. 38.

15. Ibid., p. 59.

16. Karl Marx, "Estranged Labor," *The Economic and Philosophic Manuscripts of 1844*, trans. Martin Milligan, ed. Dirk J. Struik (New York: International Publishers Co., 1964), p. 112: "Man is a species being, not only because in practice and in theory he adopts the species as his object (his own as well as those of other things), but—and this is only another way of expressing it—also because he treats himself as the actual, living species; because he treats himself as a *universal* and therefore a free being."

17. Simone De Beauvoir, "Introduction to *The Second Sex*," p. 46. Obviously, De Beauvoir's statement that women "do not authentically assume a subjective attitude" is, fortunately, becoming outdated.

18. And it is necessary for all individuals to develop an authentic subjectivity, in as much as everyone is someone else's "other."

19. Simone De Beauvoir, "Introduction to *The Second Sex*," p. 52.

20. Julia Kristeva, *New French Feminisms*, p. 167.

21. Luce Irigaray, *New French Feminisms*, p. 103.

22. Belsey, *Critical Practice*, p. 65.

23. Ibid., pp. 65, 66.

24. Simone De Beauvoir, "Introduction to *The Second Sex*," p. 46.

25. Andre Bazin, *What Is Cinema? Volume II*, ed. and trans. Hugh Gray (Berkeley: University of California Press, 1971), p. 97.

26. Simone De Beauvoir, "Introduction to *The Second Sex*," p. 45.

27. Although we are stressing the individual's distinctive "reading" of a particular film text, this is not an individualistic approach to the work of art. Our emphasis on any one individual's interpretation includes a recognition of the differences in the interpretations of other individuals. Our emphasis is on multiple readings and a collectively engendered insight.

2

Reading Eisenstein

The writings of Sergei Eisenstein on film means and film ends compose an actively "engaged" body of theory—engaged in the political transformations his country was experiencing and engaged in the personal questioning of art, of its processes, and of their interaction with the development of thought and emotion in its audience.[1] This engaged quality in his writing is signalled by various identifying marks: the rhythmic intensity manifested in the repetition, redefinition and refinement of various terms in essay after essay; the open claim to an ideological purpose; the continual grounding of film methods in the everyday realities and processes of human perception and emotion; and the eager, wide-ranging curiosity expressed through innumerable literary, scientific, and artistic references and lengthy shared quotations. And it is this openly engaged quality which both attracts the feminist film theorist to his writings and also gives her the key to their possible uses and their potentially dangerous assumptions. Eisenstein's writings announce themselves as purposive theory, as ideological weapons. This self-proclamation arouses the reader's critical awareness; it makes clear the connection between theoretical thought and cultural context. And ideally the reader will apply this awareness, recognizing the unstated assumptions and preferences concealed and/or revealed in the movement of Eisenstein's own thought.

A dark thread of contradiction runs through the fabric of Eisenstein's theory. Yet whenever the strain of this discordant hue

threatens to destroy the pattern of his thought, Eisenstein quickly brings in a whole new line of reasoning, a new harmony of color to replace the old. His work is ever shifting from one emphasis to another, with the occasional imposition of a general statement of direction, a direction meant to subsume the contradictory emphasis. His stated aim, to forge a theory or methodology that can subsume all genres or stylistic tendencies, is an example of one such statement of direction.[2] The problem with such an aim is that any theory will embody or reflect the social realities from which it emerges. These social realities include ideology, and a look at Eisenstein's use of the term ideology brings us to one of the basic threads of contradiction in his work.

On the one hand, Eisenstein openly claims his ideology. He speaks of film as an ideological weapon, "as a medium for a more perfect embodiment of lofty forms of world outlook—the lofty ideas of communism."[3] He discusses the various elements of film language in terms of their directed forcefulness. Cinema "attractions" are "aggressive moment(s) . . . the only means by which it is possible to make the final ideological conclusion perceptible,"[4] and even Soviet comedy utilizes laughter as "social exposure . . . a new kind of weapon . . . militant humour."[5] This ideology that Eisenstein is battling for is an aspiring ideology, a revolutionary aim. In his historical moment, it exists, therefore, on a conscious level in the minds of the Soviet people his films will reach.[6] His revolutionary goals include collectivity in the filmmaking and the film viewing process, the conscious and active participation of the spectator in the film's theme or movement, and an art whose purpose is not to be a reality substitute, but rather to embody the process of constructing reality.

However, while Eisenstein presents the values and aims of a socialist ideology within his films and his theoretical writing, his methods and eventually the movement of his own thought are expressions of another type of ideology. Georg Lukacs has pointed out that a penetrating critique of existing social relations, of the status quo, can only come from a position of marginality, from the oppressed class.[7] The aspiring ideology mentioned above proceeds from the same source. But there is another definition of ideology, and that is, "the image a society gives of

itself in order to perpetuate itself."[8] To the degree that socialism had been already absorbed into the emotional and thought
processes of his contemporaries, Eisenstein's work also embodies elements of this ideology of self-preservation. And to the
extent that socialism had not been absorbed, his work embodies unrecognized elements of the preexistent, pre-revolutionary
ideology of his society.

So if Eisenstein's theory is caught between the conflicting influences of these ideologies, we must be able to see the signs
of strain or the tension points. One of the most fundamental of
these conflicts centers in Eisenstein's theory of cinema form and
function. I have not separated the question of film form from
film function because their juxtaposition is at the center of this
conflict. We might also label this conflict as dynamic process
versus the organic whole.

Eisenstein's earliest thoughts about art grew from his familiarity with constructivism, with Pavlov's reflexology, and from
his rejection of naturalism in the theatre. Constructivism was a
reaction to the "deceit" of the image, the illusions of reality which
naturalistic theatre provided and which seemed, to Eisenstein,
an escape or a diversion from the material life at hand. Eisenstein, looking back on this period, says:

All around was the insistent demand to destroy art, substitute materials and documents for the chief element of art—the image, do away
with its content, put constructivism in the place of organic unity, replace art itself with practical and real reconstruction of life without any
fiction or fable.[9]

His interest in Pavlov developed into a lifelong concern with
the ability to make a direct and immediate appeal to the senses
through a work of art, and with the emotional and intellectual
impact that could be effected through these sensual impressions.

Already we can begin to see the seeds of contradiction in Eisenstein's theory. He holds that the work of art, the film, is a
product, a material construct, assembled by the collective filmmaker, and presenting a vision of reality as ordered by the socialist ideology. There is no need to copy nature, to imitate

reality, for the reality in the artwork emerges from its procedure. The work itself *is* material reality for it embodies the application of ideological critique to actual physical experience. When the audience experiences this constructed art, they participate in the creative process. They experience the juxtaposition of object, physical gesture, colors, and sounds, and they create the concept that can be deduced from these juxtapositions. Eisenstein contrasts this idea of art with a naturalistic art, whose audience is lulled into a dream-like state, accepting a pre-fabricated vision of experience with its pre-existing conceptual content. This audience does not consciously create meaning and deduce ideology; it accepts a vision.

However, while Eisenstein speaks for the conscious participation of the audience in the dynamic process of the film, he also becomes more interested in the film's ability to elicit a conditioned response, a physiological reaction from its spectators. He views the process of thought, of emotion, and, in a mirroring fashion, the process of art as proceeding through assembly or through chains of perceptions, associations and images. When a writer stages the crucial scene of a novel at midnight, that writer is relying upon a chain of associations and expectations that the reader may connect with that hour.[10] When a film director selects the dominant tones for a particular sequence, that director will rely on the emotional and experiential associations the spectator attributes to those colors. Similarly, a montage sequence relies upon the cumulative effect of one image juxtaposed with others; this physical and temporal juxtaposition causes the spectator to correlate the images and arrive at the sequence's content through a chain of impressions.

Although Eisenstein is aware that each individual spectator will pull her associations from a different bank of memories and experiences, he expects that each spectator will nevertheless arrive at the same final concepts. He relies upon cultural context and reflex physiology as a constant determinant. This reliance allows Eisenstein the assurance that his viewer is actively involved in the film process while at the same time it serves his need to impress the director's vision upon the audience. In other words, the spectator does participate in the creative process, but only as she follows in the filmmaker's footsteps. There is no

suggestion that the spectator may arrive at an individual and distinctive conclusion based on the particular associations and images the films call forth for her:

And, indeed, each spectator creates an image along the representa-
tional *guidance suggested by the author*, leading him *unswervingly* to-
wards knowing and experiencing *the theme* in accordance with his own
personality, in his own individual way, proceeding from his own experience, from his own imagination, from the texture of his associations, from the features of his own character, temper, and social status. (Emphasis mine)[11]

I find it rather incredible that amidst all this individual experience and personal texture, Eisenstein does not allow for a
personal or individual conclusion. The conflict of ideologies
discussed earlier accounts for this lapse. Where ideology is a
potential, an aspiration, a revolutionary aim, it arises from the
experience and insight of individuals whose marginal existence
in relation to the status quo enables them to penetrate its self-
created and self-serving version of social relations.[12] Revolutionary action is dependent upon those divergent perceptions,
the unpredicted insights. But once an ideology begins to be absorbed into the fabric of social expectation, it starts to rely upon
homogeneity of perception and the expected response.

For Eisenstein, socialist ideology waivers between these two
poles and this accounts for the tensions within his thought. He
proclaims his interest in bridging the gap between spectator and
performer and his desire for an audience actively and consciously participating in the creative process. On the other hand,
the social program, the content of the socialist ideology appears more important to him than this form, this collective
choice. From an emphasis upon dynamic process, Eisenstein
moves to a greater and greater stress upon the organic unity of
the work of art. He continues to delineate his theories of montage, of the juxtaposition of images and the subsequent emergence of concepts. In fact, his theories of montage grow more
complex and subtle, especially as cinema develops the capacity
for sound and for color. His theories of vertical and horizontal
montage allow for a counterpoint, harmony, and polyphonic

synthesis of all the film elements. Yet he seems less interested in collision, his original cinematic equivalent for the dialectic's thesis and antithesis, and more interested in the synthesis of which all the cinematic elements partake. Granted, within the dialectic, synthesis cannot exist without the progression through thesis and antithesis, but Eisenstein's emphasis seems to clearly shift from the *process* of the dialectic to its synthetic *outcome*. As Andrew Tudor points out in *Theories of Film*, Eisenstein gradually moves away from the dialectical model for his theory. Tudor sees this shift as an expression of Eisenstein's inability to allow an inflexible adherence to form to limit the development and scope of cinema language.[13] While it is true that Eisenstein is unafraid to contradict himself and to change his stand on an issue as his thought develops, I think this shift in emphasis is also an expression of the self-preserving ideology, the status quo ideology.

In an external sense, Eisenstein's theory and his films are of course influenced or rather, limited by the development of a rigidly defined and state-enforced "socialist realism" in the 1930s. Obviously, this is an example of ideology imposing itself from the top down or from the center outward, rather than arising from a marginal perspective, from people in a revolutionary movement. However, a concern for content or theme rather than process, this separation of the two, is echoed in several areas of Eisenstein's theory—enough areas to suggest that this emphasis is not entirely imposed from the outside.

I have already discussed Eisenstein's insistence that the viewer's conscious and active process of assembling associations and impressions within a work of art necessarily results in the single and predetermined theme that the artist intends. Obviously, this premise assigns greater value to the theme than the process. The members of the audience become as students who participate in their own education (that is, the film experience) but who are not allowed to discover their own, new truth. An emphasis upon the physiological impact of rhythms, color, movement, and sound is a further refinement of this directed, even manipulative, process.[14]

The development of Eisenstein's theory of intellectual cinema provides more insight into the ideological tendencies of his

thought. In his writings of 1929, Eisenstein suggests the possibility of a kind of "filmic reasoning":

While the conventional film directs the *emotions*, this suggests an opportunity to encourage and direct the whole *thought process*. . . . a purely intellectual film . . . achieving direct forms for ideas, systems, and concepts, without any need for transitions and paraphrases.[15]

This theory was part of the cinematic experimentation of the 1920s. Eisenstein, and others, were trying to move away from the bourgeois individualism and romantic illusions they saw in the traditional narrative theatre. A cinema that would juxtapose concepts directly, as a director juxtaposes images in montage, would bypass the ideological determinism of the standard narrative.

In his essay, "A Dialectic Approach to Film Form," Eisenstein cites two sequences from his films which illustrate the concept of intellectual cinema.[16] Both examples are from *October*, and although they both are related to their narrative moment within the film, the action in these sequences occurs in the viewer's mind rather than on the screen. Eisenstein, characteristically, is concerned with the film's impact on the viewer and with his ability to draw the viewer into the creative experience.[17] However, even in these instances where the spectator is led to "individual conclusions" concerning the sequence and its theme, Eisenstein's emphasis is on the director's ability to direct thought as he or she directs emotions and physiological reactions.[18] In a later discussion of one of the same sequences, Eisenstein draws a connection between physiological and intellectual response, linking "the motion of a man rocking under the influence of elementary metric montage . . . and the intellectual process within it, for the intellectual process is the same agitation, but in the dominion of the higher nerve centers."[19] So once again, the film's theme or content is Eisenstein's chief end and the process is of interest only as a dynamic means to this end. He does not see that the process itself may be an end, that it may be the source of new and truly revolutionary content.[20]

As historical conditions changed and "Socialist Realism" re-

placed the avid experimentation of the 1920s, Eisenstein withdrew much of his theory of intellectual cinema. He proposed the reacceptance of plot and story[21] and even a replacement of the "mass as hero" with a new understanding that "collectivism means the maximum development of the individual within the collective."[22] We know that the state's pressure was exerted upon Eisenstein to amend his "formalist" theories and to produce sympathetic narratives which would reflect the new status quo ideology of socialism. His later writings, his rejections of earlier rebelliousness and his reacceptance of the "story" must be read in the light of this awareness.

And yet, I have pointed out that even in his early and freely conceived theory, Eisenstein was more concerned with calling forth a specific response in his audience than with serving as catalyst for a free and active creative process in each viewer. Although some of this concern is a result of Eisenstein's commitment to the ideals of socialism, I believe much of it is, interestingly, due to his fascination with aesthetics. Its attraction for him was art's capacity to "grip" its audience, to evoke pathos and to take the viewer out of him or herself. In other words, he was attracted by art's power to elicit a specific response. As he explains in *Notes of a Film Director*, the art that he determined to master for political ends, eventually mastered him. Art, the "goddess" he thought he could *use* for his own purposes, became "no longer the queen I was seducing but my merciless mistress, my despot."[23] If in the beginning he had viewed art not as woman to be controlled for his own preexisting designs, but as a method of perception, a way of looking beyond the concepts he already held, perhaps he never would have been caught between his ideology and his aesthetics.

We have been examining Eisenstein's tendency to valorize content or theme above the process of his art and, in fact, his tendency to separate the two. The "process" I am referring to is the viewer's experience of the art and, for Eisenstein, this process is actually a reexperiencing of the artist's creative practice. But now, let's shift this focus from process and theme to form and content. Rather than the viewer's experience of the theme, let's examine Eisenstein's views on the origins and suitability of a particular film's form or means for expression of the

theme. This has always been a fundamental question of aesthetics and, as may be expected, Eisenstein's views on this issue are revealing.

In his earlier writings on montage as film form, Eisenstein focuses on the dialectic:

The foundation for this philosophy is a *dynamic* concept of things:

Being—as a constant evolution from the interaction of two contradictory opposites.

Synthesis—arising from the opposition between thesis and antithesis.

. . . In the realm of art this dialectic principle of dynamics is embodied in CONFLICT. . .[24]

Montage, as an expression of the dialectic's conflict, was a way for Eisenstein to unite form and content. He saw the dialectical principle as both the method and the content of a world philosophy—"a *dynamic* concept of things." Nevertheless, even as Eisenstein united form and content through montage, even when he declared that truth lay in the constant evolution of being, he still was unwilling to allow the form itself to generate, with the spectator, an idea of this truth. He still insisted that the filmmaker embody his or her theme or content within a dialectical form, a montage sequence that would lead the viewer to the same theme. Eisenstein, even then, was unwilling to trust his own theory, unwilling to allow the audience to freely experience the dialectical form of a montage film.

In his later writings, as a result of both the constraints of "Socialist Realism" and the development of Eisenstein's own thought, this need to control and direct form in the service of a preexisting, rather than an evolving content, becomes more apparent. Eisenstein begins to draw a clear line of demarcation between the realm of form and that of content. He never ceases to realize the potential power of form as a cinematic tool, or even a cinematic weapon. But the valorization of content and the sense that form *serves* content become more obvious. He separates the two, as well as their areas of effectiveness, in his 1935 essay, "Film Form: New Problems:"

The affectiveness of a work of art is built upon the fact that there takes place in it a dual process: an impetuous progressive rise along the lines of the highest explicit steps of consciousness and a simultaneous penetration by means of the structure of the form into the layers of profoundest sensual thinking.[25]

Although this quotation goes on to refer to the unity of form and content, its thrust is obviously the division of the two concepts. Eisenstein's separation of the realm of conscious ideas from that of sensual impression and form is of particular interest. Earlier in this essay, Eisenstein discusses Hegel's theory of the "a-priority of the idea," later reversed by Marx and his theory of dialectical materialism. However, Eisenstein goes on to explain that the artistic process appears to follow the "Hegelian formula, because the idea-satiation of the author, his subjection to prejudice by the idea, must determine actually the whole course of the art-work."[26] He follows this with the admission that the "author's" ideas are, of course, "a reflection of social reality."[27] What Eisenstein fails to articulate, due to his separation of form from content, is that form is also a reflection of social reality and a determinant of the artist's ideas. Form is not simply a structure that follows organically from the ideological content of an art-work; it is, itself, a social construct which helps to determine the message an art-work conveys. The artist may unknowingly contradict his or her own intention through the use of traditional forms. Form serves an ideological function as well as theme, and a theme has already been, to some extent, determined by the form of the language in which it is formulated by the artist.

To summarize, what I am saying is that Eisenstein appears to miss a step in his analysis of form and content. He states his aim: "to raise form once more to the level of ideological content."[28] He fails to recognize that ideological content has already been unconsciously shaped and determined by the form of our verbal and imagistic language when the artist brings this content to his or her creative work—and that the process of conveying this content through artistic form is a process of altering and determining anew what the content will become—and that the viewer's creative process entails another alteration

or determination of the final interaction of form and content. In other words, any neat division of the two concepts will lead to a "chicken-or-the-egg" situation where one element or the other will be misrepresented.

I began this discussion by calling attention to the socially, politically and personally "engaged" quality of Eisenstein's theoretical writings on film. This quality has directed us to the conflicts or tensions in his thought. We have located points where the aims of a visionary ideology are exchanged for the aims of a self-preserving ideology of the status quo. We have identified his inability to allow process to determine theme or to allow form to exert control over content; instead form and process must serve content and theme. And there are other conflicts in his thought: his ambivalent attitude toward collectivity and toward audience independence are examples. In each case, his commitment to the content of socialist ideology, as *he* sees it, prevents him from observing its revolutionary process.[29] And yet, it is his interest in these very problems, his insight into the unrecognized power of form and process in art, of collective practice, and of the spectator's role in the creative experience, that attract the feminist film theorist, filmmaker, and film viewer to his work. Eisenstein's preoccupations can provide points of departure for the development of a feminist film theory, and the contradictions in his thought can serve as a map of potential dangers in that endeavor.

One of Eisenstein's most consistent and revealing preoccupations is the development and the elaboration of his montage theory. Feminist uses for montage become apparent as we uncover the patterns of thought and the assumptions that underlie this theory. Ultimately, montage is based on a sort of paradox or contradiction; it is a Janus-like concept, fronted by the two faces of particularity and commonality. Montage, in its juxtaposition of two images or shots, implies both conflict or "collision," and correlation or connection. Both of these aspects are useful to the feminist. Eisenstein defines art's function: ". . . to make manifest the contradictions of Being. To form equitable views by stirring up contradictions within the spectator's mind, and to forge accurate intellectual concepts from the dynamic clash

of opposing passions."[30] This reflects the "collision" or conflict within montage. The filmmaker may use montage to bring together images that jar the viewer's sensibility and therefore, bring the viewer's ideologically engendered expectations to light. The use of shock or the "unexpected" rouses the viewer to a more active, more conscious viewing and reasoning process. While the conflict or juxtaposition of surprising images may bring our expectations and assumptions to light, they may simultaneously encourage the viewer to see connections or find commonalities hitherto unnoticed. In his essay, "Word and Image," Eisenstein writes of "that newly revealed feature of the film strips—that, no matter how unrelated they may be, and frequently despite themselves, they engendered a 'third something' and became correlated when juxtaposed according to the will of an editor."[31] For feminism, as for any radical critique of culture, it is necessary to perceive the bonds between various members and sectors of society as well as the disguised contradictions within their roles.

And yet, Eisenstein's theory of montage presents problems when we attempt to use it for feminist ends. One such problem is Eisenstein's refusal, in his theory, to accept ambiguity in his montage sequences. He expects his method "to forge accurate intellectual concepts," and always "according to the will of an editor." He does not allow for the viewer's distinct and individual experience of a particular sequence, nor can he envision a work of art that exists as an open-ended, multiply conceived and multiply perceived creative process. Eisenstein's conception of the film as a lived experience is useful to the feminist, but his insistence on a directed, complete and self-sufficient statement within the art-work is a danger. It too easily lends itself to manipulative purposes. One of film's most effective and least easily detectable methods of manipulation is this construction of an artificial unity. A world is presented, both determined by and illustrating a certain set of rules. Certain realities can therefore be easily "written out" of the script. This subtle deletion is the same process women have faced and fought in their efforts to reveal the "gap" that is woman in the literary tradition.

In addition to his emphasis on montage in the service of a

higher unity, Eisenstein has developed a cinematic application for the literary device, synecdoche. Synecdoche refers to an artist's substitution of a part for a whole, the evocation of the whole and the emotions related to it by means of a selected part or detail. Eisenstein explains that this device can only be effective "in cases where the detail, the part, the particular episode is typical. In other words, when it reflects the whole like a piece of broken mirror."[32] Obviously the device is very effective within montage sequences. Eisenstein cites the example from *Potemkin* when the surgeon's pince-nez, caught among the ship's ropes and leads, suggests the fate of the man himself after he is thrown overboard by the angry sailors. The difficulty or danger involved in this technique is the underlying assumption that the part *is* typical of the whole. Eisenstein often relies on this assumption, both within an art-work itself and also among those who collectively work to construct it.

In *Notes of a Film Director*, for example, he reveals a tyrannical trick he used when working with many anonymous actors on a film. During a crowd scene, he calls the name of an actor he does know, asking for a more energetic performance. This deceives the other actors, allowing them to believe that the director is carefully watching each one of them and causing the actors to improve their performance. A harmless and humorous device, we might say. But at another level, it suggests an assumption that one actor is typical of the whole group, just as one image may evoke an entire situation. Obviously, synecdoche is a valuable tool for the creative artist, feminist or not. But Eisenstein's use and misuse of it suggest guidelines for our development of feminist process in filmmaking and film viewing. In fact, one of the most important uses of synecdoche may simply be the viewer's awareness of it. This awareness becomes a tool or a method for the critical deconstruction of a film text and the exposure of its premises. Just as the absence of woman may be disguised by construction of an artificial unity or harmonious structure within an art-work, so may the use of synecdoche conceal the actual particularity and variance within a group who are evoked by a single, "typical" detail.

As his montage theory grew more sophisticated, Eisenstein developed the concept of vertical montage. He defines vertical

montage as "a montage that links different spheres of feeling—
particularly the visual image with the sound image, in the process of creating a single, unifying sound-picture image."[33] Eisenstein compares this visual-and-sound montage to his concept of polyphonic montage. In the silent cinema, polyphonic
montage referred to the distinct and carefully orchestrated development of many visual elements, simultaneously. Color, light,
rhythm, and so forth would each have an individual course to
follow, an individual movement to develop, and yet these
movements would work in tandem to develop the "general
sensation" of the entire sequence.[34] Eisenstein's emphasis here
is on the purposive construction of the sensation or theme the
filmmaker wishes to convey. He breaks down the cinema sequence into its various elements or modes of effectiveness, only
to reassemble them in a manner to best serve the film's theme.
So, although he desires first to "sever the passive everyday
connection between (for example) an object and the sound it
makes," he does so only to "undermine the stagnant 'order of
things' for the sake of expressing *my* (Eisenstein), the author's,
attitude to this order of things.' "[35] In other words, Eisenstein
uses montage to reveal and to undermine our unselfconscious
expectations concerning the *sense* of our world. He exposes the
ideologically constructed nature of this order. And yet, every
line within a montage sequence serves *his* "general sensation"
or theme. Eisenstein stresses the pathos, the effectiveness, of
visual and sound constructs; he points to the crucial role the
spectator plays in the creative process. But he is unwilling to
allow that the spectator may bring his or her own interpretation to the film. He explores the role and function of the viewer
only so the viewer may be better controlled and directed.

Eisenstein believes this control and direction may be best effected by an assembling and organizing of film elements within
an organic whole. He is fascinated by the idea of synaesthesia,
the blending or merging of various sensual impulses to create
a forceful simultaneity of perception.[36] This interest mirrors many
other aspects of Eisenstein's thought. He is forever dismantling
an experience in the hope that he may reassemble it in a directed, multiply perceived fashion. For example, his theory of

intellectual cinema was an attempt to merge our sensual response to a sequence with our intellectual response. And his development of polyphonic and vertical montage was an effort to separate and then re-orchestrate the various elements of a film sequence that they might more fully and pointedly express a particular theme.

His attempt to analyze the process and development of human thought is similarly patterned. He splits our experience into a primitive sensual thinking and more highly developed logical thought. (These divisions appear similar to but not interchangeable with Freud's primary and secondary process thought, and Lacan's imaginary and symbolic realms.) His aim for the artist is to separate and analyze these two processes, in an effort to recombine them in the workings of the film. For the feminist, Eisenstein's attention to a non-linear, more cumulative, less abstract thought process—sensual thinking—is quite suggestive. It can be worked into the multiply structured, materially based language that theorists such as Mary Daly and the French feminists are trying to develop. However, once again, Eisenstein, although aware of its power, is not willing to allow the sensual and imagistic aspect of film language to develop freely. He must attempt to structure this affective form according to a predetermined and narrowly defined content. And so the spectators do not really play the active and conscious role that Eisenstein claims for them.

But let's look a bit closer at the process Eisenstein calls sensual thinking. Why is it so important to him and how does he expect to embody it in the film process? We are aware of his fascination with the direct emotional and physiological power of the aesthetic experience. He knows that the communication of a theme by means of logic, of rational discourse, is not nearly as effective as the simultaneous communication of that same theme through sensual and emotional discourse, as well. His aim is to use these different levels of discourse together, for a common end. We have already noted that his neat separation of the logical from the material and the emotional is a false dichotomy. Logic and reason are constructions of our cultural and material experience. Especially as the realm of logical discourse

has traditionally been considered a male realm, this is an important observation for the feminist who hopes to use portions of Eisenstein's thought.

However, his elaboration of "sensual thinking" is useful to the feminist in her exploration of language, especially Eisenstein's concept of "inner monologue" or "inner speech." In the essay, "A Course in Treatment," and later, "Film Form: New Problems," he suggests the ways film can be used to embody the process or movement of a character's thought, and to convey ideas, an interpretation of reality, without sacrificing the "warmth" and the dramatic appeal of a "story."[37] Eisenstein views "inner monologue" as a way to achieve some of the ends of his by then discarded intellectual cinema—i.e., the direct communication of ideas with the force of emotional and physiological stimulus.

So just what is "inner monologue" for Eisenstein, and why is it of interest to the feminist film theorist? Eisenstein defines "inner monologue" as a montage sequence that intercuts film representations of a character's "feverish race of thoughts" with the scenes of the outward narrative.[38] It is a way to destroy the "distinction between subject and object in stating the hero's re-experience. . . ."[39] Obviously, for the feminist who is concerned with the way personal experience interacts with the larger cultural conditions, and with the "subjectivity" of individual experience, Eisenstein's concept is quite useful.[40] For Eisenstein, however, reality itself, in a concrete and objective form, still and always does co-exist with this "inner monologue."[41] He is aware that a work of art must embody the artist's relation or attitude toward the object or situation portrayed, but he also assumes that the object or situation itself, in some pure form, is also conveyed through the film. (This is the point where Eisenstein draws closest to the sometimes antithetical theories of Bazin.)

In his theory, though *not* in his films, Eisenstein stops short of expressing that an object exists in as many ways as it is perceived and experienced, and that the various patterns of human perception determine the so-called "reality" of an object. Through a Critical Subjectivity, discussed in chapter 1, we never reach the final, the ultimate meaning of any situation; we only

experience it in multiple ways and approach a more useful interpretation of it by following the paths of tension and conflict in those multiple perceptions.

Eisenstein comes close to this realization when he discusses his method for the synchronization of the senses with a montage sequence. When searching for a way to mesh plastic and tonal elements, he discovers:

> To relate these two elements, we find a natural language common to both—movement. Plekhanov has said that all phenomena in the final analysis can be reduced to movement. Movement will reveal all the substrata of inner synchronization that we wish to establish in due course. . . . Let us move from exterior and descriptive matters to matters of an inner and deeper character.[42]

This method, finding the links between different elements in the way they move, can be applied in a larger sense. The process, the movement, of various experiences or of several individuals' perceptions is the "place" where we may find the links and the commonalities between them. It is in process that we reveal ourselves and that we experience ourselves. The "content" may differ, but our methods of perception and experience, or even the *fact* of perception and experience itself, provides a starting point, a place to begin exploring differences and making connections. Eisenstein knew this, at one level. He placed a great deal of emphasis on the *way* his viewers would experience a montage sequence. He did not, however, allow for the real differences within perception which result from individual and social experience. He was aware of the importance of audience "milieu" but he had the tendency to generalize its effect.[43] As well, his intention was not to allow his audience the freedom of participating actively in the creative process of film. Rather his intention was to direct his audience to an experience of *this* creative process—the experience designated by the filmmaker.

For the feminist filmmaker, film theorist and film viewer, a look at Eisenstein has provided numerous avenues for the development of a film praxis. We are initially attracted by the socially "engaged" quality of his writing. He not only feels the

connection between theory and practice, between art and life, but he openly acknowledges his intentions and perspectives. He proceeds to offer directions or perhaps, the kernels of a vocabulary for our unfolding theory. Montage points to the necessary but tension-ridden harnessing of conflict and correlation, particularity and commonality—a dual perspective essential for anyone who hopes to penetrate the ideologically constructed "unity" or "organicism" of their society. Eisenstein's attention to collectivity is an attempt to transform the traditional individualism of artistic endeavor, although his recourse to the concept of "typicality," within the art-work and among the viewers, is a simplification of this very complex concept. His inability to allow for ambiguity and multiple perspectives within his art keeps him from a truly collective process. Eisenstein's own individualist commitment to his truth does not allow him to comprehend the multiple and individual perceptions which can coexist within a varied and collective artistic experience.

He does, however, feel an attraction to and fascination with a synaesthetic film language, one that stimulates multiple sensory responses and that progresses through a cumulative, nondifferentiated process. He recognizes the importance and effectiveness of a physical and material base for his film's rational content. These preoccupations point the way, or perhaps more accurately, *echo* the concerns of contemporary feminists who are exploring the possibilities of a "feminine" language, an alternative style of expression that might substitute for or serve as a corrective to the linear, absolutist rigor of traditional logical discourse. An important aspect of this new language is its attention to the multiplicity of individual realities, and Eisenstein's film equivalent of the "inner monologue" suggests possible directions and meanings for this development.

I suppose most significantly for feminists, Eisenstein views art as a process *in time* for the viewer, as well as the maker. And he stresses the important, the critical role the spectator plays in the film experience. He may not yet have been ready to surrender his film and its "meaning" to his audience, but he did recognize and encourage their active participation in the process of his art. And, as we discussed in chapter 1, the decision to surrender control was really never his to make.

NOTES

1. Lillian S. Robinson, "Dwelling in Decencies: Radical Criticism and the Feminist Perspective," *Sex, Class and Culture* (Bloomington: Indiana University Press, 1978), p. 3. This critical analysis applies to Eisenstein's theories of cinema but certainly not to his films.

2. Sergei Eisenstein, *Film Form: Essays in Film Theory*, ed. trans. Jay Leyda (New York: Harcourt Brace Jovanovich, 1949), p. 147.

3. Sergei Eisenstein, *Notes of a Film Director*, trans. X. Danko (New York: Dover Publications, 1970), p. 7.

4. Sergei Eisenstein, *The Film Sense*, ed. trans. Jay Leyda (New York: Harcourt Brace Jovanovich, 1975), p. 231.

5. Eisenstein, *Notes of a Film Director*, pp. 111, 112.

6. Eisenstein, *Film Form*, p. 245.

7. Georg Lukacs, *History and Class Consciousness: Studies in Marxist Dialectics*, trans. Rodney Livingstone (Cambridge, Mass.: MIT Press, 1971), pp. 69–70.

8. Bill Nichols, *Ideology and the Image: Social Representation in the Cinema and Other Media* (Bloomington: Indiana University Press, 1981), p. 1. This concept can be related to Althusser's theories of ideology (Louis Althusser, *Lenin and Philosophy and Other Essays*, 1971). Althusser speaks of "ideological State Apparatuses" and film, as mass media, is one of them. These apparatuses help "to represent and reproduce the myths and beliefs necessary to enable people to work within the existing social formations." (Catherine Belsey, *Critical Practice*, London: Methuen & Co., 1980, p. 58.) In other words, the aim is *not* revolutionary change.

9. Eisenstein, *Notes of a Film Director*, p. 14.

10. Eisenstein, *Film Sense*, pp. 20, 21.

11. Eisenstein, *Notes of a Film Director*, p. 78.

12. This marginality may be due to economic conditions, sex, race, etc. Class is not the only type of marginality that allows for a critical perspective.

13. Andrew Tudor, *Theories of Film* (New York: Viking Press, 1973), pp. 27–32.

14. Eisenstein would argue that this is not manipulation for the viewer is actively and consciously involved in the film process. However, Eisenstein does not allow for individual conclusions. The outcome is predetermined by the successful artist. Perhaps, the problem with this theory is less one of film manipulation and more a problem of Eisenstein's mistaken ideas about the variability of human perception.

15. Eisenstein, *Film Form*, p. 62, 63.

16. Ibid. pp. 61, 62: In this long section of his text, Eisenstein describes two famous sequences from *October*, both examples of intellectual montage. In the first, Eisenstein depicts and mocks Kerensky's ascent to power by intercutting subtitles of progressively higher military ranks into repeated shots of Kerenscky climbing the same set of stairs. In the second example, Eisenstein offers a representation of Kornilov leading troops into Petrograd. The rhetoric of this march is both patriotic and religious. Eisenstein calls this assumption of a holy cause into question by interrogating the idea of god, intercutting a series of images of deities, from the most contemporary to the primitive. In both of these examples, there is no doubt that Eisenstein's montage raises many questions for the film viewer, but he may not have anticipated the actual range and diversity of response his film would elicit.

17. Eisenstein, *Notes of a Film Director*, pp. 133, 134.

18. Eisenstein, *Film Form*, p. 62.

19. Ibid., p. 82.

20. This point is related to Eisenstein's concept of cinema realism. He is aware that film is constructed and that therefore its version of reality is constructed as well. He continues to speak of realism not, however, as the product of the filmmaker's visions and ideals, i.e., as the filmmaker's reality. Nor does he speak of film realism in terms of the precision in its imitation of nature. Rather his gauge of "realism" is in the film's capacity to *convince* the viewer. Once again, we are faced with this curious conflict in Eisenstein's thought. He is extremely concerned with the film as an experience for the viewer, but his emphasis is upon how the viewer may be convinced or directed or manipulated, rather than on what the viewer, herself or himself, creates from the film and in response to the film.

21. Eisenstein, *Film Form*, p. 17.

22. Ibid., p. 16.

23. Eisenstein, *Notes of a Film Director*, pp. 15, 17.

24. Eisenstein, *Film Form*, pp. 45, 46.

25. Ibid., pp. 144, 145.

26. Ibid., pp. 126, 127.

27. Ibid., p. 127.

28. Ibid., p. 124.

29. This is not a conflict peculiar to Eisenstein. As I stated earlier, any ideology tends toward self-preservation once it begins to be absorbed into the fabric and thought of a society.

30. Eisenstein, *Film Form*, p. 46.

31. Eisenstein, *Film Sense*, p. 9.

32. Eisenstein, *Notes of a Film Director*, p. 28.

33. Eisenstein, *Film Sense*, p. 73.

34. Ibid. p. 78.

35. Eisenstein, *Notes of a Film Director*, pp. 125, 126.

36. Eisenstein, *Film Sense*, p. 148. For Eisenstein, this synaesthesia suggested the ability to experience one sense impression as equivalent to another: to hear color, for example.

37. Eisenstein, *Film Form*, pp. 84–107 and 122–149.

38. Ibid., p. 103.

39. Ibid., p. 104.

40. Questions arise at this point concerning the degree to which "subjectivity" is culturally determined. A look at Althusser's and Lacan's theories will be useful in answering these questions—See chapter 1 of this text.

41. Eisenstein, *Film Form*, p. 151.

42. Eisenstein, *Film Sense*, p. 82.

43. Eisenstein, *Film Form*, p. 245 and Julia Lesage, "Feminist Film Criticism: Theory and Practice," *Sexual Stratagems: The World of Women in Film*, ed. Patricia Erens (New York: Horizon Press, 1979), p. 145.

3

Reading Bazin

The typical comparison and discussion of the film theories of Sergei Eisenstein and the film theories of Andre Bazin center around their varying attitudes toward "reality" and art. In his essay, "Two Types of Film Theory," Brian Henderson writes: "Bazin begins with the real but, unlike Eisenstein, does not go beyond it; he never breaks with the real in the name of art."[1] Henderson goes on to explain that Bazin's insistence on the relation of the smallest piece of film to the real restricts him to a "theory of shots," rather than a theory that could open up the questions of form in relation to the text of an entire film.[2] I would like to go one step further and suggest that the limitations of Bazin's theory lie not only within the film text itself, but also in the film's relation to its context, the society within which it occurs.

Bazin and Eisenstein are both aware of the filmmaker's role in constructing the meaning of his or her work of art. Bazin admits that "realism in art can only be achieved in one way—through artifice."[3] Even in his discussion of the neorealist, Vittorio De Sica, Bazin writes: "Though this *mise-en-scene* aims at negating itself, at being transparent to the reality it reveals, it would be naive to conclude that it does not exist. Few films have been more carefully put together."[4] Eisenstein's recognition of art as a construct allows him to use it as an "ideological weapon." He endeavors to create an experience of reality that will illustrate his ideological perspective. Bazin is also aware that the filmmaker and the film viewer will bring their political and so-

cial expectations to any work of art. Unlike Eisenstein, he allows for more varied interpretations of any particular film. And yet, he believes that some absolute and existential experience of reality, *physical* reality, must still be communicated. Sometimes Bazin refers to this experience as the "integrity" of reality and sometimes he refers to it as the "ambiguity" of reality. Nevertheless, for Bazin, it always exists before and beneath any ideological perspective the film may embody. In the following quotation, Bazin is describing Italian neorealism and yet, his point underlies his evaluation of film in general:

Whence the director's art lies in the skill with which he compels the event to reveal its meaning—or at least the meaning he lends it—without removing any of its *ambiguity*. Thus defined, neorealism is not the exclusive property of any one ideology nor even of any one ideal, no more than it excludes any other ideal—no more, in point of fact, than reality excludes anything.[5]

The problem here is not that Bazin denies the artist's active manipulation of the raw materials and the instrument of film art, nor is it that Bazin fails to see the imprint of each individual artist and each viewer on the film experience. The problem, rather, is that Bazin does not see that our experience of "reality" itself is construed; there is no pure reality that can be reached if we strip away enough layers of ideology and experience. We can never be totally free of our "ways of seeing."[6]

Bazin's arguments concerning "realism" become rather fuzzy and even self-contradictory when we try to sort them out. In some lights, he appears to offer a rich fund of insight, distinctions, and directions for the feminist film theorist and film viewer to pursue. Let the light shift slightly, however, and certain predispositions become visible, throwing into question all that has already been adopted. He speaks, for example, of the "ambiguity" of reality, of its all-inclusiveness, and the fact that there is never one single "reading" or interpretation for a particular film. For Bazin, unlike Eisenstein, this uncertainty and suggestiveness of an image are positive attributes. They prevent one ideology or viewpoint from possessing the image. Its mystery is preserved.[7] In the instance of Welles' *Citizen Kane*, Bazin de-

scribes the functioning of ambiguity in this way: "The uncertainty in which we find ourselves as to the spiritual key or the interpretation we should put on the film is built into the very design of the image."[8] So this "uncertainty" is actually a form of verisimilitude, for "reality" itself, according to Bazin, is multiple and endlessly suggestive.

For the feminist, this theory can be extremely useful, but first, we must be aware of its negative implications. Critics of Bazin will hasten to point out the idealistic nature of his thought, its almost mystical—and therefore ideologically cooptable—quality. Encourage mystery and we discourage analytic ability and critical insight. Proclaim art and the "reality" it supposedly reveals as all-inclusive and marked by ambiguity, and we effectively disarm the spectator. We discourage attempts to probe a film for the ideological mindset behind it. We put forward the illusion of a pure reflection of reality in art. The other side of this theoretical coin reveals Bazin's recognition of the spectator's active role in the creative process. For instance, in making a case for depth of focus, Bazin has this to say about the viewer:

[Depth of focus] implies, consequently, both a more active mental attitude on the part of the spectator and a more positive contribution on his part to the action in progress. While analytical montage only calls for him to follow his guide, to let his attention follow along smoothly with that of the director who will choose what he should see, here he is called upon to exercise at least a minimum of personal choice. It is from his attention and his will that the meaning of the image in part derives.[9]

Although this may seem a refreshing change after Eisenstein's efforts to direct the viewer's emotional and thought processes, it also suggests the beginning of another contradiction in Bazin's thought. If the viewer constructs her own meaning for a particular image or series of images, what becomes of the ambiguity of reality? Instead we are left with innumerable, individual yet unambiguous, readings of the film. Unless the film actually directs its viewer to question her reading, to recognize the image as a possible source for multiple readings, and to thus become aware of the ideological tendencies manifested in her

particular reading—unless the film does these things, it is not communicating a useful ambiguity. Bazin seems to vacillate between the suggestion that the possibility of varying interpretations is ambiguity enough, and the suggestion that beneath and beyond these interpretations must lie a deeper ambiguity, an ambiguity of physical appearance.

We have shown that the first of these suggestions results in no ambiguity at all, but rather a multitude of unambiguous versions of reality. The problem with the second suggestion is that it implies there is physical reality, a "physiology of existence," that exists without reference to a perspective, without reference to an ideological, social, personal viewpoint.[10] Bazin describes this "phenomenological" realism, once again, in his celebration of Italian neorealism; he writes: "The relation between meaning and appearance having been in a sense inverted, appearance is always presented as a unique discovery, an almost documentary revelation that retains its full force of vividness and detail."[11] Bazin simply does not see that appearance itself is a variable, not a constant, to use the mathematical terminology of which he is so fond. He does not realize the extent to which his writing and his thought are embedded in an ideological perspective.

However, we can begin to recognize the limitations of Bazin's thought, while at the same time salvaging those concepts that seem most useful and suggestive for the feminist. Let's begin by taking a closer look at his thoughts about the "integrity" of the image, a concept introduced in the preceding paragraph. This idea is most clearly and fully developed in his essays on Italian neorealism. Bazin points to the sophistication behind neorealist films, despite their apparent simplicity and almost documentary quality. He explains that these filmmakers were critical of the narrative devices, the artificial plot developments, and all the dramatic techniques utilized in traditional films. Like the early Eisenstein, these filmmakers wanted to break free from the tyranny of the story, and instead of holding their audience by means of narrative manipulation, they would require the viewer to actively select details and interpret scenes, to draw a sense out of life. Characteristically, Bazin expresses this concept most clearly by means of a metaphor:

One can apply the same argument to the stones of which a bridge is constructed. They fit together perfectly to form an arch. But the big rocks that lie scattered in a ford are now and ever will be no more than mere rocks. Their reality as rocks is not affected when, leaping from one to another, I use them to cross the river. If the service which they have rendered is the same as that of the bridge, it is because I have brought my share of ingenuity to bear on their chance arrangement; I have added the motion which, though it alters neither their nature nor their appearance, gives them a provisional meaning and utility. In the same way, the neorealist film has a meaning, but it is *a posteriori* to the extent that it permits our awareness to move from one fact to another, from one fragment of reality to the next, whereas in the classical artistic composition the meaning is established *a priori*: the house is already there in the brick.[12]

So we see that the neorealist filmmakers were fomenting a "revolution in narrative."[13] The problem, however, is that instead of interrogating the narrative and its technique, encouraging an audience awareness, the neorealists, according to Bazin, of course, simply replaced these techniques with others, just as consciously chosen, but appearing less studied, less predetermined. Bazin describes this method in his analysis of De Sica's *Bicycle Thief*, where he praises De Sica's "*contriving* to give the succession of events the *appearance* of an accidental and as it were anecdotal chronology," (emphasis mine),[14] and a few paragraphs later: "Thus the thesis of the film is *hidden behind* an *objective* social reality which in turn moves into the background of the moral and psychological drama," (emphasis mine).[15] In other words, although the manipulation of traditional narrative is penetrated and discarded, a new type of manipulation takes its place. The filmmaker is still trying to achieve the appearance or the experience of "reality."

Feminists will find this insight particularly appropriate. Bazin's analysis here is very similar to the analysis and work of those feminist filmmakers who adopted a "cinema verité" aesthetic in the 1960s and early 1970s.[16] The aim was to present real women actually talking about their *real* lives. It was assumed that an unmanipulated camera would somehow record a deeper truth than is possible in narrative films where the story automatically reflects ideological assumptions, subtle though they

may be. Bazin, similarly, believed that film well-used would treat each event, "according to its phenomenological integrity."[17]

So although Bazin did not pretend to think that the neorealist's camera was "unmanipulated," and although he did not deny the artifice involved in any attempt to recreate "reality," he did believe that a certain pure and "ambiguous" physical truth would shine through an image. Bazin seems to want it both ways. He recognizes the artifice of film but he does not see the need for its exposure. Instead, he promotes a style of filmmaking that is even more subtle in its construction. And at the same time, he believes there is an uninterpreted and pure "reality," a truth in appearance that the camera, by its mechanical nature, records and reveals. Bazin believes in a physical, although "ambiguous", reality that exists beyond and before ideology. He believes that a film viewer or a filmmaker brings his or her ideology to the raw material of appearances and then creates various interpretations of it. Therefore, it is always possible to strip away these ideologically engendered meanings and to return to the pure reality. This is the point at which Bazin himself becomes the victim of ideology, an ideology of self-preservation that requires him to see the world in a certain way, not to look beyond appearances and recognize the way his perception of concrete reality has already been constructed. He locates the "ambiguity of reality" in the various interpretations we might bring to its appearance, but not in our perception of the appearances themselves.

Bazin's thoughts concerning the potential integrity of the film image and the ambiguity of reality seem to favor a kind of cinema of trust—a cinema that attempts to never jar the viewer from the sense that he or she is watching real events. At first glance, there may seem to be something of a contradiction here. The very films that Bazin praises most highly, those of Italian neorealism, are films that eschew the narrative devices which ordinarily sweep the viewer into the film's sequence of events. Bazin recognizes that the attempt to recreate the ellipses and the extraneous details of actual experience, the sense of temporal duration, and the occasional inconsistency and impenetrability of actual people may distance the viewer at first. After all, audiences are accustomed to predetermined, preselected and

predigested cinema. But Bazin is not prepared to sacrifice all dramatic needs. In fact, he warns Visconti of the dangers of pushing his audience too far in *La Terra Trema*. After an insightful and sympathetic analysis of the film, he finally cautions: "The aesthetic of *La Terra Trema* must be applicable to dramatic ends if it is to be of service in the evolution of cinema."[18] Bazin believes that the rejection of certain narrative traditions for the sake of authenticity is a worthwhile and desirable evolution. The audience will learn to experience and make sense of the film in much the same way they experience and make sense of their own lives. The extra effort insures greater authenticity. Add to this Bazin's concern to preserve some of the dramatic structure and we have a cinema that, as mentioned above, attempts to preserve the viewer's sense that he or she is watching real events.

This effort to preserve an illusory construct is illustrated in other areas of Bazin's thought, as well. We have discussed his attitude toward the films of Italian neorealism. But what about other schools of filmmaking? What about genre films, the western in particular, about which he wrote so much? Or what about film adaptations of theatrical pieces, of novels, and even of paintings? In each case, Bazin is consistent in his call for authenticity and his attack on the synthetic and the artificial. This is not to say that he requires *Henry V* to be filmed in England and France, or that he requires the filmmaker to actually record a stage production of the play. He does not ask the director to be faithful to the literal place and action of a novel or play, nor does he ask that the film serve as a mere documentation of a particular performance. Bazin's realism is more subtle and sophisticated than that. He wants the film to be faithful to the form it embodies.

For instance, in his essay on *The Diary of a Country Priest*, he writes: "In this case the reality is not the descriptive content, moral or intellectual, of the text—it is the very text itself, or more properly, the style."[19] Similarly, in his essays on film adaptations of the theatre, he focuses on the differences he sees between the audience's experience of a film and of a play. He then asks that the screen version of a play attempt to find equivalents to the "theatrical quality."[20] In the case of the western,

Bazin recognizes the genre itself as a mythic phenomenon. He asks, therefore, not that the film recreate an actual likeness to the American West, but rather that it preserve and respect the myth. He mocks what he calls the "superwestern": "a western that would be ashamed to be just itself, and looks for some additional interest to justify its existence—an aesthetic, sociological, moral, psychological, political, or erotic interest, in short some quality extrinsic to the genre and which is supposed to enrich it."[21] These added qualities have nothing to do with the myth itself, the original *raison d'être* and attraction of the western. Bazin praises those filmmakers who display a kind of "sincerity" in their treatment of the genre, who reveal "a touching frankness of attitude toward the western, an effortless sincerity to get inside its themes and thereby bring to life appealing characters and to invent captivating situations."[22] These directors will, of course, bring their own attitudes and ideas to the myth, but they will never *use* the myth to serve other ends. The film exists, first, as a western, according to Bazin, in the same way that the Italian neorealists allow their films to exist, first, as documents of actual experience (again, according to Bazin).

In all the above examples, Bazin is concerned with preserving a construct, with conveying its authenticity. Be the construct of a novel, a play, a painting or a myth, Bazin wishes it to appear real and whole for the audience, just as De Sica presents the agonizing search of Bruno and his son for a stolen bicycle. It is the same desire to preserve the wholeness of experience that drives Bazin in his criticism of montage and its analytical breakdown of an event or an image.

Bazin's essay, "Marginal Notes on *Eroticism in the Cinema*," provides the exception that proves the rule. Here Bazin discusses this book by Lo Duca and its analysis of the similarities between film viewing and dreaming. Bazin moves from this premise to a discussion of the function censorship plays in the creation of the erotic. He even provides an analysis of the film viewer's identification process, an analysis that anticipates many of Laura Mulvey's observations concerning scopophilia in the essay, "Visual Pleasure and Narrative Cinema."[23] Finally, however, near the conclusion of his essay, Bazin writes: "There are no sex situations—moral or immoral, shocking or banal,

normal or pathological—whose expression is *a priori* prohibited on the screen, but only on condition that one resorts to the capacity for abstraction in the language of cinema, so that the image never takes on a documentary quality."[24] Here we have Bazin actually calling for abstraction, asking that a film draw attention to its artifice. He himself must have felt the way this statement jarred with his other theory for the remaining paragraphs in this essay are devoted to a questioning and doubting of his own statement. He finds several contradictions in his position but he cannot bring himself to resolve them. I think his inability to settle this issue satisfactorily springs from the subject itself.

Bazin's attitude toward eroticism leaves much to be desired by the feminist reader. First, he defines the erotic film as "one that is capable of provoking the audience to desire the heroine sexually and of keeping that desire alive."[25] In other words, the audience is exclusively male (or male-identifying women? Surely he was not thinking of lesbians) and the object of desire is exclusively female. In his discussion of film identification he writes: "The actor winning the woman gratifies me by proxy."[26] Again, it is only the male for whom this eroticism is designed, and Bazin sees the film as a means of sexual gratification.

When he discusses the theatre, however, all this changes. The male audience does not identify with the male actor's gratification, but rather competes with it. Speaking of a strip tease (which in Bazin's mind could only refer to a woman), Bazin insists that the woman must undress herself for "she could not be undressed by a partner without provoking the jealousy of the entire male audience."[27] One, of course, would never wish to do that for, after all, the erotic element exists *for men and their pleasure*. Perhaps the "documentary quality" Bazin fears in film eroticism is too close to the theatrical experience. The male viewer would no longer be able to simply identify with the hero's seduction of the woman. He would be all too aware of its actuality and his jealousy would be aroused. I think Bazin's proprietary attitude toward women and the consequent competitiveness with other men lead to this only instance where he contradicts his plea for authenticity. Or perhaps, this is no contradiction at all. Perhaps Bazin knows that the arousal of com-

petitive and jealous feelings will disrupt the film's illusion of reality. In this case, authenticity may have to bow to the filmic abstraction.

We have been discussing Bazin's attraction to those films that tend to preserve the *wholeness* of a myth, a theatrical or painterly composition, or even the neorealist's evocation of temporal duration and the illusion of a non-differentiated flow of events. Certain concepts and experiences seem to exist as unified wholes for him, possibly opaque, certainly "ambiguous" and suggestive of various interpretations, but whole nonetheless. He discourages the filmmaker's analysis and deconstruction of these whole entities into montage "cells." Although he recognizes that the viewer must analyze events and select details in order to comprehend the event or the image, he places a certain value and faith in the initial impression of the whole.

In his essay, "In Defense of Rossellini," Bazin defines not only neorealism but also his own perspective: "Neorealism is a description of reality conceived as a whole by consciousness disposed to see things as a whole."[28] Seeing Bazin as a man "disposed to see things as a whole" is illuminating. It unites his attitude toward film "realism" with his other analyses.

For example, in "Entymology of the Pin-Up Girl," he sees through this phenomenon, identifying the economic and ideological uses to which the pin-up has been put. He reasons that: "A wartime product, a weapon of war, with the coming of peace the pin-up has lost her essential *raison d'être*."[29] Thus, the pin-up must take on a new purpose and Bazin divides this new purpose into the two categories: "eroticism and morality."[30] Assuming the first of these needs no explanation (or perhaps more explanation than we can attempt here), let's look at the second. Bazin explains that the pin-up is used to promote "post-mobilization domestic virtues" by means of " 'pin-up mothers' and 'pin-up babies,' " for example. In his analysis here, Bazin understands the way erotic images are harnessed to other causes, be they military or domestic, in the hopes of driving the latter with the former's energy. What he fails to recognize or point out is the equation of domesticity with morality. And he seems similarly at ease with the objectification of women's bodies for

political and social ends. He recognizes what is happening but he remains unoffended, for after all, such practices are commonplace within a sexist ideology—and Bazin is disposed to see that ideology as a whole, as "reality."

Similarly, in his discussion of *The Outlaw* by Howard Hughes, Bazin attributes its ban to the American censors' view that "It is forbidden to despise women."[31] Not only does this evaluation fail to consider the fact of widespread misogyny in traditional cinema (just take a look at Molly Haskell's *From Reverence to Rape* or Marjorie Rosen's *Popcorn Venus* to review how women have been pushed and pulled, objectified and subordinated throughout film history[32]), but it also refuses to acknowledge that if Bazin is correct about the censorship of *The Outlaw*, we might wonder about the degree of fear and repression that would force such a concealment. In other words, again Bazin recognizes the way films and images work but he is unable to disengage himself sufficiently so that he might question the underlying assumptions.

If another example is necessary, we need only review his interpretation of the myth of the western. Bazin recognizes the centrality of the woman to this construct, but he fails to recognize that this is a male's version of woman and that it serves certain male fantasies and ambivalences. Instead, he interprets the woman's role according to the fantasies it serves for him. He does not stand outside of the sexual ideology of which both he and the film partake. He writes: "To engender respect for women more was needed than the fear of a risk as trifling as the loss of one's life, namely the positive power of a myth. The myth of the western illustrates, and both initiates and confirms woman in her role as vestal of the social virtues, of which this chaotic world is so greatly in need."[33] Here, not only does Bazin accept the western's attitude toward women as a type of "respect," he accepts without question an ideology that denies women status as active, choosing individuals by "raising" them to the status of icons—icons who supposedly will be "respected" and "worshipped." Once again, Bazin is "disposed to see things as a whole." He sees the ideologically constructed unity of meaning and appearance. He recognizes how the con-

struction works internally but he does not stand back far enough to see the assumptions and prior conclusions upon which it is based.

Thus far in our efforts to penetrate the method of Bazin's thought, we have identified his tendency to preserve unities, be they illusions of reality or mythic constructions. But this concept, alone, is a simplification of Bazin's perceptual and analytic process. Francois Truffaut has called him a "superlative dialectician,"[34] and his translator, Hugh Gray, writes of "his capacity to bring a dialectical brilliance . . . to the defense of lost causes or at least causes in great need of friends."[35] These comments can serve as introduction to another aspect of Bazin's thought, a particular and characteristic style of reasoning we find in many of his essays and articles.

In "The Myth of Monsieur Verdoux," Bazin writes: "There are some theorems in geometry whose truth is only finally established when their opposites have been proved."[36] It is this model which Bazin follows, not only in his analysis of Chaplin's Verdoux, but also in his essays on censorship, on Robert Bresson, on film adaptations of painting and theatre. Bazin will take an idea or an analysis that appears to be a direct contradiction of his own position. He will follow its arguments and its logic through, and finally he will use this fully developed "contradiction" to support his original thesis.

For example, in his analysis of *Monsieur Verdoux*, Bazin develops each of Verdoux' characteristics, pointing to the fact that they are reversals of "Charlie's" characteristics. The fact of their opposition, however, serves to tie Verdoux more closely to the "Charlie" character, to reveal their common origin and their relationship. Bazin sees Chaplin's film as a kind of trick and accusation played on his audience. When Verdoux is finally led to the guillotine, Bazin sees "Charlie": "The fools did not recognize him. In order to force society to commit this irreparable blunder, Charlie has decked out the simulacrum of his opposite. In the precise and mythological meaning of the word, Verdoux is just an avatar of Charlie".[37] Even in this analysis where Bazin notes the oppositions and contradictions between *Monsieur Verdoux* and Chaplin's other films, his purpose is to pre-

serve the *wholeness* of the myth, the "realism" and logic within the terms of Chaplin's argument.[38]

In a similar fashion, Bazin often points to the way censorship is used to serve the aims of cinematic eroticism,[39] and he explains that film adaptations of novels, plays, and paintings are often most realistic when they appear least to reproduce the situations and settings of the original work.[40] Rather, they offer a new, very different composition which somehow serves as a kind of translation or equivalent to the theatrical, novelistic or painterly *form*. In these cases Bazin once more explores contradictions and differences in order to reassert the original concept or the *whole*.

For the feminist, this insight into Bazin's thought processes is particularly suggestive. We have seen that as a man "disposed to see things as a whole," Bazin's analyses are doomed to a certain shortsightedness, certain blindnesses. He sees the contradictions, even the dialectics of a phenomenon or theory, but only *within* the broad outlines of the whole. Contradictions exist within a theory but they never push Bazin outside of the theoretical construct itself. These contradictions serve only as added complexities within that construct. If he were to stand outside the whole, his facility for tracing the lines of contradiction *and* the connections within a theoretical construct would be invaluable. For it is within the tensions and the oppositions of thought and experience that we find our critical insight—the closest thing we have to truth. Bazin does acknowledge multiple perspectives but he always believes in the universal and ambiguous reality that exists prior to these multiple interpretations. If Bazin would have taken one step further and moved behind that wall of "reality," he might have recognized the political and social values and assumptions that shaped his so-called " 'phenomenological' realism."[41]

NOTES

1. Brian Henderson, "Two Types of Film Theory," *Movies and Methods*, ed. Bill Nichols (Berkeley: University of California Press, 1976), pp. 396, 397.

2. Henderson, *Movies and Methods*, p. 397.

3. Andre Bazin, *What Is Cinema? Volume II*, trans. Hugh Gray (Berkeley: University of California Press, 1971), p. 26.

4. Bazin, *What Is Cinema? Volume II*, p. 68.

5. Ibid., p. 87.

6. John Berger, *Ways of Seeing* (London and Harmondsworth: British Broadcasting Corporation and Penguin Books Limited, 1980).

7. Andre Bazin, *What Is Cinema? Volume I*, trans. Hugh Gray (Berkeley: University of California Press, 1967), p. 37.

8. Ibid., p. 36.

9. Ibid., pp. 35, 36.

10. Ibid., p. 133.

11. Bazin, *What Is Cinema? Volume II*, p. 87.

12. Ibid., p. 99.

13. Ibid., p. 89.

14. Ibid., p. 52.

15. Ibid., p. 53.

16. E. Ann Kaplan, "Interview with British Cine-Feminists," *Women and the Cinema: A Critical Anthology*, ed. Karyn Kay and Gerald Peary (New York: E. P. Dutton, 1977), p. 396.

17. Bazin, *What Is Cinema? Volume II*, p. 52.

18. Ibid., p. 45.

19. Bazin, *What Is Cinema? Volume I*, p. 136.

20. Ibid., p. 115.

21. Bazin, *What Is Cinema? Volume II*, pp. 150, 151.

22. Ibid., pp. 155, 156.

23. Laura Mulvey, "Visual Pleasure and Narrative Cinema," *Screen* 16, no. 3, Autumn 1975 and Bazin, *What is Cinema? Volume II*, p. 174.

24. Bazin, *What is Cinema? Volume II*, p. 174.

25. Ibid., p. 166, 167.

26. Ibid., p. 174.

27. Ibid., p. 173.

28. Ibid., p. 97.

29. Ibid., p. 160.

30. Ibid.

31. Ibid., p. 166.

32. Molly Haskell, *From Reverence to Rape: The Treatment of Women in the Movies* (New York: Penguin Books, 1978) and Marjorie Rosen, *Popcorn Venus* (New York: Avon Books, 1974).

33. Bazin, *What Is Cinema? Volume II*, p. 145.

34. Ibid., p. vi.

35. Ibid., p. 8.

36. Ibid., p. 113.
37. Ibid., p. 108.
38. Ibid., p. 105:

The critic quoted above [*La Revue des Temps Modernes*] attacks Chaplin's performance, accusing him of failing to escape altogether from the comic format of his former character, of hesitating, not choosing one way or another, between the realistic interpretation that the role of Verdoux demands and the conventions of a "Charlie." The fact is that in this instance realism would add up to illusion. Charlie is always there as if superimposed on Verdoux, because Verdoux *is* Charlie.

39. Ibid., pp. 169–175.
40. Bazin, *What Is Cinema? Volume I*, pp. 76–143 and 164–169.
41. Bazin, *What Is Cinema? Volume II*, p. 87.

4

Directions for Feminist Film

Our discussions of Eisenstein and Bazin have brought us only so far: we have an idea of what our aims might be in the project of feminist filmmaking and film viewing—that is, to construct a film that "means" multiply and to encourage and develop as active spectators. We have also noted some of the ideological barriers that have faced past filmmakers and film theorists who moved in this direction (whether or not they named it a "feminist" project). Now we must begin to develop film strategies and a specific analysis of the spectator's existent and potential role and process in the film experience.

To begin with, I will suggest some questions or focuses around which our feminist filmmaker might organize her text. Perhaps more to the point, these may be the questions around which a feminist viewer organizes her reading of a particular film, or by which she tests and determines her ideological analysis of this film. Once again, I stress that these are simply suggested directions; they are not intended as categorical imperatives. I have derived these focuses from my readings in feminist theory and criticism, as well as my reading and viewing of current feminist literary and film texts. I have organized these suggestions around two pairs of ideas: conflict and gap, particularity and commonality.

Let's begin with conflict and gap. We have said that a woman may begin to develop a critical subjectivity by noting and interrogating the contradictions within the position constructed for her through ideology and language. Following this line of

thought, I have noted that the oppressive and restrictive representations of women found by feminist film theorists (as well as literary and social critics), fall primarily within these two categories of conflict and gap. Women are either expected to live within predetermined and conflicting roles, or they are excluded altogether and displaced. The difficulty with which we recognize these contradictions and gaps reveals the extent to which we live within a world ordered by language and the ideology language represents. The contradictory expectations become invisible for each role exists within a normalizing and exclusive discourse. While experiencing the demands of a particular role, we are thinking/speaking/living within a discourse that is structured around the self-evidence and the necessity of its specific reasoning.

E. Ann Kaplan develops this idea in her defense of psychoanalysis as a tool for feminist film analysis:

Psychoanalytic discourse may indeed have oppressed women, in the sense of bringing us to accept a positioning that is inherently antithetical to being a subject and to autonomy; but if that is the case, we need to know exactly *how* psychoanalysis has functioned to repress what we could potentially become; for this we must master the terms of its discourse and ask a number of questions.[1]

In other words, we must directly address this discourse and its manner of ordering experience in order to make visible the gaps (the repressions) and the contradictions within it, or in its relation to other dominant discourse—political, social, religious, scientific.

We need films that juxtapose these contradictory and sometimes mutually exclusive discourses, that reveal the conflicting assumptions upon which they are based. These juxtapositions must occur in the *form* of the film as well as its explicit *content* (if such a distinction in emphasis is useful). A version of Eisenstein's "Intellectual Montage" might be resurrected here, although its purpose would be multiple and open-ended rather than focused and predetermined.[2] The "truth" of these sequences will lie within the contradictions revealed, and not within an alternative proposed.

In a film like Robert Benton's *Kramer vs. Kramer*, Meryl Streep's character faces such a conflict in roles. We can easily imagine a film of the "women's picture" genre, wherein the neglected wife stays with her preoccupied and ambitious husband, serving as his helpmate and doormat while single-handedly raising their son. She, of course, would be miserable though saintly while her husband became an alcoholic or a successful executive with serious health problems, and the son would grow up with a self-destructive ambivalence toward his own needs for fulfillment. However, in *Kramer vs. Kramer*, the wife refuses this role, goes off to find her own kind of success and a sense of competence, leaving the husband to realign his values, discover his nurturing abilities, and develop a warm relationship with his son. Everyone profits from her action, except the wife herself, who sacrifices her son to her husband's new role as responsible father.

I am not suggesting that one scenario is "right" while the other is "wrong," but rather that in each case, the woman is faced with a no-win situation. The roles she is expected to serve, the needs she is expected to satisfy, are contradictory, but this is clear only when we juxtapose differing perspectives as we did above. As we shall discuss, the viewer can bring this critical perspective to any film and the filmmaker can utilize formal strategies to encourage it.

As for the gaps, the places where women are *not*, their exposure is similarly important. Certain realms of women's experience are left unaddressed, or substitutions are found which further disguise the omission: for example, Kaplan explains that "motherhood has been repressed on all levels except that of hypostatization, romanticization, and idealization."[3] Such gaps are insidious. The critical viewer must either notice and question "that which is not there"—the mother's perspective in *Kramer vs. Kramer*, for example—or the viewer must find a way to get outside of an apparently seamless world view, to recognize that which has been repressed and displaced. For example, James Brooks' 1983 film, *Terms of Endearment*, is purported to treat the relationship between two women, a mother and a daughter, and the performances of Shirley MacLaine and Debra Winger are indeed compelling. However, after reflection one

realizes that the mother-daughter relationship is merely the context or the occasion for the actual film content—that is, the relationships between these two women and their respective male lovers. These men are the subject of most of the women's exchanges and the reason for most of their decisions. We think that we have a film about two women, but all we have learned about are the relationships these women have with men. The former has been displaced by the latter; our attention is redirected, often without our noticing, and the gap goes unrecognized.

Films that reveal and/or counteract these "structuring absences" are needed. Strategies are being developed to this end. For instance, films may remain relentlessly within a single point of view; there is no "suture," or stitching of the viewer's perspective into the shot-reverse shot pattern of traditional narrative film. There is a resounding isolation of the character who is not integrated into the answering perspective, society's return glance, as well as of the spectator who never can lose herself in an illusory construction of a "whole world."

Chantal Akerman's *Jeanne Dielman, 23 Quai du Commerce, 1080 Bruxelles* (1975) is an example of such a film: Annette Kuhn explains:

> the refusal of reverse shots in the film entails a denial of the "binding-in" effect of the suture of classic cinema: the spectator is forced to maintain a distance in relation to both narrative and image, constructing the story and building up narrative expectations for herself. The familiarity of Jeanne's tasks and the precision with which they are represented, combined with the refusal of suture, serve to free the look of the spectator.[4]

In this type of film, we experience the "gap" by filling it. We try not to place the woman within a societal construct that smoothly, typically, eases her out.

Another way to reveal the absence is by placing unexpected demands upon a woman's role, within the traditional narrative set-up. Ask the traditional "heroine" to *act*, to rebel against the limits of her role. This is another way of revealing the gap by

filling it. The audience's surprise at our character's disregard for the boundaries of her role may force them to recognize their otherwise invisible expectations.

This is the strategy most often adopted by those filmmakers working within the classic narrative tradition. Examples include films like Gillian Armstrong's *My Brilliant Career*, about a young Australian girl with artistic aspirations, or John Cassavetes' *Gloria*, about a woman who works with and against organized crime in her efforts to protect a child, or Colin Higgins' *Nine to Five*, about three women office workers who take on the oppressive labor practices of a large firm. In each of these cases, the filmmaker tends to give with one hand while taking away with the other. The very fact of the unusual circumstances and the unusual roles in which these women characters are presented, raises new questions and startles the audience into a new position. However, the farcical story lines (in *Nine to Five* three women hold their boss captive in his own home with an elaborate harness and leash), the glamorous accoutrements (in *Gloria*, Gena Rowlands runs, leaps, and kills in pink satin suits with spike heels), and the arbitrarily limited alternatives facing these characters (in *My Brilliant Career* the young woman must choose between "Love" and "Career"), tend to reinforce preexisting stereotypes. This tendency, however, is not unavoidable and seems to spring largely from the production and distribution constraints of commercial cinema.

Our efforts to reveal, to *make visible* the conflicts or contradictions and the gaps or absences in film's representation through a variety of film strategies encourage and rely upon the development of critical subjectivity. The validity of these film sequences lies not in the positing of alternative truths or viewpoints, but rather in the revelation of the spaces between our expectations and the world portrayed. The aim is not to construct a whole and single world, but to suggest the multiplicity of possibility and the recognition that these possibilities exist simultaneously. This concept is difficult for us to grasp and accept, largely because our language is based on an order of selection and focus. There is a linearity to the logic reflected in our discourse and thus, the viewpoint posited here necessitates

the development of a new language, or more properly a new attitude toward language. The discussion of multiplicity to follow will develop this issue of language further.

But first, let's return to the second suggested focus for feminist film: commonality and particularity. We have noted that the development of critical subjectivity entails the recognition of contradictions or tension points within an individual's ideological context. One approach to this process involves the perception of connections or common areas in institutions or societal attitudes that are ordinarily perceived as quite distinct.

This can occur at the personal level or the institutional level. Connections can be drawn, for example, between the experiences of women, of racial minorities and of the poor. We can find emotional commonalities in the experiences of men and women, or we can find structural commonalities in the dynamics of teacher-student relationships, sexual relationships, and therapist-client relationships. In this last case, however unwittingly, commercial films from George Cukor's *My Fair Lady* to Louis Jilbert's *Educating Rita* to Marshall Brickman's *Lovesick* have played around this idea. By whatever means, be it humor or music or slapstick comedy, such films disguise this commonality, even as they raise it, by normalizing it, trivializing it, contextualizing it. The exposure of these commonalities requires, most significantly, a critical viewer. Cinema strategies can be employed, however, to encourage such awareness. For example, in *Sigmund Freud's Dora: A Case of Mistaken Identity* (Anthony McCall, Claire Pajaczkowska, Andrew Tyndall, Jane Weinstock), the sexual content of the analyst-analysand interchange is blatantly and humorously symbolized, so that it stands out from the "narrative" (such as it is):

The form of the dialogue and the cinematic strategies suggest the symbolic sexual union of Freud and Dora: we now see both Freud and Dora only from chest to thighs; Dora's hands hover around her pelvis and she is holding a maroon bag (her vagina?), while Freud is holding out into the frame a phallic cigar.[5]

Furthermore, Dora eventually ends this sexual dynamic by *choosing to leave*, thereby calling more attention to this problem-

atic relation. Both narrative sequence or plot and *mise en scene* (visual symbols, composition) are employed to draw attention to the connection between sexual and therapeutic relations.

On the other hand, the feminist filmmaker and viewer may encourage the recognition of distinctions or differences in institutions or individuals or attitudes that are ordinarily thrown together. In Helke Sander's film, *The All-Round Reduced Personality*, for example, we watch uncomfortably as Edda, on her way to work in the morning, must disentangle herself from the arms and legs of her daughter. The girl clings to Edda's neck, torso, and clothing, and finally another woman must pull her in one direction while Edda pulls herself in the other. The cries and whining, the tangled extension of legs, arms, and Edda's long scarf, like an umbilical cord which must finally be cut, Edda's exasperation—all these factors combine to create an unusually evocative sequence, despite its brevity. I suggest that much of this moment's power derives from its portrayal of a mother, decisively, purposely, and freely leaving her child. Now, in context, she is not abandoning the child: the child will be well-cared for and is well-loved; and Edda will return in a few hours. But the fact remains that a distinction is made in this sequence: a woman is choosing work in addition to motherhood and, however briefly, she even chooses her working role instead of her mothering role. Separating these two identities—woman and mother—reveals their discreteness and raises all kinds of questions and emotional responses.

This double process of perception—the recognition of commonality and particularity—can be focused outward into an individual's societal context, or it may be turned inward, revealing the commonalities and particularities between oneself and others. The application of this organizational principle or perceptual directive to film can be developed if we turn back to Eisenstein and some of his methods. Eisenstein recognized this dual function—the revelation of connections and of contradictions—in his theory of montage. Certainly his emphasis upon "collision" is clear, the juxtaposition of images or parts of images that in their very conflict suggest a "third something," a new idea.[6] Eisenstein's theory of vertical montage rests upon the determination to "sever the passive everyday connection

between [for example] an object and the sound it makes,"—the relevation of difference, of particularity.[7]

Alternately, montage can *reveal* or *construct* connections between ideas or objects that are ordinarily considered unrelated. We see this most clearly illustrated in examples of "Intellectual Montage" as, for instance, the many visual metaphors for Kerensky in Eisenstein's film, *October*: the mechanical peacock, the statues of Napoleon, and so on. Thus, montage may serve the dual perception of particularity and commonality. However, the juxtaposition of images or portions of images alone may prove limiting; similar connections and distinctions may be made at the level of the scene or sequence, or through the juxtaposition of related characters. No matter what the form, however, the important point to remember (and this is a *departure* from Eisenstein) is that the purpose of this process is not to suggest a single and true perception of the commonalities and the particularities between a group of women, a group of men and women, or a set of social attitudes. Rather this process will set up a system of resonances, a series of perceptual patterns, none of which is fully accurate, and all of which rely for their insight upon an understanding of the others. Just as a perspective line drawing of a cube may appear to be directed upward to the left or downward and to the right, depending upon the relations a viewer perceives between the lines and the spaces between them, so can the film viewer's perceptions of common areas and differences between characters shift depending on where the viewer is positioned in relation to those characters.

Our feminist film's objective is to provide multiple viewpoints within the text itself, and multiple vantage points for the viewer/interpreter, revealing the multiplicity of perspectives and the manner in which they may be suggested and/or constructed by the film's method. A particular camera angle, for example, may suggest a specific emotional attitude to the majority of viewers. Our aim is not only to employ varying angles within the film so as to complicate the emotional content, but also to recognize, value, and encourage the capability or tendency of any individual viewer to interpret these camera angles in distinctive ways.

Thus, what our feminist film is trying to provide is the op-

portunity for and encouragement of multiple perspectives. These multiple perspectives are essential for the development of a critical subjectivity. Rather than a cinematic language that constructs a viewpoint by cutting out alternate perspectives or by discrediting these alternatives, I am positing a language that conveys multiplicity. If language is a "system of differences with no positive terms," if it names objects only by differentiating them from other objects, then each and every term derives its meaning only from its juxtaposition or interaction with other terms. A language of multiplicity will make this interaction and dependence apparent. Instead of a language that seeks to create meaning by focusing, selecting, narrowing down a proposed concept, this language attempts to open out into various directions, to suggest new connections and interrelations.

Take, for example, the language of the feminist theorist, Mary Daly. She will employ "words" such as "see/name," "invasion/elimination," "portrayed/betrayed," "a-mazing," and "gyn/ecology."[8] Her slashes and hyphens and juxtaposed words allow each sentence to be read in a number of different ways, each reading commenting on the others. Similarly, the puns and "double-entendres" of Helene Cixous or Luce Irigaray or Monique Witig encourage the reader to think and rethink each phrase, finding many different and non-exclusive interpretations. Take, for example, Irigaray's essay title, "Ce sexe qui n'en est pas un," (This sex which is not one) with its multiple readings.[9] Much has been made of this style of writing, explaining that it reflects and expresses the essential plurality of women. I find this a restricting and ahistoric interpretation. Rather I would suggest that this multiplicity is the means to, and the outcome of, the development of critical subjectivity. And since women have been and are in a marginal position with regard to the discourse and values of society, it is to be expected that they will be among those who come to this plurality of vision and expression. The very contradictions within their lives necessitate it.

So if we have suggested a language that is non-linear and multiple, that holds conflicting propositions in tension and allows them to illuminate each other, how can this language be expressed in film? Let's examine a few suggestions. Once more,

the juxtaposition, the bringing together of different images through montage, makes Eisenstein's favorite a possible method. However, whereas Eisenstein used montage to suggest a single, predetermined concept (though his intention was such, in fact his montage sequences are rich in multiple interpretations), our use of montage might be freer and more open-ended. Some of this open-endedness will be the inevitable consequence of individual viewer's distinctive interpretive styles. Beyond this, the filmmaker may juxtapose a string of images, each of them relating in a different way to the others. Instead of simply intercutting the image of a deposed ruler with the image of a shattered icon, add to this sequence the image of chaos and starvation that follows the deposition as well as the joy among the triumphant troops. In other words, rather than using montage to make a point and to direct the viewer's thoughts in a predetermined direction, use montage to construct and contradict simultaneously, to make connections and suggest distinctions. Startle the viewer with the juxtaposition of seeming opposites.

Obviously, this "montage" I am describing is not limited to the intercutting of images. Chantal Akerman uses such a strategy, juxtaposing lengthy sequences, in *Jeanne Dielman, 23 Quai du Commerce, 1080 Bruxelles*. Here Akerman presents several days in the life of her main character, a single mother who supports herself and her son through prostitution. Akerman films the daily routine of this woman, played by Delphine Seyrig, in relentless detail. We know at what time she will rise, the sequence of her morning toilette, how she spends her days, the sounds of her purposeful steps in the hall, the composure, the self-enclosed quality of her characteristic expressions, and so on. We are taught, through repetition of events, in a certain sequence, filmed from a certain angle, to expect and even to depend upon the continuation of this routine. Rather than being bored by the pattern, our expectations are scaled down to the point where these minute gestures and habitual tasks become the stuff of the narrative for us. Thus, when the routine is altered, the pattern broken, however slightly, we fear, and come to fully expect, catastrophe. Here Akerman has encouraged her audience to develop a set pattern of expectation, even of nar-

rative need, through her careful use of detail, of repetition, of duration and of restraint. Then, however, she calls attention to this expectation and need, and even to the strategies that encourage it, by disappointing our expectations, by denying us the routine we have come to expect. Akerman has not offered a specific interpretation of the film events. In fact, critics and viewers have argued over what "triggers" the disruption of routine and ultimately, the film's violent climax. More to the point, however, Akerman has used the careful juxtaposition of like and unlike sequences, in a particular order, to stimulate expectation and to disappoint that expectation, thereby calling attention to the ways a film's content can encourage an audience's assumptions and needs, allowing certain events to appear "normal" or even "desirable" simply due to their repetition in a stable context.

Again, following the complexities of Eisenstein's theory, the filmmaker may not only juxtapose such sequences, but also colors, directions, rhythms and tonalities. Particularly, points of view may be compared and connected. Discussing the work of Jean-Louis Baudry, James Roy MacBean writes:

Thus, in this argument, the design of the camera lens has as its goal the achievement of "Renaissance perspective". . . . And this Renaissance perspective—with its illusion of limitless space and its ability to *place* the spectator where it wishes, instead of leaving his eye free to wander and to create multiple relations among the elements of an icon, for example—thus offers the ascendant bourgeoisie, particularly the industrial bourgeoisie, an ideological tool expressly suited for passing off as reality the image it wants the world to have of itself and of the existing socioeconomic system.[10]

To counteract this "innate" tendency in the camera, points of view may be multiplied and juxtaposed and contrasted. Although any camera angle and distance will automatically "place" the viewer, the filmmaker can counteract and interrogate this placement by providing multiple vantage points, and as we shall see in the next section, multiple identifications.

Before we discuss the uses of multiple identifications and the ways a filmmaker may encourage them, let's take a look at the process of identification itself and some of the problems it poses.

Identification is the process whereby a particular viewer loses track of her own world and temporarily feels tied to the experiences and feelings of a character within a film. The viewer may become so involved with the needs and desires of a particular character that she releases any larger view, any broader perspective she may have on the character's situation. She finds herself "wanting" things within the film that would prove self-destructive and self-defeating if transferred to her own life. For example, in a standard Hollywood-made film like *Ordinary People* (directed by Robert Redford), she may find herself identifying with the boy's pain and hating/blaming the mother. Regardless of the fact that the viewer herself may be a mother, and regardless of the fact that the film mother's behavior issues from a pain and a victimization that is just as real as the son's, and despite the fact that the film, like our society, offers little insight or attention to the mother's experience, our viewer finds herself divided against herself, through her identification.

The filmmaker has many devices at his or her disposal that can encourage the viewer's identification with a particular character. For example, the use of shot-reverse shot editing can "stitch" the viewer's viewpoint into the fabric of the film, leaving no separate space for the viewer to inhabit. Similarly, the repetition of shots from an individual character's point of view, or the continual tracking of a moving character and close-ups of a character's face serve to focus the viewer on that character's experience and to urge the viewer to "speculate" (of course, this occurs at a more emotional than an intellectual level) upon what that character feels. Identification is further encouraged if the character we are following seems vulnerable or endangered, or if the character clearly experiences an intense desire. Intense emotions make the character more accessible and more "human" to the viewer (provided the emotions are not outside a generally acceptable range).

Obviously, all these methods for encouraging identification can become manipulative and antithetical to the viewer's attempt to develop a critical subjectivity. Instead of perceiving and recognizing contradiction, the viewer is encouraged to remain within a specific perspective, that of the character with whom the viewer identifies. Following Althusser's thinking, the sub-

jectivity of our viewer is constructed as it is merged with that of the character. A further problem with this identification is that it encourages an individualistic perspective, as opposed to an awareness of collective identity and a shared human experience. The viewer identifies with a particular character and *then* turns to face the rest of the film's world. There is an individualistic drawing of lines—you and me against the world. Once again it becomes apparent that such a film experience does not lead to the development of critical subjectivity; instead of perceiving the relative validity of many perspectives, our viewer is locked into one point of view and her emotional continuity is dependent upon her ability to remain within that viewpoint.

Part of the attraction or inducement to identification is the pleasure it affords the viewer. Not only is there the "escape" that is typically attributed to the experience of popular culture; there is also the sensation of union, of connection with another human being: "The pleasure of the cinema lies in its reconstruction in the spectator of an illusory sense of this imagined early experience of unity," (i.e., the union of mother and child).[11] This is not the same as the collective identity suggested above. Rather it is an attempt to have it both ways; the spectator constructs a union with one character and then protects this individualized space from all others, or the spectator constructs a union with the world view, the social pattern portrayed within the film and then feels no need to challenge this pattern of perception. E. Ann Kaplan refers to this experience as "the pleasure that usually comes from the manipulation of our emotions (particularly around the Oedipus complex in the case of commercial cinema—the reliance of narratives on Freud's family romance) . . . [the] pleasure in recognition."[12] There is pleasure in this recognition for such films offer us a perspective on our emotional experiences that is in sync with the perceptual paradigms inherent in our language, our other cultural experiences, our education, and so on. Rather than being challenged to see and feel the mother's side of things in *Ordinary People*, for example, a perspective that would threaten our righteous sense of ourselves as misunderstood and insufficiently loved and that would challenge our expectations that mothers ought to be all-loving, all-patient, and certainly have no personal needs—

rather than face this disconcerting view, we prefer the plea-sures of a film that reinforces our expectations.

These pleasures in identification are reinforced and compli-cated by the "pleasure in looking" that Laura Mulvey first dis-sected in her essay, "Visual Pleasure and Narrative Cinema." [13] We have already mentioned the power of the camera's posi-tioning, the sequencing of shots and the camera's tracking, for example, to encourage a specific identification by directing the spectator's look or point of view. Beyond this pleasure in iden-tification, in recognition, in union, there is the scopophilic pleasure, the objectifying, controlling gaze. As Mulvey has pointed out, this gaze can be broken down into the look of the camera, of the characters within the film, and of the audi-ence—and each of these looks is often voyeuristic and predom-inantly male, in that its origin or its point of view is that of man looking at/acting upon a woman. [14] This analysis raises another problem within the process of identification for the female spectator, for with whom is she to identify—the agent of the controlling look or its object, the man or the woman?

Recognizing these problems in the identification process, the editors and writers of the *Camera Obscura* collective have tried to work out an alternative experience: "What we felt we needed was not a person to identify with but situations in which we could imagine ourselves, within a structure of distanciation which insures room for critical analysis." [15] The collective posits a "substitution . . . on the basis of conscious, recognized sameness, rather than emotional identification." [16] This empha-sis on conscious activity is crucial for the development of criti-cal subjectivity, but there are still other problems with the col-lective's formulations. As Christine Gledhill points out in her essay, "Recent Developments in Feminist Criticism," we can-not assume that the viewer will necessarily place herself in the film's situation and engage in a critical analysis of this process, any more than we can assume that the viewer will necessarily identify emotionally with a character in a classical Hollywood film. Gledhill writes:

The issue raised here is whether the audience is as automatically taken over by the identificatory mechanisms of mainstream cinema as the

anti-realist position suggests, or whether there is not a considerable degree of work required on the part of the audience in negotiating what a particular fictional world offers according to where they are placed in society. Similarly, although it is clear that the view of the media as "a window on the world" must be firmly resisted, it is not clear that the audience, even while accepting that view as a general proposition, automatically accept it on any and every occasion.[17]

So we are working with two lines of thought here. On the one hand, we have pointed to the attractions and the dangers of the identification process. On the other hand, we are reminded that any particular viewer does not *necessarily* identify with the characters a film puts forward. This second point is crucial to prove and develop the concept of critical subjectivity. If we question when and why we identify with a particular character, and when and why we do not, and if we compare our answers to these questions with other viewer's answers, we will begin to recognize the lines of contradiction and tension within a film's world view, between that world view and the experiences of its spectators.

However, it is useful to realize that despite our freedom *not* to identify, a film has many techniques at its disposal which encourage us to fall in with a particular character's experience. Judith Mayne points to this fact when she describes her experience with the film, *Kramer vs. Kramer* (directed by Robert Benton):

Like most people at the movie theatre, I was invested in *Kramer vs. Kramer*, that is, I was intrigued by the film, moved at the appropriate moments. But by the time the house lights had come on at the film's conclusion, I began to think that I had been had. What interests me is that precise moment when, my nose still runny from that emotional investment, I say: This is appalling. I have just "embraced" a film, and then there comes the moment of disavowal.[18]

It is important—and not necessarily inevitable—that the "moment of disavowal" is experienced. The development of critical subjectivity, the encouragement of a conscious questioning of our film experience, fosters this moment of recognition.

Perceiving the need for our viewer to develop this conscious,

critical attitude and to apply it to all film, classical Hollywood and anti-realist alike, what remains for the feminist filmmaker to undertake? Should she attempt to discourage all emotional identification, to hold her film and its characters ever at arm's length, or to adopt the *Camera Obscura* collective's suggestion that the viewer be provided with a "generalized 'she'," a character for which she can substitute herself without losing herself in emotional identification?[19] Or should she forget about the whole question, aware that a filmmaker can never be *sure* of leading a viewer to a particular insight or experience, and trusting to the viewer's critical awareness?

Obviously, each filmmaker will answer these questions in a somewhat different fashion, but I will offer some suggestions here that I think mesh well with the theory of critical subjectivity already proposed. Contrary to the *Camera Obscura* collective, I will suggest that emotional identification may be useful and is not necessarily or ultimately manipulative. Let our filmmaker continue to utilize those film techniques that encourage identification but utilize them *multiply*. Present a film's experience from differing viewpoints, each presented sympathetically. Allow the viewer to enter and experience *contradictory* perspectives. This experience of contradiction will encourage a *dual consciousness* in the viewer. Not only will she feel and see the logic within many viewpoints, she will recognize their incongruity, thus pulling her out to a critical distance. From this critical distance, she will begin to recognize the plurality of experience and the "truth" in the spaces between contrasting viewpoints—all the lessons of critical subjectivity.

In her analysis of "alternative film practices" E. Ann Kaplan defines what she calls the "theory film," explaining it attempts "to replace pleasure in recognition with pleasure in learning—with cognitive processes, as against emotional ones."[20] The multiple identification I posit here is an effort to avoid this dichotomy between thought and emotion. Rather it is the very process of conflicting emotional identifications that triggers the viewer's cognitive processes. If our subjectivity, as viewer, is constructed as we are incorporated into the film's world through the film's address, then this multiple address denies us an unproblematic entry. As we shall see in chapter 5, Márta Mészá-

ros uses this strategy quite forcefully in her film, *Women*. The viewer is suddenly, jarringly pulled out of her point of view/her identification with the film's main characters, when Zsuzsu, the child, literally shatters the film's final scene with her screams of pain and denunciation. We are suddenly forced into another perspective as the film ends, throwing the entire film experience into question.

In this film, the viewer's identification can suddenly shift, however fleetingly, from the mother to the child, deconstructing and constructing the viewer's sense of self in relation to these different points of view. What are the implications of this process for the viewer's sense of sexual identification? In her discussion of "spectator-text relations," Annette Kuhn credits Laura Mulvey with addressing the issue of a "gendered subjectivity."[21] Again, if our subjectivity is constructed through the filmic address, what identity exists for women? Our identification with the film's positive agent must be with the male protagonist and our recognition of ourselves, as women, must be with the sexual object, the passive muse—or worse, the woman who takes action and is then punished for her transgression. If a "gendered subjectivity" has existed for the female spectator, it has been conflicted and painful. However, if a filmmaker encourages the multiple identifications and presents the multiple perspectives suggested above, across gender lines, then the question of a "gendered subjectivity" recedes in significance. Difference is emphasized and affirmed in all its manifestations, and active empathetic identification with adults, with children, with men and women can develop. In fact, the gender categories become shockingly inadequate in the face of such a multiplicity of potential identifications.

Now if the pleasures of identification can be recouped for feminist film, what about the "pleasure in looking?" As we discussed earlier, this scopophilic pleasure is a pleasure in objectification and control—that is, the objectification and control of the woman viewed. It should become apparent that as soon as a process of multiple identification encourages the spectator to incorporate male and female perspectives into his or her sense of self, such a single-mindedly exploitative pleasure will be thrown into question. The viewer who has allowed herself to

be incorporated into a female character's world view will find it difficult to surrender that self to objectification and fetishization—won't she? E. Ann Kaplan might disagree for she explains:

The domination of women by the male gaze is part of patriarchal strategy to contain the threat that the mother embodies, and to control the positive and negative impulses that memory traces of being mothered have left in the male unconscious. Women, in turn, have learned to associate their sexuality with domination by the male gaze, a position involving a degree of masochism in finding their objectification erotic.[22].

Whether or not the individual woman does find such "objectification erotic," the feminist filmmaker is faced with a problem in presenting women's bodies. The choices seem to be identification with the (male) character looking at/objectifying the body of another (female) character or identification with the (female) character's sense of self as an object-to-be-viewed. Are there alternative ways to approach the "pleasure of looking" and what strategies exist or can be developed to implement these alternatives?

Kaplan herself raises one such alternative: "Some recent experimental (as against psychoanalytic) studies have shown that the gaze is first set in motion in the mother-child relationship. But this is a *mutual* gazing, rather than the subject-object kind that reduces one of the parties to the place of submission."[23] What elements might be present to allow for or encourage this "mutual gazing?" For one thing, the look might have the potential to be returned. The character being viewed has a "point of view," if you will, or a subjectivity that can be portrayed in response to that of the character who looks. Once again, the process of multiple identification encourages such an awareness in the viewer. But what if each character's point of view is simply the objectification of the other? Or what if our filmmaker wants to present a character who identifies with this "to-be-looked-at-ness," rather than a character who looks back? And what about the look of the viewer? How can his or her gaze be mutual when the film never looks back?

"Mutual gazing" implies an interactive process whereby the

viewer is also the viewed and the viewed one is also a viewer, a process wherein my sense of self is determined by the reflection of myself I receive from you as well as by the relation between myself and the world which I project onto you. Such a complex equation requires more than the filmmaker's active encouragement of multiple identifications. It requires the viewer to address consciously the process of identification itself, the process of interacting with a particular film. The viewer looks at her own process of looking. As we shall see in chapters 6 and 7, Yvonne Rainer and Helke Sander both use numerous strategies to call attention to the viewer's process of film viewing while yet offering narrative and identificatory pleasures.

For instance, a filmmaker may try to pull the viewer in and out of the identificatory process, thereby encouraging, once again, a dual consciousness. Alain Resnais achieves something like this in his film, *Mon Oncle d'Amerique*, where he intercuts narrative passages with a pseudo-scientific commentary on human behavior. The viewer is pulled in and out, identifying and then critiquing. In this way, the viewer is personally "engaged" or invested in the film's characters, while at the same time, she is asked to see through their behavior. The advantage in this method is that, unlike many films that, in good faith, attempt to undermine the manipulation of identification and end by boring and alienating their audience, the viewer can actually become involved with the film and its characters. In addition, this method, as well as that of multiple identification discussed above, encourages the viewer to remain aware of a shaping and creating hand, that of the filmmaker. In fact, the filmmaker actually shares her process of identification and distance *with the audience*. The manifestation of conflicting viewpoints *within* the film serves to expose the choices the filmmaker makes—when to stay with a particular character; when to a cut to conflicting perspective; when to pull back from the narrative; and so forth. This exposure of the filmmaker's process, in effect, provides the spectator with the tools necessary to dismantle the illusion.

The viewer's dual consciousness is quite useful in designing an approach to the film's larger narrative, as well. Narrative becomes suspect in a feminist critique due to its construction of an exclusive world view, an illusory realm complete with clo-

sure and invisible seams. The feeling of wholeness and authenticity makes it all the more difficult to detect ideological exclusions or inclusions. If our feminist filmmaker *uses* narrative and allows it to "feel real," while simultaneously exposing its construction, the viewer will have to develop a dual consciousness. Like the world view she lives within every day, this film world feels real but is ideologically constructed. By moving the viewer in and out, plunging her into a narrative passage and then pulling back, providing an alternate version or an alternate perspective, the viewer is asked to recognize the filmmaker's choices. And once she perceives the filmmaker's choices, our viewer will be ready and better able to make her own.

I mentioned earlier that even the most traditional of films might trigger a perception of contradiction and of multiple perspectives if our spectator brings a critical subjectivity to the viewing experience. All the possibilities for feminist filmmaking explored in the preceding pages are merely suggestions for future experimentation and would be relatively useless without an appreciation of the film viewer's active role as spectator. We have already explored the subjectivity of the individual viewer and discussed the ways in which this subjectivity may be constructed through the perception of contradiction and multiple "realities." We discussed the concerns and methods a feminist filmmaker might develop in order to encourage this process of recognition. Now I will suggest that we approach our viewer's film responses with some of the same concerns and questions with which we earlier approached the film itself.

If our film is to center around the issues of conflict and gap, let's look for the same structures within our viewer's response, and within and between the responses of various viewers. There will be "structuring absences" in one woman's responses to a film, just as there may be such absences or gaps within the film text. Similarly, there will be commonalities and particularities between the responses of various viewers of the same film. Such questioning of individual responses and interpretations allows for and encourages an awareness of the ways in which the viewer's perspective is a construct, reflecting internal consistencies and patterns, and determined to a large degree by the viewer's context. Similarly, another viewer's perspective may be

equally consistent within itself and yet may reflect a very different social context. The analysis of these responses and their juxtaposition reveals the contradictions and multiplicities that encourage a critical subjectivity. In her essay, "Feminist Film Criticism: Theory and Practice," Julia Lesage writes: "The audience's milieu is always to some extent historically/temporally/spatially/socially different from the maker's milieu, and the audience brings its experience with its milieu to its judgment of a film."[24] She proceeds to suggest that feminist film criticism take, as one of its projects, the alteration of the audience milieu. The questioning and juxtaposition of individual viewer's responses will contribute to just such a change, as it makes viewers aware of their own process and of the choices they are *not* making consciously within their film responses.

Another aspect of the "audience milieu," as well as the "filmmaker's milieu," is the whole accumulation of films, the collective cinematic text, of which any film partakes. Brian Henderson defines this "principle of intertextuality" in *A Critique of Film Theory*: "This means, oversimply, that no text is isolated, discrete, unique, and that none is self-originating. Every text is a combination of other texts and discourses, which it 'knots' in a certain way and from a certain ideological position."[25] If we follow this concept further, we can posit that this collective cinematic text, through its contradictions and inconsistencies and when viewed critically, may form a body that deconstructs itself. Narrative film and manipulative identificatory processes, then, need not be banned from our film repertoire. Rather, the audience may learn to view such a film as part of this collective body, and thereby see the gaps, the conflicts, and the multiplicity of perspective within this intertextuality that serve as an internal critique. For example, Rainer Werner Fassbinder's *Ali: Fear Eats the Soul* gathers much of its social and political impact from its juxtaposition with Douglas Sirk's *All That Heaven Allows*. And Chantal Akerman's *Golden Eighties* must resonate with blurred and collective memories of the classical Hollywood musical in order that the viewer might recognize her humor and the way in which the filmmaker choreographs that experience as well as the dance numbers. More generally, accumulated memories of film romances work to create a pattern

of expectation that new films may work with or against, depending upon their maker's motivation and perspective. The point is, each film's impact is determined to a large degree by the past film experiences, associations, and the critical awareness of the film viewer.

Obviously, my emphasis is on the viewer's role in creating her own film experience. Earlier I suggested that certain film methods might encourage a constructive and active dual consciousness in the film spectator. Now I will add that, whether or not such films are made, the dual consciousness or the critical subjectivity of the feminist film viewer can and must develop. B. Ruby Rich explains that:

> for a woman today, film is a dialectical experience in a way that it never was and never will be for a man under patriarchy. Brecht once described the exile as the ultimate dialectician in that the exile lives the tension of two different cultures. That's precisely the sense in which the woman spectator is an equally inevitable dialectician.[26]

I will add that for women to develop an "authentic" subjectivity, for feminist film viewers and filmmakers to take control of their cinematic experience, that "inevitable" dialectical process must become a *conscious* one.

NOTES

1. E. Ann Kaplan, *Women and Film: Both Sides of the Camera* (New York: Methuen, 1983), p. 24.

2. See discussion of this revised montage in text at note 6.

3. Kaplan, *Women and Film*, p. 201.

4. Annette Kuhn, *Women's Pictures: Feminism and Cinema* (London: Routledge & Kegan Paul, 1982), p. 174.

5. Kaplan, *Women and Film*, p. 147.

6. Sergei Eisenstein, *The Film Sense*, ed. trans. Jay Leyda (New York: Harcourt Brace Jovanovich, 1975), p. 9.

7. Sergei Eisenstein, *Notes of a Film Director*, trans. X. Danko (New York: Dover Publications, 1970), p. 126, 127.

8. Mary Daly, *Gyn/Ecology: The Metaethics of Radical Feminism* (Boston: Beacon Press, 1978), pp. 56, 71, 84, 6, xiii.

9. Elaine Marks and Isabelle de Courtivron, eds., *New French Feminisms: An Anthology* (New York: Schocken Books, 1981), p. 99 (see note).

10. James Roy MacBean, *Film and Revolution* (Bloomington: Indiana University Press, 1975), p. 322.

11. Christine Gledhill, "Recent Developments in Feminist Criticism," *Quarterly Review of Film Studies*, vol. 3, no. 4, Fall 1978, p. 476.

12. Kaplan, *Women and Film*, p. 138.

13. Laura Mulvey, "Visual Pleasure and Narrative Cinema" in *Women and the Cinema: A Critical Anthology*, ed. Karyn Kay and Gerald Peary (New York: E. P. Dutton, 1977), p. 415.

14. Kaplan, *Women and Film*, p. 30.

15. "Yvonne Rainer: An Introduction," *Camera Obscura: A Journal of Feminism and Film Theory*, no. 1, 1976, p. 59.

16. Ibid., p. 68.

17. Gledhill, "Recent Developments," p. 474.

18. Judith Mayne, "The Woman at the Keyhole: Women's Cinema and Feminist Criticism," *New German Critique*, no. 23, Summer 1981, pp. 40, 41.

19. "Yvonne Rainer: An Introduction," p. 68.

20. Kaplan, *Women and Film*, p. 138.

21. Kuhn, *Women's Pictures*, p. 159.

22. Kaplan, *Women and Film*, p. 205.

23. Ibid.

24. Julia Lesage, "Feminist Film Criticism: Theory and Practice," in *Sexual Stratagems: The World of Women in Film*, ed. Patricia Erens (New York: Horizon Press, 1979), p. 145.

25. Brian Henderson, *A Critique of Film Theory* (New York: E. P. Dutton, 1980), p. 217.

26. B. Ruby Rich, in Michelle Citron et al., "Women and Film: A Discussion of Feminist Aesthetics," *New German Critique*, no. 13, Winter 1978, p. 87.

THEORY IN PRACTICE

Introduction

In the following chapters, I will provide a discussion of recent works by filmmakers Márta Mészáros, Helke Sander, Yvonne Rainer, and Marleen Gorris, incorporating where appropriate an application of the concepts of multiple perspectives, Critical Subjectivity and dual consciousness—concepts developed and defined in Part I.

In her essay, "The Avant-Garde and Its Imaginary," Constance Penley writes:

Stephen Heath has argued that "deconstruction is clearly the impass of the formal device" and that a socio-historically more urgent practice would be a work not on "codes" but on the operations of narrativization which for him means "the constructions and relations of meaning and subject in a specific signifying practice." We have one example of a politically motivated avant-garde practice which addresses itself exactly to this area—the recent work of several women filmmakers focusing on feminist concerns is less a work on "codes" and "perceptual processes" than it is on narrative, fiction and the construction of another subject-relation to the screen.[1]

The filmmakers Penley goes on to name as examples of this politically engaged cinematic practice include Yvonne Rainer among them. She does not mention, however, Helke Sander, Márta Mészáros, or Marleen Gorris, possibly because their work remains closer to the "realistic" model. In my discussions of these four filmmakers, I hope to suggest the degree to which they are all actively involved in transforming the narrative form and

its relation with the viewer. In each film—most apparently in Rainer's work and to the least degree, or most subtly perhaps, in Mészáros' film—these artists are encouraging their viewers to approach these films in a new, more aware and more consciously active fashion.

These filmmakers encourage this active spectatorship by addressing the strategies and impact of cinematic form; by addressing a subject matter that falls outside the realm of traditional narrative categories; and by consciously structuring ambiguity into their texts. But do these efforts then mark these films as "feminist"? And if so, how do "feminist" films differ from other experimental or non-traditional films? Does a "feminist" film have to be made by a woman, as these films are? And does "feminist" film have to be "politically motivated?" In other words, the choice of which films to include in this text inevitably suggests the question, "When is a film a feminist film?"

I selected these four films for a variety of distinct reasons. They are all relatively recent films, made by women who are aware of feminist issues. Their subject matter and their formal strategies exemplify many of the suggested strategies I posit for feminist filmmakers in Part I of this text. As well, I wanted to call more attention to the films of women directors, to encourage their more frequent screening. However, to say then that these are "feminist" films is to miss the point.

The feminism I address in this study is a "way of seeing," a mode of perception, of seeing multiply. It may or may not be "politically motivated" but it is a political act. For many feminists, the origins of this mode of perception can be traced to the specific experience of women's oppression, and yet they now bring this perspective to their entire realm of knowledge and experience. Thus, a film becomes a feminist experience when the viewer brings this mode of perception to it. A filmmaker may do many things to encourage this type of viewing, as we have discussed, but in the end, the film viewer may resist such strategies, or the film viewing context may cancel their impact. On the other hand, a filmmaker may desire total control of the film viewer's response and the maker may use many strategies to generate a single film reading, and yet the spectator may escape this director's grasp.

Thus the question is not "Is this a feminist film?" but rather "Is this viewer enjoying a feminist experience of this film?" Feminism is not *in* the film anymore than a single meaning is *in* the image. Similarly, the question "How does feminist film differ from experimental film?" is inappropriate here. This question tries to subtract apples from oranges. The experience of a film is quite distinct from the film itself. And, the experience of making a film is distinct from that film, as well. A filmmaker may bring a multiple perspective to her subject, but that does not insure the spectator will do so also.

This is not to say that the project of feminist filmmaking is futile, that the viewer will see what the viewer wants to see so why bother. On the contrary, we have already discussed the way culture contributes to the maintenance of a status quo ideology through the reflection/construction of the subject. We have also said that this relationship need not be inevitable and that the way to shatter this distorting mirror is through Critical Subjectivity—the encouragement of multiple perception and the effort to consciously address the ideological constructions. Certainly the viewer may resist these efforts, but at some level they may begin to resonate with the rest of her film viewing experiences. And the discussion of the film viewing experience—in texts like this, at film screenings, and among friends—can also trigger a new relationship to the cinema.

The chapters that follow are just such a discussion and it is my hope that they might trigger questions, multiple response, and a more active relationship to any film experience. Thus, I want to encourage an active relationship, on the part of the reader, with my text.

I recognize that my analysis of these films reflects my own personal, social, and political experience. In an attempt to encourage a Critical Subjectivity in my readers as they approach this text, and in myself as I receive their responses, I will here attempt to note some of the patterns and motives I observe in my analyses and in my style.[2] I want to call attention to the role I have played here as author.

To begin with, I use phrases like "to begin with" and "now let's look at . . ." I intend this attempt at a friendly, colloquialism in several ways. First, I hope to invite my readers into my argument, to lighten and humanize the tone when I can.

Second, I want to remind myself that I am writing *to* someone and not just for my own perusal; I want to remember to try to be clear and to avoid falling into a personal mythology and vo-cabulary. Finally, such transitions and asides encourage me in my writing and thinking process, perhaps because they give the sense of movement and logical progression. Much like narra-tive transitions in film, however, this sense of logical progres-sion is my own construct.

I also tend to use the first person plural pronoun a good deal and again, I do this for several reasons. For one, I find the ex-clusion of all personal pronouns not only false, but also stylis-tically cold. But the prolonged use of "I" often makes me un-comfortable; it feels solipsistic. A sense of audience is very important to me as I write and the use of "we" is a convenient fiction to that end. I do not intend this "we" as coercive, forc-ibly incorporating the reader into my text, but rather as an op-timistic invitation. I ask my readers to come along with me in my thinking for the next few pages, to try to see things from my perspective. But I fully expect that these readers will see my ideas from within their own perspectives, as well, encour-aging, again, an awareness of multiplicity.

As well, when referring to the film viewer, I regularly use the third person feminine pronouns—she and her. It would be easy, but not entirely accurate, to say that I use these pronouns in the generic sense, just as most communicators use the ge-neric "he." However, I believe that the common use of mas-culine pronouns has an impact on readers, an impact of exclu-sion. The female reader is not invited into the discourse except insofar as she is willing and able to identify herself with the masculine pronoun and with the exclusive company of men, nor is the male reader encouraged to see himself in the company of women as he approaches the text. Therefore, I intend my use of the feminine personal pronouns as an inclusive gesture, an explicit invitation to women readers, to enter into the text. I also hope to jar my readers, both male and female, into recognizing the "gap" in many texts—the absence of explicit reference to the female reader—by filling that gap. I recognize that, in using this strategy, I risk the alienation of those readers who may feel I am simply replicating and reversing an exclusionary tactic. I

believe the potential positive impact outweighs this risk, however, particularly in this context—that is, a text which emphasizes the recognition and validation of difference.

Finally, in my analyses themselves, I notice my tendency to
see thematic patterns and formal strategies as functioning in
more than one way. (Note my frequent use of apposition.) I read
things multiply, with multiple implications, perhaps account-
ing for my attraction to the theory I set out in the first part of
this text. I have difficulty excluding any perspective altogether,
although my preferences become apparent. I am attracted to
syntactical patterns such as: "Just as . . . is true, so is . . ." I
find myself struggling to communicate a simultaneity, a multiplicity of responses to a particular sequence or formal strategy.

Any reader of the following chapters would probably notice
some or all of these tendencies without my explicit reference to
them. I do so not merely to provide a key to my idiosyncracies
or personal style, but rather to encourage that kind of a reading. An awareness of the writer and her personal choices allows and encourages a more active and engaged reading, just
as an awareness of the filmmaker's hand detracts from the il-
lusionism of the cinema. And this awareness does not imply a
deficiency in the film or the written text so much as a recognition that to be an individual is to construct from and within a
particular context. This awareness, ideally, will lead to a broad-
ening of this context when possible and to an acceptance of the
existence of alternative contexts.

NOTES

1. Constance Penley, "The Avant-Garde and Its Imaginary," *Camera
Obscura: A Journal of Feminism and Film Theory,* no. 2, p. 25.
2. See chapter 1, note 4.

5

Márta Mészáros and *Women*: Learning to Accept Multiplicity

In his essay, "Narrative Space," Stephen Heath suggests that "a politically consequent materialism in film" today might be "work on the constructions and relations of meaning and subject in a specific signifying practice in a given socio-historical situation, a work that is then much less on 'codes' than on the operations of narrativization."[1] In other words, despite the "codes" that Heath himself pays lip service to in his rhetorical style, a politically "engaged" cinema will pay less attention to formal devices that seemingly exist autonomously and ahistorically *within* a film text, and will pay more attention to the way these devices interrelate with and color specific subject matter, and the way these devices and this subject matter is "read" by a specific, historically and politically situated audience.[2] This is a cinema that is very much concerned with and aware of its spectators, that is constructed less as a formal innovation and more as a catalyst for new and multiple interpretations and insights. As Constance Penley describes it, this is "less a work on 'codes' and 'perceptual processes' than it is on narrative, fiction and the construction of another subject-relation to the screen."[3] The cinema called for here by Heath and Penley allows room for a wide range of formal styles and methods of addressing the subject. In fact, Heath explains that:

As its most effectively critical, moreover, [this] work may well bear little resemblance to what in the given situation is officially acknowl-

edged and defined as 'avant-garde;' in particular, and in the context of the whole account offered here of film and space, it may well involve an action at the limits of narrative within the narrative film, at the limits of its fictions of unity.[4]

Following this prescription for a "politically consequent materialism in film," a film practice that engages its audience through forms of narrative, let us turn our attention to the 1977 feature film, *Women* (or *The Two of Them*), directed by the Hungarian filmmaker, Márta Mészáros. In accord with Stephen Heath's prediction, this film has never been seen as a part of the cinema avant-garde. In fact, Amy Taubin wrote in 1978: "Formally, the film is not of particular interest. It is socialist realism, but a delicate and subtle working of that form."[5] And yet socialist realism, with its implications of an objective representation of verifiable "reality" and of a single meaning that is easily accessible, is grossly inadequate as a categorization for this film.[6] Despite her apparent reliance on narrative structure and the absence of jarringly disruptive formalist strategies, Mészáros has assembled a film that is quietly subversive. Her film is based, structurally, thematically, and to a lesser degree, formally, on the breakdown or loss of order, not in the service of a despairing anarchy—although the film is steeped in a mood of sadness—but as a suggestion of new roles, new and multiple relations that might exist within, between and among her characters. In his recent book, *The Altering Eye—Contemporary International Cinema*, Robert Kolker characterizes today's Hungarian filmmakers with the following: "Their films provide one way of examining the possible conjoining of areas of experience—the subjective and the political—that in Western film are usually kept distinct."[7] In this film, Mészáros dismantles political, social, familial, and personal structures in order that this overlapping of "conjoining of areas of experience" may occur.

In the following chapters, I try to emphasize the cinematic strategies feminist filmmakers have used to encourage multiple readings of a particular film text and a dual consciousness in the individual spectator.[8] Obviously, despite a filmmaker's attempt to stimulate such a active and constructive spectatorship—or perhaps more accurately, due to the degree to which

any viewer already constructs her viewing experiences to suit her particular needs and defenses—the filmmaker has no ultimate control over the film each audience member "sees."[9] Discussions of film form, however, can be dangerously misleading in this regard. Because, for instance, I am describing an observable manipulation of the film camera or an observable editing decision, and because such formal choices are not credited with the emotional and identificatory charge that film characters and their narrative worlds are assigned, my observations appear to be somehow "objective" and less personally problematic. Now there are many reasons why this is a false interpretation. Foremost of these is the way in which a particular culture within a particular historical moment develops its own ideologically determined 'ways of seeing;' Bill Nichols writes of this phenomenon:

We have discussed how perception comprehends the physical world in a habitual manner that can be called a way of seeing . . . we have spoken of the construction of images as a representation of a way of seeing as well. Photographic images of films that reproduce many of the perceptual cues used in encountering the physical world, or correlates of them—images within the vast stream of style known as realism—place before us an objectified token or trace of the very categories of meaning we initially constructed . . . the habitual or coded nature of perception obscures our own active role in perception.[10]

Thus, to the degree that our perceptions are ideologically determined, they are not "objective." On the other hand, to the degree that an individual's perceptions, within her cultural context, are colored by her own personality and experience, by her "identity theme," they also are *not* "objective."[11] Finally, if the viewer identifies herself with the camera and its placement, there are times when the film suture may be rent apart, when the spectator herself may refuse to assume the offered point of view.[12]

In light of this clarification, an analysis of film content (to the extent that it can be separated from film form), is more easily recognized as the construction of a particular critic and his or her individual preoccupations and perceptive abilities. Thus, of all the film discussions offered here, my reading of Mészáros'

Women may be the most recognizably personal and the easiest with which to argue. In these ways, it is also most clearly in alignment with the call for self-proclaimedly individual film analyses as a stimulus to multiplicity of perception and the development of Critical Subjectivity. With all this in mind, I will proceed to my discussion of *Women*.

I stated earlier that Mészáros' film is based on the breakdown or loss of order, be it through external changes or internal recognitions. This theme, the loss of order, can be read as the most banal of potential premises. For example, Archer Winsten writes for the *New York Post*: " 'Women'. . . is a Hungarian film, directed by a woman, Márta Mészáros, and dealing with two women and their troubled marriages. . . . The picture investigates the emotional turmoil stirred up by a drunk and does it extremely well." And John Dodd writes for the *Edmonton Journal*: "Mészáros's *Women* deals honestly . . . with the joys and disappointments of the search for human warmth in a modern industrial society."[13] Or it can be read as an unsettling, open-ended and painfully comprehensive critique of social and personal relations. As you have probably guessed, I see the film as the latter, and although my examination of its content and themes will yield this interpretation, it is the film's technique and primarily, its overall structure that, for me, require such an analysis.

Women is constructed of situations and circumstances that may easily be mistaken for the over-used and over-determined plot devices of cinematic attempts at commom denominator emotionality: a married woman's mid-life crisis; an inattentive husband who takes his wife for granted; the destruction an alcoholic causes within his marriage; unfulfilling work situations; the child who gets lost in the shuffle of the parents' marital struggles. In fact, the film opens with perhaps the most significant and yet the most potentially misleading of these emotional frameworks.

One morning, Mari arrives at the women's work hostel where she is supervisor, only to receive a cablegram from her husband, summoning her home. Already viewers are primed for an "event of significance." Mészáros has gradually built up to this moment. The film has opened with a long, hazy shot of

the hostel where Mari works. She first appears, a small, dark, indistinct shape walking toward the glass doors of the institution. Mészáros cuts to a close-up of a woman's face, looking left, and then to Mari entering from the left. As the two women begin to talk, beginning an interview on their feet, the camera stays with them and follows them into the hostel's interior. All this has followed fairly standard cinematic style, allowing the effacement of the camera's presence and encouraging the viewer to focus on the women and their progress through the interior space. Things begin to become more complicated now, however, as more and more women, all workers, begin to appear. The camera holds back a bit, allowing Mari and her interviewee to be seen, moving into the group of women who are entering from all directions. Mészáros creates the sense of life and work in process, as the solitary and indistinct silhouette that was Mari is pulled immediately into this work day world. At this point, however, the camera moves in closer to Mari as the cablegram is delivered. The interviewee keeps talking at Mari, making demands, and other women continue to move around and behind her, but Mészáros is closing in on Mari. Her habitually self-composed expression begins to take on a new suggestiveness as she reads the cable. We, as viewers, are not allowed to see its contents. Mészáros has led our attention from the long, establishing shot to close-up, focusing our interest on Mari and then drawing us into her crowded, everyday world. The anticipation and suspense that surround the cable and the disruption it causes in the sequence-in-process create a specific expectation in the viewer. Accustomed as we are to the narrative gimmick, the single event selected by the writer or the filmmaker to serve as a kind of objective correlative or an emotional watershed, we *expect* that the cable is the harbinger of the film's emotional catalyst.

With all these expectations, we follow Mari home by train. The news we learn there is everything a critic could have hoped for dramatically. Mari arrives home to her husband, Feri, and her grown daughter and son, to learn that her mother has died. The death of Mari's mother, rife with emotional and psychological implications, is a shadow that will hang over our viewing and analysis of this film, particularly after the expectations

Mészáros has quietly developed. What fascinates me about Mészáros' film, however, is that although I can read this death in the most obvious and unrevealing ways as the motivating event or the catalytic plot device in *Women*, the truth is that I did not do so until after the fact. Actually, every move Mari makes in the film—her maternal role toward Juli, the young, rebellious worker; her questioning of her husband and her marriage; her conflicts of authority at the hostel; her increased awareness of her own sexuality; her fear of growing older; and her reluctance to quit her job and move back home—could be interpreted as part of her reaction to her mother's death. Mészáros even tempts us to this analysis by privileging this death through its position in the narrative.

And yet, Mari makes sense in this film, without the fact of her mother's death. In fact, one of Mészáros' strengths (not only in this film but also in *Nine Months* and *Adoption*) is her capacity for suggesting the emotional and intellectual interiority of her women characters; they become self-creating individuals, autonomous to the degree that any human being can be autonomous. Mészáros accomplishes this in a variety of ways. At the most obvious level, she films narratives centered around women characters and their experiences. Although in this film she follows the experiences of two women, two men and a girl child, her most emphatic focus is clearly on the women and in particular, Mari. And yet, Mészáros' method in encouraging this focus is distinctive and significant. She does not privilege the experiences and realities of her female characters in the traditional way. Dominant cinematic practice might enlist the viewers' identification and emotional investment by means of the shot-reverse shot pattern. We would be allowed to see what the character sees, thereby joining our experience and sense of an event with that of this character; we would be offered a ready-made interpretation of the event and, due to our emotional identification with the character, we would be more likely to accept this character's viewpoint. Mészáros has a different set of aims; rather than encouraging us to identify with her characters, to blend our perspectives with the characters' perspectives, she wants us to *look at* and *into* her characters, to learn to

understand them, to sympathize with them, but nevertheless to respect their autonomy, their separateness from us.

Mészáros achieves this through her camera patterns. Her film progresses through dialogue, by means of conversation, rather than physical action. And although Mészáros has a knack for capturing the expressive detail and the characteristic gesture, she focuses primarily on faces. Still, these are no "talking heads." She brings her camera close as her characters speak, eliminating all distractions or extraneous particulars. She focuses tightly and then she holds. Rather than flashing back and forth to catch every reaction shot, to instill a sensation of continuing action or movement, to remind constantly that this character is only acting/talking in response to another character, Mészáros allows her speaker to think, to work through an idea or an emotion. It is not that Mészáros is denying that her characters exist *in relation to* other characters; at careful intervals she will punctuate her extended close-ups with brief full shots, establishing the characters physicality, their proximity, and their "narrative space." In fact, these full shots are often carefully choreographed to reveal concretely the emotional and social dynamics of an encounter; Amy Taubin describes this as Mészáros' "psychological dynamizing of space" and gives examples of these

very brief long shots in which a dramatic and complex relationship between two characters is drawn in just a few seconds through the placement of their bodies in a space and through one or two gestures. In one of these scenes, the two women undress for the first time in the same room and the strength of the curiosity about and fascination with another woman's body is revealed in about three seconds. In another, Mari is left lying alone on the floor after unsuccessful lovemaking with her husband and the sense of abandonment is almost palpable.[14]

These brief shots remind us of her characters' social and personal context, and yet with her prolonged close-ups, Mészáros manages to preserve and communicate the sense of their discreteness, their individual identities that are not simply a response to this particular encounter but rather a product of many encounters, many influences over a period of time. Mészáros

allows her characters, particularly her women characters, a *history*. They exist not only in reaction shots, but as coherent beings; in an interview in *Hungarofilm*, Mészáros herself said: "It's people's inner world, above all else, that I'm interested in."[15]

In a discussion of "The look," Annette Kuhn writes of Laura Mulvey and

her argument that, as far as the look is concerned, the element of spectacle in dominant cinema may at times work against the flow of the narrative by halting it in favour of moments of erotic contemplation of the image; and that, as representation, woman may often operate on the side of spectacle and therefore constitute a potential disturbance to the spectator's voyeuristic/narcissistic identification. The assumption here is either that the spectator is male or—a more complex position—that cinematic address works to constitute the spectator as such.[16]

Mészáros, with her full face close-ups, constructs just the kind of image that may "work against the flow of the narrative," and yet these images are not the eroticized, fetishised close-ups of which Kuhn writes: "In classic cinema, the woman-image is typically fetishised both by means of lingering close-ups which, through interrupting the flow of the narrative, constitute woman as spectacle, and also by means of the glamorous costumes, make-up, settings and lighting surrounding female stars."[17] Mészáros eschews this latter; Marina Vlady, who plays Mari, talks of *Women* in an interview with Dan Yakir:

I try to find films—and this is partly why Marta's film is so important to me—that enable me to lift the mask, remove everything that is the attribute of seduction in the cinema: make-up, costumes. We accentuated the harsh light to show me as a tired woman. . . . It's very difficult to achieve this, because most people aren't prepared to face themselves as they are in real life. There is such a strong cinematic tradition that idealizes people.[18]

As for the "lingering close-ups which . . . constitute woman as spectacle," Mészáros has found her antidotes. For one, her close-ups frequently occur during conversations—long, reflective conversations—and "spectacles" do not talk. Mészáros gives

her women *language*. And when she offers the image of a silent woman, it is invariably at a point in the narrative when this character is confronting an intense emotional experience, a point when we, as spectators, are likely to be most concerned with what she is thinking and feeling and what she is seeing, rather than with our looking at her. Which brings us back to the death of Mari's mother, one occasion of such silent close-ups and the point from which we began this rather lengthy digression.

The preceding paragraphs have been an attempt to analyze how Mészáros manages to thwart the schematic significance of Mari's mother's death in her film's narrative. I have noted that although Mari's behavior and motivations within the film can be seen as part of a clear and predictable reaction to this death, Mészáros allows this behavior to make sense, to reflect an intricate and self-creating identity apart from this obvious emotional catalyst. The effect Mészáros achieves here is to complicate her subject matter, to give it multiple contexts. At the level of personal psychology, Mari's discontent can be read as her effort to readjust her sense of her own identity now that the role of daughter has been taken from her. But at a social and political level, her discontent and her dissatisfaction with her marriage is rooted in an emotional (and later an intellectual) recognition of the inadequacy of the role she, as woman/wife/mother, is expected to fill. Mészáros wants her film to cut both ways—personally and politically. If we read the film only at the level of personal psychology, Mari's pain is trivialized into "mid-life crisis." On the other hand, if we read *Women* only as a social and political critique, we miss all the subtle complicities Mészáros explores, the way a character's personal and emotional life must enter just the right conjunction with her social and political position before she can recognize the tacit lies and the unstated oppression in which she is participating.

Mészáros' construction of multiple contexts for her characters and her subject matter serves to encourage in her viewers the Critical Subjectivity discussed in chapter 1 of this text and in chapter 4:

A woman may begin to form a subjectivity for herself when she sees the gap between herself and the version of woman society reflects back

to her, and when she stops trying to unite with this distorted reflection. The development of this critical subjectivity relies upon the perception of contradiction, and therefore this project is in opposition to a world view or an art "Disposed to see things as a whole." . . . Accepting Althusser's hypothesis, that our points of view are created by the ideology in which and through which we exist, we must still recognize that these points of view will differ according to our position with that ideology and that our position will vary according to context.[19]

Mészáros illustrates this Critical Subjectivity by constructing a narrative that, when analyzed schematically, offers a wholly consistent if somewhat predictable interpretation, and by simultaneously employing formal strategies that deflect our attention from this schematic reading, encouraging us to see and feel personalities at work in her film, personalities that transcend the inexorability of the narratives in which they are situated.

And Mészáros further thwarts the spectator "disposed to see things as a whole"[20] by providing yet another context through which to read the significance of the death of Mari's mother. I have already suggested that Mészáros constructs her film around the breakdown or loss of order; Mészáros herself, describing the inspiration for this film, explained: "I did have an idea—or rather, I was curious to find out just what it is that holds a family together. Once the regular, accustomed relationships between people cease."[21] Mészáros, in this interview and in her film, makes apparent the obvious sources of upheaval in Mari and Feri's marriage: her decision to return to work (a decision made "before" the film's action begins); Feri's business assignment in Mongolia, necessitating a long absence; perhaps even the fact that their children are grown and leaving home. Unstated, but perhaps equally or more significant, is the effect the death of Mari's mother has on *Feri*. Through references and conversational comments, without ever showing us the family situation, Mészáros has suggested an order that existed before this death. We know Mari's mother helped out at home, but perhaps more significantly for Feri, she was a womanly and maternal presence there. With her loss, his world is imbalanced; he needs Mari to fill this gap. Simply by juxtaposing

events, without overtly calling attention to these possibilities, Mészáros suggests the fragility of this familial balance. Feri participates in its disruption as much as Mari, through his assumptions and his needs.

This discussion of the multiple significances of the mother's death in Mészáros' film has perhaps suggested some of her concern with the personal and social dynamics of familial relationship. In fact, each of the orders that is threatened within this film is an example or parody of family patterns: Mari and Feri's marriage; the family unit of Juli, Janos, and their daughter, Zsuzsi; the hierarchy of authority in Mari's work hostel. In each of these cases, characters find themselves incapable of filling the roles that are expected of them. Mari cannot be the mother/housekeeper that Feri expects and he cannot accept her new independence. Juli and Janos are alternately dependent upon and resentful of the child/parent relations they act out with each other. In his bouts of drinking, Janos plays the foolish child to Juli's long-suffering maternity. In their sexual relations, they both are children who cannot resist, but after intercourse, Janos carries the sleepy Juli to her bed and tucks her in, the fatherly chasteness of his actions reinforced by the fact that Juli, unable to cope with his alcoholism any longer, is staying with Mari while Janos returns home alone. Unexpectedly, however, after tucking her in and speaking fondly of her child-like qualities to Mari, Janos begins to angrily denounce her deception and infidelity. Dependent as he is upon her, he resents the necessary fact of her autonomy. Similarly, Juli and Janos both find themselves incapable of filling the parental role they expect of themselves, ostensibly for the sake of their child, Zsuzsi. When the three of them attend a dance at the worker's hostel, Juli forces an insincere smile, explaining to Janos that Zsuzsi likes to see them happy together. As she says this, the camera that has framed the two of them in a medium close-up pans downward to reveal Zsuzsi, embracing the lower torsos of both her parents, looking ahead abstractedly with the hint of a quiet smile about her lips. This abrupt shift in perspectives, in point of view, shoves the viewer into another attitude toward this couple. Their transparency becomes all the more tragic. At other times, Juli runs away from the drunken Janos, leaving Zsuzsi to watch his

pain, or Janos, unable to cope, leaves Zsuzsi at the hostel for Juli. Neither of them are quite able to hold the family structure together, but, in fits and starts, they try to preserve the facade—a facade in which Zsuzsi, of course, can no longer believe. Finally, relations among the women at the workers' hostel follow the patterns and the "pecking order" of sibling rivalry in a large family. The women have a common background; they were all poor village girls. As some of them—Mari's assistant, the party inspectors—begin to work their way into the hierarchy of authority, they assimilate the prejudices of their new colleagues and try to distance themselves from an origin of which they are ashamed. They treat the other workers, their charges, with an inflexibility and lack of empathy that springs from their own resentment of past slights, much as older siblings visit their suffering upon the younger. Mari, attempting to supervise these women with more gentleness and less rigidity, reminds the authorities of their common backgrounds, calling for a family model within the hostel. The irony is that the conflicts that exist already *do* follow the patterns of familial relations; the order Mari calls for is simply an ideal—one that does not exist in any of the actual families we explore in the film.

Thus, the breakdown of order that Mészáros examines is that of an *assumed* order, an "ideal" order her characters have posited for themselves as a model (or rather they have learned this order). She reveals the failure to achieve this order in Mari and Feri's established relationship, in Juli and Janos' newer marriage, and as well, in the State's attempt to provide its own version of a home for the hostel workers. In each case, the conflicts develop when characters attempt to force themselves or others to assume the roles dictated by the form—the "ideal" order they expect of themselves. Mari wants Feri to be her lover. Feri wants Mari to live up to his idea of the wife and mother. Janos wants to find the success and satisfaction in his work that he believes to be his due. Juli wants Janos to exemplify the responsibility and discipline she expects of a husband and father. Both of them pretend to be a family, "for the sake of" the child. The supervisors at the hostel want to distance themselves from a background and identity they resent, by distancing themselves from the women who share their roots.

On the other hand, the relationships that work in this film exist outside the familiar order. Mari's friendship with Juli is, of course, the major example of this. Their relationship defies all expectations; they seemingly have very little in common. There is no place for such an intense friendship between two married women; they are supposed to devote their lives, their time, to their families. But beyond this, they are from different generations; they are worker and manager; and most significantly, they appear utterly dissimilar in personality. Mészáros describes them thus:

Mari is fortyish, still attractive, a woman with confidence and poise whose life is well-ordered: . . . Juli, an irregular, erratic person who lives a scandal-ridden life and seems to have a peculiar capacity for messing things up. . . . The two women couldn't be more dissimilar in character. One is blonde, largely built, a sedate, level-headed person; the other, a petite brunette, taut, a tense, strange soul.[22]

Still, even though there is no familiar model for their relationship, or perhaps because there is no pattern of expectations, these two women manage to offer each other a varied kind of interaction.

Initially, Mari and Juli confront each other at the hostel, Mari wearing her authority uncomfortably and Juli well-defended in her armor of hard rebelliousness. They argue in Mari's office over Zsuzsi: Mari explains that children are against the hostel regulations while Juli points out she has no other place to go. In anger and frustration, the two of them lash out at each other: Mari stands firmly on the rules; Juli taunts "You're all like that;" Mari orders her out of the office, punctuating her demand with a shove that emphasizes the difference in stature between the two. Mészáros uses her camera as if it were her sensibility in this scene; the camera backs away, in contrast to the familiar full face close-ups, as the women begin to assume the typical roles of manager and worker, parental authority and child. They have ceased to see the actual individual before them, seeing instead a role, a pattern of behavioral expectations. The camera remains high and distant as Mari pushes Juli out the door; it pans around to follow their movement from this high angle,

subtly suggesting a shifting ground and space. At this moment when Mészáros' two characters most closely exemplify the order of the worker/manager relationship, the enforcement of hostel regulations, her camera comes up "TILT," suggesting imbalance and upheaval. As soon as Mari closes the door upon Juli, however, she leans against it, as a child might listen through the door of her parent's room. The camera moves in closely and Mari opens the door, revealing the sobbing Juli. Mari, throwing away all regulations, invites Juli and Zsuzsi to share her apartment with her, and the camera returns once again to *its* familiar order of facial close-ups. The two women exchange shy and tearful smiles.

In this scene, Mészáros has dramatized the existing "order," the roles Mari and Juli are expected to play—expect themselves to play—within the hostel. And through her camera movements and her character development, Mészáros establishes that these roles are inadequate. In fact, the scene's resolution, its restored order, is based upon a totally irregular situation—a situation against the regulations, against the characters' expectations and against ours. This new order or relationship between the two women follows no set pattern. Mari often seems a maternal figure for Juli, providing her with a temporary home, protecting her from other hostel authorities, encouraging her to take responsibility for her marriage and her child. Juli, for her part, plays the child to Mari's concern, sullenly refusing to see Janos, exacerbating her situation in the hostel by playing insulting pranks on her superiors. On the other hand, when Mari becomes drunk and upset after Feri stands her up at the hostel party, Juli takes control, arranging for Mari's train ride home; Mészáros offers a lovely and telling image of the two of them huddled together in the warm glow of the night train's artificial lighting, Mari curled under Juli's arm, her head at Juli's breast. Similarly, there are times when Juli's personal and emotional honesty and daring set her up as the older woman's teacher, stirring thoughts and feelings in Mari that she never allowed herself before. Finally, there is an eroticism between the two women, an unself-conscious affection and physicality that neither character needs to acknowledge verbally. The strength, vitality, and stability of their relationship—its "order"—spring from

the fact that they play multiple roles for each other, all roles for each other. Mari and Juli still experience conflict, but these conflicts do not carry the weight of guilt and resentment for unfulfilled patterns of expectations. Mészáros continues to emphasize, with her dialogue, her juxtapositions and her framing, the familial patterns within relationship: mother/daughter, daughter/mother, siblings, lovers. She posits, however, in Mari and Juli's relationship the release from fixed expectations and the affirmation of multiplicity. This multiplicity exists in each relationship she examines, but only with Mari and Juli does it go unresented and is it given free rein.

Within the narrative of her film, therefore, Mészáros suggests the restraints and the hypocrisies required within traditional family structures, and she emphasizes the salutary vitality of relationships that exist outside of these traditional structures, allowing for flexible and multiple modes of interaction. Turning from this thematic analysis now, at the structural level of her film, Mészáros also emphasizes the need to question assumed interpretations and to allow for multiple, even contradictory perspectives on experience. Annette Kuhn, writing of Realist women's film, has written: "As dominant cinema, their realism rests on the credibility of texts which construct identifications for the spectator on the levels of character and narrative, within a fictional world constituted as coherent and internally consistent."[23] Mészáros, certainly not an avantgarde filmmaker, appears to partake of this category described by Kuhn. She does question the "coherent" and "consistent" world order of her characters, but from *within* a "coherent" narrative. Seemingly, an awareness of this film as a construct, even an ideological construct, must come from the awareness and active attitude of its viewers. Despite the camera sensibility we have discussed, the unusual use of prolonged close-ups and brief, choreographed full shots, the film's over-all impression is one of realism; these formal strategies are quiet, subtle. Yet Mészáros has constructed a finale for her film that openly addresses the film's construction of a consistent world perspective by suddenly, jarringly throwing the narrative into a new frame.

The film has been quietly, sadly working its way to a de-

nouement: Feri has left for Mongolia and Mari, resolutely, continues to work at the hostel, two decisions that imply the end of their marriage; Juli, Zsuzsi, and Mari have settled in together at the hostel and Janos, after yet another violent bout of drinking, has finally committed himself to an institutional "cure." Mari and Zsuzsi have gone to visit Janos after Juli stubbornly, tearfully, and painfully has refused. The scene at the hospital is graphic and appalling: vacant looking men are forced to undergo aversion therapy and Janos, hurt by Juli's absence and painfully aware of his own circumstances, lashes out at Mari, borrowing all his ugly insults from the traditional "order"—men's resentment of their own dependence upon women, a misogyny born of the oedipal conflict. Despite Mari's orders, Zsuzsi has wandered through the hospital and has seen her father, crying disconsolately and being sedated. When the two return to a worried Juli at the hostel, Mari attempts to soothe her friend, insisting that everything is all right. At this point, with everything winding down to a quiet if despairing close, Zsuzsi begins to scream—Zsuzsi who has spoken almost not at all throughout the film and who has been an ever present, if easily ignored, observer. She is suddenly given a voice and at Mari's assurance that all is fine, she screams: "It's not true! Nothing is true! You all lie!" If we have been talking about orders subverted, perspectives limited, and communication attempted across the barriers of expectation and traditional roles, then Mészáros has been leading up to Zsuzsi's scream—but so quietly, so delicately that it shocks us, shakes us loose from the consistent perspective we have been developing. The appearance of order, new or old, is shattered by a scream that retrospectively privileges the child's perspective and throws into question the balances we were constructing through Mari and Juli's relationship. Mészáros is affirming nothing if not complexity, and the child's sudden accusation does not make the selection of a truth any easier. In fact, it makes us conscious of the perspectives we have developed through the film and also of the existence of perspectives we have overlooked. Mészáros' conclusion is very clever; it pulls us out of the narrative perspective, the point of view, we have assimilated without pulling us out of the film entirely. She manages to incorporate her

multiple perspectives and dual consciousness into the narrative structure. As viewers, we are pushed to an awareness of the complexity of her story and the inadequacy of any one version, and yet, unlike much of the film avant-garde, Mészáros does not shove us right out of the film. She still allows us a "content," albeit a complex and indefinite one.

Finally, through this film conclusion, Mészáros not only adds an entirely new dimension or perspective upon women's narrative; she also disrupts the order she herself has constructed—that is, a narrative focused upon and through the experience of Juli and Mari. But just as Mészáros reveals the patterns of sibling rivalry and child/parent dependency in all her characters' interactions, not to eliminate these patterns but rather to eliminate our *denial* of them—so Mészáros confronts Mari's perspective, for example with Zsuzsi's, not to supplant the former entirely, but rather to allow an awareness of multiplicity in the characters' experience and that of the viewer. Thus, Mészáros' brand of cinematic realism does not forsake Critical Subjectivity through the construction of a "fictional world constituted as coherent and internally consistent." Rather she asks for the development of a Critical Subjectivity, not only in her viewers but in her characters as well.

NOTES

1. Stephen Heath, "Narrative Space," *Questions of Cinema* (Bloomington, Indiana: Indiana University Press, 1981), p. 64.

2. Lillian S. Robinson, "Dwelling in Decencies: Radical Criticism and the Feminist Perspective," *Sex, Class and Culture* (Bloomington, Indiana: Indiana University Press, 1978), p. 3.

3. Constance Penley, "The Avant-Garde and Its Imaginary," *Camera Obscura: A Journal of Feminism and Film Theory*, no. 2, p. 25.

4. Heath, "Narrative Space," p. 64.

5. Amy Taubin,"Womenfriends," *The Soho Weekly News* (September 7, 1978).

6. See Lee Baxandall, ed., *Radical Perspective in the Arts* (New York: Penguin, 1972).

7. Robert Phillip Kolker, *The Altering Eye—-Contemporary International Cinema* (Oxford: Oxford University Press, 1983), p. 324.

8. See chapter 4 of this text for discussion following note 19.

9. Norman N. Holland, *Poems in Persons: An Introduction to the Psychoanalysis of Literature* (New York: W. W. Norton & Company, 1973), pp. 47–50.

10. Bill Nichols, *Ideology and the Image: Social Representation in the Cinema and Other Media* (Bloomington, Indiana: Indiana University Press, 1981), p. 35.

11. Holland, *Poems in Persons*, pp. 47–50.

12. "The Apparatus: An Introduction by Bertrand Augst" and "The Apparatus" by Jean-Louis Baudry, *Camera Obscura: A Journal of Feminism and Film Theory*, no. 1, pp. 97–126. There are times when the spectator may actively prevent herself from being incorporated or "sutured" into the film text: I have refused "suture" in the "Slasher" films when I am encouraged to assume the point of view of the killer.

13. Archer Winsten, " 'Women' Looks at Marriages Gone Bad," *New York Post* (October 6, 1977) and John Dodd, "Film's 'Socialist Realism,' a Pleasant Change," *Edmonton Journal* (February 15, 1980), p. C–12.

14. Taubin, *The Soho Weekly News* (September 7, 1978).

15. " 'Mary and Julie' and Márta Mészáros," *Hungarofilm* (1977), 2 Bulletin, p. 18.

16. Annette Kuhn, *Women's Pictures: Feminism and Cinema* (London: Routledge & Kegan Paul, 1982), p. 61.

17. Ibid.

18. Dan Yakir, "Coming of Age," *The Soho Weekly News* (September 7, 1978).

19. See chapter 1 of this text, for discussion following footnote 24.

20. Andre Bazin, *What Is Cinema? Volume II*, ed. trans. Hugh Gray (Berkeley: University of California Press, 1971), p. 97.

21. " 'Mary and Julie' and Márta Mészáros," p. 15.

22. Ibid., p. 13.

23. Kuhn, *Women's Pictures*, p. 136.

6

Helke Sander's *Redupers*:
Personality-In-Process

It is difficult to begin talking about Helke Sander's 1977 film, *The All-Round Reduced Personality ("Redupers")*, without also talking about the novelist and essayist, Christa Wolf. Wolf, living and working in the German Democratic Republic (GDR), provides Sander's film with both a framework or context for its themes, and also an argument or challenge by which to define itself.

Much of Wolf's writing centers around the difficult and unending but, for her, very necessary effort of self-definition, or more properly, self-construction. We can see this effort reflected in the very titles of her works: *The Quest for Christa T.,* "Self-Experiment," "Interview with Myself," "Diary—Aid to Work and Memory," to name a few.[1] Her long essay, "The Reader and the Writer," is a painfully and painstakingly honest, yet purposive effort to reexamine, redefine and reaffirm the usefulness, and in fact the necessity, of prose writing. After an exploration of the supposed "death of writing" and an introspective analysis of the potential truth or falseness of experience presented in the written text, Wolf arrives at the need for an "epic prose" that:

> has the courage to think of itself as an instrument, sharp, accurate, attacking, changing, to be used as a means, not as an end in itself. . . . Epic prose should be a genre which undertakes to penetrate along paths not yet traveled into the innermost parts of this individual, the reader of prose. . . . The voice of another person, in prose,

can reach this region, it can be touched and opened up by language, not in order to gain control of it, but to set free spiritual forces[2]

This definition of epic prose can serve as an effective guide for the reading and analysis of Wolf's own writing. Her writing is, in its form and content, a "quest for Christa Wolf." In fact, she closes her analysis of the nature and uses of prose with the assertion and the hope that "It [prose] helps mankind to become conscious subjects."[3] This working toward self-recognition and self-realization can work its way into a narrow, self-absorbed and self-protective individualism, or it can work toward the development of Critical Subjectivity, an awareness that her "innermost" Self is distinct, a synthesis of all her experiences and thoughts, and that this very distinctness suggests a similar unique validity for every other Self.[4] Wolf writes that prose "should be incorruptible in its insistence on the one and only experience and not violate the experience of others; but it should give them the courage of their own experiences."[5].

This purpose puts Wolf in accord with the analysis of subjectivity and the goals of a feminist aesthetic we discussed in chapters 1 and 4. And, it also provides us with a key or a way into Helke Sander's *Redupers*. Sander's film is, in many ways, an effort to recognize and construct a Self for its main character, Edda Chiemnyjewski (and, to whatever extent the film is autobiographic, for its maker, Helke Sander[6]). As well, we shall see that the film's form, its pattern of "exposition," bears a strong resemblance to Wolf's style. And finally, Sander herself punctuates her film with quotations, spoken and read, from Wolf's essays.

In addition, however, to the aspects of form and theme which author shares with filmmaker, Wolf also provides Sander with a challenge. Wolf's defense and even celebration of prose writing comes at the expense of the film medium. If through prose we can imitate and carry through an exploration and interrogation of our deepest selves, an exploration whose findings and whose categories will be constantly shifting as we continue to discover that the foundations of our selves are false bottoms, that the very act of looking alters and expands the selves there are to see—if prose can do all this, Wolf feels that film, on the

contrary, can only show one scene at a time, that it simplifies, universalizes, and concretizes all the multiply and wonderfully faceted experience that prose can uncover. For Wolf, film is the medium of "miniatures," the neatly finished versions of our experience that we carry and exchange so that we may feel safe and in control of our pasts:

At one time one was afraid to touch them [one's memories], afraid of burning one's fingers on them; now they are cool and smooth, some of them artistically polished, some especially valuable bits have cost years of work, for one must forget a great deal and rethink and reinterpret a great deal before one can see oneself in the best light everywhere and at all times. . . . But we are in the habit of calling it "remembering" when we show people these prettily made pieces of arts and crafts and call them genuine, so that they can show their market value and measure up with the other pieces on show; and *the more like these others they are the more genuine they are said to be* (emphasis mine).[7]

There are really two criticisms here of the process of miniature-making we call remembering and, by Wolf's analogy, of film: Wolf criticizes first the freezing of experience, cutting it off from the continuum and the changes in our lives and our perceptive processes; and second, she criticizes the universalizing of experience and emotion. She believes that prose can express a continuum of experience, a strand of continually self-correcting and self-expanding representation that can simultaneously present and distinguish the time of the experience described, the time of the writer's narrative process, and the time of the reader's reading: Wolf's prose "overcomes the dichotomy of realism and modernism by bridging the gap between experience in the world and experience in literary language. It overcomes the dichotomy of narrator and narration by differentiating the various modes of temporal experience."[8] In addition, she believes that prose can express an individuality so unique, so distinct, so uncompromising, that rather than read ourselves into it, we as readers will be encouraged to see the variations and lines of our *own* selves. And for Wolf, the film camera cannot allow for this continual re-evaluation and redefinition of Self; it cannot present an individual so distinct and deeply felt that we cannot incorporate it into our own fantasies of Self. Film, like our min-

iatures, is too finished and concrete; an image projected is an image remembered and believed. And film is too physically compelling; once we enter and scene we are unwilling to let the boundaries or the colors shift. We cannot go beyond this projected presence to find the emotional absences. Or so Christa Wolf argues, finally charging that "prose should try to be unfilmable."[9]

Now when Helke Sander adapts Christa Wolf's thematic and formal concerns to film, she cannot help but come face to face with Wolf's reservations and critique of the cinematic medium. In the following discussion, however, we will see that Sander has developed film equivalents for many of Wolf's prose techniques. And where Wolf uses the metaphor and example of cinematic limitations to delineate and celebrate the uses and necessity of prose writing, Sander rather incorporates prose passages from Wolf and other writers into her film, allowing the sum of these parts to equal a greater whole. Finally, where Wolf's writing is marked by an intelligent idealism and a moving purposiveness, Sander's film is colored rather by a quiet irony that although no less creative in its form, seems a bit more skeptical? more patient? with regard to its ultimate influence.

In her essay, "Female Narration, Women's Cinema: Helke Sander's *The All-Round Reduced Personality/Redupers*," Judith Mayne finds the film's center to be the construction of a female subject. She sees this work as a process of integration, of drawing connections between disparate voices and situations, and finally of distillation: she concludes that the film ends when "our perception of the public sphere of Berlin has been transformed, from the flat anonymity of a tracking shot to a still image representing depth; from the proliferation of voices to the single female voice that analyzes and reflects."[10] Although this description of movement from surfaces into depth, or from the "public sphere" to the "space of fiction," clarifies Sander's film, I see the pattern of "exposition" as more complex. Rather than this purposive movement from surface to depth, the film's movement is a continual alternation between the two. It shifts from movement in time, or a temporal continuum, to movement into space, or depth—and then it shifts back again. Sander creates a continual vacillation between these two *kinds of pro-*

gression (rather than between two realms, as Mayne suggests), and neither has meaning without the other. This pattern of progression is remarkably consistent with the process we find in Christa Wolf's prose. Her writing flows as if in a stream of consciousness, picking up pieces of the writer's "present" experience, of her past, of dreams and associations, and then it pauses or hovers when these bits of experience and thought collect around an idea or a question. At these moments, she "dives," to use her own metaphor, and tries to plumb the depths of this particular concept.[11] Wolf uses this method of writing not because she naively thinks it best "captures" the experience of "reality," but rather because she recognizes it as a *tool* for probing and creating the experience of Self. Sander uses this method in much the same way and, what's more, the shifting perspectives built into it encourage the perception of multiplicity, and of commonality and particularity we have linked with a feminist aesthetic.

Let us begin our discussion of *Redupers* by setting the scene. Edda Chiemnyjewski (played by Sander herself) is a free lance photographer and a mother, living in West Berlin. She is a member of a group of women photographers and she is politically aware. The closest thing to plot development or standard narrative focus that we find in the film is the city officials' selection of Edda's photography group to do a sort of public relations series of photographs on the city. Other pieces of information are supplied or suggested in passing: a woman named Carla appears to live with Edda and helps care for Edda's child, Dorothea, although we do not know what sort of arrangement the two women have; Edda takes a lover, Werther, for a time; she has trouble making ends meet financially; she is known by friends in a local bar; and so on. The film is built of fragments, seemingly picked out at random. The greatest depth and detail and development in the film are devoted to the women's photography project and to the portrayal of Edda at work. The greatest sources of continuity in the film are the repeated use of long tracking shots of the city, of its walls, and of The Berlin Wall, and the frequent sound of a radio announcer's voice broadcasting new items and commercials. Interspersed among the fragments of Edda's life, Sander distributes still shots, some

of Edda's photographs, and a map of East and West Berlin. Passages from various German writers, most prominently Christa Wolf, are recited to the viewer or sometimes appear printed on the screen. There is one particularly striking sequence when Sander cuts "quoted" sequences from films made by contemporary women filmmakers into the image of a page of newsprint, with a voice-over reading of a family letter. Finally, Sander makes occasional use of a third person female narrator who provides information about Edda herself and about her photography project. These are the "ingredients" of Sander's film, ingredients that are assembled along the double axes of movement in time, a temporal continuum, and movement into space, or depth (movements which are not, of course, exclusive).

Sander's film opens with the titles in black and white: "Berlin, March 1977." A specific historical and geographical location is established. We are placed in time. When the moving images appear, our awareness of time is maintained. *Redupers* begins with a long tracking sequence, revealing flattened images of graffiti-scarred walls, quiet store fronts, empty sidewalks. The solidity and impenetrability of this extended facade is occasionally and disorientingly broken when the camera tracks past a gap in the street front where an alley extends back into the screen's space. We catch a glimpse of children playing in the distant space; we are treated to a moment of depth and activity until the camera slides past. Despite these glimpses of depth, the prevailing impression is of a continual movement too swift to allow us to focus in or hold on to any moment, yet slow enough to create a desire and an expectation that such a focusing and pause will occur. Time passes with the street front buildings, and we develop an impatience, an eagerness for the film to open up. The image is relentlessly two dimensional and our collective memories of films and narratives gone by promise that we soon will be able to slide in between two of these buildings to find a world of three dimensional and fictional space.

Soon this expectation is tested and teased. The tracking slows; we catch our breath, waiting for a "situation" to develop. But no. The camera car is simply preparing for a right turn. Simultaneously, we become aware of several things: the camera is

given a physical, tangible reality when our attention is drawn to the vehicle in which it is mounted (without our ever having to *see* that vehicle); the dream-like, evenly measured time of our film viewing experience is forged to the "real world" time of a camera on a car in a Berlin city street; and finally, the right turn into the screen that promises depth provides only a renewed two dimensionality as the tracking begins again. Now, however, we have become conscious of our present, the time of our viewing experience, as we became aware of the film's own time, tied to the pace of the camera's car. Simultaneously, we become aware of these different temporal realms, even as they come closest together. Thus, the viewer feels the reality of her own experience of time through her recognition of another's (in this case, the camera's or the filmmaker's) experience of time.

We can see this identical process in a passage quoted from Christa Wolf:

I am writing this sitting at the duty desk in my room in the Hotel Rossiya; with the present in my mind, for example, the river down below and all the real and dreamt-of experiences connected with it, I write about something that happened before and while doing it, feeling my way along a chain of associations, I remember not only earlier events but also past thoughts and memories, even to the point of thinking that *all this might be important in the future (which at this moment is the present)*, [emphasis mine].[12]

The last phrases of this passage not only weld Wolf's sense of her writing present to what *was* her future, they also link the reader's present ("which at the moment is the present") to Wolf's earlier concept of the future: when Wolf was writing this passage, in her present, the present of any reader reading it, was Wolf's future. In other words, her phrase speaks, within its context, to the shifting realms of her temporal experience (Wolf's past, present, future) but it also speaks out from the page, making the reader aware of her own time because of its overlap with that of Christa Wolf. The very precision with which Wolf's time is portrayed, or that of Sander and her camera, teaches the reader and viewer to be aware of her own temporal experience.

So what does this mean with regard to the film's double axes of a temporal continuum and depth? And how are this film's double axes distinct from any representation of experience over time? Let us take this second question first. We might say that any film (or novel or other expressive form) that partakes of a narrative structure simply has to present activity over time—a temporal continuum—as well as a particular character or situation in enough depth that the viewer/reader will become emotionally involved. To a certain extent, this is accurate, of course. Typically, however, the sense of temporal continuum will be sacrificed in order that the audience may become absorbed into the film's fictional depth. Often we are aware of time and its passing only at the beginning of a film, before the camera has found its subject. Or if a film is organized around the flashback, we most likely become aware of this temporal setting at the start and again at the close of the film; throughout the bulk of the viewing experience, however, we are absorbed in the film's present, unaware of either our own temporality or that of the film's subject. Some films, of course, may flash back and forth in time and even here, our attention is so focused on our main characters that these shifts in time usually do not break our concentration, and we do not remain conscious of the layers of time involved in any narrative experience: that is, the time of the experience portrayed, the time of narrator and/or artist expressing it, the time of the audience viewing it. Of course, there are exceptions to this rule. We do, for instance, become aware of time passing if a film bores us or if it makes us too uncomfortable. And since my description here has related primarily to the classical film, the film whose ideal viewer is the unself-conscious viewer, another exception is obviously the avant-garde film and films that experiment with self-reflexivity. Helke Sander's *Redupers* partakes of this experimental category of filmmaking, without doubt, and yet she clearly has not rejected narrative altogether. Her film is an interesting amalgam.

This brings us back to our earlier question: what does Sander's ability to make the spectator aware of her own temporal experience while viewing *Redupers* mean? How does it relate to the film's double axes of a temporal continuum and of depth? As we noted earlier, the opening sequence of *Redupers* creates,

in the viewer, an expectation or an eagerness that we may soon focus on a subject or a situation, in depth. We want to become absorbed into the film's narrative. And although Sander does eventually offer us a main character, Edda Chiemnyjewski, and some details of her life, we are continually pulled back from this movement into a narrative depth. Just as we are able to align ourselves with Edda and a particular activity she undertakes, we are forced back into that same camera car, forced to experience the sense of time, the frustration of time passing, that Edda must feel getting from one place to another. Once again, we not only become aware of the actual feeling of temporality in Edda's life, we also become aware of our own time passing in the darkened theatre.

Thus the viewer experiences the shift from movement into depth to movement in time at two levels. She experiences it first in the life of the film's subject, Edda; the viewer senses the reality of waiting, of fragmentation, of disparate experience in Edda's life. Rather than using narrative to falsify her character's life by constructing an artificial coherence and purposiveness, Sander uses it creatively, brokenly, to convey the pieces of any life that may or may not be unified by the imaginative Self. Similarly, the spectator becomes conscious, through this movement in time and into depth, of her own activity and that of the filmmaker. The spectator may still *feel* the experience of the main character as the film probes Edda's situation in depth, but the subsequent withdrawal into "real time," the lived time of waiting for the camera to get from here to there, pulls the spectator back out of the film again. We become aware, first and most obviously, of the filmmaker's hand, of her control and manipulation of this experience. We also become conscious of our own desire to be *in* the film, our unconscious efforts to condense time and to reconstruct experience in its most economical and emotionally satisfying form. We find time to think and to analyze the film as we watch scenes of the city passing by; we enter into an intellectual relationship with the material portrayed and with its form. And we become very conscious of a sense of physical space, of geography, of the actual distances that exist in this city and between the scenes of this woman, Edda's, life. Finally, our own thought processes are revealed to us, the way

we alternate between *experience in depth*—our experiences and all their associated memories, imaginings, expectations, projections—that feel timeless or simultaneous, and *experience in time*—the awareness of time passing, of details, experience, thoughts all sliding past often with no discernible pattern. This last is the dual process of becoming a subject, of "coming-to-oneself" that Christa Wolf develops in her writing, as much through her form as through the "content" of her essays.[13] And this process is an instance of the *dual consciousness* posited, in chapter 4, as a possible means and end for feminist filmmaking.[14]

We could locate and develop many examples, from *Redupers*, where Sander plays with this alternation between a temporal continuum and a movement into depth. Her use of a third person narrator, for instance, illustrates this effect. At various points throughout the film, a woman's voice will speak over specific images, providing information, insight and sometimes analysis or interpretation. The voice is disembodied and unidentified. It speaks with an authority because it cannot be tied to a particular point of view or a particular set of needs, defenses, and desires. Again, as Judith Mayne has pointed out, Sander reflects Christa Wolf's insights in *The Quest for Christa T.*: "I understand the secret of the third person, who is there without being tangible and who, when circumstances favor her, can bring down more reality upon herself than the first person: I."[15] The authority of this voice is enhanced by its seeming freedom from temporality. It exists outside of the film's time and therefore its observations and analyses appear to partake of a truth that Edda herself could never feel sure of. Edda's life exists within the flow of time and she finds it difficult to make the pieces of her existence fit coherently within that temporal continuum. There is never enough time, for work, for relaxation, for her child. Many of the glimpses of Edda's life which the film provides are illustrations of this frustration: Dorothea clinging to her mother's neck in the morning as Edda reluctantly leaves for work; Edda attempting to join an aikido class and finding herself unable to attend regularly; Edda always working at a furious pace, always attempting to do two things at once. The press of time, the seeming shortage of time, diminish Edda's sense of control in her life. She hasn't time for much of what she desires; she

hasn't the time to think and respond to her life as she wishes. But we learn this not from Edda, but from the narrator who exists outside of time, who has the leisure to reflect and who therefore seems to speak from a more controlled and coherent viewpoint. Her freedom from time allows her a depth of insight; she explains that Edda wishes for the time to think about how the state should be run and about biochemistry and physics.

When the narrator speaks, her insights give depth to the spectator's conception of the main character. Sometimes she draws lines of connection between various experiences in Edda's life, or sometimes she only names them; but at any rate, she speaks as the consciousness of depth in Edda's life, the awareness that can stand back from the flow of time and move deep into the Self instead, much as Christa Wolf "dives" into these same depths. In fact, we can view this third person narrator as a part of Edda, as one of her own voices, just as Wolf's Christa T. sometimes wrote of herself in the third person.[16] And although Christa Wolf will tell us that this kind of movement into depth is necessary for the process of Self-construction, Sander uses the medium of film to complicate the process. She uses a kind of vertical montage, juxtaposing the narrator's voice with images of the fragmented moments of Edda's life *in* time. Although the narrator's analysis in depth seems timeless, Sander makes us aware that nothing is, that all exists within the temporal continuum and that even as we construct an order for the pieces of our lives, new pieces have been added to the collection.

For example, as the narrator tells us of Edda's financial difficulties, we see her taking many more pictures than she will be able to sell; as the narrator tells us Edda cannot afford to work, gratis, for the many political activists who come to her, we see Edda continuing to listen to them, trying to work something out; as the narrator speaks abstractions about Edda's empathetic interest in the lives of other women, we *see* her interacting with elderly women at a political reception—we sense the shifting personal emotions in such an encounter. The abstractions become meaningless; they do not speak to the needs, defenses, and desires Edda is trying to gratify. As well, the use

of a disembodied narrator to provide our glimpses into the depths of Edda's self, emphasizes a kind of disjointedness or lack of integration, a struggle within the process of "coming-to-oneself."[17] These insights appear to spring from a source outside of Edda's consciousness. Edda/Sander's continual expression of sad irony only reinforces this sense of difficulty, and the lack of resolution in the film's conclusion seals the viewer's, as well as Edda's, fate. We recognize that the moments of insight into the depths of Edda's character, those moments of Self-construction, exist only within a temporal continuum that is unraveling them even as they are stitched together. Christa Wolf's polished "miniatures" cannot survive such a shifting base, and Sander has found a way to crack the surface of her images, defusing the impression of permanency and universality of which Christa Wolf accuses them.

Sander's need to crack these two dimensional surfaces accounts, as well, for her fascination with walls, barriers, boundaries, and even still photographs. These flat images and surfaces seem to prevent a movement into depth and to ensure instead an accumulation of two dimensional pictures. We see this in the repeated long tracking shots of the Berlin Wall. And yet Sander uses these surfaces dialectically; her emphasis of their two dimensionality and impenetrability counteracts these very attributes. When confronted with seemingly over-long tracking shots of a flat wall, we begin to recognize a depth and significance in the structure. The graffiti scrawled across its surfaces not only communicates its particular message, but also reveals a new meaning in the wall itself. The wall becomes a placard, a newspaper, and its very existence as a barrier points up the need for greater communication. Edda and her photography group design a series of photographs of Berlin, two dimensional pictures whose purpose is to penetrate the very images they present. When these women photograph the Berlin Wall, their aim is to present the "chinks in the wall," the places where the barrier becomes the occasion and even the impetus for seeing connections between the people of East and West Berlin.

For example, Edda displays parallel shots of an East Berliner with his "prize possession," his automobile, and of a West Berliner in the same position. She displays parallel shots of sub-

way graffiti, official and unofficial. And she presents a high angle shot of the Wall, revealing the communication possible
between one East Berlin window and a West Berlin window.
This series of photographs allows the viewer to see the areas of
commonality, the links between the lives of East and West Ber-
liners. We see that the Wall is a false barrier in a sense, that in
many ways the Wall serves to create a *similarity* of experience
in these different people. Again, Sander tries to crack the surface of the Wall's image, to show the contradictions within it.

Edda's photography group follows the same pattern: in their
efforts to reveal the similarities and connections between East
and West Berlin (making connections is ever a feminist goal),
they themselves erect a barrier, a curtain, only that they may
draw it aside to reveal anew, freshly, the world on the other
side of the wall. They know that framing an experience often
allows it to be seen in a new way—the very goal of Edda's photography and Sander's filmmaking. Sander's skepticism and
irony, however, prevent her from presenting these strategies
with the determined optimism that Christa Wolf displays about
her prose. Sander's women are disappointed by the effect of
their curtain; it is an anti-climax. As Edda smiles her sad smile
into the camera, we may suspect that Sander feels a similar
skepticism about the effect of her films. And yet she not only
continues to make them (she began making films in 1966), she
also frames them with quotations from Christa Wolf, a writer
whose purposefulness is uppermost.

Sander's (and Edda's) attempt to use framing as a strategy to
reveal new meanings in an image, especially a two dimensional
image, is displayed again through the insertion of still photographs into her film sequences. Once again, she uses a flat and
frozen image to point out its opposite, depth and flux, by means
of their absence. Sander allows us to see what is missing by
emphasizing what is there. For example, when Edda attends a
civic function, a reception for the elderly, we see her mingling
with the crowd, talking and dancing with them, taking pictures
of the bureaucrats giving their addresses, and so on. Meanwhile, the third person narrator informs us that Edda finds it
difficult to take only the "marketable" pictures; she tries rather
to really understand and record the *quality* of the event. This

scene is then followed by a series of still photographs presumably taken, following Edda's example, in an attempt to "capture" this quality. In this sequence, the irony exists on several levels. First, of course, we recognize that the photos the papers want from Edda reveal little about the lives of these elderly people or even about their reception; in fact, the papers do not want to examine these lives. Rather, they are interested in recording and reporting the "line" the bureaucrats feed them. Second, we have just learned in a previous sequence that Edda can barely clear enough income to support herself and her daughter. What's more, we know that the cost of materials is a major difficulty for her, and yet she cannot keep herself from taking "unprintable" photographs. But finally, and most disturbingly, Sander's irony extends to the photos of the reception themselves. After following Edda, on film, as she moves about the banquet hall and speaks with various guests, we find the still photographs at the close of this sequence somehow false and inadequate. They are frozen, lifeless—like Wolf's "miniatures"—and they lack the layers of complexity and political critique we found in Sander's juxtaposition of a narrator's analysis, *pictures* of Edda taking pictures, and the changing scene of the reception itself. Edda's commitment to and respect for individual experience has not only proved to be impractical, but ineffective as well. Sander has used what Wolf would call the "medium of Miniatures" to criticize miniature-making. By "framing" her still photographs between strips of "moving pictures," she has pointed up their inadequacies. If these photographs reveal anything, they reveal Sander's attempt to show Edda in a particular way. The photos display Edda interacting with the guests, trying to be one of them. We quickly realize that these photos could not have been taken by Edda for they are "candid" shots of herself. This, of course, implicates the filmmaker, and all the more so when we realize how neatly these photos fit the narrator's earlier analyses of Edda's tendency to try to "imagine the sorrows and passions of others." Thus, Sander's use of these photographs not only points up the impossibility of any attempt to pin down experience outside of moving time, but it also calls our attention once again to the role of the filmmaker. Once again, Sander questions the ideas

and images she herself offers the viewer. She attempts to emphasize the layers of time and multiplicity of interpretation in any representation of experience, hoping all the while that her viewers will turn these insights back onto *Redupers* as well.

Although there are many more examples of Sander's play with still images and the impression of two dimensionality—her use of maps, of printed texts, of paintings in an art gallery, for example—let us focus on only one more instance. As part of their Berlin series, Edda's group took photographs of common city scenes and blew them up to billboard dimensions. The enlarged photo we see in the film depicts a lone car parked against the Berlin Wall. Edda and some of the other women experiment with possible locations for the huge photo. Three of them stumblingly carry the unwieldy frame about the city.[18] Sander's playful image allows the viewer to feel that these women are struggling with their political ideals and commitments, that they are not always in control. And although, once again, they are trying to place a frame around an image that we might see it more clearly, they are afraid that their photograph will not even be noticed among the many billboards advertising various products. Sander shows us how difficult it is to create images that are not cooptable. Edda finally rests when she has brought the huge photograph to the spot where it was taken; she places the image beside the parked automobile it represents. If any context allows us to see the ironies and political complexities of this photograph, it is this one. Sander juxtaposes the scene and the image Edda has made of it—or more accurate, she juxtaposes *her* film image with Edda's—and we, the viewers, finally begin to really look at the photograph. We begin to see all the assumptions that are inherent in our ability to see as *natural* and *ordinary* this image of a parked car in front of the Berlin Wall. We recognize that the image of the Wall and all it implies has been absorbed into our consciousness. It no longer startles us. Sander knows how difficult it is to shake us free from our "ways of seeing," so she provides her viewer with a whole series of image juxtapositions instead of simply the final example. The viewer can follow the *process* Edda and the other women experience as they try to find the most effective location for their photograph. And finally, even this process is open-ended; no

voice-over analysis is offered and the sequence is unresolved as it melts into the women's next project. There is no hint that a new understanding has or has not been achieved. It is all up to the viewer.

Perhaps the most dramatic and surprising example of this open-endedness and of the film's emphasis upon multiple viewpoints occurs later on. The screen becomes filled with several columns of newsprint. This is a familiar image to us by now, for we know Edda is always listening to or reading the news. This time, however, we do not see Edda, and cut into the frame of newsprint are three smaller frames, each revealing sequences from recent films by women directors: *The Executioner* by Ursula Reuter-Christiansen, *Film About a Woman Who . . .* by Yvonne Rainer, and *Invisible Adversaries* by Valie Export.[19] Over these images we hear the narrator's voice saying, "Obsessed by daily life as other women see it," and then reciting a letter to Edda from "Aunt Katherine." The letter offers Edda encouragement in her photography and her feminism, and provides scraps of news, all in the sketchy but endlessly suggestive style we often find in letters from relatives. This sequence makes explicit what has been implicit thus far. In one frame, Sander has joined three separate film sequences, each dealing with some aspect of women's experience. Although the content of these sequences is verifiable (see note 19), it is not the point. As the sequence passes, the viewer is able to focus on all the strands of information that are presented. We cannot read the newsprint, watch three different films, and listen to the voice-over (or in some cases, read the sub-titles). The best we can do is focus on one or two strands, while trying to catch occasional scraps of material from the others. And this is precisely the point: it is impossible to capture all the versions of reality, all the separate narratives that exist around any one event or at any one moment for all the individuals who experience it. It is even impossible to follow all the strands of implication and association and memory and expectation that exist around a particular event for just one individual. Sander's entire film has been trying to suggest this idea. It offers us fragments of Edda's life in depth and then pulls back to show all of her life sliding by in time, never pausing long enough for an event to

have only one meaning or interpretation. As soon as we have constructed an analysis for one aspect of her life, we pull back to see that this aspect has changed, has accumulated new resonances and new tensions. Similarly, in this scene, we are offered pieces of experience in the films and in Aunt Kate's letter that in themselves suggest several political and personal critiques; together, at any moment, these images and words also offer an interlocking sort of analysis. They reflect upon one another. And finally, even as we develop an analysis of the relation between a certain set of images and words, these images and words have slid past us and changed.

This sequence captures, in a few moments, the process of Sander's entire film, and this quotation with which she concludes *Redupers* can shed light on this particular sequence as well:

I don't want to go any further. Anyone who asks about a person's diary must accept the fact more is concealed than said. It was not possible to speak about plans, clearly set forth in the diary, that have arisen, been changed, dropped again, come to nothing, or were carried out, unexpectedly suddenly there, complete. And it wasn't possible to bring into focus through strenuous thought the stuff of life that was very near in time. Or the mistakes made in trying to do this. And, of course, no mention of the names that appear once or more often in the diary.[20]

Here Sander is comparing her film with Wolf's conception of the diary: "work, training, a means to remain active, to resist the temptation to drift into mere consumption . . . an aid to work and memory."[21] *Redupers* certainly helps us "resist the temptation" to "mere consumption." Sander does not allow us that indulgence. She steadfastly retains the gaps, the incoherencies, the inexplicable emphases, and the shifting perspectives of any individual life. She allows Edda what narrative structure there might be in anyone's life, yet tries not to falsify her experience for the sake of plot. Sander aims to avoid those traps that Wolf claims for film: a tendency to universalize and concretize experience. By presenting Edda's experience with all the ellipses and loose ends of a diary, Sander discourages her audience from constructing the kind of whole picture they might identify with. Sander's viewers may sympathize with and care

for Edda, but they see her as distinct and still in flux. Edda is not a "finished work," a concrete entity. She is a character whom Sander portrays as still constructing herself and being constructed by her experiences.

In *Redupers*, Sander manages to present the open-endedness of experience and the commonalities and particularities that exist across so-called "Walls." She suggests the gaps in our understanding of experience by encouraging us to *see again*, to find hidden meanings in an image through juxtaposition and framing. She urges us to see her film, Edda's life, and our own viewing experience as "works in progress"—specific, shifting, inconclusive. Her experiments in form allow her to answer Christa Wolf's criticisms of the film medium, even as she adopts many of Wolf's ideas about the construction of the subject. All of these means and ends reflect the feminist aesthetic we discussed in chapter 4, and yet Sander's film retains its own very distinct flavor of irony and sad humor, as evidenced in her title. Still, Edda is perhaps less the "all-round reduced personality" and more the "personality-in-process"—certainly not a bad place to be.

NOTES

1. "Self-Experiment: Appendix to a Report" may be found in *New German Critique*, no. 13, Winter 1978. "Interview With Myself" and "Diary—Aid to Work and Memory" can be found in: Christa Wolf, *The Reader and the Writer—Essays, Sketches, Memories* (New York: International Publishers, 1977).

2. Wolf, *The Reader and the Writer*, p. 201.

3. Ibid., p. 212.

4. See the discussion of critical subjectivity at the end of chapter 1 of this text.

5. Wolf, *The Reader and the Writer*, p. 193.

6. Hints of partial autobiography occur throughout the work: Sander herself plays the main character; Sander is a filmmaker and Edda is a photographer; through her film's form and through the inclusion of particular quotations from Christa Wolf, Sander suggests that her work may be likened to a diary (see the concluding remarks in *Redupers* quoted at the end of this chapter).

7. Wolf, *The Reader and the Writer*, pp. 190, 191.

8. Myra Love, "Christa Wolf and Feminism: Breaking the Patriarchal Connection," *New German Critique*, no. 16, Winter 1979, p. 47.

9. Wolf, *The Reader and the Writer*, p. 193.

10. Judith Mayne, "Female Narration, Women's Cinema: Helke Sander's *The All-Round Reduced Personality/Redupers*," *New German Critique*, nos. 24–25, Fall-Winter 1981–82, p. 171.

11. Wolf, *The Reader and the Writer*, p. 179.

12. Ibid., p. 180.

13. Ibid., p. 77.

14. See the discussion of dual consciousness following note 19 in chapter 4 of this text.

15. Mayne, "Female Narration, Women's Cinema," p. 155 and Christa Wolf, *The Quest for Christa T.* (New York: Farrar, Straus & Giroux, 1970), p. 170.

16. Wolf, *The Quest for Christa T.*, p. 170.

17. Wolf, *The Reader and the Writer*, p. 77.

18. The image precedes Paul Mazursky's use of the same idea in his 1978 film, *An Unmarried Woman*. In that case, Alan Bates' "gift" of a huge canvas carried a certain amount of his resentment with it. Therefore, Jill Clayburgh's being buffeted by winds on a Soho corner seemed to be as much a result of Bates' irritability as her decision to live independently. In Sander's film, the women have chosen their political aims and methods and yet they still appear slightly overwhelmed by them. More of Sander's irony. Self-definition does not ensure complete control.

19. Mayne, "Female Narration, Women's Cinema," p. 165:

In each screen we see a segment from a woman's film: a close-up of a woman from Ursula Reuter-Christiansen's *The Executioner* (Denmark, 1972); the beach scene from Yvonne Rainer's *Film About a Woman Who. . .* (U.S.A., 1974), in which man, woman and child rearrange themselves as if for a series of snapshots; and a kitchen scene from Valie Export's *Invisible Adversaries* (West Germany, 1976) in which a woman cuts up a fish and insects and opens a refrigerator to reveal a baby inside.

20. Wolf, *The Reader and the Writer*, p. 75.

21. Ibid., pp. 70 and 75.

7

How To Have Your Narrative and Know It, Too: Yvonne Rainer's *Film About a Woman Who . . .*

In her film work, Yvonne Rainer dances around a number of so-called dichotomies: classical narrative cinema and the cinema of the avant-garde; humanism and formalism; autobiography and fiction; symmetry and randomness; the "moving picture" and the still shot; the dramatic persona and the performer. Add to this list one more pair, simultaneously and appropriately personal and political: the aims of the feminist movement and of the individual female artist. Looking at this final pairing, you might say there is no reason, there *should* be no reason why these two would be in conflict. Rainer would probably say the same thing of the preceding list; and it is precisely her process of working through these other "dichotomies" that has brought her individual work closer to general feminist concerns. The content or themes in her work, her film strategies, and the overall structure of her films all serve to encourage the dual consciousness, the multiplicity of perspective and the Critical Subjectivity, posited earlier as aims of a feminist aesthetic.

In her second feature length work, *Film About A Woman Who . . .* (1974), Rainer manages to hold the opposing terms of these dichotomies in a balance. Writing about this film, B. Ruby Rich notes that it "is best described by its own title,"[1] a title that

implies a story, a narrative, while withholding all specifics. And this seeming contradiction is actually Rainer's resolution of our first dichotomy, classical narrative cinema and the cinema of the avant-garde. Rainer begins from the premise that narrative film, with its language of illusion, serves to draw the viewer into a single perspective, to build her into an ideological construct; this is a premise generally accepted among artists and audiences of the avant-garde. Rainer has said: "My whole emphasis has been to avoid any clear continuity. . . . There's some kind of sleight of hand going on in the way we don't want to give a clear message; yet by leaving the interpretation of what we do to the audience, we wish to free it, rather than manipulate it."[2]

In this quotation, we hear Rainer's claims for an anti-narrative; we hear of her desire to "free" her audience. And yet we also hear that this strategy entails a certain "sleight of hand." After all, there is a kind of "clear message" in the very attempt to avoid such messages. Rainer, in her film, openly *owns* this ambiguity. She plays with her own work's tendency to provide messages, and with the viewer's tendency to look for them. And it is in the viewer's tendency to search out meanings, it is in this tendency that we find the other side of our original dichotomy. Rainer begins with the anti-narrative stance of the avant-garde, but her probing brings her to two new realizations: first, that she cannot be free of all intention in her creative process, that she *is* communicating a message, perhaps despite herself, and second, that the narrative process is not a one-sided manipulation, that the viewer will actively shape the materials of life and art into an order, whether or not Rainer allows her film to do so. Rainer perhaps reveals the narrative structure as a mere *construct*, but she also affirms the pleasures of this structure and recognizes it was a way, perhaps the only way we have, to respond to our experiences. And finally, Rainer reveals narrative structure as a means to an emotional satisfaction, without positing it as a set organization or hierarchization of actual people and experience.

Now the preceding has been all very well as a general description of Rainer's approach to narrative, but how does she construct this balance within the film? To begin with, the raw material of her film is that of a traditional love story: two women;

two men; domestic scenes; scenes of lovemaking; arguments; idyllic interludes (at the beach, of course); social gatherings and so on. Yet these ingredients are often fragmented and juxtaposed, in unexpected sequence, with spoken and/or written texts that comment upon, analyze, or completely depart from the projected images. And in Rainer's words, the four protagonists "in varying combinations and in a variety of indoor and outdoor locations—'play out' the valences of their interdependencies in word and gesture, gaze and stillness, in 'unhinged fragments of reality' (to use Louise Brooks' phrase) further fragmented by distortions in speed, time, placement of objects, and bodily orientations."[3] Rainer's use of these descriptive strategies is in perfect accord with the modernist move toward a cinema of self-reflexivity, a cinema that calls attention to its material nature, to its existence as an ideological product.

The Camera Obscura Collective elaborates upon this movement and its use for feminism:

We felt that the feminist problematic—the complex and ambiguous permutations of male dominance/female submission—could not be presented as a political, and therefore changeable, problem using the conventional—that is to say, the dominant—modes of representation. We had come to question the political effectiveness of films which depended on emotional identification with characters. What we felt we needed was not a person to identify with, but situations in which we could imagine ourselves, within a structure of distanciation which insures room for critical analysis.[4]

Rainer's fragmented structure certainly offers this "distanciation," and her characters do not invite personal identification from the viewer. Rather her characters "function as types;"[5] through narration, they are identified as "he" and "she" only. They have no other names, and "he" can and does refer to both male characters simultaneously and alternately. Similarly, we never are certain which woman is "she," at any particular moment. Rainer's characters rarely speak "in sync" with their images, and often their words are distanced through the use of an off-screen narrator, speaking in third person. The acting style is flat and unfocused. All of these strategies discourage the

"manipulative" emotional identification of classical narrative cinema.

In the preceding paragraph, we have noted just a few of the strategies Rainer uses to dissociate her film from traditional narrative. Yet despite her desire to avoid the "manipulation" inherent in this form, she still, just as surely, lays claim to many of the strategies and pleasures of narrative. For example, as mentioned above, her film is based, although loosely, on a narrative situation: the shifting relationships between and among two women and two men. And although they do not fit into a single coherent whole, several relatively lengthy sequences follow an exaggerated version of narrative chronology. For example, perhaps half way into the film there is a sort of "story within a story," titled "An Emotional Accretion in 48 Steps." Introducing this section, Rainer's text suggests that if we trace this "particular series of faux pas" back to its origins, perhaps we might be able to unravel the complexities and miscommunications between this particular "he" and "she;" perhaps we can "set it right." Then follows a series of numbered frames, describing in still images, moving pictures, narrated passages and printed texts, a sequence of events leading to an argument and eventually a reunion between two lovers. The sequential causality implicit in narrative structure is taken to its extreme here, with forty-eight numbered steps. There is a purposefulness in this sequence with its attempt to "get to the bottom" of this relationship and its motivating desire to "set it right." Here Rainer is placing an exaggerated emphasis on the narrative assumptions of sequential causality and of linear purposiveness. This emphasis is self-reflexive; it calls an amused and ironic attention to the whole process (one of the numbered steps asks the viewer in a printed text, "Do you think she could reason her way out of a paper bag?"). And yet, there still *is* a narrative here. Despite Rainer's ironic distance, there is a purposiveness and, speaking of this film, even Rainer herself has said: "If anything can be said to be exemplary in this work, it is the idea that self-scrutiny can function as an active and positive principle."[6] Rainer may poke fun at this principle, she may tease out its circularity with characters who end in the same place where they began, but she also clearly believes it to be a necessary,

perhaps an unavoidable process. At the same time that she makes visible the rigidities and oversimplifications of a narrative structure, she also paints her viewer squarely inside the borders of such a structure.

Rainer is relying upon the cultural training of her particular audience. She knows that the audience her work will reach is an audience that has been raised upon the formulaic stories of television, of supermarket novels, of commercial film—that is, of mass culture. She further knows that her audience lives in a society where the privileged mode of thought and discourse may be described as linear, goal-oriented, and hierarchically ordered. She knows that at the merest hint of a plot, or of characters, this audience will set about filling all extraneous bits of the film into a coherent narrative pattern. And at the barest suggestion of a purpose and an order, her audience will busy itself with a constructing meaning.

Rainer is counting upon this response for several reasons. On the one hand, the viewer's tendency to find a story in her film is the very response that allows Rainer to critique the narrative structure. She makes our activity visible to us by naming it, by exaggerating it, and by thwarting it. We see this in the numbered sequences that call attention to our expectation of a sequential causality, for example, or in the printed questions that speak out of the frame to the viewer, making us *conscious* of our involvement in the film's events—questions such as, "Who is the victim here?" projected over the image of three women on a sofa.

On the other hand, while Rainer makes us aware of narrative's seductive strategies, she also emphasizes the degree to which we are active agents in our own seduction. The intricate balance between manipulation and active agency is articulated in one of the film's opening textual passages. While watching our four protagonists as they sit side-by-side on a sofa, watching a slide show,[7] the narrative speaks, presumably about one of the two seated men: "Then he thinks about her: his very gaze seems to transform her into a performer, a realized fantasy of herself." Here we have a self-conscious statement about the power, the control that falls to the "bearer of the Look."[8] We transform experience into a performance—or a selected narra-

tive—dependent upon what we desire to see. A moment later in the film, however, we read this printed text: "This stage of his life as a captive audience-for-one seems based in artifice and as such must sooner or later come to a close. He sighs to himself, 'such delicious artifice. Nowhere is captivity less painful or more complete.' " Here Rainer focuses upon the limitations of the controlling gaze; the one who looks is now referred to as a "captive." He is a captive of his own self-created and self-enclosed world. Rainer admits the pleasures of this captivity while stating its contrivance.

To make all of this even more intricate, these two statements exist *within* a narrative structure. If we read them only within their narrative context (the story of the relationship between two lovers), we ourselves serve as a "captive audience" in that artifice. Yet if we read them out of that context only, as a warning against narrative manipulation, we become a "captive audience" to Rainer's efforts at communicating this "clear message." Rather, we might read these statements *in and out* of the narrative. We might shape the narrative through our viewing process while becoming aware of that process; we might note Rainer's attempt to communicate the complexity of the viewer/performer relationship while enjoying that relationship with the film itself. In other words, we might resist either extreme: the film will not be a world unto itself in which we immerse ourselves, nor will it be solely a self-reflexive trick or warning against that immersion. Rainer plays back and forth, encouraging us to have her film both ways.

Thus, Rainer's film encourages the dual consciousness we posited, in chapter 4, as a possible strategy for a feminist film aesthetic.[9] While viewing *Film About A Woman Who. . .*, we move in and out of the narrative structure, and in and out of an emotional identification with the experiences of the film's characters. Earlier, however, I explained that Rainer uses her narrative structure as a means to an emotional satisfaction in the viewer, without requiring that the viewer accept a particular ordering or interpretation of the film's events. Rainer employs camera movement, fragmented spoken and written texts, music, pacing, and images, a wide spectrum of strategies, in such a way as to evoke the patterns and rhythms of narrative. The

film's various sequences do not fit together into a coherent and unified whole, or rather they can be fitted together in a variety of ways. The identities of her characters seem to shift and alter, to exchange themselves; Rainer has concretized the drama of "sliding signifiers." We have the broad outlines of a narrative, but the specifics keep changing; some of them are never offered at all. And *yet*, despite all this mutability and indefiniteness, the willing viewer can experience a version of narrative satisfaction. There is no single story; the viewer is free to actively create the links and transitions within a plot, to fill in the very literal gaps in the story, and to resolve the seeming contradictions. The film allows for, or even requires, multiple readings in two ways. First of all, each reader is free to construct her own story from the film's jumbled pieces, thereby ensuring as many possible readings as there are willing viewers. Second and more significantly, Rainer encourages her audience to enjoy the release and resolution of narrative without ever pinning down the specifics of her "plot." The viewer achieves a kind of satisfaction that does not require certainty and specificity; it coexists with multiple perspectives. B. Ruby Rich hints at this process when she writes: "In *Film About A Woman Who. . .* it is the abstracted narrative that advances the emotion instead of the traditional model of emotion advancing a superimposed plot."[10]

But how does Rainer encourage this emotional satisfaction? It's as if she strips away all the flesh from a story line and locates the underlying structure, the skeleton. If the most conventional narrative is built upon an introductory exposition, gradually accumulating complications, a series of climaxes which build toward a final confrontation, its resolution and denouement, Rainer asks what kind of pleasures do we find in this structure? To begin with, there is a pleasure in recognition; we see ourselves and our emotions and our difficulties in this construct. There is the security we experience when a sequential causality is demonstrated; we feel as if experience is manageable, comprehensible, and even predictable. There is the vicarious release derived from the witnessed confrontation. And there is the feeling of acceptance and restored order derived from narrative resolution. It is not my intention here to analyze the

"pleasures of the text"; this has been done well in many book length studies of the narrative and related forms.[11] However, I do want to simply note some of these pleasures so that we might recognize Rainer's efforts to evoke them.

If we begin by looking at the pleasure of recognition, Rainer's strategies and their purposes immediately become very clear. We have already noted the familiar ingredients in *Film About A Woman Who. . .*; B. Ruby Rich has listed and identified these ingredients as the recipe for melodrama:

> In conversation with a friend, we posited the existence of a set of elements which are intrinsic to women's film melodramas and so implicit as to force a feminist critique: the presence of a woman at the center of the film; a domestic setting, usually the site for domestic conflict; an ellipsis of time to allow for the development of emotion, always central to the drama; extreme verbalization, which replaces physical action as the means of communication for the now-interior movement; and finally, the woman's ultimate decision to release her emotions. . . . This set of elements can . . . be traced throughout *Film About A Woman Who . . .* with such regularity and frequency as to indicate that Rainer must be credited with serious revitalization of melodrama, surpassing mere parody or homage.[12]

Thus Rainer elicits the pleasures of recognition through both form and content. We recognize the conventions of her form, of melodrama, and therefore we feel comfortable, secure in our expectations from this film. Similarly, we recognize the subject matter, the emotional strivings and conflicts of Rainer's characters, and therefore we begin to feel that we can identify with their experiences.

Rainer manages, however, to thwart both these tendencies. For her, the confidence with which we ease ourselves into the standard narrative forms should be a warning signal. If this signal goes unheeded, critical awareness is suspended and all our expectations are fulfilled. Similarly, a content into which we can project ourselves and our habitual readings of experience serves too easily as reinforcement for a status quo ideology.

Rainer calls attention to this seduction by naming it within her film: just after "An Emotional Accretion in 48 Steps," her title reads, "Only in movies can you send your mind away."

But her purpose here is not simply to block this comforting immersion in the familiar. Her purpose is not to hold her audience in a constant state of critical awareness and distrust of the "cinematic capability."[13] Rather, Rainer wants to encourage a balance, in her viewers, between conscious critique and the pleasure of a personalized narrative satisfaction. Her process is complicated and often appears contradictory in its struggle to find this balance: the preceding quotation, for example, reads differently in the light of Rainer's second line: "Only in movies can you send your mind away. *For some reason*, she was embarrassed by her reverie" (emphasis mine). And this text follows a long, slightly hypnotic sequence; there has been little action, less spoken dialogue, printed texts with little detail, a stretch of black leader, and a lengthy passage of recorded opera from Bellini. In other words, the sequences preceding this quotation have been calculated to *encourage* reverie.

Now we could surmise from this that Rainer has been playing a rather condescending trick on her viewers, drawing us into reverie and then teasing us for the same, suggesting that this reverie is cause for embarrassment. I, however, suggest that her intentions here are far more complex. She wishes us to be *aware* of our reveries as personal constructions, triggered by the film's machinations, yet nevertheless pleasurable and a source of insight when examined. By naming our reveries—"Only in film can you send your mind away"—she encourages this examination. Rainer simultaneously triggers the feeling of personal recognition in her viewer, recognition of form and content; thwarts that recognition, encouraging a critical self-consciousness through strategies of cinematic reflexivity; and yet allows space and time for personal reverie, an *actively* created structure of narrative pleasure.

For example, early on in the film there is a relatively long narrated sequence. It follows a series of seemingly unconnected frames of still photographs—family wedding pictures, shots of women and men, of varying ages, in varying configurations; and images of the two couples, our protagonists. We, the viewers, do not necessarily know that these photos display the actual families of the film company; these connections are not apparent. At any rate, there ensues a series of fragmented,

unfinished sentences that seem to follow a single narrative line, that is, internal narrative. They follow a woman's reflections concerning the course of her relationship with a certain man. What seem to be crucial portions of her reverie are deleted, however, and the narration looks something like this:

First an emptiness like a great white bird soared through her. Then she began to think about particulars—the quality of his intelligence at the moment..........., his insight into the nature of her struggle, his refusal to go along with her desperate................ He had dragged it all out of her. Now she had to pay. Yet it was a relief that he was now carrying the ball. It was *his* turn to.......... and not dance the fandango in .... And there was still so much she didn't know, which, if known, might have made her act differently. How much of the prob-lem of their differences was real and how much was a smokescreen to conceal..........? Her mind clouded when she tried to answer.

   She had set him an impossible task.".......... to allow me to .... when I need to," she had told him. He had reminded her that *she* was not so...... of *his*....... She pleaded special circumstances. They argued. His voice was hard and curt.

The die seemed cast. Yet in some way she trusted him. He would............. They would meet again. If only he would say, "But we really ...." Which was all very well for *her* to say, having jumped the gun in...........

   Then that terrible accusation of his. She couldn't even repeat it, it........... Yet it posed another question: "Is it possible that I have really........ that I will never make.......... Only in this way.............survive." So be it. There are worse ways to live. Being so......... may very well............ , however, little conviction.

And finally, she grew calmer, almost resigned. They had both been......—her terror and the ....—slowly eroding.................and regard him.................and pleasure.[14]

This long text, narrated by a man although describing the thoughts of a woman, in many ways can serve as a microcosm of Rainer's film. It illustrates much of her method, despite the fact that it is primarily a verbal sequence. [15]

   Initially, this sequence can be extremely frustrating for the film viewer. I felt as if crucial pieces of information had been de-leted from the text. How could I know these characters, iden-tify with their experiences, if all specifics were withheld by the

filmmaker? And yet, I recognized the *form* of the character's re-flections. Certain phrases, by virtue of their status as cliches, triggered little bells of emotional recognition and of association: "Now she had to pay," for example, and "He was now carry-ing the ball." These cliches represent metaphorically the kind of intricate and continually shifting balance, the constant weighing and transferring of blame, of guilt, of responsibility that characterizes emotional relationships. Without pinning down the specifics of this particular couple, Rainer has elicited a feel-ing of emotional familiarity from me, and I am faced with a choice: I can either try to fill in the blanks, the ellipses, in this textual passage, thereby *consciously* constructing a specific nar-rative that will co-exist with all the other narratives constructed by other viewers, or I can allow myself the generalized, non-specific emotions and pleasures of this narrative structure, without forcing anyone's story to fit its contours.

Either choice implies a kind of conscious multiplicity, but the second is a bit more complex, for here Rainer "reassures us without compromising either us or herself."[16] Here the viewer can experience the pleasures of recognition, the security of an assumed causality, the vicarious release of confrontation, and the renewal and acceptance of resolution—she can experience this cycle of emotions without ever pretending that it explains or resolves her lived experience, or that of anyone else. There are syntactic patterns, for example, that reflect the emotional balancing act between this unidentified "he" and unidentified "she", without providing specific details: for example, " '.........to allow me to.........when I need to,' she had told him. He had reminded her that she was not so....... of *his*........." Without knowing the content of their charges, we recognize the familiar game of claim/counter-claim that this couple is playing. As well, there is the structure of the entire passage that moves from a woman's consciousness of sensation ("emptiness like a great white bird"), to her reflection upon "particulars" of the man she loves, to a description of their interaction—the personal revelations, the accusations, the confusion, to the climactic confrontation ("that terrible accusation"), and finally to accep-tance and renewed attraction. Not only is this structure re-peated several times throughout the film—"An Emotional Ac-

cretion in 48 Steps," for example, and the final printed confrontation which is projected over the closing image of waves breaking upon a shore—but it also reproduces the most conventional narrative structure. And yet Rainer avoids the usual specificity; I felt I had glimpsed some of the contradictions and complexities of human relationships, that emotions had been opened up before me, and *yet*, that I had been able to derive a sort of renewed hope and restored energy, without the necessity to oversimplify, to force experience into categories where it did not want to go. Rainer is aware of narrative as an ideological construct reflecting an epistemology based upon a linear logic, the assumption of a comprehensible, expressible and exclusive "reality." At the same time, however, she recognizes the emotional needs narrative can serve. The minds and feelings of her viewers can be engaged through narrative in a more active, more intense fashion than through the unrelentingly cold anti-narrative posited by much of the film avant-garde.

So Rainer has it both ways. She fragments her narrative. She brackets it by exaggerating its own tendencies (through numbered sequences, for example, or an overwhelming operative score that drowns out all else). She calls attention to its formulas and cliches by visually punning them: for example, the cliche phrase "He was now carrying the ball" is visually echoed in an intricately symmetrical series of dance passages, late in the film, featuring a man, a woman, and an ubiquitous rubber *ball*; the male and female dancers pass the ball back and forth, using it as a prop and a support. Yet, despite this emphasis upon Rainer's formulas and cliches, the viewer is still invited into the world of the narrative. Rainer's reflexive strategies are all the more powerful, because her viewers have the opportunity to become emotionally engaged; a dual consciousness is encouraged.

We have been discussing Yvonne Rainer's use of narrative in *Film About A Woman Who . . .* In other words, we have been discussing the theory and the form of her work. And although form *is* content, to varying degrees in all film, it is time we turned our attention to some of the themes around which Rainer builds her film. These include the interrelation of love, sex, and per-

formance; an analysis of the act of looking; and the anatomization of experience into small moves, countered and balanced against the answering moves of lovers, friends and fellow performers.

Let's begin with a look at the last of these—the anatomization of experience into small moves, countered and balanced against answering moves—for this theme is actually the essence of the film's process. (Again, form and content are forever, hopelessly blurred.) Again and again, the film's sequences are based upon this approach, this analysis of experience. Immediately, obviously, we recall "An Emotional Accretion in 48 Steps," a sequence introduced with an expression of intention, the hope that by tracing this "series of faux pas" to its first cause, it might be "set right." The entire sequence is a flashback, a memory of experience. Its breakdown into forty-eight pieces, then, is a perspective, an analysis imposed on experience from outside it.

Rainer never claims that this is the only way to view events, and in fact, she does criticize this perspective, or at least complicate it, by her inclusion of multiple viewpoints. We hear of and see this relationship played out often from "her" perspective, but sometimes from "his." Rainer's method within this sequence, as well as her introduction to it, makes us aware that this anatomization of experience is but one way of looking at it. However, this method is gradually, implicitly valorized in her film simply through repetition.

For example, the dance sequences at the close of the film are based upon this same method—the gradual accumulation of small moves, answered by and alternating with the moves of one's partner. These dances are set to quietly beautiful, seemingly simple piano sonatas, composed by Edvard Grieg, compositions that, almost unnoticed, build to a climax and then resolve themselves into their original phrases. A young man and woman dance to these pieces. First one dances and then the other. Occasionally they dance together in carefully balanced configurations. Sometimes still poses are alternated. The total effect is one of symmetry, balance, the gradual accumulation of simple gestures and poses, until the music brings them to a climax, an intensity that is finally absorbed into the sonata's res-

olution. Of course, these dances serve as emblems, as metaphors for the film's "plots," the dance of emotional relationships.

And there are other examples of this approach to experience, this anatomization: Rainer's frequent use of a series of still photos, rather than moving images; her dissection of the shower murder in Hitchcock's *Psycho* into a dramatic sequence of still shots; her projection of a photo of the Luxembourg Gardens, accompanied by this text: "The places for sitting in the Luxembourg Gardens are individual chairs rather than benches. So one can make small adjustments in placing oneself in relation to a companion or the total view;"—and we could find other examples. The effect of this method seems to be, however, a simultaneous emphasis on the importance of small, distinct moves—the atoms of our experience—and an indication that these moves are not completely within our control, they are hopelessly complicated by the answering, balancing moves of our partners, or that our interpretation of a still depends as much on those stills that precede and follow it, as on the still itself.

There is both hope and hopelessness in Rainer's analysis. The attempts to break down, analyze and understand our experience are repeated over and over; there is a determined purposefulness that remains undaunted. And yet Rainer emphasizes the difficulty, even the futility of this attempt at analysis by revealing the varied and multiple perspectives that we bring to any event. What seems necessary and possible finally, is a continual awareness, a constant weighing and balancing of one move against another. In the end, no single dogma or belief system is adequate; this is articulated in the film when Rainer, as narrator, reads the following passage:

She would like to engage in politics, but she can't decide whether to join the big women or the hunch-twats. The big women have a lot to offer, but she has discovered essential weaknesses in their proposal to use wads of counterfeit money for . . . doorstops? What is this . . . boxtops? Oh . . . box-stops. Neither is she attracted to the naive notion of hunch-twats that every connection brings bed-chains. Not that it's a matter of victims and oppressors. She simply can't find alternatives to being inside with her fear or standing in the rain with her self-contempt. How long can you go on this way, mmm? You still think it's all going to come out right, don't you? For instance, if your get up

in the morning and feel your feelings well enough you will receive the right gifts from heaven without ever having to ask for them or even define them. It should be smooth sailing now, right? Just deciding which side you're on should insure that all the best things in life will beat a path to your door, right? After all, you've paid your dues, haven't you? What do you want?

Her pretense of innocence must end. Nothing is new anymore, thank god. Now at last she can use her head and her eyes. If the mind is a muscle then the head is a huntress and the eye is an arrow.[17]

Here the narrator expresses an ironic attitude toward the passage's protagonist and her naive notion that one can make an either/or choice, once and for all, about anything in life. In other words, this process of analysis and of evaluation, this anatomization of experience must continue. No permanent answers will be achieved; this would mean stasis and stasis is the end of the dance. Rather, as the structure of Rainer's film reflects, there will be repeated cycles. A series of small steps will rise to a climax and then be resolved in a temporary balance—but there is no ending.

And appropriately, Rainer's film "ends" in flux, in process, rather than in certitude. Projected across the image of waves breaking on the shore, we read the text of another conflict building between our "he" and "she." We read the "terrible accusation" and of a slap across the face, the music reaches the pitch of its crescendo, and then, after a pause, the emotions are resolved into the sonata's quiet conclusion. The text of the argument concludes: "She sighs with relief. Now that she knew the truth about her feelings she was free to love him again." The balance is restored between the two lovers through awareness, but nothing permanent is achieved. Rainer emphasizes this in her final text, "You could always have an ocean ending," projected over the image of the waves breaking on the shore. The ocean gives the impression of permanence, but, of course, it is ever changing. In addition, Rainer's address to the audience in this final text emphasizes the arbitrariness in her conclusion; you *could* have an ocean ending, but then again, you could *not*. And the use of the second person personal pronoun draws the viewer more actively into the construction of narrative satisfaction. There is no lasting resolution here, simply the

opportunity to rest. And obviously, Rainer is playing with the narrative cliche of "ocean endings," a convention whereby films and novels borrow the evocative powers of nature as a bolster to their artifice.

After discussing the film's conclusion, we may feel a certain reluctance at turning once more to its themes. Still there could be no method of analysis more appropriate, more faithful to the film's cyclical process. Earlier I mentioned the film's analysis of the act of looking and its exploration of the interrelation of sex, love, and performance. These two thematic concerns are closely linked, of course, for it is the act of looking that determines the performance-quality of experience. In her essay/interview, "Yvonne Rainer on Feminism and Her Film," Lucy Lippard writes:

A Woman Who begins and nearly ends with the actors and actresses sitting before a screen watching themselves and others on slides (still photographs being one further remove from life than motion pictures). The audience is immediately and firmly reminded that here, and throughout the film, we are seeing neither life nor live performances, that we are looking at looking, rather than looking at things happen.[18]

The scenes Lippard refers to make very literal this "looking at looking." We watch the four protagonists lined up on a single sofa, boy/girl/boy/girl, staring intently ahead; we look at them looking at. . . . At first, in the film's opening scene, we do not know what they are looking at. A rhythmic light and shadow falls across their faces but this seems appropriate to the sound track, sounds of a raging thunderstorm. When the camera provides an answering reverse shot to these four on the sofa, however, we realize that the pattern of light is not lighting, but rather the reflected glow from the projected slides.[19] Rainer's use of projected still photographs reemphasizes the act of looking, this time our *own* looking, for our natural attempts to create links and transitions between the photos and the characters in this scene, as well as among the photos themselves, points up our active agency in the constructive process of looking. Rainer frequently films stills in a sequence (as in the quotation from *Psy-*

cho) and even series of posed actors, allowing the motion picture camera and its moving film to serve as a concretized metaphor for our own viewing process. As the film links these series of frozen images, so does our process of looking actively construct, through persistence of vision, the semblance of seamless action from thousands of separate frames. Rainer emphasizes the constructive nature of looking, the way viewed experience is once again made up of a series of small steps, of still images.

But why does Rainer take such pains to emphasize the act of looking? Constance Penley, in "The Avant-Garde and Its Imaginary," discusses Lacan's analysis of the Look in "Du regard comme object petit a." She examines Lacan's claim that the act of looking implies the experience of separation from what is seen, making the seen *other*. And yet, Penley explains: "There is, then something in vision nowhere mastered by the subject: the look of the other pre-exists the subject's look; the subject's visual field is always organized in relation to the other's look that it is not."[20] In other words, implicit in our act of looking is the definition of self as opposed to other, which in our sense is an act of control and in another sense is the experience of being controlled, determined by what we expect to see—that is, the expectation of ideology. Rainer, by calling attention to the way we construct the film's visual field as well as to the way we are constructed by it, and by thwarting our expectations of ideology, encourages an awareness in her viewer that defies Lacan's seeming determinism.

This awareness that defies determinism could easily be seen, along with the encouragement of a Critical Subjectivity, of a dual consciousness in the viewer, and of multiple perspectives, as the fulfillment of a feminist aesthetic. Rainer herself has repeatedly demurred when interviewers and critics have attempted to label her a feminist. In an interview with Lucy Lippard, Rainer explains this reluctance:

Well, to feminists I always say I'm not [a feminist] and then I wait for them to tell me that I am and then I end up agreeing with them. . . . I should stop playing this game and just stand up on my hind legs and admit it. It's just that I guess I make a distinction for myself. I

didn't come to be an artist or an independent person directly dealing with this female experience through the women's movement, so somehow I'm reluctant for that reason to proclaim myself.[21]

This statement brings us back to our introductory statement of a seeming dichotomy: that is, between the aims of the feminist movement and of the individual female artist. In Rainer's work we have a demonstration that these aims and their methods need not be in conflict. In fact, the "individual" female artist exists only in context, be that context patriarchal society, the avant-garde in film and dance, and/or the women's movement. None of these excludes the other, and it demands a finely developed Critical Subjectivity to negotiate one's way through these shifting perspectives and their distinctive discourses. In fact, a feminist analysis of art or anything else derives its unique complexity from the fact that it must balance simultaneous and multiple perspectives while still retaining its distinct shape and unity, like an atom holding its positive and negative charges in equilibrium. And isn't this continual weighing and balancing of counter moves what we have found Rainer's film to be? Rainer resolves dichotomies by focusing on the dynamics, the spaces in between, and in this process, she creates the forms and strategies of a feminist aesthetic.

NOTES

1. B. Ruby Rich, "The Films of Yvonne Rainer," *Chrysalis, A Magazine of Women's Culture*, no. 2, p. 117.

2. Annette Michelson, "Yvonne Rainer, Part One: The Dancer and The Dance," *Artforum*, vol. 12, no. 5, p. 62.

3. "Appendix: Rainer's description of her films," *Camera Obscura: A Journal of Feminism and Film Theory*, no. 1, p. 72.

4. "Yvonne Rainer: An Introduction," *Camera Obscura*, no. 1, p. 59.

5. Ibid.

6. "Yvonne Rainer: Interview," *Camera Obscura*, no. 1, p. 95.

7. This emphasis upon "looking at looking" is a theme we will explore later in the chapter. See quotation at note 18.

8. Laura Mulvey, "Visual Pleasure and Narrative Cinema," *Women and the Cinema: A Critical Anthology*, ed. Karyn Kay and Gerald Peary (New York: E. P. Dutton, 1977), p. 418.

9. See chapter 4, following reference to note 19 of this work.

10. Rich, "The Films of Yvonne Rainer," p. 119.

11. References with regard to these "pleasures of the text" might include: Roland Barthes, *The Pleasure of the Text*, trans. Richard Miller (New York: Farrar, Straus & Giroux, 1975); Frank Kermode, *The Sense of an Ending: Studies in the Theory of Fiction* (New York: Oxford University Press, 1967); Lionel Trilling, "The Fate of Pleasure," *Beyond Culture: Essays on Literature and Learning* (New York: Harcourt, Brace, Jovanovich, 1965), pp.50–76.

12. Rich, "The Films of Yvonne Rainer," p. 119.

13. J. Dudley Andrew, *The Major Film Theories: An Introduction* (New York: Oxford University Press, 1976), p. 4.

14. Yvonne Rainer, *Work 1961–73* (New York: New York University Press, 1974), p. 255–257.

15. In fact, Rainer handles the various codes or cinematic tracks at her disposal—spoken texts, printed texts, voice-in-sync, soundtrack music, still images, moving pictures, even black leader—in a very evenhanded fashion. She privileges all of them, alternately, and she disrupts the continuity in all of them as well. Treating each track as a kind of object to be manipulated, of equal importance with any other track, is an inheritance from Rainer's roots in Minimalism and dance; the Camera Obscura Collective (in "Yvonne Rainer: An Introduction," *Camera Obscura*, no. 1, p. 55) writes: "The interchangeability of objects—that is to say, the use of object-as-object—could be seen as a correlate of aleatory composition in dance movement. The literalist-minimalist aesthetic as it was applied to dance signalled an attack on the narcissistic, virtuosic, emotive, regal, dramatic, decorative view of performance. Rainer's alternative view of performance was as a kind of work or task, and as neutral—". Still, in her films, Rainer complicates this process and the "object-as-object" also packs a narrative punch.

16. Rich, "The Films of Yvonne Rainer," p. 120.

17. Rainer, *Work 1961–73*, pp. 264, 265.

18. Lucy R. Lippard, *From the Center: Feminist Essays on Women's Art* (New York: E. P. Dutton, 1976), p. 277.

19. This characteristic punning across the cinematic codes is Rainer's humorous reminder that the simultaneous experience of visual and aural tracks does not ensure their intended causal relationship. The sound of a thunderstorm does not *necessarily* mean we are to assume its coincidence with our four characters sitting on a sofa.

20. Constance Penley, "The Avant-Garde and Its Imaginary," *Camera Obscura*, no. 2, pp. 22, 23.

21. Lippard, *From the Center*, pp. 268, 269.

8

Feminist or Tendentious?
Marleen Gorris' *A Question of Silence*

In the preceding chapters, we have discussed films that, to
varying degrees, encourage multiple readings of their narratives; shifting identifications with their characters; an awareness of the filmmaker's hand in the construction of the texts;
and therefore, a Critical Subjectivity on the part of each viewer.
It is crucial now, I think, to address a film that appears more
openly and more controversially tendentious. Annette Kuhn
explains that, "Filmmakers may have a political investment in
certain interpretations of their films, and thus seek to delimit
readings."[1] Such a tendency may seem implicit within the feminist film project: politically motivated filmmakers will intend
to generate certain "politically correct" interpretations of their
films. And yet this appears to contradict a major thesis of this
book—that feminism exists in the film reading, not the film text,
and that a feminist film reading is one which seeks to hold contradictory perspectives in tension.

A Question of Silence (1982), the first feature film by Dutch
writer/director, Marleen Gorris, can serve as a case in point in
our exploration of this apparent contradiction. Critical response
to this film revolves around the question of its tendentious-
ness:

First-time film maker Marleen Gorris's film polarizes its audience; many
will dismiss it as a feminist tract, but it is far more than that—

The feminist cause will not be well served by *A Question of Silence*—

"A Question of Silence,". . . is both a feminist movie, and a thriller. Yet, it goes beyond those categories, and becomes a deeply human, poignant drama—

Sounds weighty, but rookie director Gorris leavens her social study with subversively original humor—

A Question of Silence proceeds by dialectics rather than didacticism—[2]

Whether the critics love it or hate it, they all feel compelled to address the questions: "Is this film 'feminist,' a 'tract,' 'didactic'—in other words, 'political'?" or "Is it 'human,' 'dialectical,' more than a 'political statement'?"

The implicit assumption here seems to be that if the film is tendentious, we will be justified in dismissing it. Only if it presents a totally "balanced," "fair-minded" picture of all events and characters do we need take it seriously. On the one hand, such a response negates the degree to which individual viewers may respond and interpret the film text in different ways. Perhaps more insidiously, however, buried in such a response is the assumption that most film is *not* tendentious or does *not* present a distinct ideological viewpoint. As well, this expectation of a "balanced" and "fair-minded" representation entails a denial of the degree to which any film exists within a certain cultural, societal, and historical frame. No film is an island, to which the viewer responds as if in a vacuum. We all bring our experience and our contexts with us. In other words, a critical portrayal of a husband's behavior in a world which validates that behavior may be more "balanced" and "fair-minded" than an empathetic portrayal of that same behavior.

Thus it seems that Gorris' film must be read in its societal and historical context and, in that context, her film is oppositional: it derives much of its impact through its juxtaposition with and reaction to the status quo. And in a strange fashion, the very extremity of its content insures a certain multiplicity in viewer response. This is not a film that will lull the viewer

into acceptance of its premises. I found myself thinking, wondering, questioning its logic even as I felt its inexorable inevitability.

Briefly, the film is based upon the murder of a male shopkeeper by three women who happen to be in the boutique together one day. Christine is a young mother whose frustration and loneliness in her marriage have brought her to a nearly catatonic state. She rarely speaks and her movements are slow and blunted, robotic, except when she caresses her infant child. Annie is a waitress in a neighborhood diner. She is in her forties, divorced, and she talks and laughs loudly and incessantly. There is a cynicism, an intelligence, and a desperation in her manic expressiveness. Andrea is a young, educated business secretary. She knows more than her employer and she knows that, too. Her self-expression reveals neither the desperate laughter of Annie nor the pained silence of Christine, but rather an intelligent, articulate, and relentless contempt. The women have never met before, nor have they known the shopkeeper. Ostensibly the attack is triggered when the shopkeeper catches Christine shoplifting. As he draws the stolen article from her bag, she defiantly takes it back and grabs another garment as well. The shopkeeper is stunned, and as the other shoppers—all women—stop to watch, Annie and Andrea each take an article of clothing from the racks and broadly stuff it into their purses. The three women, slowly and in silence, gather around the man and begin to beat him, deliberately, calmly, and without hesitation.

The extremity of this situation, the film's premise, insures that virtually any plot summary begins as mine has, and yet, Gorris builds her film upon a different narrative. The film opens with and is structured around the experience of Dr. Janine Van de Box, the psychiatrist who has been appointed by the court to determine the mental state of the three accused murderers. Block by block, the film is constructed of symmetrical, balanced sequences. We listen as Janine interrogates each of the women, in turn and repeatedly, and gradually she comes not only to understand their actions but to identify with them as women.

Responding to this film, the critic and viewer can put the brutal murder aside, soft-pedaling its radical nature, and emphasizing

"the other plot," Janine's consciousness-raising. The murder becomes more of a plot device, therefore, a difficult metaphor which allows a more easily accepted point to be made. Or, the critic and viewer can get stuck on the film's so-called biases; Carrie Rickey speaks with Gorris on this point:

> She [Gorris] describes the typical response to her film, both at home and abroad: "Its critics complain that there's not a nice man in it." She deadpans, mimicking a finger-pointing male critic, "It would have made your film much stronger if you hadn't stereotyped the men." Then, lapsing into her own voice, she observes, "That's like saying, 'if there is one good man, then all's well with the world because I am that man.' "[3]

Each of these critical approaches seems to miss the film's best points. They both position and read the film within certain preexisting and standard measures of "realism," "poetic license," and "morality." Perhaps the more revealing approach to the film—and the approach most in sync with the process of feminist criticism I explore in this text—is to ask "why was the film made in this way?" and "what questions are raised by the film's radical content and its deliberate, symmetrical form?" These questions help us to see the film less as a single and tendentious statement, and more as an occasion for multiple perspectives.

In fact, if Gorris had wished her viewers to sympathize unquestioningly with the three murderers, if she had intended to lead her viewers unswervingly to certain thematic conclusions, she would have made a very different film. In the *Monthly Film Bulletin*, Sheila Johnston writes that this film moves its viewers "with the methods—allusion, association—of the most classical narrative."[4] I would argue that Gorris modifies these methods and utilizes some of Eisenstein's strategies—vertical montage and intellectual montage, and subversive laughter, for example—to create a distinct effect. She manages to communicate to her viewers a sense of the inevitability of the narrative action, even a desire for that action to be played out, without requiring an answering and unreflective audience commitment to that action. The viewer is caught up in the action, enjoying its rhythms

and balance, even desiring its inevitable resolution, just as a listener comes to anticipate and actively desire the resolution that develops organically from a passage of music. And yet Gorris insures a certain distance or awareness on the part of this same viewer, encouraging a reflection, an active questioning, the generation of multiple perspectives.

So how does Gorris achieve this uneasy balance? Let us look first at the level of narrative structure. Gorris constructs her film of numerous "equivalent" sequences arranged and balanced symmetrically. For example, the film opens with "the crime," a brief, supposedly playful scene of attempted intimacy, poor timing, and missed connections between Janine and her lawyer husband. If this film contains a metaphorical murder, this is it. The two players are at home, on the sofa, and the camera tracks around from a side view to a head-on perspective, giving us, the viewers, a clearer vantage point. (Gorris' camera is frequently this obliging, revealing "what's important" with a directness that almost calls attention to itself in the difficult context of this film.) The scene centers around an effort at communication, at connection, which is manifested as a competition, a power struggle between husband and wife. He is reading and she wants to get his attention, to play. She tries to distract and arouse him and he seems to respond, only to shift positions with his book. In annoyance, Janine takes her pen and pantomimes a thrust to his chest, drawing the pen down toward his genitals until her husband leaps to attention and they begin to embrace. The scene is brief and light, ending with laughter and kisses, yet Janine's pantomime is disturbing. Even more disturbing is the fact that it is her feigned violence, not her playful affection, that connects with her husband. And as the film proceeds, we will observe that it is this type of muffled yet competitive power struggle—although verbal rather than physical—that characterizes Janine's relationship with her husband.

Getting back to the larger structure of the film, this opening "scene of the crime" is followed by six brief scenes, introducing the three murderers, *after* their crime and the "crime" we have just witnessed. The first three of these scenes reveal in sequence and in context, the film's characters: Chris in her liv-

ing room with her child; Annie working at the diner; and Andrea taking dictation from her employer. After identifying the
three women and providing some significant, suggestive details in each of their contexts, Gorris offers three more short
scenes, in the same sequence, revealing the arrest of each of
the three women. The pattern of the film is quickly established.
Gorris seems to build her film of blocks of information, each of
them similar in some ways to the other blocks: first, Christine
is introduced, then Annie, and then Andrea; first Christine is
arrested, then Annie, and then Andrea. In a similar fashion,
we are offered symmetrical scenes of Janine interviewing first
Christine, then Annie, and then Andrea, again and again.

These building blocks function in a number of ways. Initially, they provide a sense of security, of balance, for the viewer.
We know how the film will proceed and in the midst of quite
a radical content, we experience the calming influence of order.
As well, this symmetrical progression adds to the viewer's experience of narrative inevitability. No matter how shocking the
material treated, we come to expect and desire each new block
of information, for it is a necessary part of the symmetry of the
whole. And yet, each sequence concludes with a number of
questions still unanswered. Janine cannot persuade Chris to
speak to her, for example, and Andrea continues to deny that
there were witnesses to the murder. Similarly, the murder itself is depicted in a series of flashbacks, each of them revealing
a bit more than the last, yet each of them stopping just short
of total disclosure. By this method, Gorris ties her audience into
the narrative, enlisting our curiosity and stimulating our desire
for the narrative to play itself out. Each sequence ends without
completely satisfying our interest and so we are drawn further
and further into the story—a standard narrative strategy. At the
same time, however, Gorris denies us certain typical narrative
satisfactions, thereby encouraging a certain awareness and distance in her viewers.

Perhaps most significantly, Gorris often denies her viewers
the satisfactions of the shot-reverse shot paradigm, the return
look that allows the viewer to slip smoothly into the film's exchange. In Janine's initial interview with the accused Christine,
the camera keeps a disconcerting distance from the suspect. We

see Janine, in close-up, as she asks her questions, but there is no answering reverse shot of Christine. Instead, the camera is more distant and Christine sits at right angles to the doctor, only occasionally turning her head quickly to glance at Janine after a particularly misguided or painful question. This lack of connection is even more disconcerting to a viewer who most closely aligns herself with the psychiatrist. Janine provides the thread of continuity in the narrative; she is the locus of change and at least initially, she seems the more reasonable of the main characters—after all, she has not committed a brutal murder. It is because we are most easily drawn to Janine that her isolation from other characters, their unresponsiveness, is all the more noticeable and uncomfortable to us. And this isolation develops as a theme.

Beyond the disruption of the shot-reverse shot pattern—a disruption all the more unsettling because of this pattern's apparent suitability for depicting the analyst-analysand exchange—Gorris often presents Janine, alone in her study, listening again and again to the tapes of her interviews with Annie and Andrea. As we listen to the disembodied voices and laughter, the irony of this non-communication reinforces the viewer's sense of Janine's isolation, and of our own distance from the film's characters. Similarly, Christine's refusal to speak, the "question of [her] silence," imposes another isolation upon us, the viewers. And Gorris' imagery reinforces this experience: the camera often keeps a surprising distance from her speaking subjects; she creates an almost rhythmic visual refrain of characters turning their heads, suddenly, jarringly, when a speaker's words strike home—a startling attention that serves to point up the extent to which these characters are otherwise unconnected; and she uses repeated shots of a character standing at a window, her back to the scene's supposed "action" and her eyes fixed, unseeing, upon the opaque surface.

This experience of isolation, of disconnectedness, in the midst of a relatively standard narrative format is significant. Gorris coaxes her viewers in and out of the film. Her symmetrical narrative structure lulls the viewer into compliant expectation, just as her extreme content drives the viewer to fight this very acceptance. She disrupts the shot-reverse shot paradigm, simul-

taneously encouraging and thwarting the viewer's expectation of connection between two characters and between viewer and the film. Her strategies lead to a questioning of standard tests of rationality and patterns of logic. The film "rejects rationality on the entirely admissable grounds that the commonsense assumptions which underpin it—'it's only clear'/'there's no doubt'—are the weapons of a patriarchy which controls not only by repression (the police, the penal system) but also, more insidiously, through ideology."[5] In other words, Gorris uses the forms of classical film narrative to draw us into her story and then, just as we begin to expect a certain "logical," "obvious" resolution, she changes her focus. She draws the camera and us away from the supposed "action." She points to a new center, a different train of thought. In effect, she constructs a "new logic;" the terms of syllogism are unexpected because she focuses her film on unexpected questions. Perhaps the best demonstrations of this process are Gorris' treatment of the murder itself and of the courtroom debate.

The murder itself is drained of all frenzy, of all surprise. To begin with, all knowledge of the murder is after the fact. There is a definitiveness about the act and as viewer, I never had that familiar sense that "if only . . . this would never have happened." The murder has already been committed before the film commences and we hear the coroner's very detailed, very dispassionate description of the fatal beating before we see the scene in flashback. Gorris offers the murder in a series of flashbacks, each proceeding a little further with the account of the deed. These flashbacks are accompanied by a playfully ominous, quickly moving musical score. Gorris' camera is disconcertingly obliging in these scenes, panning from woman to woman, making sure that we know where everyone is and that we understand exactly how the scene progresses. And finally, when we are actually confronted with the murder, her camera stays unswervingly with the faces and moves of the three women. Once the shopkeeper falls, we do not focus on his body again. The women's faces remain perfectly calm, composed, and purposeful. There is no frenzy, no uncontrolled emotion, no flinching.

As we mentioned earlier, the use of a series of incomplete

flashbacks stimulates the viewer's curiosity. We are drawn into the event and we begin to actively desire its resolution. In other words, we want to see the murder. As well, the fast-paced musical score, particularly in contrast to the quiet, more serious tones of much of the film's sound track, excites us and draws us into the scene's events. The bright, garish, toystore colors of the boutique and its display racks add to our desire/expectation of action. But this desire/expectation is stirred at the visceral level, as well as at an intellectual or even an emotional level. The pace is light and quick, almost playful, and we want something to happen.

But when it does happen, Gorris' depiction of the beating is "stylised through a deliberate, almost ritual execution," and she refrains from building a bond of passionate empathy and identification between her characters and the viewers.[6] We have caught glimpses of Christine, Annie, and Andrea's everyday lives and we are aware of their personal frustrations. Gorris has not, however, portrayed them as helpless victims. She has not developed their personalities and experiences over time, building toward this outburst of violence. Rather, she has used a sort of shorthand in communicating the family and professional frustrations these women face; Gorris clues us in to their only too typical experiences without drawing us into the individual characters' perception of those experiences. We remain observers for we do not see these characters change and suffer, and we learn of their situations, for the most part, third-hand—we listen in as Janine repeatedly interviews each of them. As well, the immediate catalyst for the murder is seemingly rather trivial: a shopkeeper catches Christine shoplifting. We have not shared Christine's day with her, leading up to his event. Similarly, the murder itself is so calm, so dispassionate, failing to enlist a frenzied emotional identification from the viewer. And the killing is prolonged over time; this is no sudden, impulsive gunshot but rather a measured, determined beating. And although Gorris never presents us with a sensational and bloody image of the dying man, neither does she shy away from the physical details of the murder. The coroner's account is so detailed, that we, the viewers, can picture the damage done by each of the women's blows and kicks. Thus, Gorris avoids an

immediate, emotional response to a violent image while she nevertheless communicates an intellectual and imaginative recognition of the scene's significance. She refrains from the fast cutting, the bloody images, the emotional frenzy common to much movie violence—strategies which stimulate sensation, not reflection—while she still conveys the physical detail and the horrible permanence of the women's act.

So Gorris uses standard movie techniques to draw us into the scene: flashbacks, musical score, imagery, and color. At the same time, she thwarts our expectations of other narrative techniques by denying us the fast editing, violent imagery, explicit motivations, and invitations to emotional identification to which we are accustomed. The use of standard strategies prevents us from resisting/rejecting her difficult content out of hand. The denial of other expected strategies prevents us from becoming so absorbed in the difficult content that we fail to really see it. In other words, Gorris is trying to strike an uneasy balance. She wants our attention, our investment in her narrative, but she also wants us conscious, intellectually aware. Her strategies encourage the dual consciousness, the Critical Subjectivity we have posited as elements of feminist film viewing.

Rather than a tendentious film, Gorris' film now seems a problem film, a film that raises questions precisely because of the extremity and apparent bias in its subject matter. That subject matter suggests a whole host of questions while her formal strategies lead us off in another direction. While the film's explicit content may lead us to question the women's relationship with the murder victim—and by extension with men—the film's form focuses our attention on the murderers' relationships with each other, with Janine, with women. For example, Gorris' depiction of the murder focuses not on the mutilated body of the victim, not on the violent relation between the killer and the killed, but rather on the experience and behavior of the women performing the murder, and on the responses of the women who witness it.

Similarly, the film *story* triggers questions like "what did the shopkeeper do to deserve such violence?" and "why did three women who had never met before join together so instinctively to perform this act?" and "how can viewers—particularly the

male viewers—respond to this film without fear and hostility?" However, the film *form* grants the narrative premise an air of cool, measured, deliberate and inevitable fact. The climactic courtroom debate is perhaps the most succinct demonstration of the manner in which this film shifts the terms of our reasoning, suggesting the irrelevance of our typical line of questioning. After a seemingly interminable procession of male witnesses, none of whom have "witnessed" anything, and whose testimonies Gorris cuts together into seamless, senseless babble, Janine is finally called to testify as to the accused women's mental health. The doctor, to the surprise and horror of the court, defends the mental soundness of the three women, and by her "defense," she convicts them of sanity and of power. The women are caught in a patriarchal trap: the doctor's "defense" assures them of the harshest sentence. Gorris has turned the courtroom "rationality" upside down. And when the prosecutor, in exasperation, attacks Janine with the question, "what if three men had killed a female shopkeeper?", all the women— the accused, the murder witnesses who have each appeared for the trial and Janine—burst into laughter. The laughter is startling, disconcerting, seemingly inappropriate, and utterly contagious. It breaks the tension and it startles the viewer out of the context, encouraging us to think again, to reflect. Gorris attempts to call our attention to the utter irrationality of the prosecutor's logic, to use "militant humour" in an effort to disrupt this logic.[7] Mary Daly has analyzed four "male methods of mystification," one of which is precisely this "reversal" attempted by Gorris' prosecutor.[8] It is an effort to deceive, to obscure the basis of the argument by reversing its elements. The film murder has everything to do with the gender-based oppression of women, the economic servitude of women, and the silent isolation of women. To reverse the roles as the courtroom prosecutor suggests is to render the act unrecognizable (not to mention the ironic and painful fact that violence directed against women by men is by far more frequent than its reverse.)

Thus, we found a number of ways in which Marleen Gorris plays her film content off against her film form, encouraging an

active questioning of the typical "ways of seeing" a particular event, and of the typical ways of experiencing a particular formal strategy. We have raised a number of questions that grow out of this film's difficult subject matter and the film viewer's possible experience of that subject matter. I suggest that Gorris prevents her viewers from resisting the subject by using certain familiar, even seductive, film strategies, and yet she thwarts that seduction again and again, encouraging an actively critical perspective in these same viewers. In this way, Gorris encourages multiple perspectives in her viewers.

However, *A Question of Silence*, like any other film, does not insure a particular spectator response. The questions I raise, the tensions I identify between form and content, are not necessarily the tensions and questions other viewers will experience. And although a filmmaker may wish to encourage a Critical Subjectivity in her spectators through the depiction of multiple perspectives, the most effective way to stimulate this active questioning is through the sharing of distinct, individual responses to a particular film. In this text, I have tried to offer some suggestive approaches to a group of specific films in the hopes that these ideas might trigger more discussion and greater self-consciousness on the part of the film viewer. For most of all, Critical Subjectivity is a process of perception, and in that sense, it is never complete. Just as dreams accumulate interpretations and meanings for us in the reflected light of each new experience, so our analyses of films change and develop in the light of new insight and extended sympathy. And the feminist film experience is the affirmation of this expansiveness, this construction of the self that names itself not "in opposition to" all "other" readings of a text, but rather identifies itself—simultaneously, complexly—in a multitude of meanings.

NOTES

1. Annette Kuhn, *Women's Pictures: Feminism and Cinema* (London: Routledge & Kegan Paul, 1982), p. 190.

2. Linda Gross, "Filmex Reviews," *Los Angeles Times*, Saturday, April 23, 1983, Part 5, p. 2; Janet Maslin, "Film: Silence of Killers," *New York Times*, March 18, 1983, C3, p. 132; Peter Stack, "Three Women Who

Murder a Man on the Spot," *San Francisco Chronicle*, Friday, October 21, 1983, p. 71; Carrie Rickey, "Three Women Kill a Man—'For No Reason,' " *San Francisco Sunday Examiner and Chronicle*, November 11, 1983, p. 32; Sheila Johnston, "De Stilte Rond Christine M. (A Question of Silence)," *Monthly Film Bulletin*, vol. 50, no. 589, February 1983, p. 48.

3. Rickey, "Three Women Kill a Man—'For No Reason,' " p. 32.

4. Johnston, "De Stilte Rond Christine M. (A Question of Silence)," p. 48.

5. Ibid.

6. Ibid.

7. Sergei Eisenstein, *Notes of a Film Director*, trans. X. Danko (New York: Dover Publications, Inc., 1970), pp. 111, 112.

8. Mary Daly, *Gyn/Ecology: The Metaethics of Radical Feminism* (Boston: Beacon Press, 1978), p. 8.

APPENDIX

Film Credits and Distributors

WOMEN

Director:	Márta Mészáros
Screenplay:	Ildikó Koródy
	József Balázs
	Géza Bereményi
Music:	György Kovács
Cinematography:	János Kende
Cast:	Mari: Marina Vlady
	Juli: Lili Monori
	Zsuzsi: Zsuzsa Czinkóczy
	Feri: Miklós Tolnay
	Janos: Jan Nowicki
Length:	94 minutes

Hungary, 1977, Dialog Studio, color

Distributor:	New Yorker Films
	16 West 61st Street
	New York, NY 10023
	(212) 247–6110

THE ALL-ROUND REDUCED PERSONALITY ("REDUPERS")

Director:	Helke Sander
Screenplay:	Helke Sander
Cinematography:	Katia Forbe
Photographs:	Abisag Tüllmann

Film Editor: Ursula Höf
Sound: Gunther Kortwich
Cast: Edda: Helke Sander
                                      With: Joachim Baumann
                                            Frank Burckner
                                            Eva Gagel
                                            Ulrich Gressieker
                                            Beate Kopp
                                            Andrea Malkowsky
                                            Gisland Nabakowsky
                                            Helga Storck
                                            Gesine Strempel
                                            Ronny Tanner
                                            Abisag Tüllmann
                                            Ulla Ziemann
                                            Gisela Zies
Length: 98 minutes
Federal Republic of Germany, 1977, Basis-Film/ZDF, black and white
Distributor: The Cinema Guild
                                      1697 Broadway
                                      Suite 802
                                      New York, NY 10019
                                      (212) 246–5522

FILM ABOUT A WOMAN WHO . . .

Director: Yvonne Rainer
Cinematographer: Babette Mangolte
Film Editors: Babette Mangolte
                                      Yvonne Rainer
Performers: Dempster Leech
                                      Shirley Soffer
                                      John Erdman
                                      Renfreu Neff
                                      James Barth
                                      Epp Kotkas
                                      Sarah Soffer
                                      Yvonne Rainer
Length: 105 minutes
United States, 1974, black and white
Distributor: Film-Makers' Cooperative
                                      175 Lexington Avenue

New York, NY 10016
(212) 889–3820

A QUESTION OF SILENCE

Director:	Marleen Gorris
Screenplay:	Marleen Gorris
Cinematography:	Frans Bromet
Film Editor:	Hans Van Dongen
Music:	Lodewijk De Boer
Cast:	Janine: Cox Habbema
	Christine: Edda Barends
	Annie: Nelly Frijda
	Andrea: Henriette Tol
	Janine's husband: Edyy Brugman
Length:	92 minutes
Holland, 1982, Sigma Films, color	
Distributor:	Quartet/Films Incorporated
	440 Park Avenue South
	New York, NY 10016
	(212) 679–5533

Selected Bibliography

Althusser, Louis. *Lenin and Philosophy and Other Essays*. Trans. Ben Brewster. New York: Monthly Review Press, 1971.

Andrew, J. Dudley. *The Major Film Theories: An Introduction*. London: Oxford University Press, 1976.

Arnheim, Rudolf. *Film As Art*. Berkeley: University of California Press, 1957.

Augst, Bertrand. "The Apparatus: An Introduction by Bertrand Augst." *Camera Obscura: A Journal of Feminism and Film Theory*, no. 1 (1976), pp. 97–101.

Barry, Judith and Sandy Flitterman. "Textual Strategies: The Politics of Art-Making." *Screen*, vol. 21, no. 2 (1980), pp. 35–48.

Barthes, Roland. *Elements of Semiology*. Trans. Annette Lavers and Colin Smith. New York: Hill and Wang, 1981.

———. *The Pleasure of the Text*. Trans. Richard Miller. New York: Farrar, Straus & Giroux, 1975.

Baudry, Jean-Louis. "The Apparatus." *Camera Obscura: A Journal of Feminism and Film Theory*, no. 1 (1976), pp. 104–126.

Baxandall, Lee, ed. *Radical Perspective in the Arts*. New York: Penguin Books, 1972.

Baxandall, Lee and Stefan Morawski eds. *Marx and Engels on Literature & Art: A Selection of Writings*. St. Louis: Telos Press, 1973.

Bazin, Andre. *What Is Cinema? Volume I*. Trans. Hugh Gray. Berkeley: University of California Press, 1967.

———. *What Is Cinema? Volume II*. Trans. Hugh Gray. Berkeley: University of California Press, 1971.

Belsey, Catherine. *Critical Practice*. New York: Methuen & Company, 1980.

Berger, John. *Ways of Seeing*. London and Harmondsworth: British Broadcasting Corporation and Penguin Books Ltd., 1980.

Bergstrom, Janet. "Enunciation and Sexual Difference (Part I)." *Camera Obscura: A Journal of Feminism and Film Theory*, nos. 3–4 (1979), pp. 33–70.

————. "Rereading the Work of Claire Johnston." *Camera Obscura: A Journal of Feminism and Film Theory*, nos. 3–4 (1979), pp. 21–32.

Bordwell, David and Kristin Thompson. *Film Art: An Introduction*. Reading, Mass.: Addison-Wesley Publishing Co., 1979.

Cahiers du Cinema. "John Ford's *Young Mr. Lincoln*." *Screen*, vol. 13, no. 3 (1972), pp. 5–44.

Camera Obscura editors. "Yvonne Rainer: An Introduction" and "Yvonne Rainer: Interview." *Camera Obscura: A Journal of Feminism and Film Theory*, no. 1 (1976), pp. 53–96.

Chodorow, Nancy. *The Reproduction of Mothering: Psychoanalysis and the Sociology of Gender*. Berkeley: University of California Press, 1978.

Daly, Mary. *Beyond God the Father: Toward a Philosophy of Women's Liberation*. Boston: Beacon Press, 1973.

————. *Gyn/Ecology: The Metaethics of Radical Feminism*. Boston: Beacon Press, 1978.

Deren, Maya. "An Anagram of Ideas on Art, Form and Film," (1946) reprinted in George Amberg, ed. *The Art of Cinema: Selected Essays*. New York: Arno Press, 1972.

————. "Cinema as an Art Form," *New Directions*, No. 9 (1946), reprinted in Charles T. Samuels, *A Casebook on Film*. New York: Van Nostrand Reinhold, 1970, pp. 47–55.

Dinnerstein, Dorothy. *The Mermaid and the Minotaur: Sexual Arrangements and the Human Malaise*. New York: Harper & Row, 1976.

Dodd, John. "Film's 'Socialist Realism' a Pleasant Change." *Edmonton Journal*, February, 15, 1980, sec. C, p. 12.

Eisenstein, Sergei. *Film Form: Essays in Film Theory*. Trans. and ed. Jay Leyda. New York: Harcourt, Brace, Jovanovich, Inc., 1949.

————. *The Film Sense*. Trans. and ed. Jay Leyda. New York: Harcourt, Brace, Jovanovich, Inc., 1975.

————. *Notes of a Film Director*. Trans. X. Danko. New York: Dover Publications, Inc., 1970.

Eisenstein, Zillah R., ed. *Capitalist Patriarchy and the Case for Socialist Feminism*. New York: Monthly Review Press, 1979.

Erens, Patricia. *Sexual Stratagems: The World of Women in Film*. New York: Horizon Press, 1979.

French, Brandon. *On the Verge of Revolt: Women in American Films of the Fifties*. New York: Frederick Ungar Publishing Co., 1978.

Gilbert, Sandra and Susan Gubar. *The Madwoman in the Attic: The Woman Writer and the Nineteenth-Century Literary Imagination.* New Haven: Yale University Press, 1979.

Gledhill, Christine. "Recent Developments in Feminist Criticism." *Quarterly Review of Film Studies,* vol. 3, no. 4 (Fall 1978), pp. 457–493.

Gross, Linda. "Filmex Reviews." *Los Angeles Times,* Saturday, April 23, 1983, Part 5, p. 2.

Haskell, Molly. *From Reverence to Rape: The Treatment of Women in the Movies.* New York: Penguin Books, 1974.

Heath, Stephen. *Questions of Cinema.* Bloomington: Indiana University Press, 1981.

Henderson, Brian. *A Critique of Film Theory.* New York: E.P. Dutton, 1980.

Holland, Norman N. *Poems in Persons: An Introduction to the Psychoanalysis of Literature.* New York: W. W. Norton & Company, 1975.

Johnston, Claire, ed. *Notes on Women's Cinema.* London: Society for Education in Film and Television, 1973.

———. "The subject of feminist film theory/practice." *Screen,* vol. 21, no. 2 (1980), pp. 27–34.

Johnston, Sheila. "De Stilte Rond Christine M. (A Question of Silence)." *Monthly Film Bulletin,* vol. 50, no. 589 (February 1983), p. 48.

Kael, Pauline. *Taking It All In.* New York: Holt, Rinehart and Winston, 1980.

———. *When the Lights Go Down.* New York: Holt, Rinehart and Winston, 1975.

Kaplan, E. Ann. *Women & Film: Both Sides of the Camera.* New York: Methuen, Inc., 1983.

Kay, Karyn and Gerald Peary, eds. *Women and the Cinema: A Critical Anthology.* New York: E. P. Dutton, 1977.

Kermode, Frank. *The Sense of an Ending: Studies in the Theory of Fiction.* New York: Oxford University Press, 1967.

Kolker, Robert Phillip. *The Altering Eye—Contemporary International Cinema.* Oxford: Oxford University Press, 1983.

Kuhn, Annette. *Women's Pictures: Feminism and Cinema.* London: Routledge & Kegan Paul, 1982.

Lacan, Jacques. *Ecrits: A Selection.* Trans. Alan Sheridan. New York: W. W. Norton & Company, 1977.

Lippard, Lucy R. *From the Center: Feminist Essays on Women's Art.* New York: E.P. Dutton, 1976.

Lorde, Audre. *Uses of the Erotic: The Erotic as Power.* Brooklyn: Out & Out Books, 1978.

Love, Myra. "Christa Wolf and Feminism: Breaking the Patriarchal Connection." *New German Critique*, no. 16 (1979), pp. 31–53.

Lovell, Terry. *Pictures of Reality: Aesthetics, Politics and Pleasure.* London: British Film Institute, 1980.

Lukacs, Georg. *History and Class Consciousness: Studies in Marxist Dialectics.* Trans. Rodney Livingstone. Cambridge, Mass.: MIT Press, 1971.

MacBean, James Roy. *Film and Revolution.* Bloomington: Indiana University Press, 1975.

Marks, Elaine and Isabelle de Courtivron, eds. *New French Feminisms: An Anthology.* New York: Schocken Books, 1981.

Marx, Karl. *The Economic and Philosophic Manuscripts of 1844.* Trans. Martin Milligan. Ed. Dirk J. Struik. New York: International Publishers Company, 1964.

" 'Mary and Julie' and Márta Mészáros." *Hungarofilm Bulletin*, no. 2 (1977), pp. 13–18.

Maslin, Janet. "Film: Silence of Killers." *New York Times*, March 18, 1983, C8, p. 132.

Mast, Gerald. *A Short History of the Movies.* Indianapolis: Bobbs-Merrill Educational Publishing, 1976.

Mayne, Judith. "Female Narration, Women's Cinema: Helke Sander's *The All-Round Reduced Personality/Redupers.*" *New German Critique*, no. 24–25 (1981–82), pp. 155–71.

———. "The Woman at the Keyhole: Women's Cinema and Feminist Criticism." *New German Critique*, no. 23 (1981), pp. 27–43.

Mellen, Joan. *Women and Their Sexuality in the New Film.* New York: Dell, 1973.

Michelson, Annette. "Yvonne Rainer, Part One: The Dancer and The Dance." *Artforum*, 12, no. 5 (1974), pp. 57–63.

Mulvey, Laura. "Visual Pleasure and Narrative Cinema." *Screen*, 16, no. 3 (1975), pp. 6–18.

Nichols, Bill. *Ideology and the Image: Social Representation in the Cinema and Other Media.* Bloomington: Indiana University Press, 1981.

———. *Movies and Methods: An Anthology.* Berkeley: University of California Press, 1976.

Penley, Constance. "The Avant-Garde and Its Imaginary." *Camera Obscura: A Journal of Feminism and Film Theory*, no. 2 (1977), pp. 3–33.

Rainer, Yvonne. *Work 1961–73.* New York: New York University Press, 1974.

Rich, Adrienne. "Compulsory Heterosexuality and Lesbian Existence." *Signs: Journal of Women in Culture and Society*, vol. 5, no. 4 (1980), pp. 631–60.

———. *Of Woman Born: Motherhood as Experience and Institution*. New York: Bantam Books, 1977.

———. *On Lies, Secrets, and Silence: Selected Prose 1966–1978*. New York: W. W. Norton & Company, 1979.

Rich, B. Ruby. "The Films of Yvonne Rainer." *Chrysalis, A Magazine of Women's Culture*, no. 2 (1977), pp. 115–27.

Rich, B. Ruby, et al. "Women and Film: A Discussion of Feminist Aesthetics," *New German Critique*, no. 13 (1978), pp. 83–107.

Rickey, Carrie. "Three Women Kill a Man—For No Reason.' " *San Francisco Sunday Examiner and Chronicle*, November 11, 1983, p. 32.

Robinson, Lillian S. *Sex, Class and Culture*. Bloomington: Indiana University Press, 1978.

Rosen, Marjorie. *Popcorn Venus*. New York: Avon Books, 1973.

Rosenblatt, Louise M. *The Reader, the Text, the Poem: The Transactional Theory of the Literary Work*. Carbondale and Edwardsville: Southern Illinois University Press, 1978.

Saussure, Ferdinand de. *A Course in General Linguistics*. Trans. Wade Baskin. New York: The Philosophical Library, 1959.

Smith, Sharon. *Women Who Make Movies*. New York: Hopkinson & Blake, 1975.

Stack, Peter. "Three Women Who Murder a Man on the Spot." *San Francisco Chronicle*, Friday, October 21, 1983, p. 71.

Taubin, Amy. "Womenfriends." *The Soho Weekly News*, September 7, 1978.

Trilling, Lionel. *Beyond Culture: Essays on Literature and Learning*. New York: Harcourt, Brace, Jovanovich, 1965.

Tudor, Andrew. *Theories of Film*. New York: The Viking Press, 1973.

Vogel, Amos. *Film As a Subversive Art*. New York: Random House, 1974.

Winsten, Archer. " 'Women' Looks at Marriages Gone Bad." *New York Post*, October 6, 1977.

Wolf, Christa. *The Quest for Christa T.* New York: Farrar, Straus & Giroux, 1970.

———. *The Reader and the Writer—Essays, Sketches, Memories*. New York: International Publishers, 1977.

———. "Self-Experiment: Appendix to a Report." *New German Critique*, no. 13 (1978), pp. 109–31.

Wollen, Peter. *Signs and Meaning in the Cinema*. Bloomington: Indiana University Press, 1972.

Wood, Michael. *America in the Movies or "Santa Maria, It Had Slipped My Mind!"* New York: Delta, 1976.

Yakir, Dan. "Coming of Age." *The Soho Weekly News*, September 7, 1978.

Index

About the Author

MARY C. GENTILE is Assistant Director at the Office of Career Services and Off-Campus Learning at Harvard University. She is the author of articles on feminist writers and feminist education appearing in *Learning Our Way: Essays on Feminist Education* and *Maenad: A Women's Literary Journal.*